China Forever

**POPULAR CULTURE AND
POLITICS IN ASIA PACIFIC**

Series Editor
Poshek Fu, University of Illinois at
Urbana-Champaign

*A list of books in the series
appears at the end of this book.*

China Forever

The Shaw Brothers and Diasporic Cinema

Edited by

POSHEK FU

UNIVERSITY OF ILLINOIS PRESS

Urbana and Chicago

∞ This book is printed on acid-free paper.

Library of Congress Cataloging-in-Publication Data
China forever : the Shaw Brothers and diasporic cinema /
edited by Poshek Fu.
p.   cm. — (Popular culture and politics in Asia Pacific)
Includes bibliographical references and index.
ISBN 978-0-252-03273-8 (cloth : alk. paper)
ISBN 978-0-252-07500-1 (pbk. : alk. paper)
1. Shaw Brothers (Hong Kong) Limited.
I. Fu, Poshek
PN1999.S43C45   2008
791.43095125—dc22   2008002175

Contents

Acknowledgments

This is the first English-language book devoted to the study of a single Chinese-language film studio in a global historical context. It grew out of a conference, "Constructing Pan-Chinese Cultures: Globalism and Shaw Brothers Cinema," held at the University of Illinois at Urbana-Champaign in October 2003. I want to thank the Chancellor's Office, College of Liberal Arts and Sciences, Center for Advanced Study, Department of History, Humanities in a Globalizing World Initiative, Illinois Program for Research in Humanities, and the Unit for Cinema Studies for their financial support. Many friends and colleagues, at Illinois and beyond, gave me help and encouragement. They include James Barrett, Antoinette Burton, Christine Catanzarite, Chuek Pak-tong, Stephanie Po-yin Chung, David Desser, Peter Fritzsche, Francis Gateward, Law Kar, Lily Kong, Daisy Ng, Kent Ono, Jerry Packard, Vijay Prashad, Charles Stewart, Liesel Wildhaen, Shelley Wright, Gary Xu, Sai-shing Yung, and particularly Masumi Iriye and David Roediger. Thank you also to actress Cheng Pei-pei for her wonderful participation.

I am most grateful to Lane Harris and Jeff McClain, whose talent and able assistance were critical to the completion of both the conference and the book. Tonglin Lu and David Wang offered helpful suggestions on the preparation of the manuscript. I also thank Joan Catapano of the University of Illinois Press and Colin Day of Hong Kong University Press for their confidence in making Shaw Brothers into a book.

As always, my family has supported my work with their humor and curiosity about Chinese diasporic cultures.

The Shaw Brothers Diasporic Cinema

POSHEK FU

The globalization of Chinese-language cinemas has inspired a great deal of critical attention in recent years. This attention has largely been focused on the period since the 1980s, which was marked by the rise of New Wave cinemas in China, Hong Kong, and Taiwan. This critical trend should not be confused, however, with the historical trajectory of Chinese cinemas. As early as the 1960s, the Hong Kong–Singapore based Shaw Brothers Studio had already created an extensive business network that produced and distributed films for a global pan-Chinese public. Its mobility of capital and market development across national borders had played an enormous role both in the transformation of Hong Kong (and to a lesser extent Taiwan and Singapore) from a small, local film industry to a transnational cinema second in production only to Hollywood and in the shaping of cultural outlooks and aesthetic sensibility of Chinese audiences around the world. As director Ang Lee recently revealed, the shaping influences of *Crouching Tiger, Hidden Dragon* were the numerous Shaw Brothers costume dramas and musicals he watched as he was growing up in Taiwan in the 1950s and 1960s.

Despite the importance of the Shaw Brothers Studio in the history of pan-Chinese cinemas there have been until recently very few systematic studies of it in any language.[1] This oversight owes in part to the post-1980s emphasis of current scholarship on Chinese-language cinemas and in part to the paucity of research materials on the studio. Based on newly available sources (particularly the recent release of many Shaw Brothers films in DVD formats by Celestial), this collection is the first critical study in English to explore and assess the social history and cultural apparatus of the Shaw Brothers Studio;

the various production and marketing strategies it pursued in establishing a global film empire appealing to the diasporic Chinese community; the context and limitations of some of these strategies; the transformative effects of its business vision and studio system in the media culture of Hong Kong, Taiwan, and Southeast Asia; the intersection between cultural production and political changes in its drive to business expansion; and the racial and ethnic politics of its efforts to connect to the non-Chinese U.S. market (especially the connection of its kung fu films with African American popular cultures).

Shanghai-Singapore-Hong Kong

The Shaw Brothers Studio originated in Shanghai as the Tianyi (Number One) Film Company. It was founded in 1925 by four Shaw (in Chinese, Shao) brothers—namely Runje (Zuiweng), Runde (Cunren), Runme (Renmei), and Run Run (Renren or, more popularly known, Yifu). In an attempt to expand into the overseas Chinese markets in Southeast Asia (mainly Singapore-Malaya, Thailand, and Vietnam), Runme and Run Run moved to Singapore in 1928. In less than a decade, the two brothers succeeded in forming close partnerships with diasporic Chinese business leaders to build a regionwide distribution circuit in Singapore-Malaya. Under the name of Shaw Brothers Ltd., they distributed films from Tianyi as well as other Shanghai and Hong Kong companies. By the early 1930s, with a circuit of about thirty theaters under their control, Runme and Run Run guided Tianyi's production strategies to focus on the Southeast Asian Chinese market, which was dominated by Cantonese-speaking audiences. In 1934, Tianyi moved to Hong Kong to expand Cantonese film production, and, in 1936–37, it reorganized under Runde, who replaced Zuiweng (the eldest brother returned to Shanghai to look after the family interests) as studio head. Reflecting its new business strategy, the studio was renamed Nanyang (South Sea; i.e., Southeast Asia) Studio. Throughout the 1930s and 1940s, the relationship between Nanyang in Hong Kong and the Shaw Brothers Ltd. in Singapore-Malaya was markedly transnational. Taking advantage of the British colonial network (e.g., the Hong Kong and Shanghai Banking Corporation and shipping routes in the region), the territorial boundaries between both cities were continuously transgressed. Although Nanyang's operation depended on the steady cash flow and distribution network of Singapore, the Shaw Brothers Studio could not accumulate its capital and continuously expand without the constant supply of commodities, skills, and equipment from Hong Kong, Shanghai, and Guangdong.

By the 1930s, hence, the Shaw Brothers had linked British Hong Kong, China, and Southeast Asia into a transnational network of entertainment businesses. This mobility of capital and goods was in fact characteristic of overseas Chinese business culture in Southeast Asia (and also in North America), which privileged pragmatism, family connections, and flexibility of capital formation. Whether it was in the form of trading, mining, or revenue farms, usually with support from colonial powers, since at least the eighteenth century, Chinese capital, goods, and labor moved with great fluidity across the region in search of profits; central to these movements were often family or lineage networks. For example, the legendary tycoon Loke Yew, father of film magnate, and future rival of the Shaws, Loke Wan Tho, arrived in Singapore from Guangdong in 1858 with the help of kinsmen and went on to amass a great fortune through investments (in tin and rubber, among others) throughout the Strait settlements linked to China, Hong Kong, and Europe by means of the intricate network of economic and social exchanges he created with Chinese lineage groups, various colonial powers (e.g., British and Dutch), and local power elites.[2] So, too, the Shaw Brothers exemplified the cosmopolitan and boundary-crossing business culture of diasporic Chinese capitalists in the realm of mass entertainment.

The Shaw Brothers entertainment business continued to expand until World War II, during which many of their properties in both Hong Kong and Singapore-Malaya were destroyed by the Japanese. It recovered quickly after the war. By the 1950s, it developed into what can be called a trans-Asian empire that included theme parks; dance halls; film studios of Chinese and Malay languages; a massive distribution network importing films from Hong Kong, India, Europe and the United States; and a circuit of more than 130 theaters throughout Southeast Asia. Their dominance in the mass entertainment business of the region was, however, challenged by the Cambridge-educated Loke Wan Tho's Singapore-based Cathay Organization, which gained increasing market shares in postwar Asia by means of its circuit of upscale theaters and the urbane, sophisticated films produced by its new studio in Hong Kong, the Motion Picture and General Investment Group (founded in 1957). The rivalries between these two diasporic Chinese business powers in the 1950s and 1960s extended from Southeast Asia to Hong Kong, transforming the film culture and business of Asia-Pacific in the process.[3]

Movietown

Many scholars have argued it was the Shaw Brothers' drive to crush their rival that brought Run Run Shaw to Hong Kong in 1957 to reorganize the production facilities. Because Runde Shaw ran Nanyang Studio with a conservative hand, its products lacked the kind of glamour and sleekness of those of MP

& GI and lagged behind in market shares. In order to strengthen the Shaws' position in the competition, Run Run took over the studio (by buying out Runde) and renamed it the Shaw Brothers Studio.[4]

I believe there were other reasons behind the reorganization, however. These were to do with the loss of the China market and the political changes in postcolonial Southeast Asia. After World War II, many former European colonies in the region became independent. Their struggle to create a national identity out of a colonial past and a racially and ethnically diverse population marked the Chinese as so-called aliens and threatened to exclude them from the imagined communities. In the 1950s and 1960s, antagonism against Chinese was rampant throughout Southeast Asia. In Indonesia, for example, the majority of Chinese there were denied citizenship (until the 1980s). While declaring English to be the privileged language of the city-state, Singapore lashed out against the "tax fraudulence" and "yellow culture" of the Chinese-owned film industry and imposed stringent censorship and an exorbitant tax on imported films.[5] These deteriorating business conditions coincided with the loss of a supply of films from China. The founding of the People's Republic of China in 1949 led to a nationalization of the cinema industry. Its products were limited and its overseas distribution tightly controlled by a few

Shaw brothers in Hong Kong. *Left to right:* Runde, Runme, and Run Run Shaw.

so-called leftist studios in Hong Kong. To ensure a steady supply of Chinese-language films to its sprawling distribution circuit and to open new markets beyond Southeast Asia, Runme and Run Run Shaw decided to reorganize the studio facilities in Hong Kong. To them, the colony created an attractive production base because of its low taxes, favorable labor conditions, political stability, open access to Taiwan and other Chinese communities across the world, and concentration of filmmaking talents, who included many recent exiles from postrevolutionary Shanghai.

The rivalries with Loke Wan Tho, then, added fuel to the changing business conditions that drove the Shaw brothers to reformulate their business strategies and marketing structure. These strategies centered on the ideas of modernity and globalization. In a widely circulated promotion article in 1964, the Shaw Brothers publicists appropriated the May Fourth new cultural rhetoric of linear progress to proclaim that the world had entered a "new age" (*xin shidai*) of modernity as a result of the recent developments in science and technology. Filmmaking had to "modernize" itself in order to meet the "changing entertainment needs of the tens of millions of audiences from different Asian nations." And so, the Shaw Brothers set out to build a modern film studio in Clear Water Bay, Hong Kong. In 1965, Movietown boasted fifteen stages, two permanent sets, a color film development facility, and all sorts of state-of-the-art film equipment imported from Europe and the United States. By building the largest and best-equipped studio in the history of Chinese filmmaking and by launching Chinese-language cinema into an age of color and widescreen (Eastmancolor and Shawscope), the Shaw Brothers was thus the modernizing force that led the transformation of Hong Kong cinema from an old age of traditional production into a new cinema of modern sensibility and cutting-edge technology.

Run Run Shaw also brought modern studio system and capitalist management techniques to Movietown. He used all means possible to recruit major film talents in Hong Kong, particularly studio executives and actors and directors exiled from Shanghai. Among these recruits were Saint John University alumnus Raymond Chow, who soon became Run Run Shaw's top advisor, stars Li Lihua and Lin Dai, and directors Yue Feng and Li Hanxiang. A school was also set up in Movietown with a Mandarin-speaking teaching staff from Shanghai to train new acting talent. By the mid-1960s, Movietown boasted more than 1,300 employees. Based on the U.S. Fordist-Taylorist model of industrial organization, Movietown was run like an assembly line, with Run Run Shaw overseeing every part of the operation and making all decisions, that was operated on the principles of rational management, cost efficiency, professionalization, and standardization of the production process in pursuit of maximum profit. To have rational control over its labor force, except for a few big stars and directors, all of its employees were required to live in the Movietown dormitory and subjected to the disciplinary regime of stringent contracts, strict rules, and low pay (but some stars, like Cheng Pei-pei, liked the simplicity of dormitory life). Thus Shaw Brothers Studio was often referred to by industry insiders as "dream factory" (*meng gongchang*). Along with his stress on mass production, Run Run Shaw understood the importance of branding in the entertainment business. He succeeded in identifying the studio in the public mind with lavish production values and advanced technology by launching a series of ambitious, lavishly made costume films in the late 1950s and early 1960s, which included Li Hanxiang's *Kingdom and the Beauty* (*Jiangshan meiren,* 1959), *Enchanting Shadow* (*Qiannü youhun,* 1960), and *Love Eterne* (*Liang Shanbo yu Zhu Yingtai,* 1963), which were all enormously popular in Chinese communities across the globe. Indeed the modernization of the Shaw Brothers Studio was part of its effort toward globalization of Chinese-language films.

Going Global

Globalization marked a new shift in the Shaw Brothers Studio's business strategies, which also required a change in its production policy. In fact, the most obvious change of the studio after Run Run Shaw's reorganization was the change from an emphasis on Cantonese to Mandarin in its productions. In the first years of its operation, the Shaw Brothers Studio made films in both languages, but by the mid-1960s, Mandarin clearly became the official language of the studio.

Why privilege Mandarin production? I think the reasons lie in an admixture of business calculation and cultural nationalism that belied an ambition to build a global Chinese cinema. If the ascendancy of the Shaw Brothers Studio to power in Hong Kong represented what historian Du Yunzhi calls "the domination of Hong Kong cinema by Southeast Asian film industry," this domination had brought with it a cosmopolitan, border-crossing consciousness typical of many diasporic Chinese capitalists, which was to transform the vision and structure of Hong Kong cinema industry. In this regard, the Shaw Brothers represented a part of the global network of diasporic Chinese business and culture that played a significant role in Asia's transition to modernity.[6] As diasporic Chinese capitalists with properties and business connections throughout Asia and across the Pacific, it was probably part of the Shaw Brothers' plan to turn the crisis engendered both by the political changes in Southeast Asia and by the loss of the China market into an opportunity to go global.

Run Run Shaw most likely had already in his mind the vision of expanding his entertainment empire globally when he came to Hong Kong in 1957. It meant establishing new market networks beyond Southeast Asia and thereby fulfilling the dream of making Chinese-language cinema, like Hollywood, a world-class cinema to be consumed and acclaimed by a global audience.[7] This dream, embodying the modernizing logic inspired by the nationalist desire of catching up with the West and becoming an equal member of the international community of powers, had been dreamed by great Chinese movie tycoons such as Zhang Shankun and Li Zuyong since the 1930s. Living away from home and under an alien culture, most diasporic Chinese, whether in Hong Kong or Southeast Asia or the Americas, were nationalistic and culturally drawn to the homeland (consider the roles they played in the Anti-Manchu Revolution and the War of Resistance against Japan). Run Run Shaw was no exception; his cultural nationalism was naturally mixed with business ambition.[8] As described by publicity articles, it was the Shaw Brothers' goal to expand transnationally, extending its film empire from Southeast Asia to the whole Asian region and eventually to the global market. This was inspired both by "profit motive" and by its sense of "cultural and national missions," which was "to introduce through celluloid images to people of different races and linguistic backgrounds the cultural and artistic traditions of China."[9] Indeed, to go global was to break into the developed markets of Europe and, particularly, the United States. In his frequent interviews with both Chinese and Western presses in the 1960s, Run Run Shaw repeatedly declared the studio's goals in terms of cultural nationalism. It aimed to "bring the East into the West" by leading Chinese cinemas out of the racial ghetto of Chinatowns into the global market and coproduction with film companies around the world "on an equal footing" as a way to declare the entry of China into the global community of national cinemas.

It should be clear in this context why Mandarin production was privileged by the Shaw Brothers Studio. The Shaw Brothers had made huge profits from Cantonese films in Southeast Asia; however, from a nationalist perspective, it was, after all, a dialect that appealed to a parochial, localized market. In fact, the nationalist government had tried to include in its nation-building agenda efforts to ban Cantonese cinema in the 1930s. Mandarin, however, was the national language (*guoyu*), the language that represented the modern nationhood of China and embodied the collective sensibility—Chineseness—

of ethnic Chinese around the world. It represented China to the world. To go global, therefore, to bring Chinese-language cinema to a worldwide audience, the Shaw Brothers Studio adopted Mandarin as its business language. The training center in Movietown emphasized Mandarin classes to teach the studio's mostly Shanghainese- or (later) Cantonese-speaking actors and actresses the national language and switched to all-Mandarin production by the early 1960s. Unlike Zhang Shankun or Li Zuyong, the Shaw Brothers had the vision, the resources, and a systematic business plan to build a global Chinese cinema. They enjoyed intimate connections to the diasporic Chinese business network in the region that crisscrossed national boundaries and had intimate access to trans-Asian financial powerhouses such as the Hong Kong and Shanghai Banking Corporation. They could also easily mobilize people and goods between Hong Kong and Singapore and, after decades of importing Hollywood, European, and Indian films to Southeast Asia, had business ties with major studios beyond the Pacific. From the 1950s to the 1970s, Movietown in Hong Kong became the Shaw Brothers' base from which they struggled to build a global Chinese cinema.

In retrospect, the Shaw Brothers Studio was most successful in constructing a pan-Chinese film culture in the diaspora by means of its little-challenged domination over the Chinese-language cinema industries around the world. At the height of its power from 1960 to 1973, the studio was also successful in building what can be called a trans-Asian entertainment network, with movements of capital, technology, and personnel across the Asian region, a success that led to the later transformation of Hong Kong into the capital of the regional cinemas. Its globalization efforts in the West, however, succeeded mainly in increasing the visibility of Chinese-language cinema in the international film festival circuit. It stopped short of gaining a foothold in the mainstream markets in Europe or the United States. This varying success brings to light the production and marketing strategies of the Shaw Brothers as well as the global capitalist system in which they pursued their business goals.

The principal means of the Shaw Brothers to expand its cinema network into the West were participation in international film festival circuits and coproduction with major film studios in Europe and the United States. These strategies were not different from many non-Western cinemas that sought to globalize production but lacked name recognition and access to the established market structure in the West. From the Shaw Brothers' perspective, coproduction with Hollywood had the added benefit of strengthening its operational standards. In fact, Run Run Shaw was enthusiastic in challenging the global hegemony of Hollywood by bringing Chinese cinema to the West; he invariably expressed his enthusiasm in terms of nationalism. In a press conference in Taiwan in the early 1960s, for example, he insisted that he would work with Western film studios on an "equal basis" as a way to "declare the entry of the Chinese cinema" into the global community of national cinemas.[10]

Japanese cinema was commanding a star attraction in the Euro-American film festival circuit at the time (most notably historical films by Akira Kurosawa and Kenji Mizoguchi). Shaw Brothers planners believed this was due largely to the sumptuous display of an exotic "Oriental flavor" (*dongfang secai*) in their films, whose mystical charm and old stories appealed to audiences in the West. Because the origin of Eastern civilizations was in China, they argued, Chinese cinema should reach out to the audience as the purest and most authentic representation of "Oriental flavor."[11] At the same time, Run Run Shaw frequently explained to the public that the way to globalize Chinese cinema was to emphasize its cultural difference: that was its "Chinese flavor" (Zhongguo weidao) because it was this difference that "attracted the global audience."[12] It was therefore no coincidence that all of the films Shaw Brothers sent to compete in the Cannes Film Festival and San Francisco International Film Festival, including Li Hanxiang's *Enchanting Shadow, Yang Guifei* (Empress Yang, 1962) and *Love Eterne*, were lushly made costume epics set in an unspecified past. Their publicity also centered on the twin themes of cherished cultural tradition and authentic "Oriental flavor" in the Shaw Brothers films and highlighted the nationalist mission of the studio to help the globe "understand China and Chinese culture."[13] Similarly, all the stars accompanying Run Run Shaw to the film festivals appeared in fancy traditional costumes (e.g., Li Lihua dressed as Empress Yang) to underline the authentic Chineseness of their films. While raising curiosity about Chinese-language cinema, however, these films took no major prizes at the festivals. They achieved no critical successes as the Shaw Brothers hoped. As one critic for the 7th San Francisco International Film festival (1963) wrote of her reaction to the costume opera drama *Love Eterne*: "Exquisite beauty of the Chinese (Formosa) countryside captured in this poetic story of doomed love . . . provided a restful interlude in the Film Festival, almost exclusively concerned with war and grim problems of contemporary life. . . . Its musical tradition of Chinese opera lacks commercial appeal for most Western audience. The camerawork is superb. The depth of color through the changing season and the wisps of fog in the landscape have all the quality of fine Oriental art."[14] Perhaps it is this "quality of fine Oriental art" that won it a Special Citation; similarly *Yang Guifei* won the award for Best Interior Cinematography in Cannes in 1962 for its sumptuous display of imperial Chinese settings and fashions. Both prizes were marginal, and both films did not exhibit in the United States until after 1965 and, similar to most other big-budget Shaw Brothers historical epics like Li Hanxiang's *Bai se zhuan* (White Snake), *Jiangsan meiren* (Empire and the Beauty), and *Hua Mulan,* only within the confines of Chinatowns. A quick check of *Variety* between 1960 and 1965 revealed that there was not a single Chinese-language film shown in New York City or San Francisco, which were the "gateway[s] to the American foreign film market."[15]

If the Shaw Brothers film presence was marginal in the Euro-American film festival circuit, it played only a minor role in the various coproduction projects involved with British and Hollywood studios. The Shaws had developed extensive connections with major Western studios like Warner Brothers through distributing their films in Southeast Asia and other investment deals, but none of them seemed to be interested in extending their business interests beyond that of marketing to Asia. In the few coproduction projects we know of, the partnership was invariably unequal. The role of Run Run Shaw was seemingly a supportive one. He provided mainly technical supports, studio facilities, and local knowledge to the Western partners when they made films in Hong Kong or Singapore (to enhance the exotic appeal of their products). Aside from learning up close the Western production procedures, he made profits out of such deals by acquiring their exclusive distribution rights to these films in Asia and rights to use their sets and original scripts for his Mandarin-language productions.[16] Thus, despite his dream and efforts, Run Run Shaw was able to attract only some attention to Chinese-language film in the Euro-American world, and his position in the film business there was marginal.[17]

Unlike its marginality in Euro-American film festival circuits, Shaw Brothers was at the center of what came to be a trans-Asian cinematic network linked by market, film festivals, joint production, and movement of people and capital. Beginning in the 1950s, the Shaw Brothers began the practice of hiring, on mostly short-term contracts, directors, cinematographers, sound recorders and special effects technicians from Japan (mainly affiliated with Shin Toho, Daiei, and Shochiku Studios) to improve the standards and efficiency of its studio system and to try to open the Japanese market. These so-called Japanese expatriates brought in new filmmaking technologies (e.g., Nishimoto Todashi assisted Li Hanxiang with widescreen camera and color cinematography in making his historical dramas like *Love Eterne*) and helped

Movietown expand into various popular genres such as musicals (notably Inoue Umetsugu) and spy thrillers (e.g., Nakahira Ko). The Shaw Brothers also sent young directors (e.g., Gui Zhihong) and rising stars (e.g., Cheng Pei-pei) to Tokyo for training. At the same time, throughout the 1950s and early 1960s, the Shaw Brothers lent scriptwriters and technicians to Shin Toho and Daiei to help them produce historical films of Chinese subjects (e.g., Kenji Mizoguchi's *Yokihi* or *Empress Yang Kwei Fei*) and distributed their films to markets across Southeast Asia. Japanese studios such as Shochiku also enjoyed the technical and financial support of the Shaw Brothers when they shot films on location in Hong Kong (e.g., Nomura Yoshitaro's *Bomeiki* or *Refugees*) in exchange for distribution rights outside Japan.[18]

The Shaw Brothers and Japan also joined hands in creating what became the most important film festival in the Asia-Pacific. Co-organized in 1953 by Daiei Studio head Nagata Masaichi and Run Run Shaw with the alleged purpose of promoting unity and elevating production standards of Asian cinema, the Asian Film Festival (originally named Southeast Asian Film Festival) was held annually among its members, which included Hong Kong, Japan, Taiwan, Korea, Singapore, Malaysia, Burma, the Philippines, and Vietnam. Its aim was to become the Asian equivalent of the Cannes and Venice Film Festivals, a prestigious event at which filmmakers competed and made business deals. Throughout the 1960s, the Shaw Brothers (which represented Hong Kong and, as Malay-language film producer, Singapore) dominated the film festival, taking away most of the major Golden Harvest Awards (i.e., Best Picture, Best Actress, and Best Director). This domination expanded its business networks with other Asian film industries and made Movietown in Hong Kong (particularly after the decline of Japanese cinema) the center of modern film cultures in the region—thus its sobriquet, "Hollywood of the East." Partnership with other Asian film producers was a major part of the Shaw Brothers' strategies in the 1960s, both to increase its production capacity and to open up new markets in the region. Unlike its primarily subordinate relations with Euro-American (and Japanese) film companies, the Shaw Brothers dictated the terms of coproduction with various Asian partners. For example, its partnership with Shin Productions allowed it to conduct location shooting near Seoul, South Korea, where (unlike Hong Kong) open land and cheap labor were abundant (thus Yue Feng's *Da ji* or *The Last Woman of Shang* [1964] involved more than 5,000 locally hired extras), whereas coproduction with Thai, Filipino, Vietnamese, and Indonesian film companies (e.g., Luo Wei's *Eyu he* or *Crocodile River*, 1964) enabled the Shaw Brothers to evade all kinds of anti-Chinese film laws in these nations and opened the markets there. All these coproduced films were made in two versions (with different leading stars and languages) and were highly popular in Hong Kong (for their exotic sceneries) as well as other parts of Asia (for the Shaw Brothers stars and Shawscope).[19] Besides coproduction, the Shaw Brothers constantly acquired new talent from its Asian partners to keep up with its production needs. In the 1960s, Taiwan, naturally, provided Movietown with the largest number of Mandarin-speaking actors, directors, and writers.

Constructing Diasporic Chinese Cinema Cultures

Inasmuch as it had only a marginal role in the Euro-American world, the Shaw Brothers succeeded in launching Hong Kong into the capital of pan-Chinese cinema, producing and marketing films for the consumption of ethnic Chinese around the globe since the 1960s. Besides the discussed purpose of representing the modern nationhood of China to a desired global audience, the Shaw Brothers adopted Mandarin as its official language, which was also a strategy that aimed to construct a pan-Chinese culture. In a comparative discussion of diaspora, William Stefran theorizes that diaspora builds together by a consciousness of being an "ethnic, racial or religious community." The strength of a "homeland myth," which can be defined by an imagined connection to the ancestral homeland through (among other things) the belief of a distinct language and historical memory, is instrumental to the development of this "diasporic consciousness."[20] With a distinct script system and as the national language of China, Mandarin became the fundamental framework within which the Shaw Brothers brought together a Chinese diasporic community. Indeed Shaw Brothers was most successful in projecting this pan-Chinese community through constructing the consciousness of a cultural China in its films—an imagined homeland expressed by principally an invented tradition, a shared past, and a common language—that appealed to the nostalgia and nationalism of Chinese audiences around the world. As Run Run Shaw told an interviewer about his production policy: "I make movies to satisfy the desires and hopes of my audience; and the core of my audience is Chinese. What they desire to see on the screen are folklore, romances and popular subjects in Chinese history with which they are already familiar. . . . They miss the homeland they have left behind and the cultural tradition they are still cherishing."[21] Moreover, most major Shaw Brothers planners and directors, including Run Run Shaw's trusted advisors Li Hanxiang and Zhang Che, were associated with the circles of so-called literati from the south (*nanlai wenren*), intellectual exiles from China after 1949. Their roots were in the mainland, their political sympathy was with the nationalist state in Taiwan, and they saw Hong Kong as merely a temporary refuge in which they turned their nostalgia and alienation into creative energy, making films to celebrate and perpetuate the Chinese culture in diaspora. Thus, making popular subjects and familiar themes from what came to be claimed as the Chinese cultural tradition with a markedly celebratory, nostalgic ethos, and in the Mandarin language, had become the guiding principles of Shaw Brothers productions.

In fact, all the big-budget and most successful Shaw Brothers films were romances, folklore, and (after 1965) martial arts subjects, notably Li Hanxiang's *Empire and the Beauty* and *Love Eterne* and Zhang Che's *Du bei dao* (*One-Armed Swordsman,* 1967) and King Hu's *Da zui xia* (*Come Drink with Me,* 1966), drawn from the Chinese popular tradition. In close examination, whether they are feminized scholars or masculine heroes, virtuous beauties or woman warriors, the main characters in these films are all invested with values and desires closely paralleled with an idealized morality supposedly existent in traditional China: notably filial piety, chastity, purity, and loyalty. For example, Fang Gang (Wang Yu) in *One-Armed Swordsman* is a filial son who remains unfailingly loyal to his *shifu* (master) despite the pains and humiliations he has to suffer after being ostracized from the school; and in *Empire and the Beauty,* a village girl, Li Fengzhe (Lin Dai), is so virtuous and chaste that the emperor (Zhao Lei) defies political conventions to try to marry her. Moreover, these films are always set in an unspecified time in the past and an unspecified place in China (mostly in the north or in Jiangnan-Lower Yangtze delta). This dehistoricization of space and time projects an image that evokes the imperial grandeur, majestic landscape, or rural idyllic of an imagined land that is China. These are evident, for example, in the opening sequences in *Empire and the Beauty* in which the imperial palace is so elaborately and meticulously reconstructed as to create a sense of awe and astonishment in the audience, whereas the scenes of the Jiangnan countryside where Li Fengzhe and the emperor fall in love, like those in *Love Eterne,* evoke a romanticized landscape filled with beautiful lakes, charming people, and idyllic life. Embedded in a familiar aesthetic of popular stories and folk music (notably Huangmei opera), these characters and settings contributed to the construction of a China that was at once idealized and ahistorical (and thereby unchanging). This imagined changeless China held enormous appeal to ethnic Chinese audiences around the world, They found in Shaw Brothers films a China forever in the midst of all the political turmoil and personal displacements and with which they could continue to identify despite their life in the diaspora.

It is therefore no coincidence that in the 1950s and 1960s the Shaw Brothers films were particularly popular in Taiwan, where tens of thousands of mainland Chinese had exiled there with the Nationalist regime. Their nostalgia for China and cultural anxiety found some relief in Shaw Brothers films, which had begun to enter the Taiwan market in the late 1950s. All Huangmei opera films were box-office sensations, and *Love Eterne* in particular turned the island into what the local press dubbed a "city of fanatics" (*kuangren cheng*). The film showed to full houses for more than half a year in 1963; many people saw it more than a hundred times and memorized every scene and song in it. The phenomenal success of *Love Eterne* helped put an end to the hegemony of Hollywood in Taiwan and enabled Shaw Brothers to dominate the market there (it also enabled the rapid growth of a Taiwan Mandarin film industry in the mid-1960s). This was an important market as Taiwan had the largest Mandarin-speaking population in the world (outside of the mainland), and it was seen during the 1950s and 1960s (i.e., Cold War in Asia) as the capital of a global struggle to preserve Chinese civilization from the ravages of Chinese Communism. Indeed, recognizing the popularity of Shaw Brothers Mandarin films and its projection of a China that was unchangingly virtuous, the Nationalist regime in Taipei made it the official representative of "Free China" in the global film festivals circuit.

People lining up in front of a Taipei, Taiwan, movie theater to buy tickets for *Love Eterne.*

Along with the conquest of the Taiwan market, Shaw Brothers extended its business to other areas of the pan-Chinese world. To make sure Chinese in different countries and speakers of various dialects could appreciate its Mandarin production, the studio put in Chinese (and sometimes also English or Spanish) subtitles in all its films. In Hong Kong, even though most of its population was Cantonese-speaking migrants from South China, the Shaw Brothers rose to predominance in the 1960s. Its new technology, aggressive marketing, and image of a changeless China combined to push Cathay to the margin (which went into rapid decline after the death of Loke Wan Tho in 1964) and drove the Cantonese film industry to its demise. As a journalist remarked, Shaw Brothers productions gave the local audiences such a "thrilling experience" that they left the low-budget Cantonese-language cinema (mostly in black and white) en masse, and, for the first time in Hong Kong's history, "Chinese [Mandarin] films become as popular as Hollywood imports." In the late 1960s, Cantonese films stopped production altogether.[22] The same trend happened in Chinese communities across Asia-Pacific, Europe, and the Americas as well. Even though most of the overseas Chinese spoke various dialects, they were thrilled by the lavish production values of Shaw Brothers films and enthralled by the mythologized China represented in them. In fact, the Shaw Brothers magazine *Nanguo dianying* (Southern Screen) during the 1960s was filled with reports on Penang, Manila, San Francisco, or London Chinatown theater owners visiting Movietown to make deals on distribution rights.[23] Thus, in the 1960s, the Shaw Brothers created a transnational network that linked all Chinese outside postrevolutionary China into a cultural community in which images of a mythical China reigned.

Localizing China

A few years after its launching of the "Age of Martial Arts" (*wuxia shiji*) in 1965, Shaw Brothers made a breakthrough in its globalization efforts by breaking into the mainstream U.S. market with the kung fu drama *Five Fingers of Death* (1965), directed by Korean expatriate Cheng Chang Ho. This was a low-budget film, and it was quickly overshadowed in the U.S. market by the phenomenal success of Bruce Lee. The subsequent popularity of English-dubbed kung fu films in the 1970s in Africa, Latin America, and the African American communities in the United States extended the Shaw Brothers' global reach. Yet the 1970s was actually a decade of enormous challenges, limited accommodation, and steady decline for the Shaw Brothers that led to its shift of operation to television in the early 1980s. A major challenge was the rapidly changing conditions of Hong Kong as well as other markets in the pan-Chinese world. In Hong Kong, the convergence of the "economic miracle" and the demographic changes—whereas in the 1950s the majority of the population was born outside Hong Kong, in 1971 most were born locally, and almost all of them were younger than 30—created a popular consciousness of what novelist Xi Xi called "My City." The colony was intricately connected to Great Britain and China, yet in the minds of the young generation, it was a community with its own culture and identity that were distinct from either of them.[24] This growing local consciousness was reinforced by the emergence of culture magazines and newspaper supplements devoted to issues and concerns particular to the local community and by the rapid rise of the television industry (after the founding of HKTVB in 1965), which built its Cantonese-language programming around the life and sensibility of the locals. Particularly popular was the HKTVB news broadcast that brought events and voices around the city into the living rooms of most people's houses, enabling them to participate in imagining a local community. (Similar consciousness also emerged in different ways in Singapore, Malaysia, Taiwan, or other Chinese communities around the world.)

All these changes created enormous challenges to the Shaw Brothers Studio, whose production strategies and marketing structure had been anchored in its conception of a global pan-Chinese community. Reflecting the colony's demographic changes, the studio had since the late 1960s lost to death or retirement many of its top stars, directors, and technicians who migrated from Shanghai after 1949. As migration had largely stopped since the 1950s, and the Taiwan film industry began to prosper in the late 1960s, the Shaw Brothers had to seek replacement mainly locally. Local talents were recruited in large numbers throughout the 1970s. Among them included directors Chor Yun (Chu Yuan) and Kuei Chih-hung (Guei Zhihong) and action actors Ti Lung (Di Long), David Chiang (Jiang Dawei), and Chan Kun-tai (Chen Guantai). Whether they were veterans from the now-defunct Cantonese cinema or new to the film profession, none of them appeared to have been hired to bring their local experience and sensibility to the films made at Movietown. Remaining on the top of the studio hierarchy was Run Run Shaw, who continued to have absolute control over what films to make and how to make them.[25]

Nonetheless, this marked the beginning of what director Zhang Che calls the process of "localization" (*bengdi hua*) of the Shaw Brothers.[26] I would argue that this process was marked by limited strategic accommodation to changes in the pan-Chinese market of which Hong Kong was an increasingly important part. Taiwan had been a major market for the Shaws' cinema, but the maturity of its film industry in the late 1960s took away a significant part of its market shares. Similarly, the diasporic market in Southeast Asia was under pressure by the continuous surge of nationalism and communist revolutions (e.g., Vietnam) in the region, whereas its market control in Chinatowns across the Western world faced challenges from the revitalized Cantonese cinema in the mid-1970s (more later). A larger but varied audience was emerging in Hong Kong. It offered a lucrative market of four million people in 1971, half of them between the ages of 10 and 35, an age group of peak movie attendance. In fact, a hit in the colony could readily gross more than $1 million and easily recoup the production cost (which rarely exceeded $700,000 to $800,000). Hence, an observer remarked, "what Hong Kong likes looms [increasingly] large" in the Shaw Brothers' production strategies.[27] But the rapid changes in the city in the 1970s made it a market vastly different from that of the 1960s, when the ticket-buying audience for the most part identified with a remote China, allowing the Shaw Brothers to "Mandarin-ize" the film industry. In the 1970s, the growing local consciousness set off a development toward what can be called a "Hongkongization" of Hong Kong cinema. This development involved, among others, a revival of the Cantonese-language cinema and an obsession with Hong Kong. Growing out of an increasing identification with "My City," it was an obsession to give cinematic expression to the experiences, concerns, attitudes, and fantasies of the local community. What was its history? How was it different from other Chinese communities and European colonies? What did its people want, and what were their hopes and dreams? No language was more effective in projecting local experiences and sentiments than the language most of the locals spoke in everyday life: Cantonese dialect. Hence, it is no coincidence that Cantonese began during this time to gradually overtake Mandarin to become the dominant official language of the film industry. It is in this sense that the 1970s have often been referred to as the "transition period" paving the way for the creation of the Hong Kong cinema that we know today.[28]

In this context, the localization of the Shaw Brothers production seemed a limited, halfhearted strategy to protect its market hegemony in Hong Kong. The localization was both a natural process of generational changes and a historical response to structural changes in the local film market: to try to reach the larger, younger, more affluent, and local-born audience. This process proved to be difficult, however. The difficulty was compounded by the emergence of a rival film studio, the Golden Harvest, founded by Raymond Chow, a former top lieutenant of Run Run Shaw. With a flexible subcontracting production system, and more sensitive to the growing local consciousness among the young generation, Golden Harvest produced a series of high-grossing films in the 1970s, such as Bruce Lee's *The Way of the Dragon* (*Menglong guojiang*, 1973) and Michael Hui's *The Private Eyes* (*Bangjin bai liang*, 1976). These films, many of which were in Cantonese dialect, either projected a modern, anticolonial sentiment or satirized the local experiences with modernity. Golden Harvest rose quickly to challenge the Shaw Brothers' hegemony. Similarly, Cantonese-language filmmaking came back to life after suffering more than a decade of debasement and decline. Participating in the discussions of the meaning and experiences of the local community, a number of independents in the mid-1970s turned out some thoughtfully made social dramas like Wu Si-yuan's *Anti-Corruption* (*Lianzheng fengbao*, 1975) and Leung Po-chi's *Jumping Ash* (*Tiaohui*, 1976). For example, although *The Private Eyes* and *Jumping Ash* grossed more than $8.5 million and $3.6 million, respectively, the Mandarin Shaw Brothers historical epic *Forbidden City* (*Qing guo qing cheng*, 1975) earned only $2.5 million.[29] The popularity of these "new-style" Cantonese-language films led to the emergence of the New Wave cinema and the revival of the local dialect industry in the 1980s.

Shaw Brothers was apparently less in tune with the gradual formation of local identity in the colony. Its strategy of localization turned out to be a strategic emphasis on localizing China in the new context rather than obsessing with Hong Kong. By localizing China, I mean an effort to make the idea of pan-Chinese cultures continuously relevant to the local conditions. Indeed, throughout the 1970s, the Shaw Brothers continued to churn out martial arts movies (both kung fu and *wuxia*—or knight errant—types), despite the increasing lack of market appeal in Hong Kong. A few exceptions were Chor Yuen's evocative adaptation of Gu Long's anxiety-ridden, apolitical martial arts novels (e.g., *The Magic Blade* or *Tianya, Minyue, Dao*, 1976) and the kung fu epics by Zhang Che and Lau Kar-leung. The Shaw Brothers' unchanged policy was believed to be both a result of its inflexible studio system that thrived on mass production of similar subjects and the profitability (mainly because of low production costs) of martial arts movies in other parts of its global market, particularly Southeast Asia and the United States. But I want to argue that the Shaw Brothers' insistence on making martial arts subjects was perhaps also a result of its attempt to localize China for a changing audience.

Zhang Che's notion of localization aptly reflected the studio's approach. He remembered that he came up with the idea in the early 1970s when he realized that to expand market shares in Hong Kong it was imperative to mobilize local flavors and perspectives to film production. Hence, he recruited more young local actors and began to place folklore, myths, and the martial arts tradition of South China in his new works (the most famous of which included *Shao-lin Martial Arts* or *Hongquan yu Yongchun*, 1974, and *Disciples of Shaolin* or *Hongquan xiaozi*, 1975), which, perhaps ironically, were all made in Taiwan. Like his earlier works, Zhang's "localized" films were well choreographed and filled with stylized violence and tragic heroism, but they highlighted southern-styled fighting techniques (i.e., Hongquan) and Guangdong folk cultures. They also sought to capture the modern ethos of the new Hong Kong audiences by featuring young, rebellious male characters fighting in search of self-expression and social justice. As critics pointed out, however, these films revealed Zhang's limited knowledge of the popular traditions of South China. And their themes continued to be structured around the aesthetics of masculine strength and the values of male bonding, loyalty, and romantic idealism that had been recognized as the signature style of the director (since his *One-Armed Swordsman* of 1967).[30] There also remained certain dehistoricized and nostalgic qualities typical of Shaw Brothers production in the setting, atmosphere, and narrative structure of these films, functioning to invite identification with a mythical China. It is therefore clear from these Zhang Che films that the Shaw Brothers envisioned localization basically as a strategy of repackaging and reformulating its products to reenhance the relevance of their pan-Chinese vision and values to the rapidly changing local condition. It was, in other words, a strategy of limited accommodation.

If Zhang Che came from Shanghai and his works reflected this diasporic experience, a new local-born director's films can be even more revealing of the Shaw Brothers' strategy. Kuei Chih-hung learned his craft in the 1960s from some Japanese directors hired by Run Run Shaw to improve the efficiency of the production system. He brought to some of his best works an obsession with Hong Kong and a passion for individuality. These orientations conflicted with the studio, however, and the resultant tensions brought to light the limits of the Shaw Brothers' policy of localizing China. Combining social drama, kung fu action, and a setting in a new town, low-income public housing district, Kuei's *The Teahouse* (*Chengji chalou*) was one of the most popular Shaw Brothers films of the period. Released in 1974, it tells the story of a group of recent immigrants (from China), under the leadership of Big Brother Cheng (Dage Cheng, played by Chan Kun-tai), who open a restaurant that quickly becomes a center of action against problems plaguing the local community. Obviously, the local community here represents "My City," and the restaurant a community of citizens devoted to "building a brave new world." But this obsession with Hong Kong is everywhere compromised by a strong attachment to the Chinese tradition popularized by the Shaw

Brothers. The film put the blame for the city's rising crimes on the lack of muscle of the colonial legal system (particularly the abolition of the death penalty) and the corruption of the pro-British elites. To solve the problems, it calls for a return to the traditional principle of restoring social order by harsh laws. The vehicle to change the legal system is not social movement or institutional change but Big Brother Cheng, who appears as a contemporary version of a typical Shaw Brothers *wuxia* (knight errant), using violence in the name of the poor and disadvantaged. And the restaurant staff becomes, in effect, his followers. Reminiscent of Zhang Che's works, the restaurant is a community dominated by men whose relationship is bound by the traditional values of hierarchy, loyalty, and courage. This explains Big Brother Cheng's ambivalence toward the gangsters who prey on and terrorize the local community: On the one hand, he detests their criminal violence; on the other hand, he is drawn to their tradition of male bonding and *jianghu yiqi* (cherishing loyalty). Hence, he cannot accept the offer from the police to work together to get rid of the gang violence. At the end, the police see him as part of the gangland network and the gangs see him working for the police, and both sides want him in their service or dead. To survive with integrity, he leaves the community to seek refuge in—as we find out in the sequel, *Dage Cheng* (*Big Brother Cheng*, 1975)—the rural idyllic of the New Territories. Thus, the local problems of the colony have become only a new context in which the Shaw Brothers' vision of Chinese values and traditions were projected.

The Teahouse was a box-office success; its success derived mainly from its action-packed narrative and the thrills of some of the fighting scenes (which were shot in the Zhang Che–styled slow motion to exciting effects). As with all Shaw Brothers pictures in the 1970s, it came nowhere near the box-office fortune of Cantonese-language films from such rivals as Golden Harvest, which soon included on its payroll the new superstar Jackie Chan and extended its markets to Japan and Korea. The Shaw Brothers' inability to capture and fully accommodate to the growing local consciousness of Hong Kong audiences was exacerbated by their stress on cost cutting and streamlining of production staff. In the context of structural changes in the pan-Chinese market conditions, the Shaw Brothers began to decline after more than a decade of domination over Hong Kong cinema, during which time it began to grow rapidly and expand globally. Indeed, the quality and market shares of Shaw Brothers products declined steadily until the mid-1980s, around the time of the death of Runme Shaw, when Run Run Shaw began to shift his energy to the operation of HKTVB and rented out large

Big Brother Cheng and his followers in *The Teahouse*. (Courtesy of Celestial Pictures Ltd.)

parts of the Movietown lots to television opera production. From this point on, the Shaw Brothers Studio largely ceased operation. In its stead, television has become the central vehicle of the Shaw Brothers' efforts to construct a global market on the basis of localized programming and pan-Chinese distribution network by means of satellite broadcasting and video rental.

Indeed, a study of the Shaw Brothers is enormously important for our understanding of the complexity of issues and themes concerning the history, politics, diasporic network, global business, identity construction, and pan-Chinese cultures of Chinese-language cinema. For example: To what extent was the Shaw Brothers business a continuity of Chinese business practices? In what ways did its pan-Chinese film community coincide with the global Chinese diasporic business network? What was the role of the Shaw Brothers in Cold War politics in which the Taiwan Nationalist state tried to lead a pan-Chinese alliance against Chinese Communism in the mainland? What were the gender politics and nationalist ideology of the Shaw Brothers Huangmei opera and martial arts film genres? In what ways did the Shaw Brothers help us better understand the complex globalization of Chinese-language cinema today? What made the Shaw Brothers martial arts films so popular among

African American audiences at a time of rapid social and cultural changes in the United States? How did the films impact the Afro-Asian connections and the U.S. racial politics? Although most attention was on the Shaw Brothers' role in the development of Hong Kong cinema, what were its role, strategies, and geographic politics in Southeast Asia? What are the points of intersection of culture, business, gender, modernity, and geographic discourses involved in our study of the Shaw Brothers pan-Chinese cinema? What is the specific role of Hong Kong–Japan coproduction in the development of trans-Asian culture industry? In what ways does a systematic study of the Shaw Brothers pan-Chinese cinema contribute to our understanding of the current debate on the politics and processes of globalization and Chinese diasporic business networks? This collection brings together eleven film critics and scholars of various disciplines to address some of these issues. Actress Cheng Pei-pei, shortly after migrating from Shanghai to Hong Kong in 1961, joined the Shaw Brothers. A well-trained ballet dancer, she quickly rose to stardom with her dazzling performance in *Come Drink with Me* and became the leading actress of the Shaw Brothers' move into martial arts production. In the late 1960s, Cheng Pei-pei was voted by the Hong Kong press as the "Queen of martial arts film." After a long retirement from acting, she recently returned to the screen with the role of Jade Fox in Ang Lee's *Crouching Tiger, Hidden Dragon*. Here she gives us a warm reminiscence of people and life in Movietown at the height of the Shaw Brothers' power. These critical works and personal memories, we hope, will provide a framework for systematic study of the Shaw Brothers' pan-Chinese cinema and deepen our knowledge of the complex history and global connections of the Chinese-language cinema and diasporic culture.

Notes

1. Most recently, two important Chinese-language anthologies on the Shaw Brothers cinema and media have come out in Hong Kong and Taiwan: Wong Ain-ling, ed., *Shaoshi dianying chutan* (*The Shaw Screen: A Preliminary Study*) (Hong Kong: Hong Kong Film Archive, 2003); and Liao Jinfeng et al., eds., *Shaoshi yingshi diguo: wenhua Zhongguo de xianxiang* (*Shaw Brothers Media Empire: Imaging Cultural China*) (Taipei, Taiwan: Maitian chubanshe, 2003). Michael Curtin's recent book, *Playing at the World's Biggest Audience: The Globalization of Chinese Film and TV* (Berkeley: University of California Press, 2007), has an important chapter on the Shaw Brothers cinema. These works provide a strong base for a systematic study of the Shaw Brothers pan-Chinese cinema.

2. See Wang Gungwu, *The Chinese Overseas: From Earthbound China to the Quest for Autonomy* (Cambridge, Mass.: Harvard University Press, 2000), chaps. 1–2; Carl Trocki, "Boundaries and Transgression: Chinese Enterprises in Eighteenth- and

Nineteenth-Century Southeast Asia," in Aiwah Ong and Donald Nonini, eds., *Ungrounded Empires: The Cultural Politics of Modern Chinese Transnationalism* (New York: Routledge, 1998), pp. 61–82; and Lynn Pan, *Sons of the Yellow Emperor: A History of the Chinese Diaspora* (Boston: Little, Brown, 1990), pp. 128–52.

3. There are many fine studies and memoirs of Cathay and MP & GI and the rivalries with the Shaw organization, which I will not discuss here. For examples of these works, see I. C. Jarvie, *Window on Hong Kong: A Sociological Study of the Hong Kong Film Industry and Its Audience* (Hong Kong: Center of Asian Studies, 1977), pp. 35–48; Du Yunzhi, *Zhongguo dianying shi* (History of Chinese Cinema) (Taipei, Taiwan: Shangwu yinshuguan, 1972), vol. 3, pp. 123–40; Sha Rongfeng, *Binfen dianying xishi chun* (My Forty Years of Cinematic Experiences) (Taipei, Taiwan: Guojia dianying ziliaoguan, 1994).

4. See, for example, Jarvie, *Window on Hong Kong*, pp. 44–46; and Du Yunzhi, *Zhongguo dianying qishi nian* (Seventy Years of Chinese Cinema) (Taipei, Taiwan: Dianying tushuguan chubanbu, 1986), pp. 436–46. For an insider's account, see also Zhang Che, *Huigu xianggang dianying sanshi nian* (A Retrospective of Thirty Years of Hong Kong Cinema) (Hong Kong: Sanlain shudian, 1989), pp. 27–45.

5. Bernard Williams, "Singapore's Chinese Barnums Hit by New Hostile People's Party," *Varsity*, January 13, 1960, p. 13.

6. Du Yunzhi, *Zhongguo dianying shi*, vol. 3, pp. 123–24.

7. Run Run Shaw once said that he built Movietown and put so much money into making films not to make money but to "fulfill the mission of developing the Chinese cinema." See Huang Ren, "Shaoshi dianying de tese he yingxiang" (The Characteristics and Impact of the Shaws Films), (unpublished paper, 2002), p. 92.

8. See his interview for *Life Magazine* (Asia edition), "The World of Run Run Shaw," which was published in Chinese in *Xianggang yinghua*, no. 1 (January 1967), pp. 47–50.

9. "Yuandong zuida de yule gongying ku: Shaoshi" (The Shaw Brothers Studio: The Largest Supplier of Entertainments in Asia), *Nanguo dianying*, no.59 (January 1961), pp. 30–33.

10. "Shao Yifu changtan Zhongguo dianying shiye" (Run Run Shaw Discusses Chinese Cinema Business), *Nanguo dianying*, no. 78 (August 1962), p. 14.

11. Tang Yuan, "Yang Guifei" (Empress Yang), *Yinhe huabao*, no. 53 (August 1962), p. 21.

12. "Shao Yifu Zai Wanguo bolanhui" (Run Run Shaw in the World Expo), *Nanguo dianying* no. 59 (January 1963), p. 62.

13. See, for example, *Nanguo dianying*, no. 65 (July 1963), pp. 2–5.

14. Judy Stone, "San Francisco Fest Review," *Variety*, November 13, 1963, p. 17.

15. See "Foreign Films in U.S. Market," *Variety*, April 20, 1960, p. 78; "New York Foreign 'Art' Film Time Up," *Variety*, October 23, 1963, p. 1.

16. See *Xianggang yinghua*, no. 1 (January 1967), pp. 46–49.

17. Perhaps the Shaw Brothers' failure to break into the film markets in Europe and the United States reflected the larger context of global capitalist political economy in

which the Hong Kong cinema industry partook. In the 1950s and 1960s, the capitalist world system was one characterized by rigid boundaries between the underdeveloped East and the industrialized West. A dichotomous habit of mind consequent of colonialism and imperialism pervaded. Discourse of modernization—the West as the universal norm with which all the others were obliged to catch up—abounded in popular publications as varied as *Far Eastern Economic Review* or *The Economist* or *Variety*. Indeed, Hong Kong was by the mid-1960s seen in the industrialized world as a primitive sweatshop turning out cheap, shoddy goods that threatened to depress the global capitalist system. It had low standards of management and production skills and lacked well-known brand names. In order to overcome such prejudices in an attempt to strengthen Hong Kong's export economy, the colonial government launched a series of campaigns that included sending a trade ship around the world to promote economic ties with the city and encouraging local manufacturers through tax incentives to adopt Western management and marketing techniques and set up joint ventures to extend into new markets. As a marginal member in an unequal, hierarchized global capital economy dominated by superpower politics, even with their energy, financial resources, and business acumen, the Shaw brothers had only limited success in transcending the cultural and political boundaries that rigidly divided the world into North and South and East and West. Its films, big or small budget, were ghettoized in the West into a racially bounded market throughout the 1960s.

18. See Yau Shuk-ting's excellently researched essay, "Shaoshi dianying de Riben yinshu" (The Japanese Elements in the Shaw Cinema), in Laio Jinfeng et al., *Shaoshi yingshi diguo*, pp. 76–113.

19. See *Xianggang yinghua*, no. 1 (January 1967), pp. 46–47.

20. William Stefran, "Comparing Diaspora: A Review Essay," *Diaspora* 8, no. 3 (Winter 1999), pp. 255–91.

21. "Shao Yifu de dianying wangguo" (The Film Empire of Run Run Shaw), *Xianggang yinghua* no. 1 (January 1967), p. 48.

22. *Xianggang nianjian* (Hong Kong Report) (Hong Kong: Huaqiao ribao she, 1967), vol. 20, pp. 119–20.

23. See Law Kar, "Xianggang dianying de haiwai jingyan" (The Overseas Experience of Hong Kong Cinema), in Law Kar, ed., *Overseas Chinese Figures in Cinema* (Hong Kong: Urban Council, 1992), p. 16.

24. Xi Xi, *Wo cheng* (*My City*) (Taipei, Taiwan: Yuncheng wenhua, 1993).

25. See David Baird, "What Makes Shaws Run," *Far Eastern Economic Review*, no. 12 (March 19, 1970), p. 83; and I. C. Jarvie, *Window on Hong Kong: A Sociological Study of the Hong Kong Film Industry and Its Audiences* (Hong Kong: Center of Asian Studies, 1977), p. 78.

26. Zhang Che, *Huigu Xianggang dianying sanshi nian* (Thirty Years of Hong Kong Cinema) (Hong Kong: Sanlian shudian, 1989), pp. 90–91.

27. Jarvie, *Window on Hong Kong*, p. 63.

28. See, for example, Stephen Teo, "The 1970s: Movement and Transition," in Poshek Fu and David Desser, eds., *The Cinema of Hong Kong: History, Arts, Identity* (New York: Cambridge University Press, 2000), pp. 90–110; and Li Chuek-to, "Postscript," in *A Study of Hong Kong Cinema in the Seventies* (Hong Kong: Urban Council, 1994), pp. 127–31.

29. Chen Qingwei, *Xianggang dianying gongye jiegou ji shichang fengshi* (Analysis of Hong Kong Film Industry and Marketing) (Hong Kong: Dianying xuang zhou kang chubanshe, 2000), p. 14.

30. See Tian Yan, "The Fallen Idol: Zhang Che in Retrospect," in Li Chuek-to, *A Study of Hong Kong Cinema in the Seventies*, pp. 44–46; Lo Wai-lik, "Zhang Che wuda dianying de nanxing baoli yu qingyi" (The Masculine Violence and Sentiment of Zhang Che Films), in Liao Jinfeng, ed., *Shaoshi yingshi diguo* (Taipei, Taiwan: Maitian chubenshe, 2003), pp. 308–22.

1

Shaw Cinema Enterprise and Understanding Cultural Industries

LILY KONG

Films are an art, but they're also an industry. Forget that
a moment and you have a money loser on your hands.

—Sir Run Run Shaw, *Signature*, January 1981

Introduction

The Shaw Brothers hold a particular fascination for me. We share the same
Ningbo roots, a rarity in the context of predominantly southern Chinese
Singapore. Out of sheer fortuitousness, my office is housed in the Shaw Foundation Building, and my very able senior manager in the Dean's Office hails
from a Shaw family (though not *the* Shaw family). In the 2003 commence-
ment ceremony at my university, an honorary doctor of letters was conferred
on Shaw Vee Ming, son of Run Run Shaw and nephew of the late Runme
Shaw. I was the public orator.

As I researched this chapter, my fascination for the Shaws grew. They
opened up a vista that called for the exploration of a multitude of issues
about cultural industries, forefronting the production of economies, the
creation of meanings, and the defiance of dichotomies. It is impossible to do
justice to all the issues that jostle for attention in one chapter. What I intend
to do, therefore, is to offer a broad sweep, giving attention to how the Shaw
Organisation and its activities challenge dichotomous thinking and prompt
instead a recognition of the mutual constitution of culture/economy, firm/
individual, Fordism/post-Fordism, global/local, and place/placelessness. The
chapter is organized along these binaries, combining in each case larger conceptual issues with analytical insights drawn from the Shaw experience or

theoretical positions that prompt specific research questions about the Shaw Organisation that deserve further interrogation. In working with these different dichotomies, but also unraveling them to encourage a more mutually constitutive understanding of the relationship between the poles of each dichotomy, I adopt an inherently scalar approach that recognizes how the production and consumption of films occur at "multiple levels of meaning, space, time and geography."[1] The analysis that I emphasize is one that runs along a continuum, with a focus on the individual at one end and broad global processes at the other. In between, a variety of scales calls for analysis; for example, the firm, the family, the clan, the state, and so forth, all intersecting in myriad complex relations that (re)produce a cultural economy. In pulling it all together in the concluding section, I seek to spell out an agenda for research into the Asian film industry that goes beyond the scale hitherto dominating film research—that of the nation-state.[2]

The Shaw Story

The Shaw Organisation was founded in 1924 when Tan Sri Runme Shaw came to Singapore from Ningbo, near Shanghai in China. He and his brothers already owned a film company known as Unique Film Productions, also set up in 1924 in Shanghai where they produced silent films. Their intention was to expand beyond the domestic market, particularly in Southeast Asia. As distribution manager, Runme Shaw took on the task and traveled to Singapore, followed by his brother Sri Run Run Shaw. In Singapore, Runme and Run Run incorporated the Hai Seng Co. (later Shaw Brothers Pte. Ltd.), which was responsible for the distribution and exhibition of their movies, as well as those produced by other Chinese companies. From silents to talkies, Singapore to Malaysia, the brothers' film business grew from strength to strength, and by the late 1930s, all the cinemas were managed under Malayan Theatres Limited, a subsidiary of Shaw Brothers Ltd. Downturns during the Great Depression of the 1930s, the Japanese occupation of the 1940s, and the arrival of television in the 1960s presented temporary setbacks that the Shaws dealt with via a range of strategies, including diversification. By 1965 there were thirty-five companies belonging to Shaw Brothers Ltd., including Shaw Studios in Clearwater Bay, Hong Kong, the largest privately owned studios in the world, which officially opened in 1961. In 1969, Shaw Brothers Pte. Ltd. in Singapore became Shaw and Shaw Pte. Ltd., and Shaw Brothers (HK) was listed in 1971. Video piracy of the mid-1980s forced further strategies and reorganization. By 1988, the company was reorganized under the umbrella

of the Shaw Organisation Pte. Ltd. and, through its more than fifteen subsid-
iaries, operates office blocks, apartment buildings, shopping arcades, hotels,
amusement centers, and multiplexes. It has nevertheless not abandoned its
film business; today, Shaw is the leading distributor of worldwide independent films in Singapore.

Culture's Economies, Economy's Cultures

Efforts to generate thinking about the reciprocal relationship between seemingly discrete economic and cultural practices are now new. Andrew Sayer,
for example, argued for the study of the dialectical interplay of the cultural
and economic, just as Lash and Urry propositioned that "the economy is
increasingly culturally inflected [whereas] . . . culture is more and more economically inflected."[3] Specific empirical studies have also been conducted to
interrogate the intersections of culture and capital in the real estate market,
in music, and in fashion, for example.[4]

In thinking about films, a dichotomy of culture/economy is a distinction
between film texts (the social and cultural meanings in and of films) and
film business and industry (the political economy of film). But the dichotomy
is a false one for a variety of reasons. First, politics is closely weaved into
both economic strategy and cultural product; for example, the institutions
of political censorship shape both commercial product and cultural meaning, and political conditions prompt specific economic strategies and shape
cultural product.[5] Shaw ventures clearly exemplify this. The politics of the
1930s shaped the Shaws' production strategy and, hence, the cultural product
and meaning. As Zhou highlighted of 1930s Shaw enterprise, "After the attack
launched by the Japanese on 28 January 1932, Shanghai and the whole country
experienced a sea change in attitudes. Romance, *wuxia* films, and fantasies
were no longer popular. The audience turned to the left-wing, patriotic, and
progressive films." Shaw Brothers' Unique Studios at that point quickly "ad-
justed its strategy, eschewing its old line of populist culture in favour of the
new culture." It started producing movies that "propagated resistance against
the enemy and the imperialists in order to ensure the survival of China as
a nation."[6] This did not last, however. Sensing the need to relocate, by 1933
they had moved to Hong Kong and turned attention to the Southeast Asian
market, using the populist entertainment strategy they followed prior to 1932.
This culture of "political pragmatism" and "flexibility of capital formation"
characterized the Shaws' economic strategy and illustrates the integral intersections of political positioning, economic strategy, and cultural product.[7]

Second, the film message is not autonomous from the material world of film production.[8] For example, the location of capital, personnel, and technology; their spatial concentration or disaggregation; and the movement of key actors as shifts in capital occur all shape the nature of the product. Who is available, with what budget and technology to produce what kind of product and infused with what shade of meaning, involves both economic and cultural considerations. Further, competition and monopoly, the structure of ownership, and the effect of market forces on film production also affect the types of movies produced, the meanings purveyed, and their ideological influences. In short, economic questions should not be studied in isolation from the industry's ideological role and vice versa.[9] The global flow of a cultural product is therefore tied in intimately with moving currents of values and beliefs. Given the global scale and reach of the Shaw enterprise (see the section "Globalizing the Local, Localizing the Global"), the economic traffic that it has generated has also facilitated cultural flows.

Third, the use of cultural (and historical) resources to shape commercial products relies on the cultural codes of a people to sustain the capitalistic enterprise. Various observations about the Shaw enterprise spotlight this intimate interplay of the cultural and economic. For example, eldest brother Runje Shaw was a shrewd observer of human behavior, and the stories he cleverly picked to put on film were positioned to win them a strong market following. In the 1920s and 1930s, he turned popular folk legends that had long been familiar to the masses into popular films, from *Liang Shanbo yu Zhu Yingtai* (*Love Eterne*) to *Madam White Snake, Hua Mulan,* and *Qianlong You Jiangnan*.[10] It revealed how the "rational calculus of the market" was inescapably embedded in cultural roots, for the popularity of these movies relied on the cultural familiarity of the folk legends—their known storylines, their familiar moralities, their recognizable cultural values.[11] The marketing of the product would rely on the deeply embedded cultural references to and portrayals of love, filial piety, valor, and good and evil. This represented an appropriation of historical material and cultural meanings for commercial ends.

A fourth intersection of culture and economy centers on the role of commercial film in the reproduction of social and cultural ideologies and identities. Although films are often commercial products designed to reap profits, they also have social-cultural roles, both via their content and the circumstances of their screenings. Let me take each in turn.

Filmic content contributes to a discursive construction of the society and place they portray. In this, they create social and place meanings but are also the product of such meanings. Textual analyses of Shaw movies will provide broad grounded understandings of such discursive constructions, and they deserve fuller analytical attention than I can afford in a broad treatment.[12]

Apart from such textual analysis of film content, it is as imperative to acknowledge how movie screenings also contribute to a forging and maintenance of social and cultural identities. This is evident, for example, in the "Women's Only" and "Men's Only" screenings that were popular in the 1950s and 1960s. They reflected and reinforced gender roles and relationships, serving as medium and outcome of constructions of masculinity and femininity.

For many years, Shaw Brothers successfully ran "Women's Only" screenings with various female product endorsements. These events attracted hundreds of women from all walks of life. Typical promotions include the *Baby Doll* (1957) promotion, which featured a negligee fashion show; the *Seven Hills of Rome* modeling show of Italian creations by Vanity; and *The Most Beautiful Woman in the World* (1957) promotion, which had a Max Factor cosmetic expert giving free facials and makeup to patrons. An unusual promotion in 1958 attracted scores of mothers as a baby weight contest was held at the Capitol Blue Room in conjunction with the film *The Birth of a Baby.* Constructions of femininity and motherhood are not difficult to discern in these events. Conversely, "Men's Only" screenings involved macho contests, such as beer drinking or arm wrestling. Movie premiums and gifts were also tailored for the male patron. A typical example was the preview of James Stewart's *Night Passage* (1958) with Red Lion drinks given away.[13] What these examples illustrate is how commercial cinema plays important and multiple roles in purveying dominant ideology while appearing ideologically innocent or mere entertainment.[14] In brief, my intention in this section is to contribute to the growing literature that deconstructs the dichotomy between culture and economy and to illustrate how economic intents have social-cultural import in as much as the social and cultural have economic outcomes. This resonates with the views of the French Cinéthique group (based around a French journal of that name) when it condemned commercial cinema for its uncritical ideological role.

Abstraction of Firms, Agency of Individuals

Moving from the macroscale of economy, culture, and society, I turn attention in this section to a more micro analysis of the firm and individual, treating them as poles of a binary, the distance between which deserves interrogation. In neoclassical economic geography, the firm is an unproblematic given, a homogeneous unit of analysis that gives rise to economic outcomes in space. In such analysis, the firm is a unit constituting locational patterns that deserves scrutiny. Similarly, in the more radical literature, the firm is "subsumed . . . under dominant capitalist class relations such that capital's logic explains the spatial behaviour of the firm."[15] In these approaches, the "internal workings" of the firm are not the substance of study. Such treatments of the firm as a given entity still generate much important research. The "sociocultural turn" in geography, however, has also led scholars to consider the firm as a "site of power relations and power struggle among actors who may be capitalists, workers, technologists, managers, regulators, analysts, strategists and so on."[16] This has prompted the view that firms are not just abstract economic institutions but are instead "embodiments of social-spatial logics and actor-specific discursive practices."[17] Such an approach tends toward the analysis of individuals within firms as social agents in a particular time and place who shape the direction of the firm.[18] It also recognizes that firms are "internally heterogeneous and contested by different interest groups and corporate actors with varying degrees of power and access to knowledge and resources" as well as influenced by their gender, ethnicity, and culture.[19]

Understanding the Shaw Brothers movie business requires an approach that appreciates both the firm as an economic entity to be understood in terms of abstract linkages and processes and the firm as a sociocultural site to be understood in terms of relationships and tensions, constituted of a complex of individual networks and decisions. Such an approach should acknowledge the mutually constitutive relationship between the abstract firm and individual agency. How the unitary firm behaves and is located within the film industry form the substance of discussion in the next section on Fordism/post-Fordism. In the next section, I focus on individual social agents within firms, the key actors whose specific practices impact on the decisions and workings of the firm, as well as the ways in which the structure, organization, and culture of the firm impact on the individual agent's actions. I also draw attention to the relationships between individuals and the networks that they constitute in influencing the workings of firms.

Fordist Production, Post-Fordist Innovation

In the 1930s, in their foray into Malaya, Singapore, and Indonesia, the Shaws chose to produce locally, establishing studios in Singapore and buying cinemas. In doing this, they sought to control all aspects of their film business: production, distribution, and exhibition. At the peak of Shaw Studios' output in the 1960s in Hong Kong, production on a new film would start every nine days, with as many as twelve films in production at any one time. Shooting would take only an average of forty days per film.[20] This was made possible given Run Run Shaw's development of Movietown in Hong Kong from 1958, which boasted of modern technology (e.g., Eastmancolor, Shawscope) as well as the introduction of modern capitalist management techniques:

> The Shaw Brothers Studio was run like an assembly line, with Shaw himself overseeing every part of the operation that stressed rational management, economic efficiency, professionalism, standardization of production in pursuit of maximum profit. To have "rational" control over its labor force, for example, most of its 1,700 employees were required to live in the Studio's dormitory and subjected to the disciplinary regime (related to its infamous "star-making system") of stringent contract, strict rules, and low pay.[21]

This was Fordism at its best and worst. All the classic characteristics of the Fordist regime of accumulation were evident in the Shaw enterprise: the moving assembly line; the "mass workers" in large factories; economies of scale reaped through large-scale mass production; a hierarchical bureaucratic form of work organization, characterized by a centralized management; vertical integration, driven by a desire to achieve cost efficiency in production and exchange.[22] And it worked, for the mass consumption continued to support the mass production for the system to regenerate itself.

In recent years, however, a series of writings on Hollywood have signaled the permeation of post-Fordist modes of accumulation in the film industry. For example, authors have debated the continued importance of the majors, as vertically disintegrated production complexes replace the vertical integration of old. Vertical disintegration has entailed "the fragmentation of organisational elements into separate and specialized yet functionally interlinked units" as well as more active use of subcontracting.[23] It has occurred in order to externalize nonstrategic or unpredictable and variable functions and labor processes, thereby externalizing uncertainty and risk.[24] Vertical disintegration has also occurred as part of an attempt to exploit maximum variety of creative resources. Christopherson and Storper argue that, in the post-Fordist regime of vertical disintegration, majors are divested of their former productive capacity and contractual engagements and, instead, become the nerve centers of the new disintegrated networks in which skilled employees previously on studio payrolls become freelance agents.[25] Large numbers of small, flexibly specialized firms spring up in a wide range of subsectors, providing both direct and indirect inputs to the majors. This, they contend, leads to territorial localization, the formation of cultural districts with agglomeration of firms because the instability of casualized employ-ment relations and the critical need to remain in contact networks generate agglomeration tendencies. This trend of disintegration and localization is not contradictory to integration and globalization because the former is about cultural production, the latter about cultural distribution (see the section "Globalizing the Local, Localizing the Global").[26]

Beyond vertical disintegration, another sign of the advent of post-Fordist modes of production and its impact on firms is the growing corporate integra-tion or horizontal alignment, "at both national and international levels, with new alliances between broadcasters, film and television producers, publishers, record producers and so on."[27] Large conglomerates and cross-media owner-ship characterize post-Fordist accumulation. In Hollywood, this is evident in that the majors, which have traditionally concentrated on the financing, production, and theatrical distribution of motion pictures, have, over the last few decades, actively diversified operations, currently earning a substantial proportion of their revenue from specialized divisions, including TV program-ming, home video, multimedia, theme parks, and merchandising.[28] Overarch-ing communications empires combine these diverse media products.[29] These growing conglomerates may be ascribed to attempts to "internalize the syner-gies that are frequently found at intersections between different segments of the media and entertainment (and hardware) industries."[30]

The firm in Fordist and post-Fordist analysis, as outlined previously, dis-plays definite characteristics and behaves in specified ways. The Shaw experi-ence, however, suggests that Morley and Robins are exactly right in making the case that "any real-world transition beyond Fordism will inevitably be a great deal more complex, unruly and uncertain. . . . The process of trans-formation is complex and uneven, and it is genuinely difficult to establish whether the present period marks the emergence of a post-Fordist society, whether it should be characterized as neo-Fordist, or whether, in fact, it re-mains a period of late Fordism."[31]

Although pre- and postwar Shaw enterprise exhibited all the classic char-acteristics of Fordism, there were also evidences of elements deemed post-Fordist accumulation even in the early twentieth century. Further, in the late twentieth and early twenty-first centuries, evidence of post-Fordist ac-cumulation is also less clear-cut.

In the 1920s, the Shaw Brothers had already begun to engage in cross-media ownership, a strategy that has only intensified in more recent decades. When Runme and Run Run Shaw bought into cinema chains in the early 1920s, they also bought into the burgeoning and increasingly popular multipurpose entertainment parks that contained cinemas and housed cabarets, *joget* dance stages, Bangsawan stages, Chinese opera, food stalls, magic shows, and gambling stalls.[32] From the prewar days, the Shaws also maintained their own printing press called the Shaw Printing Works, which facilitated the printing of publicity materials and, later, movie publications. In Singapore, film magazines in all four languages were published under the banner of the Chinese Pictorial Review Ltd. The English-language film magazine was the very popular *Movie News*, first published in 1948 and continuing until the late 1980s when foreign entertainment magazines dominated the market. *Southern Screen*, published in Hong Kong from the 1950s until the early 1980s, was the popular monthly Chinese magazine read in Singapore, Malaysia, Indonesia, Macau, Taiwan, Brunei, Vietnam, Cambodia, Laos, Burma, the Philippines, Australia, India, Korea, the United States, South and Central America, Canada, France, and England.[33] Their ownership of a printing press and entertainment parks facilitated marketing and exhibition of Shaw movies.

In 1973, Sir Run Run Shaw launched TVB, Hong Kong's first wireless commercial TV station. Unlike the British scene of the 1980s when TV stations were cofinancing film ventures, here, the alliance worked in reverse.[34] Nevertheless, TVB complemented the work of the movie production studios, providing a means by which the movies reached a wide audience. TVB is the leading producer of Chinese-language programs in the world and has, by far, the highest viewer ratings in Hong Kong and South China, with more than 70 percent market share. TVBI (TVB International), established in 1976, supplies programs to free-to-air broadcasters, cable and satellite service operators, and licensed video distributors throughout North and South America, Europe, and the Asia-Pacific region. By 1990, it had a satellite television linkup license to establish its own distribution operations in the United States and the United Kingdom to handle home videos; by 1994, TVB (USA) Inc. was beaming its Jade Channel via satellite directly to viewers in the United States; and by 1997, it had a franchised video chain called TVB Video in Vancouver, British Columbia, with a similar one in the United Kingdom, as well as a satellite-delivered Chinese-language service in Europe. TVB also entered into a joint venture in 1999 with a Malaysian company to incorporate an Internet subsidiary company, aiming to be the dominant Chinese-language portal that will host a spectrum of net broadcasts and interactive services.[35] In short, Shaw Brothers is now Shaw Media, a part of the TVB group, and is involved in producing TV shows that are shown on Chinese cable and satellite channels all over the world and has extended the cross-media ownership from cinema to TV screen, pay-TV, satellite TV, the Internet, and DVD.[36]

If the Shaws seemed ahead of their time in displaying post-Fordist tendencies to establish a media conglomerate constituting an overarching communications empire, it prompts the thought earlier intimated that perhaps transformation between Fordism and post-Fordism is a messy, cross-cutting affair, not a linear transition. Further research is needed to explore the organization's tendency to vertically integrate or disintegrate. Preliminary information suggests that the diversification to television and other ventures coincided with a shift away from film production and a concentration on film distribution and exhibition, with the Shaw Studios lots in Hong Kong leased out to TVB and other movie production companies in the 1980s. There is, however, a potential reversion to movie production with new investments in a joint venture with Hong Kong Movie City Company to develop new movie studios, which were completed in 2007.[37] Detailed analysis of how the Shaws choose to take their enterprise ahead will help shape conceptual understanding of the transition from Fordism to post-Fordism.

Individual Agency

In focusing on the firm—its state of integration or disintegration, its scale of production, its management, its spatial relationship, and its organizational association with other firms—attention is drawn away from individual agency, the "discretionary choices of actual historical individuals."[38] Yet there is evidence to suggest the imperative role of individuals as social agents within firms, whether as corporate strategists or cultural intermediaries, or in the relationships, connections, and networks they cultivate and enjoy that facilitate their roles.[39]

Given the focus of this chapter on cultural industries, I will confine my comments to one category of individual agents particularly significant in cultural products firms, namely, the cultural intermediaries. In its original construction, Bourdieu referred to cultural intermediaries as "all the occupations involving presentation and representation (sales, marketing, advertising, public relations, fashion, decoration and so forth) and in all the institutions providing symbolic goods and services . . . and in cultural production and organisation."[40] These cultural intermediaries tend to blur conventional distinctions, such as between "personal taste and professional judgement," and leisure and work.[41] In this regard, these individuals foreground the ways in which culture shapes the economics and generates thinking about the reciprocal interrelationship of what are often thought of as discrete cultural and economic practices.[42]

As distinct from Bourdieu's conception of cultural intermediaries, Negus proposes "the suits" (senior managers, senior corporate executives, business analysts, and accountants) as another category of cultural intermediaries. They assess the economic potential of any acquisition and help monitor economic performance and commercial viability and thus mediate the process of production of cultural products. Their own relations with artists also influence the judgments they make. By participating in the construction of what is to be commercial, they, too, mediate the values through which aesthetic work is realized.

If attention in Shaw research has been given to the role of individuals, the tendency has been to acknowledge the brothers themselves. This is, of course, warranted for their larger-than-life roles in producing, marketing, purchasing, distributing, and so on—in short, for building a hugely successful movie empire. There are also others in their employ who have acted as key individual agents, however, as cultural intermediaries in both Bourdieu's and Negus's conceptions. An analysis of their roles can shed light on the contributions of cultural intermediaries. Given the management structure of the Shaw Organisation and its predecessors, several key roles would seem to deserve research attention in Shaw archives and through oral histories, such as the heads of the Publicity and Advertising Department; the Chinese, Malay, and Indian Departments; the Film Booking Department (which decided where, when, and how long a film would play in Shaw cinemas); and the chief of Shaw Printing Works. The mediating role that the marketing executive played, for example, deserves to be understood within the social and economic context of the country and company at the particular historical juncture. Thus, as explained in the Shaw Organisation's Web site:

> Promotional materials sent from major studios had to be adapted to local conditions in Singapore and Malaysia. Having to work on a tight budget, Shaw's marketing team had to be creative at the least expense. For the Federation (Malaysian) Theatres, promotional materials were usually recycled from a film's Singapore release. It was up to the publicity managers of the various management offices in Malaysia to come up with creative ways to utilise such materials and hype up a film.[43]

Relative box office successes must thus be understood in terms of the roles of such key agents in helping present and re-present products. This would, in my perspective, constitute an important question on any research agenda that focuses on film (and cultural) industries.

The agency of individuals must be understood not only in terms of the roles they perform, but also in terms of the relationships, connections, and networks they bring, establish, and develop that facilitate performance of their roles. For Bourdieu, entry into those occupations he defines as cultural intermediaries is usually via "networks of connections, shared values and common life experiences."[44] This is true, too, for the cultural producers—the artist, director, writer, and producer—not just in terms of entry into the occupations, but in myriad other ways, embedding various economic processes in networks of interpersonal relations. Indeed, relations of trust, cooperation, and mutuality ensure that economic action is not "some kind of free-floating logic or rationality" but is embedded in key social actors and their networks.[45] These networks must be understood in terms of the rationale behind their creation (e.g., ties developed to enable funding for ventures); their wider social, cultural, institutional, geographic, and historical contexts; their strength of association and the varying enabling effects; and the power relations within these interpersonal networks that "need not necessarily be highly egalitarian and reciprocal."[46] Writing about the Vancouver film industry, Coe argues that the nature of the production process is determined by interpersonal relations and that the key relationships are between producers, executive producers, talent agents, entertainment lawyers, and business affairs executives who negotiate the deals.[47]

For the Shaw Brothers, entry into the Southeast Asian market in the 1920s and 1930s was initially hampered by the lack of "networks of connections." That they were Shanghainese resulted in their being "locked out of the highly protected market by the dominant dialect factions—Cantonese, Hokkien and Teochew—which controlled local film business."[48] These businessmen imported films directly from China to show in their cinemas, and Run Run and Runme Shaw had to struggle to carve out a market share for themselves:

> With Run Run supervising Singapore, Runme took the train north to the larger towns of Malaya like Ipoh, Kuala Lumpur and Penang, in order to establish business ties with local theatre owners. Ipoh was chosen as his base from where smaller towns could be explored for business potential. These "market surveys" were done by car. With so much territory to cover, both brothers took turns driving through the night, stopping only to drink water from pipes by the road. Where a trip was particularly grueling, even Run Run's wife Mei Chen joined in as a relief driver.

Clearly, the Shaws did not originally have the business or interpersonal networks—the *guanxi* (relationships)—that would give them an easy foothold into the industry in Southeast Asia. Quite unlike the literature in Asian business networks that identifies the role of relationships in facilitating market entry, the businesses that the Shaws were to develop in Southeast Asia began from a handicapped position, one lacking in dialect ties, emphasizing the myth of unitary pan-Chinese identity.

That the business, which had been undauntedly carved out of unknown and unfriendly territory, remained so much within the Shaw family points to a need to understand the relationships within the organization as inflected by family ties. Negus, in writing about cultural intermediaries, had suggested that, in the film industry, anecdotal evidence points to the importance of family connections.[49] Besides that brief reference, however, little work has been done on how large media conglomerates may in fact function as a family firm. This opens up a range of questions about the Shaw Organisation as a Chinese family business. Researchers from a variety of disciplines have examined the phenomenon of family businesses and have foregrounded their characteristics, successes, and failures, focusing on issues such as personalism, paternalism, centralized authority structures, trust (*xinyong*), and connections (*guanxi*).[50] This research has not yet been done, but analysis of the Shaw family business should interrogate issues of conflicts and conflict management, succession and inheritance, as well as the increasing permeation of legal rationalism, professionalism, meritocracy, and credentialism with the rise of the nation-state. We already know that

> The company was run on a family management style. Each brother managed a different department in the production process. Second brother Runde was the financial controller; third brother Runme (aka Shanke) and sixth brother Run Run/Yifu were responsible for distribution and building distribution networks at home and overseas. The brothers coordinated their efforts in administration, while their talents were also given full display in the artistic field.[51]

But much more empirical research and analysis (not to mention cooperation on the part of the family) is needed to help us establish the appropriate theoretical ground between simple market and culturalist models of Chinese business strategy and structure. This area currently remains terra incognita, and is presented as a challenge, first, to students of cultural industries, and especially film industries, as a question about the role of family ties in the development of such industries, and, second, to students of family business networks, as a question about how the role of the family in the film business differs from that in other businesses.

Globalizing the Local, Localizing the Global

I have now dealt with a variety of scales, beginning with a broad consideration of economy, culture, and society, and then deconstructing that in terms of the firm, individual, and family. What are implicit in the preceding discussions are the multiple intersections of the global and local; for example, the ways in which global Fordist practices shape local management techniques and the ways in which local interpersonal ties can build global empires. In this section, I wish to turn explicit attention to global/local intersections.

Much of the literature on this issue (as it pertains to popular cultural forms like music and television) has focused on how global (often U.S.) influences lead to a homogenization of product and therefore stamp out local uniqueness or how distinctive cultural resources localize global forms.[52] This remains a worthy line of analysis and will be given some airtime later. In painting on a larger canvas, however, I would like to use the grounded data from observations of the Shaw Organisation to distill a conceptual framework for the analysis of economic and cultural globalization and localization as it pertains to the film industry. The framework insists not only on the intersections of the global/local, but also returns our scrutiny to the intersections of the cultural/economic.

Four key frames form the main bases of specific strategies of the Shaw Brothers, namely, globalizing trends, reterritorializing economies, localizing content, and creating meanings. *Globalizing trends* addresses the ways in which the organization aimed to achieve a global scale of business, the impetuses for such global ventures, and the strategy of transnational collaboration to achieve global reach. Although essentially economic in intent, intersections with the cultural are apparent in the diasporic inroads to the global and the mixed cultural-economic impetuses to globalize. *Reterritorializing economies,* in emphasizing the importance of territory in building economy, draws our attention to the local and the value of place in the production of economy. *Localizing content* constitutes the third frame of analysis and draws attention to essentially cultural strategies that result in hybridized products for local markets. Finally, *creating meanings,* a fourth frame of analysis, draws attention to the creation of local place meanings through both the production and consumption process.

Global Ventures: International Scale and Reach

One interpretation of *becoming global* is simply achieving a global business scale and reach that would warrant characterization as a global venture. I will

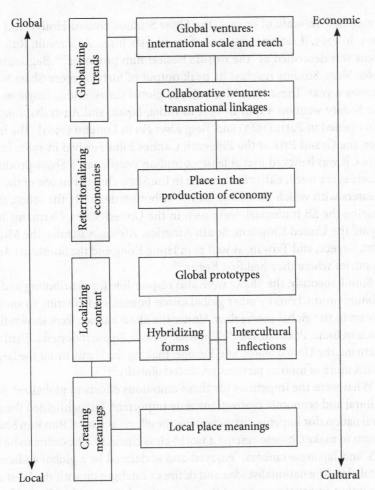

Global-local connections: insights from the Shaw Organisation.

illustrate briefly how the Shaw Organisation has achieved qualified success in this endeavor as well as explore the impetuses for such global ventures.

The Shaw enterprise was extensive in its scale of business, beginning with a regional reach and eventually extending to a global scale. Begun in the 1920s, the Shaws were already operating a chain of 139 cinemas across Singapore, Malaysia, Thailand, Indonesia, and Indochina by 1939. These were either bought, built, leased by the Shaws, or operated in partnership with their owners. By the 1970s, the worldwide cinema chain had grown to 230, dotting Southeast Asia, Hong Kong, Japan, Australia, and North

America.[53] In scale of output, the Shaw Studios rivaled Hollywood studios. In 1965, it set a new record of twenty-six films. As a result, Run Run Shaw was described as "the world's busiest film producer."[54] Beginning in 1966, Shaw Studios reached its peak output of forty or more Shaw Scope movies a year. These films also enjoyed global distribution. *Kingdom and the Beauty* went on a tour in 1961 to India, Japan, and Australia. *Empress Wu* opened in Paris (1963) and *Yang Kwei Fei* in London (1963). The latter won the Grand Prix at the Fifteenth Cannes Film Festival in 1962. In the 1970s, it was believed that at least 1.5 million people saw a Shaw-produced movie every week, either in a cinema in the Shaw chain or in one of the 600 theaters with which the Shaws had distribution deals. By the 1980s, films bearing the SB trademark were seen in the United States, Germany, Italy, Japan, the United Kingdom, South America, Africa, Australia, the Middle East, Greece, and Taiwan, as well as in Hong Kong and the Southeast Asian countries where they had first begun.[55]

Simultaneously, the Shaws were also responsible for distributing and exhibiting productions by other global movie houses, contributing to another stream in the global media flow. Under the Shaw banner were shown films made in India, Pakistan, the Philippines, Taiwan, Japan, Indonesia, Thailand, Vietnam, the United States, and Europe, making the Shaws by far the largest distributors of motion pictures produced globally.[56]

What were the impetuses for these ambitious efforts to globalize? Both cultural and economic motivations were important. Fu highlighted the cultural nationalist impetus, characterizing the efforts as part of Run Run Shaw's dream to make Chinese cinema a world-class cinema.[57] The desire to be like U.S. and Japanese cinema, "enjoyed and acclaimed by a global audience," paralleled "the nationalist idea and desire of catching up with the West and becoming an equal member of the international community." Fu attributed this to the fact that the Shaws lived away from home and under "alien" culture, and like other diasporic Chinese, developed a sense of nationalism. Given his "business opportunism and personal ambition," Run Run Shaw's nationalism found expression in cultural and economic terms: to capture the Southeast Asian, then Asian, then global market for profit motives as well as to fulfill "cultural and artistic missions." The latter entailed "introduc[ing] through celluloid images to people of different languages and races the cultural and artistic traditions of China."[58] As Fu further pointed out, "In the early 1960s, Run Run Shaw invariably expressed his enthusiasm to conquer the land of Hollywood in terms of nationalism. In a press conference in Taiwan, he declared his mission as leading Chinese cinema out of the racial ghetto,

Chinatown, into the mainstream market," and he promised to collaborate with Western film producers on an "equal basis" in order to "accelerate the entrance of Chinese cinema into the global market."[59]

How successful were the Shaws in achieving global scale? The international reach outlined previously would seem to point to the Shaw business as a thoroughly global enterprise. Yet they were not entirely successful in breaking into some markets or in securing equal partnership with companies beyond Asia or outside the "racial ghetto" in the West, so that a more appropriate assessment might be a qualified success.

In market terms, the Shaws' success was very much built on the Chinese diaspora, despite Run Run Shaw's desire to move out of the "racial ghetto." The potential of this diasporic market was already evident in the 1920s. As an example, Said pointed out how movie houses owned by Chinese were widespread in the Indonesian archipelago because, first, it was the wealthy Chinese who could afford to be producers; second, the influx of Chinese films from Shanghai showed the potential of the Chinese market and encouraged development of the Chinese film industry among overseas Chinese; and third, the Chinese recognized the need among the populace for movies that spoke to their daily lives as opposed to stories from traditional theater about princes and princesses.[60] Thus, by the 1930s and 1940s, the Shaws decided to invest in Cantonese films, "which were hugely popular among Chinese communities in Southeast Asia."[61] Zhou argued that the cinema was an important channel by which the illiterate Chinese laborers from Guangdong and Fujian clung to "their motherland."[62] At the same time, Fu showed how the Shaw movies appealed to the Chinese diaspora, which was nostalgic for the homeland, but lacked appeal for the mainstream U.S. audience because of the lack of "cultural relevance and emotional identification."[63]

These diasporic markets do not negate the globality of the Shaws' ventures and should indeed be characterized as global niche markets. This is akin to the contemporary phenomenon in which globalization has brought into existence a global media space and market. This global media space is not the same as a "world cultural convergence," or "acceptance of a single product and positioning across a wide range of geography," because the global corporation will look to "respond to the demands of particular segments of the market" while searching for "similar segments throughout the globe to achieve the scale economies that keep their costs competitive."[64] In other words, these global corporations, including the Shaw Organisation, adopt the strategy of "treat[ing] these market segments as global, not local, markets" and develop strategies that expand these specialized and niche markets to worldwide proportions rather than stamp out specific market segments in the interest of a global homogenized market.[65]

Collaborative Ventures: Transnational Linkages

Looking away from the perspective of distributive reach and market, in production terms, the Shaw Brothers achieved global reach through transnational collaborative ventures. In the 1950s, they worked with Japan, mainly through mutual facilitation of on-location shooting. Subsequently, other coproduction offers started pouring in as foreign producers were keen to share in the success of Shaw Studios. These ventures included regional players such as Taiwan, Korea, Thailand, and the Philippines. As the Shaws' reputation grew, attracting talent from the region was not an unusual feature of their productions. By 1970, among the studio's fourteen directors were Japan's Inoue Umetsugu and Korea's Cheng Chang Ho. Its performers also hailed from all over the region.[66]

By the 1970s, the Shaw Brothers were coproducing films with Western producers for the international market as well. Among their collaborations were *Dracula and the Seven Golden Vampires* (Hammer production), *Supermen against the Orient* (Indief Film Co. production), *Cleopatra Jones and the Casino of Gold* (William Tennant production), *Meteor* (Sandy Howard/Gabriel Katzka production), *Inseminoid* (Jupiter Films production), and *Blade Runner* (Ladd Company production). These coproductions helped increase total output of the studio, enabling wider reach, and raised production standards in Hong Kong, giving cast and crew from the Shaw Studios the opportunity to learn firsthand from Hollywood and Europe.[67]

Fu remains skeptical about an unmitigated evaluation of these transnational linkages, however, arguing that the Shaws' role tended to be minor in the collaboration with Euro-American producers.[68] The relationship was limited to rights to market in Asia or unequal coproduction partnership. The Shaws would provide technical support and studio facilities to the Western partners when they shot on location in Hong Kong, make profits through acquiring the exclusive distribution rights to these films, and acquire rights to use the sets and original scripts for the production of Mandarin films. In short, although there is definite evidence of transnational linkages constituting globalizing trends, there is also evidence of uneven development arising out of collaborative ventures. Theoretically, it is critical to register the point that collaborative ventures and transnational linkages are indicators of globalization of firms, industries, and economies, but the nature of the collaboration and linkage must be interrogated for a more nuanced understanding of the specific character of globalization.

Reterritorializing Economies

The surge to globalize is sometimes also combined with the localization of global form and process, suggesting that simultaneous globalization and localization is by no means a contradictory process. In this section, I wish to highlight the manner in which the local is important in the production of economy, for place matters in the ways it enables and constrains.

The Shaw Brothers certainly were aware of this fact. In the 1960s and 1970s, for example, their presence in Thailand could escalate because the free-trade policy allowed them to take control of more than one hundred exhibition halls across the country.[69] Similarly, the experience of 1949 China shaped Shaw business strategy:

> After the founding of the People's Republic in 1949, the mainland's cinema industry was nationalized. Its exports were limited and tightly controlled by a handful of "leftist" distribution companies. Thus, the supply of Mandarin films (principally from Shanghai) ended for all overseas private distributors. To ensure steady supply of Chinese-language films, both Mandarin and Cantonese, to their sprawling exhibition network in Southeast Asia, Run Run Shaw decided to upgrade and expand the production facilities in Hong Kong in order to take advantage of the low-tax, export-oriented business environment and concentration of film talents (including many émigrés from post-revolutionary Shanghai) in the colony.[70]

To summarize, although market freedom and global flows do characterize much of contemporary economic conditions, locality nevertheless shapes the context—including the politics and state policies—which has an effect on the production of the cultural economy. Even as hypermobile capital reduces the friction of geography, space and place cannot be annihilated.[71]

Beyond the place of the state, with all its enabling and constraining policies that shape conditions for the production of economy, place is significant in the (re)production of the cultural economy in yet other ways. With post-Fordist vertical disintegration, Scott argues, "With the reconstitution of production system as a transactions-intensive congeries of small and specialized but complementary firms, the agglomerative forces holding the entire complex together in geographic space were reinforced and its regional competitive advantages secured."[72] This echoes the views of Morley and Robins who point out that

Vertical disintegration results in the formation of a localised nexus of small units, often centred around one or a few dominant large companies, and involved in close contractor/subcontractor relationships, continuous information exchange and, thus, spatial proximity. The consequence of the new dynamics of flexible specialisation, with its tendencies towards spatial agglomeration, has been to give a new centrality to local economies (Courlet and Judet, 1986). It is at the level of locality that important new economic and social developments are being worked out.

The "small variations in the nature of different localities" become important, such that "the spatial matrix of contemporary capitalism is one that, in fact, combines and articulates tendencies towards both globalisation and localisation."[73]

There is as yet no research into this aspect of Shaw enterprise, which should be coupled with systematic analysis of the extent of vertical disintegration of the company. As discussed earlier, the transition to post-Fordist production does not appear to be marked by clarity and textbook systematicity, and detailed empirical inquiry into Shaw and other Asian film company experience will go a long way into a nuanced understanding of Fordist/post-Fordist practices in the film industry.

Localizing Content

In as much as economies are reterritorialized, in recent years scholars have also argued that a reterritorialization of the media is needed; that is, a relationship between media and territory deserves to be reestablished so that the media contributes to "sustaining both the distinctiveness and the integrity of local and regional cultures, against the threatening forces of 'de-territorialisation' and homogenisation."[74] In other words, scholars have argued for the localization of content of cultural products.

The Shaw experience reinforces the economic value of such localization. Their strategies in Southeast Asia, for example, met with various degrees of success, dependent on their sensitivity to local cultures. Thus, of the initial foray into Singapore, van der Heide highlighted how the lack of understanding and appropriate incorporation of local Malay culture in Shaw movies proved detrimental:

> In the late 1930s, the Shaw Brothers set up a film production company in Singapore and produced eight Malay language films. They imported used film equipment from Shanghai and employed Shanghaiese [sic] directors and

technicians. The films that they produced starred the region's best-known *Bangsawan* (popular Malay opera) players. Yet the films were not popular with local audiences partly because the Chinese directors were unfamiliar with Malay culture, such that the films had no cultural resonances for the Malay audiences. It ended Shaw Brothers' interest in film production for some time.[75]

In the late 1940s, the Shaw Brothers reentered the film industry in Singapore, and right up until the mid-1960s they worked to redevelop a Malay film industry with different strategies. Although the movies were still in Malay, this time they relied only on Chinese funding and technical expertise, while using Indian directors and keeping Malay actors. The intercultural inflections worked this time. The cross-influences of Bangsawan actors with Madras, Bombay, and Calcutta (as opposed to Shanghainese) directors weaved the Indian tradition of "melodramatic, episodic and digressive narrative" with local stories and local song and dance styles, to much better response. These transnational intercultural influences place on the research agenda issues about both the production and consumption of these hybrid forms—what elements of the different cultural styles are taken on board, and how are they "fused," and why? What new cultural space and form was being created? Why were these Indian-Malay films more popular with the local audiences than the earlier Chinese-Malay films?[76]

Apart from such intercultural inflections, the Shaw Brothers also attempted, as a second strategy, to hybridize the content of their productions to cater to specific audiences. Measures included dubbing, censoring, and incorporation of local cultural forms. In their heyday in the 1960s and 1970s, Shaw movies would be dubbed in various Chinese dialects as well as European languages for the few movies that were to be exported to Western markets. At the same time, to address local censorship issues, three versions of films would be made if they were aimed to have wide distribution: "a 'hot' version for the U.S., Japan and Europe; a 'cold' version for Singapore, Malaysia and Taiwan; and a 'medium' version for Hong Kong."[77] Further, local cultural resources would be drawn upon to appeal to senses of familiarity. Thus, in the early production of Malay films, for example, Malay pantuns and proverbs would be incorporated.

Third, the localization of global form is further evident in the ways in which global trends are adopted and adapted. Thus, in the 1960s, with the popularity of the James Bond films, the Shaws' directors saw the opportunity to adopt the prototype and harness the interest in spy movies. They began making their own brand of spy movies, with films such as *Black Falcon* (1966), *The Angel with the Iron Fist* (1966), *Special Agent 009* (1967), and *Kiss and Kill* (1967), with Hong Kong's own Paul Chang Chung as the Chinese equivalent of James Bond and leading ladies like Lily Ho and Margaret Tu Chuan as female Bonds.[78]

Creating Meanings

By now, the significance of place and locality in the production of economy and the making of cultural product should be evident. In this final section on the global/local, I focus on place and the creation of meaning. This has to do with the way in which films capture the many geographies of a place, functioning as both medium and outcome of "splintering, colliding, and merging" geographies of a place.[79] Films are a medium through which place and place meanings are portrayed, but film is not merely a "transparent medium" that is the "innocent" outcome of producers' place meanings, for three reasons.[80] First, as Kennedy and Lukinbeal point out, multiple factors affect a film's representation, "the social milieu in which it was formed; the cultural values of the film maker; the film maker's own ideological views; the need to make narrative cinema a form of entertainment; colour and lighting; the subject-matter presented; and the genre of the film."[81]

Second, an interpretive audience "reading" films ensures that the meanings intended by producers are not uncritically received. Third, the impact of a film on an audience can mold conceptions of place and place experience. As Aitken and Zonn point out, "the way spaces are used and places are portrayed in film reflects prevailing cultural norms, ethical mores, societal structures, and ideologies. Concomitantly, the impact of a film on an audience can mold social, cultural, and environmental experiences."[82] The fine tradition of work that focuses analysis on specific films or a body of films and explores the meanings of/for people and place deserves no elaboration here but certainly warrants continued research focus.[83] Often, they reflect the intersections of the global/local in the making of meanings.

Conclusion

The Shaw Brothers present abundant opportunities for research into cultural industries, identity constructions, and place meanings. Their business was, of course, not confined to movies alone, although that constituted the hub of the wheel for a long time. Their other enterprises also open up arenas for research, not least the spectacle of amusement parks, the gendered world of dance halls, the regulation of morality in cabarets and revues, and the scale and competition of international trade fairs. But although another world opens up there, I will confine my remarks to the film industry in particular and cultural industries more generally.

Using the theoretical lenses evolved through the preliminary and broad-ranging observations of the Shaw enterprise, and the agenda-setting contemplations of geographers such as John Silk, Christina Kennedy, and Christopher Lukinbeal, I wish to conclude by reflecting on key research questions that I believe deserve attention as they focus on the film industry in Asia particularly and cultural industries more generally. To do so requires that I take stock first of what kind of research currently exists. It is fair to say that much of the research has tended to focus on the historical development of the film industry in each country,[84] on issues of nationalism and cinema,[85] and on the analysis of specific personalities, particularly actors[86] and images and themes.[87]

All of this research is important and relevant, and the currents of interest should continue to shed light on Asian life and rhythms, policy, and economy. But if further insights are to be gleaned from an analysis of films and the film industry, then close scrutiny of the intersections of the global/local, culture/economy, firm/individual should be encouraged. What are the ways in which local cultural and economic spaces refract such spaces at the global scale? How are cultural meanings inseparable from the political economy of a place? How are a firm's decisions to be understood in terms of individual predilections and networked connectivities? Where does the family and the diasporic community intersect with economic production and distributive reach? Although some of these questions are already being interrogated, others deserve fuller focus.

Analyzing the Shaw Brothers and their organizations requires that we draw from a whole range of theories that span a continuum of scales from the individual to the firm, the social-cultural, the state, and the global. The interconnectedness of different scales of interaction and operation are evident from the preceding discussions, knitting the individual with the family and other social connections (such as dialect ties and Chinese diasporic networks) and weaving local place logics with global imperatives. At the same time, a more comprehensive approach to the analysis of films and film companies suggests that different analytical traditions must be adopted, such as textual analysis, literary criticism, landscape analysis, and economic analysis. This accords with Kennedy and Lukinbeal's "holistic" approach to geographic research on film, in which they argue that

[T]o develop a theory of film, it would not be enough to interpret it only in economic terms, only in terms of its distinctive technological form, or only with respect to its content and ideological effects (the predominant mode of theorising at the moment), but would require the analysis of the mediations between its political economy, its insertion into political struggles of the time, its changing cultural forms and effects, its use of new technologies, and its diverse use by audiences.[88]

In sum, films are texts as well as commercial products. Understanding Shaw Brothers cinema and its role in constructing pan-Chinese cultures therefore entails both deconstructing the texts of the films as well as understanding how their film business contributed to and depended on pan-Chinese economic networks. Thus, the student of Shaw films will benefit from analyses of both film texts (the social and cultural meanings in and of films) and the film business and industry (the political economy of film). Indeed, it is imperative that research focus on the intersections of economy, culture, society, global, local, place, politics, and policy. This will go a long way in enhancing understanding of the contributions of the film industry, in particular, and cultural industries, more generally, to economic and sociocultural life. If cultural industries are truly successful, they will contribute to income and employment as well as the quality of life and community development, not least through constructing and challenging senses of identity.[89] Cultural and urban policy can help shape the contributions of cultural industries to ensure that they are not defined only by economic rationality and a focus on financial returns but are rooted in meaningful, local cultural resources and community rhythms. This, Wynne argues, will make cultures and the arts a true investment, providing both economic returns and quality of life.[90]

Notes

This paper was first written in 2003. I would like to thank Yung Sai Shing for drawing my attention to useful material. I would also like to thank Lynette Boey for excellent assistance. The research for which this paper forms a part was funded by the National University of Singapore (R-109-000-052-112).

1. J. Hopkins, "A Mapping of Cinematic Places: Icons, Ideology and the Power of (Mis)Representation," in Stuart C. Aitken and Leo Zonn, eds., *Place, Power, Situation, and Spectacle: A Geography of Film* (Lanham, Md.: Rowman and Littlefield, 1994), pp. 47–65; Christina Kennedy and Christopher Lukinbeal, "Towards a Holistic Approach to Geographic Research on Film," *Progress in Human Geography* 21, no. 1 (1997): pp. 33–50.

2. Gerald M. Macdonald, "Third Cinema and Third World," in Stuart C. Aitken and Leo Zonn, eds., *Place, Power, Situation, and Spectacle: A Geography of Film* (Lanham, Md.: Rowman and Littlefield, 1994), p. 28.

3. Andrew Sayer, "The Dialectic of Culture and Economy," in Roger Lee and Jane Wills, eds., *Geographies of Economies* (New York: Arnold, 1997), pp. 16–26; Scott Lash and John Urry, *Economies of Signs and Space* (Thousand Oaks, Calif.: Sage, 1994), p. 64.

4. Sharon Zukin, *Loft Living: Culture and Capital in Urban Change* (New Brunswick, N.J.: Rutgers University Press, 1989); Chris Gibson and John Connell, "'Bongo Fury': Tourism, Music and Cultural Economy at Byron Bay, Australia," *Tijdschrift Voor Economische En Sociale Geografie* 94, no. 2 (2003): pp. 164–87; C. Dwyer and P. Crang, "Fashioning Ethnicities: The Commercial Spaces of Multiculture," *Ethnicities* 2, no. 3 (2002): pp. 410–30.

5. Krishna Sen, *Indonesian Cinema: Framing the New Order* (London: Zed, 1994).

6. Chengren Zhou, "Shanghai's Unique Film Productions and Hong Kong's Early Cinema," in *The Shaw Screen: A Preliminary Study* (Hong Kong: Hong Kong Film Archive, 2003), pp. 1–17.

7. Poshek Fu, "Going Global: A Cultural History of the Shaw Brothers Studio, 1960–1970" (paper presented at the "Conference on Shaw Enterprise and Asian Urban Culture: Interdisciplinary Studies and Cross-Regional Comparison," National University of Singapore, July 26–28, 2001).

8. Macdonald, "Third Cinema and Third World," p. 27.

9. John Silk, "A Rationale for Film Research in Geography" (Discussion Paper No. 11, Department of Geography, University of Reading, 1992), p. 14.

10. Shaw Brothers Web site, "The Shaw Story," http://www.shaw.com.sg/shawstory/shawstory7.htm, accessed September 15, 2003.

11. Peter Jackson, "Commercial cultures: transcending the cultural and the economic," *Progress in Human Geography*, 26, no. 1 (2002): (3–18).

12. See, for example, Paul G. Pickowicz's chapter in this book.

13. Shaw Brothers Web site, "The Shaw Story," http://www.shaw.com.sg/shawstory/shawstory7.htm, accessed September 15, 2003.

14. Silk, "A Rationale for Film Research in Geography," p. 19.

15. H. W. C. Yeung, "Regulating 'the Firm' and Sociocultural Practices in Industrial Geography II," *Progress in Human Geography* 25, no. 2 (2001): p. 293.

16. Ibid., p. 294.

17. Ibid., p. 295.

18. E. Schoenberger, "Corporate Strategy and Corporate Strategists: Power, Identity, and Knowledge within the Firm," *Environment and Planning A* 26 (1994): pp. 435–51.

19. Yeung, "Regulating 'the Firm'," p. 296.

20. Shaw Brothers Web site, "The Shaw Story," http://www.shaw.com.sg/shawstory/shawstory7.htm, accessed September 15, 2003.

21. Fu, "Going Global," p. 8.

22. James A. Robins, "Organisation as Strategy: Restructuring Production in the Film Industry," *Strategic Management Journal* 14 (Special Issue, 1993): pp. 103–18; J. Allen, "Post-Industrialism/Post-Fordism," in S. Hall, D. Held, D. Hubert, and K. Thompson, eds., *Modernity: An Introduction to Modern Societies* (Oxford: Blackwell, 1996), pp. 546–55.

23. David Morley and Kevin Robins, *Spaces of Identity: Global Media, Electronic Landscapes and Cultural Boundaries* (London: Routledge, 1995), p. 30.

24. Ibid.

25. S. Christopherson and M. Storper, "The City as Studio, the World as Back-Lot: The Impact of Vertical Disintegration on the Location of the Motion-Picture Industry," *Environment and Planning D* 4 (1986): pp. 305–20.

26. Morley and Robins, *Spaces of Identity*, p. 33. Critics of this view argue that the majors continue to play critical roles and that contemporary patterns of production in Hollywood can only be understood as an expression of the economic power and leverage of the majors. See, for example, A. Aksoy and K. Robins, "Hollywood for the 21st Century: Global Competition for Critical Mass in Image Markets," *Cambridge Journal of Economics* 16 (1992): pp. 1–22; M. Smith, "Theses on the Philosophy of Hollywood History," in S. Neale and S. Smith, eds., *Contemporary Hollywood Cinema* (London: Routledge, 1998), pp. 3–20; L. Veron, "The Competitive Advantage of Hollywood Industry," *Columbia International Affairs On Line* (1999), http://www.cc.columbia.edu/sec/dlc/ciao/wps/ve101, accessed September 15, 2003; H. Blair and A. Rainnie, "Flexible Films?" *Media, Culture and Society* 22 (2000): pp. 187–294. On the other hand, Scott sought to balance these two views, arguing that both large and small firms play important roles in contemporary Hollywood; Allen J. Scott, "A New Map of Hollywood: The Production and Distribution of American Motion Pictures," *Regional Studies* 36, no. 9 (2002): pp. 957–75.

27. Morley and Robins, *Spaces of Identity*, p. 32.

28. Scott, "A New Map of Hollywood," p. 961.

29. Morley and Robins, *Spaces of Identity*, p. 32.

30. Scott, "A New Map of Hollywood," p. 961. See also K. Acheson and C. J. Maule, "Understanding Hollywood's Organisation and Continuing Success," *Journal of Cultural Economics* 18 (1994): pp. 271–300; T. Balio, "A Major Presence in All the World's Major Markets: The Globalisation of Hollywood in the 1990s," in S. Neale and M. Smith, eds., *Contemporary Hollywood Cinema* (London: Routledge, 1998), pp. 58–73; D. Gomery, "Hollywood Corporate Business Practice and Periodizing Contemporary Film History," in S. Neale and M. Smith, eds., *Contemporary Hollywood Cinema* (London: Routledge, 1998), pp. 47–57; D. Puttnam and N. Watson, *Movies and Money* (New York: Knopf, 1998); S. Prince, *A New Pot of Gold: Hollywood under the Electronic Rainbow, 1980–1989* (New York: Scribner's, 2000).

31. Morley and Robins, *Spaces of Identity*, p. 28.

32. Bill Van der Heide, "Malaysian Movies: The Shaw Brothers Meet the Pandava

Brothers in the Land below the Wind," in Bruce Bennett, Jeff Doyle, and Setendra Nandan, eds., *Crossing Cultures: Essays on Literature and Culture of the Asia-Pacific* (London: Skoob Books, in association with University College, Australian Defence Force Academy, Canberra and the Centre for Studies in Australian Literature, University of Western Australia, 1996), p. 101.

33. Shaw Brothers Web site, "The Shaw Story," http://www.shaw.com.sg/shawstory/shawstory7.htm, accessed September 15, 2003.

34. Jeongmee Kim, "The Funding and Distribution Structure of the British Film Industry in the 1990s: Localization and Commercialisation of British Cinema towards a Global Audience," *Media Culture and Society* 25, no. 3 (2003): pp. 405–13.

35. Shaw Brothers Web site, "The Shaw Story," http://www.shaw.com.sg/shawstory/shawstory7.htm, accessed September 15, 2003.

36. Shaw Brothers Web site, "Shaw Brother's Biography," http://www.firstuniversal.clara.net/shawsbio.htm, accessed September 15, 2003; Stephanie Po-yin Chung, "The Industrial Evolution of a Fraternal Enterprise: The Shaw Brothers and the Shaw Organisation," in *The Shaw Screen: A Preliminary Study* (Hong Kong: Hong Kong Film Archive, 2003), pp. 1–17.

37. Shaw Brothers Web site, "The Shaw Story," http://www.shaw.com.sg/shawstory/shawstory7.htm, accessed September 15, 2003.

38. E. Schoenberger, "Corporate Strategy and Corporate Strategists: Power, Identity, and Knowledge within the Firm," *Environment and Planning A* 26 (1994): p. 435.

39. Pierre Bourdieu, *Distinction: A Social Critique of the Judgment of Taste* (London: Routledge, 1984); Keith Negus, "The Work of Cultural Intermediaries and the Enduring Distance between Production and Consumption," *Cultural Studies* 16, no. 4 (2002): pp. 501–15; Neil M. Coe, "The View from Out West: Embeddedness, Inter-personal Relations and the Development of an Indigenous Film Industry in Vancouver," *Geoforum* 31, no. 4 (2000): pp. 391–407.

40. Bourdieu, *Distinction*, p. 359.

41. Negus, "The Work of Cultural Intermediaries," p. 503.

42. Ibid., p. 504.

43. Shaw Brothers Web site, "The Shaw Story," http://www.shaw.com.sg/shawstory/shawstory7.htm, accessed September 15, 2003.

44. Negus, quoting Bourdieu, "The Work of Cultural Intermediaries," p. 511.

45. Coe, "The View from Out West," p. 394. See also Keith Bassett, Ron Griffiths, and Ian Smith, "Cultural Industries, Cultural Clusters and the City: The Example of Natural History Film-Making in Bristol," *Geoforum* 33 (2002): pp. 165–77.

46. Coe, "The View from Out West," p. 395.

47. Ibid., p. 397.

48. Shaw Brothers Web site, "The Shaw Story," http://www.shaw.com.sg/shawstory/shawstory7.htm, accessed September 15, 2003.

49. Negus, "The Work of Cultural Intermediaries," p. 511.

50. Siu-Lun Wong, "The Chinese Family Firm: A Model," *British Journal of Soci-*

ology 36, no. 1 (1985): pp. 58–72; Gary Hamilton, ed., *Asian Business Networks* (New York: Walter de Gruyter, 1996); Chee Kiong Tong and Pit Kee Yong, "*Guanxi* Bases, *Xinyong* and Chinese Business Networks," *British Journal of Sociology* 49, no. 1 (1998): pp. 75–96.

51. Zhou, "Shanghai's Unique Film Productions," p. 21.

52. See, for example, R. Wallis and K. Malm, "The International Music Industry and Transcultural Communication," in J. Lull, ed., *Popular Music and Communication* (Newbury Park, Calif.: Sage, 1987); L. Kong, "Popular Music in Singapore: Local Cultures, Global Resources and Regional Identities," *Environment and Planning D: Society and Space* 14 (1996): pp. 273–92; L. Kong, "Popular Music in a Transnational World: The Construction of Local Identities in Singapore," *Asia Pacific Viewpoint* 38, no. 1 (1997): pp. 19–36.

53. Shaw Brothers Web site, "The Shaw Story," http://www.shaw.com.sg/shawstory/shawstory7.htm, accessed September 15, 2003.

54. *The China Mail,* March 9, 1965.

55. Shaw Brothers Web site, "The Shaw Story," http://www.shaw.com.sg/shawstory/shawstory7.htm, accessed September 15, 2003.

56. Ibid.

57. Fu, "Going Global," p. 11.

58. Shaw Brothers Web site, "The Shaw Story," http://www.shaw.com.sg/shawstory/shawstory7.htm, accessed September 15, 2003.

59. Fu, "Going Global," pp. 14–15.

60. S. Said, "The Rise of the Indonesian Film Industry," *East-West Cinema Journal* 6, no. 2 (1992): p. 100.

61. Chung, "The Industrial Evolution of a Fraternal Enterprise," p. 4.

62. Zhou, "Shanghai's Unique Film Productions," p. 30.

63. Fu, "Going Global," pp. 14–19.

64. Morley and Robins, *Spaces of Identity,* p. 15.

65. S. Winram, "The Opportunity for World Brands," *International Journal of Advertising* 3, no. 1 (1984): p. 19; Morley and Robins, *Spaces of Identity,* p. 15.

66. Shaw Brothers Web site, "The Shaw Story," http://www.shaw.com.sg/shawstory/shawstory7.htm, accessed September 15, 2003.

67. Ibid.; Fu, "Going Global," p. 14.

68. Fu, "Going Global," pp. 14–19.

69. Boonrak Boonyaketmala, "The Rise and Fall of the Film Industry in Thailand, 1897–1992," *East-West Film Journal* 6, no. 2 (1992): p. 77.

70. Fu, "Going Global," p. 10.

71. Morley and Robins, *Spaces of Identity,* p. 30.

72. Scott, "A New Map of Hollywood," p. 959.

73. Morley and Robins, *Spaces of Identity,* p. 30; C. Courlet and P. Judet, "Nouveaux éspaces de production en France et en Italie," *Annales de la recherché urbaine* 29 (1986). See also Bassett et al., "Cultural Industries, Cultural Clusters and the City."

74. Morley and Robins, *Spaces of Identity,* p. 18. See also Kim, "The Funding and Distribution Structure of the British Film Industry in the 1990s."

75. Van der Heide, "Malaysian Movies," p. 101.

76. Ibid., pp. 102–3.

77. Shaw Brothers Web site, "The Shaw Story," http://www.shaw.com.sg/shawstory/ shawstory7.htm, accessed September 15, 2003.

78. Ibid.

79. Lisa Benton, "Will the Real/Reel Los Angeles Please Stand Up?" *Urban Geography* 16, no. 2 (1995): p. 145.

80. Silk, "A Rationale for Film Research in Geography," p. 3.

81. Kennedy and Lukinbeal, "Towards a Holistic Approach to Geographic Research on Film," p. 45; J. Gold, "From 'Metropolis' to 'the City': Film Visions of the Future City, 1919–39," in L. Burgess and J. Gold, eds., *Geography, the Media and Popular Culture* (New York: St. Martin's Press, 1985), pp. 123–43; A. Jenkins, "A View of Contemporary China: A Production Study of a Documentary Film," in L. Zonn, ed., *Place Images in Media* (Totowa, N.J.: Rowman and Littlefield, 1990), pp. 207–29; B. Godfrey, "Regional Depiction in Contemporary Film," *Geographical Review* 83 (1993): pp. 421–40; L. Zonn, "Landscape Depiction and Perception: A Transactional Approach," *Landscape Journal* 3 (1984): pp. 144–50; S. Aitken, "A Transactional Geography of the Image-Event: The Films of Scottish Director, Bill Forsyth," *Transactions, Institute of British Geographers* 16 (1991): pp. 105–18; W. Natter and J. Jones, "Pea or Meat: Class, Ideology, and Space in *Roger and Me*," *Antipode* 25 (1993): pp. 140–58; D. Liverman and D. Sherman, "Natural Harms in Novels and Films: Implications for Hazard Perception and Behavior," in J. Burgess and J. Gold, eds., *Geography, the Media and Popular Culture* (New York: St. Martin's Press, 1985), pp. 86–95; L. Ford, "Sunshine and Shadow: Lighting and Color in the Depiction of Cities on Film," in Stuart C. Aitken and Leo Zonn, eds., *Place, Power, Situation, and Spectacle: A Geography of Film* (Lanham, Md.: Rowman and Littlefield, 1994), pp. 119–36.

82. Aitken and Zonn, *Place, Power, Situation, and Spectacle*, p. 5.

83. In the context of Shaw movies, see, for example, Paul Pickowicz in chapter 4 of this book; Sai-shing Yung, "The Joy of Youth, Made in Hong Kong: Patricia Lam Fung and Shaw's Cantonese Films," in Wong Ain-ling, ed., *Shaoshi dianying chutan* (*The Movies of the Shaw Brothers: A Preliminary Study*) (Hong Kong: Hong Kong Film Archive, 2003), pp. 183–93; the English version, translated by Stephen Teo, is in Wong Ain-ling, ed., *The Shaw Screen: A Preliminary Study* (Hong Kong: Hong Kong Film Archive, 2003), pp. 221–35.

84. J. A. Lent, *The Asian Film Industry* (Austin: University of Texas Press, 1990); N. G. Tiongson, "The Filipino Film Industry," *East-West Film Journal* 6, no. 2 (1992): pp. 23–61; Jose F. Lacaba, ed., *The Films of ASEAN* (Quezon City, Philippines: ASEAN Committee on Culture and Information, Boonyaketmala, 1992); Said, "The Rise of the Indonesian Film Industry"; Sen, *Indonesian Cinema*; Lacaba, *The Films of ASEAN*.

85. K. G. Heider, *Indonesian Cinema: National Culture on Screen* (Honolulu: Uni-

versity of Hawai'i Press, 1991); Wimal Dissanayake, ed., *Colonialism, Nationalism in Asian Cinema* (Bloomington: Indiana University Press, 1994); L. Francia, "Philippine Cinema: The Struggle against Repression," in John D. H. Downing, ed., *Film Politics in the Third World* (New York: Praeger, 1987), pp. 209–18.

86. Rohayati Paseng and Tim Barnard, "The Ambivalence of P. Ramlee: Penarek Beca and Bujang Lapok in Perspective," *Asian Cinema* 13, no. 2 (2000): pp. 9–23.

87. B. S. Santos, "Idol, Bestiary and Revolutionary: Images of the Filipino Woman in Film (1979–1986)," in S. S. Reyes, ed., *Reading Popular Culture* (Manila, Philippines: Office of Research and Publications, Ateneo de Manila University, 1991), pp. 209–24.

88. Kennedy and Lukinbeal, "Towards a Holistic Approach to Geographic Research on Film," p. 34.

89. F. Bianchini, "Culture, Conflict and Cities: Issues and Prospects for the 1990s," in F. Bianchini and M. Parkinson, eds., *Cultural Policy and Urban Regeneration: The West European Experience* (Manchester, U.K.: Manchester University Press, 1993), p. 212.

90. D. Wynne, ed., *The Culture Industry* (Aldershot, U.K.: Avebury, 1992), p. x.

2

Shaw's Cantonese Productions
and Their Interactions with
Contemporary Local and
Hollywood Cinema

LAW KAR

Introduction

In 2003, Celestial Pictures began the gradual release of the Shaw Brothers film library in Hong Kong, Taiwan, Singapore, and Malaysia, to be followed later in Japan, France, and other Western countries, thus making Shaw Brothers (SB) an increasingly viable subject of study for film scholars and critics. Because the films released on DVD thus far are mostly productions from 1970 onward (only a small fraction being from the 1960s and practically none from the 1950s when productions were mostly in black and white), there are, as yet, very few studies on the Shaw productions of the earlier period, from the mid-1950s to early 1960s. In this chapter, I am going to discuss the Cantonese productions of Shaw Studio between 1955 and 1964 and compare them with its Mandarin ones as well as the productions of its rival studio MP & GI. I will analyze the rise of Shaw's Cantonese new stars, particularly the making of young idol Patricia Lam Fung, in relation to the rise of the lower-middle class and middle class; the promotion strategy behind this; and the strong influence from Hollywood.

Background

In the 1950s, Cantonese cinema was part of the daily life of the common people. People of the lower and lower-middle classes loved Cantonese movies because they vividly depicted their living situation; the poor and under-privileged were heavily exploited by the rich and powerful while the Colonial Government, either not knowing what to do or lacking the will, did nothing to alleviate the situation. Cantonese cinema was a populist cinema at that time, and it helped common people express their anger, fear, and desire; it served to guide them through their difficult lives and provide outlets for their discontent.

Starting in the mid-1950s, Hong Kong went through a period of rapid industrialization. Hong Kong was changing from an entrepôt to a city that was strong in light industry and export of local products. The number of factories increased more than fourfold from 1951 to 1962, and the number of workers increased more than threefold. In 1953, export of local products accounted for 25 percent of total export trading, but in 1962 it reached 76 percent.[1]

While the economy was progressing quickly, social improvement was moving much slower. There were three basic social problems in dire need of solutions. First, there was a housing shortage, which led to numerous other problems like water shortages, unsanitary living conditions, and insufficient medical care. Second, labor conditions were dismal; workers were badly exploited and had little to no legal protection. Finally, inflation was pushing up food prices, rent, taxes, and other fees from 1958 onward.

Yet compared with the immediate postwar years, the living standard of the common people was improving. There were more opportunities for work, and even the younger members of the family could earn wages by working in factories, offices, or at home. All in all, although the fruits of economic growth were not fully enjoyed by the lower and lower-middle classes, life was slowly getting better.

The mid-1950s to early 1960s was also the period in which the Western way of life was gradually becoming accepted as an advanced and modern way of life. Western popular music, dating, dancing, swimming at the beach, picnicking, and traveling abroad were becoming popular among residents of Hong Kong. These became regular parts of the lifestyle enjoyed by the middle and upper classes, whereas the lower and lower-middle classes dreamed of them and worked very hard in hopes of obtaining them.

It was against this background that the Cantonese cinema grew into prosperity in the 1950s and 1960s. The fast-growing number of factory and office workers was reflected in the rapidly increasing cinema population. As the people worked harder, they needed to play harder, and moviegoing was the cheapest, most accessible entertainment they could find. In light of this growing need, it is natural that Cantonese cinema gradually changed, becoming less didactic and more entertaining from the mid-1950s onward.

Cantonese versus Mandarin Cinema

Local production of Cantonese-language film started in 1933, and after the huge success of *White Golden Dragon* (*Baijin long*, 1933), made by the Shaw Brothers' Tianyi (Unique) Studio in Shanghai, more and more Cantonese films went into production. Tianyi's Hong Kong branch was among the biggest studios that made Cantonese sound films. Apart from local release, the films were also exported to Guangdong, Guangxi, and Nanyang, the Southeast Asian countries with vast Chinese communities. The Shaw Brothers also produced a large number of silent and Mandarin-language films in Shanghai and Cantonese films in Hong Kong. Taken as a whole, they had the largest distribution network for Mandarin and Cantonese films in Nanyang.[2]

After the interruption of World War II, the Shaw Brothers were among the very first to resume filmmaking in Singapore and Hong Kong, this time exclusively on the Mandarin side because the Nationalist government banned dialect cinema and forbade the export of Cantonese films from Hong Kong. Because China was a big market for Mandarin films, the late 1940s saw the emergence of a host of large and small production companies in Hong Kong that specialized in Mandarin production, most with financiers and filmmakers coming from China itself. Among them was Da Zhonghua (Great China) Film Company, where Runde Shaw (Shao Cunren) was one of the partners.

Mandarin film was not very popular in the local Hong Kong market, however, where it gained only a one-tenth to one-fifth share of the local market and some otherwise popular Mandarin films were never even released. Under these market pressures, some of the Great China productions had to be dubbed into Cantonese to appeal to the local audiences. After 1949, Mandarin film companies in Hong Kong were facing a grim future because the Communist government began to close the mainland market to overseas film productions. To survive, the Mandarin producers had to open up new markets or expand existing ones in Taiwan, Singapore, Malaysia, and Indonesia. Further, they adopted a more aggressive strategy in the local market in order to compete with the Cantonese cinema industry. But when independent companies were facing hard times in 1955 and 1956, the Singapore-based Cathay Organization decided to take up the bankrupt Yung Hwa Film Studio to start productions of its own. Two years later, Run Run Shaw (Shao Yifu) of the Shaw Brothers Company (Singapore) came to Hong Kong to establish Shaw Brothers Studio (HK), taking over what Runde Shaw's Shaw and Sons Studio had been doing in film production and injecting much capital to build a modern studio in Clearwater Bay, Kowloon. Hong Kong cinema was in transition to an era of the studio system in the following decade, a decade of severe competition between Mandarin and Cantonese cinema.

Meanwhile, Cantonese cinema was growing steadily, with average annual production exceeding 150 films in the mid-1950s and reaching a peak in the early 1960s, producing more than 200 films yearly from 1960 to 1963.[3] From then on, it was gradually pushed toward the edge of existence by the competitive Mandarin cinema, until it totally disappeared in 1972.

Shaw and Sons

Right after the anti-Japanese war, Runde Shaw resumed distribution of Cantonese and Mandarin films with his Nanyang Film Company, but after producing only a few titles, production stopped in early 1947. After four years of interruption, Runde Shaw took up production again under the name Shaw and Sons (SS).

From 1952 to 1956, SS's productions were all in Mandarin, with the exception of one Cantonese production made on location in Singapore and one in Japanese, coproduced with Toho Co., Japan. It is not difficult to explain why SS joined the fray at a time when the Mandarin film industry was facing a big crisis; productions of Mandarin films dropped drastically from twenty-seven in 1949 to sixteen in 1950 and 1951. Great China, the leading Mandarin film studio that produced forty-three films from 1946 to 1948, the largest amount by a single studio, had been forced to close down. Yung Hwa, another big Mandarin studio, was suffering financial difficulty. Yet in the wake of the closing of the Mainland China market, the Shaw Brothers had the advantage of their already well-established distribution network for Mandarin films all over Nanyang. When competitors were getting weak, it was thus the perfect time for Shaw to join in. Moreover, like all other Mandarin film companies, SS was trying to break into the Taiwan market, that great potential market for Mandarin films.

Yet Runde Shaw would not neglect the importance of the local market. In 1956, just three years after the Mandarin productions had resumed, SS managed to establish its Cantonese section and had it functioning with great efficiency.

The year 1956 was also when Cathay Organization of Singapore acquired the Yung Hwa Studio and invested a great sum to rebuild it into a modern studio, setting up a new film company, Motion Pictures and General Investment Co. Ltd. (MP & GI), in Hong Kong to take charge of the studio. Production there was soon in full swing.

Table 2.1. Shaw's Cantonese and Mandarin Productions

Year of release	Cantonese	Mandarin
1955	1	6
1956	0	11
1957	3	11
1958	8	13
1959	9	16
1960	17	17
1961	13	17
1962	4	9
1963	2	17
1964	0	15

Source: Wong Ain-ling, ed., The Shaw Screen, Hong Kong Film Archive, 2003.

Table 2.2. Cathay/MP & GI's Cantonese and Mandarin Productions

Year of release	Cantonese	Mandarin
1955	4	0
1956	3	8
1957	5	10
1958	8	4
1959	1	20
1960	5	22
1961	4	13
1962	4	11
1963	2	11
1964	2	14
1965	1	6
1966	1	6
1967	0	15

Source: Wong Ain-ling, ed., The Cathay Story, Hong Kong Film Archive, 2002.

Because MP & GI/Cathay was clearly going to be a major threat to Shaw and Sons, SS positioned both its Mandarin and Cantonese arms to fight against the rival. I shall describe and discuss the development of Shaw's Cantonese productions in detail and compare them both to those of the MP & GI and to Shaw's own Mandarin productions in order to see their interactions in the years when Hong Kong cinema was undergoing the transition to an age dominated by big studios. It is also interesting to consider how the big studios imposed a Mandarin-speaking cinema onto the local audience, which did not speak the language, only because of marketing considerations.

In fact, Cantonese cinema, which grew out of the daily life of local common people and had a long tradition of its own, has often been neglected by researchers and scholars as supposedly inferior to Mandarin cinema; such is not the case. On the contrary, Cantonese cinema in general reflected the social situation and need of the common people in a changing society and thus deserves much more socially and culturally informed research.

Shaw's Cantonese Section

Preparations for the Cantonese section started in 1955–56, during which time director Chow Sze-luk (Zhou Shilu) headed the section. Chow was a veteran cameraman who had served Shaw's Hong Kong Studios since the mid-1930s and turned to directing after World War II. A Cantonese who worked in Shanghai before coming to Hong Kong, Chow, unlike many of Shaw's Mandarin directors who came after the war, had lived in Hong Kong for more than two decades and knew much about Cantonese filmmaking.

The section started open auditions for actor/actress in 1956. Since then, an impressive group of new talents—including actresses Pearl Au Ka-wai (Ou Jiahui), Lam Yim (Lin Yan), and Patricia Lam Fung (Lin Feng), and actors Cheung Ying-choi (Zhang Yingcai), Mak Kay (Mai Ji), Lui Kay (Lu Qi), and Lung Kong (Long Gang)—have been recruited to receive extensive in-house training, such as dancing and singing.

Before the founding of the section, SS had made one Cantonese film on location in Singapore, *The Opera Boat in Singapore* (*Xing Dao Hong Chuan*) in 1955. Production from the section began in 1956 with *Pearl of the Island* (*Bao dao shen zhu*, opened on January 1, 1957), starring Pearl Au Ka-wai, a swimming champion. The film was a fully costumed adventure, with some location scenes and special effects photography done in Japan with the help of Japanese technicians. Two costume films—*The Fairy Sleeves* (*Xian xiu qi yuan*), a Chinese fairy tale, and a melodramatic horror, *The Marriage between the Quick and the Dead* (*Yinyang pei*)—both starring Patricia Lam Fung, were completed and shown in 1957 with moderate reception. Then came the third film with Lam Fung, *A Pretty Girl's Love Affair* (*Yunü chunqing*, opened April 4, 1958). It was a great hit, as was the next one, *A Virtuous Girl from a Humble Household* (*Peng men shunu*), released two months later. Since then, Lam Fung became the biggest among all of SS's Cantonese stars (Pearl Au was their number two). Shaw banked heavily on Lam by casting her in a series of films tailor-made for her and by promoting her heavily. All in all, Lam starred in a full twenty-nine out of the fifty-seven films made by the Cantonese section from 1957 to 1963.

Table 2.3. Films with Patricia Lam Fung as compared with Pearl Au Ka-wai

Year of release	Lam Fung	Au Ka-wai
1957	3	1
1958	4	3
1959	4	2
1960	10	3
1961	6	2
1962	2	1
1963	0	1

Source: Wong Ain-ling, ed., *The Shaw Screen,* Hong Kong Film Archive, 2003.

The Cantonese section worked with a much higher efficiency than its Mandarin counterpart. Out of the fifty-seven films, Chow directed twenty-three and codirected two. Although the Mandarin side had more than eight major directors, the Cantonese side had only one and a few freelancers.

Budget/Salary

According to Weng Ling-wen, who worked for Shaw's promotion department at that time, the average budget of a film produced in the Cantonese section was HK$150,000 (US$30,000), much higher than the standard production budget of other Cantonese film companies, and the working days were longer, too.[4] According to Chan Wan, the writer/director under section head Chow, however, production budget and working conditions were no better than at other companies.[5] Actor and later assistant director Lung Kong seemed to confirm Chan Wan's opinion. In our correspondence in 2003, Lung recalled that in those days Shaw's own studios were completely occupied by Mandarin productions; the Cantonese productions had to be shot in rented studios. Shooting was to be finished in fifteen to sixteen working days for a standard production and a maximum of twenty to twenty-two days for director Chow's films. The estimated budget was HK$40,000 to HK$60,000, as compared to HK$50,000 to HK$60,000 for an average Cantonese film from MP & GI. In general, the average budget of a Cantonese film from Shaw was within the average range of a low- to medium-budget film at the time.[6]

Still, the production quality of Shaw's Cantonese films was usually better than those with similar budgets, one reason being that Shaw had its own pick of stars that were usually under five-year contracts and were usually underpaid.

Creative Unit

When the section first started in 1956, there were four staff writers and one script supervisor. Writers were hired on a contractual basis with a monthly salary of HK$200. For each script accepted, HK$600 was paid, to be shared equally by the four writers. To increase the output and working spirit, in 1958 director Chow supervised the scripts himself, and the number of staff writers was cut down to two—Chan Wan and Ng Dan—then each writer could write more and gain his own full pay for each accepted script. These scripts were exclusively for in-house use, mainly for Chow's films. Directors hired from the outside were to bring their own scripts. This policy encouraged the writers to write more and faster to cater to the rising number of productions from 1959 to 1961. In addition, Chan and Ng were encouraged to learn directing by working as assistant directors or codirectors with Chow, and by 1960 both of them could work independently as directors shooting their own scripts. Chan Wan wrote sixteen scripts between 1958 and 1961 and directed three of them. Although this might not have been a healthy policy with respect to the creative/artistic level of the products, it really did work for a system that demanded minimal use of resources and maximum profits.[7]

Rise and Fall

After 1959, the number of Cantonese productions doubled, and that was the same year the logo *SS* and the name *Runde Shaw* disappeared from the Shaw screen. By late 1958, Lam Fung had reached her superstardom with four great hits, and in early 1959 she was sent to Singapore and Malaya with a crew headed by Chow to shoot three films: *The Merdeka Bridge* (*Duliqiao zhi lian*), *Bride from Other Town* (*Guobu xinniang*), and *When Durians Bloom* (*Liulian piao xiang*). They stayed there for three months, returned to Hong Kong, and did the postproduction at full speed. Then, starting in June 1959, the three films were released one by one over the next few months, and all to a very good response. That brought the working spirit of the section into full bloom. In 1960, the output was amazing: seventeen films, the same as SB's Mandarin output. The output continued to be strong in 1961 (twelve films) but dropped to just four in 1962 and only one in 1963, and by 1964 the section practically ceased to function.

Why SB slowed down the pace of its Cantonese section when it was progressing so well and in two years cut it off completely is an issue that needs further exploration. Here, I would suggest the following points for consideration:

1. In 1961, Shaw's new studio was already functioning, but in the subsequent three years total output was getting not larger but smaller. The reason was that Run Run Shaw facilitated several studios to make Mandarin epics or opera films with "Chinese pride" or spectacular musicals, all of which took much longer to produce. This was part of Run Run's tactics: using spectacular, big-budget productions (color, Shawscope, big cast, beautiful sets, full costumes, scenes of thousands of people and horses, etc.) to counterattack its rival, MP & GI, which specialized in contemporary romance and comedy. Examples include epics like *Yang Kuei Fai* (*Yang Guifei*, 1962) and *Empress Wu Tse-tien* (*Wu Zetian*, 1963), Huangmei operas like *Love Eterne* (*Liang Shangbo yu Zhu Yingtai*, 1963) and *Lady General Hua Mulan* (*Hua Mulan*) (1964), and spectacular musicals like *Love Parade* (*Hua tuan jin cu*, 1963).

2. Lam Fung left the unit after she had fulfilled her five-year contract. That was a great loss to Shaw's Cantonese section, though Run Run Shaw might not agree. In the following years, Shaw Brothers could not find another star of equal power to replace her, and the appeal of its productions dropped because of this.

3. Then in 1963, *Love Eterne* helped initiate the Huangmei opera craze all over Taiwan and Southeast Asia. This gave Run Run a trump card to advance into the Taiwan market and subdue his rivals. Since then, SB exerted its full strength in Mandarin films to finish the conquest of the Taiwan market, thus leaving behind its Cantonese productions as trivial in comparison.

4. According to Poshek Fu, committing full resources to produce Mandarin films was part of Run Run Shaw's global business strategy. "To go global, to reach for the mainstream markets beyond the Cantonese communities in Southeast Asia and Hong Kong, the Shaw Brothers Studio had to use Mandarin as its 'business language.' Speaking Mandarin indicates a cosmopolitan sensibility and an image that corresponded with the global vision of the Studio."[8]

Genres and Films

The sixty films produced by the section during its seven years of existence can be divided into six genres:

1. Opera film (seven films). These were either adopted from Cantonese opera stories, featuring opera singing, or from Chinese legends and fairy tales, with both opera singing and dancing. Examples of such include *The Fairy Sleeves* (1957) and *The Peach Blossom Fan* (*Taohua shan*, 1961). Opera films proved to be a long-lasting genre. Perhaps with a view to play it safe

with their new starlet, the first two Lam Fung films belonged to this genre. For these films, the unit provided two teachers to train her in opera singing and dancing, which she learned quite rapidly.

2. Costume film with a Western background (six films). These were adaptations or imitations of Western fairy tales or Hollywood films. It is interesting to note that although the production design, sets, and costumes were all Western styled, the stories were adapted to comply with Chinese habits and moral teachings. Pearl Au and Lam Fung were often cast in this genre, and Cheung Ying-choi, as Prince Charming, was their perfect match. Examples include *Glass Slippers* (*Boil xie*, 1959) and *The Sleeping Beauty* (*Shui guangzhou*, 1960).

3. Detective thriller/suspense (eleven films). Set with a contemporary background, strong influences in plot and style came from postwar Hollywood film noir or detective stories of the 1950s such as *Asphalt Jungle* (1950) and *The Big Heat* (1953). Pearl Au seemed to be ideal, cast as the victim or the frightened girl, with Lung Kong as the villain. Later, Pearl Au also starred in a few films as a female lead who fought the bad guys, such as *Oriole, the Heroine* (*Unfixes hanging*, 1960). Other examples include *Crime of Passion in the Hotel* (*Jiudian qingsha an*, 1958) and *Murder on a Wedding Night* (*Sharen huazhu ye*, 1958).

4. Melodrama (fifteen films). Family melodrama, or romance melodrama, both centered on a pretty, young girl. Because Lam Fung was very popular in a series of teenager movies, she was also cast in melodramatic tragedies of love or family melodramas, which were intended for the entire family rather than the just the younger generation. This might have been part of the marketing strategy—to extend her audience base to all age groups. Examples of Lam Fung's melodramas include *A Helping Hand* (*Wennuan zai renjian*, 1960) and *Love and Chastity* (*Lianai yu zhencao*, 1960). Other well-known melodramas are *The Four Sisters* (*Lan gui si feng*, 1963), with Pearl Au, and *The Mother* (*Cimu shou zhong xian*, 1961), with Pak Yin.

5. Comedy (eight films). This genre included both light comedies, playing with the sorrows and joys of the middle class, and farcical comedies. Though the plots were melodramatic and situations traditional, there was no lack of youthful elements as well: love affairs with young pretty girls, singing and dancing scenes, fancy dresses, and elaborate settings. Examples of these include *The Impossible Son-in-Law* (*Huangtang nüxu*, 1959) and *Manhunt* (*Yunu Qiu Huang*, 1961).

6. Youth film (ten films). The emergence of youth film as a genre in Cantonese cinema was something new to the Hong Kong audiences of the 1950s.

By the mid-1950s, Hong Kong audiences had seen quite a number of Holly-wood films that centered on youth—films that depicted the energy, the pas-sion for freedom, the joy of love, and the yearning for a materialist life and sensual excitement, thought to be so prevalent in the United States. Further, these films often depicted the rebellious character of young people and the familial and social impact of their rebelliousness. Films like *The Wild Ones* (1954) and *Rebel without a Cause* (1955) were either well received outright or had at least become major talking points among Hong Kong filmgoers. Some Cantonese movies in the 1950s did pay attention to the growth of youth and children, but always in an overly didactic way, quite unlike the Hollywood ones. Shaw's youth films were not really that "youthful" and "joyful" when compared with their Hollywood counterparts; there were far too many melo-dramatic elements in them. Yet because the actors and actresses were very young and there were plenty of playful scenes, these films still displayed a fresh and youthful spirit seldom found in the Cantonese movies of that time. Examples include *A Pretty Girl's Affair* (*Yunü chungqing,* 1958) and *Young Rock* (*Qingchun le,* 1959).

Shaw Brothers versus Cathay/MP & GI

In order to understand more about the changing of audience tastes and its social significance, one can compare the development of Cantonese produc-tions of the two big studios of that time.

Cathay produced Cantonese movies in Hong Kong as early as 1955, well before the founding of MP & GI in 1966. When general manager Robert Chung (Zhong Qiwen) set up MP & GI, however, he and production man-ager Stephen Soong (Sung Qi) recruited staff members and artists almost exclusively for the making of Mandarin films. According to Tau Han-fun, who was in charge of the MP & GI Cantonese productions, Chung did not put much in the way of resources and attention on the Cantonese side, leav-ing him to initiate most of the projects on his own. Lacking staff members, Tau had to rely heavily on outside directors, writers, and artists. There was only one contracted actress, Christine Pak Lo-ming (Bai Luming), and di-rectors and writers were hired on a project-by-project basis.[9] Although the Mandarin films of MP & GI were generally recognizable by the studio's dis-tinct style and were created for a core group of new stars by new directors and writers with a well-considered production strategy, the Cantonese films looked more or less similar to other Cantonese films of the time, differing only in that their production values were generally higher. Among the forty

Cantonese films, many of them were better known for their popularity and high quality rather than for their innovation or youthful spirit.

On the other hand, the Cantonese films from the Shaws were known and remembered for their bright new stars, trendy parties, fashionable dresses, and youthful energy (despite their endings, which were loaded with moral teachings), all of which contributed to a homogeneous and distinct Shaw studio style.

Shaw's more popular Cantonese productions—a large number of them the family melodramas with strong youthful elements or the so-called youth films—were not created out of thin air, however, but were following the trails blazed by MP & GI's Mandarin films of the same genres. In 1957, MP & GI's *Mambo Girl* (*Manbo nülang*) and *Our Sister Hedy* (*Si qianjin*) were so successful that a series of films in the same mold were made in the following years: *Spring Song* (*Qingchung ernü*, 1959), *Calendar Girl* (*Longxiang fengwu*, 1959), *Air Hostess* (*Kongzhong xiaojie*, 1959), and many others. What was new to these family melodramas and light comedies was that none of them were lacking in young pretty girls and boys, dancing and singing scenes, and a youthful spirit. The same was true of Shaw's Cantonese films. It is fair to say that these Shaw Brothers Cantonese films were made, in part, to counteract the huge success of MP & GI's Mandarin ones.

Shaw's Cantonese films differed from MP & GI's Mandarin films in that the former, though stylistically cutting edge, were decidedly more conservative in content. Although the youthful elements were all there, the treatments were quite different. Although the MP & GI films celebrated the joy of youth and the release of youthful energy, the Shaw Brothers films warned the young of the corruption of Western materialism, urging them not to indulge in frivolous play and love affairs, which, it was claimed, could only result in the loss of their senses. Most of all, the Shaw's Cantonese family melodramas seemed to share a constant worry about the impact of the Western way of life on the Chinese family system and ethical order. Like the Cantonese films of the 1950s, many of Shaws' Cantonese films set their main story lines amid conflicts between the rich and the poor, the downfall of a young girl from a poor family amid the temptations in the "high society," or the invasion and dissolution of a family by the evils of the modern city. If the MP & GI Mandarin films foresaw the growth of the middle class, celebrating middle-class values, and the coming of a modern way of life to Hong Kong and other overseas Chinese communities, Shaws' Cantonese films were quite dubious regarding such a future. Still, this hesitancy did not affect their popularity. The young audience of the time seemed to be satisfied merely by the trendy elements and the young idols, despite the prevalence of conservative moral teachings. It is vital here to note that these films were targeted at the lower and lower-middle classes, and thus the stories reflected the mind-set of those groups, suggesting that they were the underprivileged, that society was unfair and unjust to them, and that they had the right to enjoy life and leisure like wealthier people.

Lam Fung: "The Jewel of Shaw"

Born in 1940, Lam Fung joined the Cantonese section when she was sixteen and made her screen debut at the age of seventeen. In two years' time, she became the most beloved and fastest rising star at Shaw Brothers. Though no precise box office records can be traced, her popularity is undisputable. Although the standard showing for a Cantonese feature was just one week, Lam's *A Pretty Girl's Affair* was extended to three weeks, and the next one, *A Virtuous Girl from a Humble Household,* was shown for two weeks. From then on, Lam's films were usually not scheduled in Shaw's Mandarin theaters, so that if they overran they would not block the schedule of the Mandarin films. The *Wah Kiu Evening Post* declared Lam to be one of the top-ten stars, and she won the Golden Globe Award eight consecutive years, starting in 1958.

In 1958, a fan club called Shaw's Jade Girl Fans Association was formed to entertain the young fans of Lam Fung and two other "jade girl" new stars, Ha Wai and Tong Dan; however, it was Lam Fung who was clearly the focus of the association. By mid-1959, the association was said to have a membership of more than 30,000 teenagers. Raymond Chow, who formerly worked as a reporter for Voice of America, was recruited by Run Run Shaw to become promotion manager in 1959. He was asked to expand the group's scope by turning it into Shaw's Film Fan Club and to provide regular activities for the club members, including showings of Lam Fung's films, concerts, parties, and excursions. A monthly club magazine, *Shaw's Film Fan Club,* was specially published for the members, now not limited to females.

In spite of the broadened scope, it was always Lam Fung who occupied the center pages with her pretty pictures and a column in which she answered letters from her fans. Lam was heavily promoted in every issue as a girl from a middle-class family (though, in fact, she was not) who loved music, dancing, and acting from the age of five; who was filial to her parents; very clever and diligent in learning; and had a pure and kind heart, as in her films. It might have been Chow's idea to take advantage of the printed media as well as radio broadcasting to activate the two-way communication, and it really provoked the passion and imaginations of Lam's fans. The effects were very handsome, such that in two years' time Lam had become the "Jewel of Shaw," the most popular Cantonese actress at the studio and perhaps the most popular of all Cantonese female stars of the time.

According to Chan Wan, who wrote more than ten films for Lam Fung, he first noted the modern image of Lam and then tailor-made the role in *A Pretty Girl's Affair* for her. It is not surprising that reviewers can identify similar plots or scenes from *Blackboard Jungle* (1955), *West Side Story* (1961), or *Splendor in the Grass* (1961). Chan Wan himself admitted that he learned much from watching Hollywood films and that he used to take notes from repeated viewings of films he liked and then used them while he was writing. The film had all the fashionable elements, too: songs; various dancing numbers, from cha-cha, mambo, and rock and roll to calypso and tango, performed by Lam herself; and gang fighting with short knifes. Above all, Lam Fung's character was the most attractive thing about the film, a character modeled on Natalie Wood's Maria in *West Side Story*. *A Pretty Girl's Affair* became an immediate hit.

Indeed, Lam Fung looked very much like Natalie Wood, only younger and more extroverted. Even in a tragic role, such as the songstress in the love story *The Merdeka Bridge*, a role that recalls Vivian Leigh in *Waterloo Bridge*, Lam acted with full energy and a gaiety such that the film would not depress the audience, except for a few tragic scenes, which were alleviated by the happy ending. It was always the star quality of Lam, rather than the characters in the films, that attracted the audience. Such was the case in *First Love*, in which she played a role that was quite similar to Natalie Woods' in *Splendor in the Grass*. A girl with an innocent mind and yearning for love, she went through her sentimental journey with three boys only to realize that joy of love and cruelty of life were inseparable, and thus she eventually came to maturity. She displayed in full her youthful gaiety and frustrations, and the audience, who knew well that she could make it through all the hardship, only waited to applaud her in the end. It could not be a tragedy with Lam Fung as its star.

Throughout her thirty films for Shaw Brothers, Lam Fung played many different roles: high school student, poor factory girl, cigarette vendor in the streets, songstress in nightclubs, wild rich daughter, office lady turned teddy girl, from teenager to young lady to mature woman. In her roles, she was typically cast as a happy, strong, independent girl who knew how to work and play and was eager to enjoy life, while at the same time exhibiting good virtues. On occasion, she was cast as a fallen angel or woman in distress who finally overcame all difficulties, but it was very seldom that she appeared as a wholly tragic figure. It was this screen image that distinguished her from other actresses. From the postwar years to the early 1950s, good-hearted women who suffered or filial daughters who knew only hard work and no play were still the prevalent images on screen. There were some femme fatales, vamps, or teddy girls, and even a few fighting women, but the dominant female figures were those who appealed to the audience for sympathy rather than applause or envy. Lam Fung's image of a Westernized, modernized female was thus something new but not inaccessible to Hong Kong audiences who were familiar with Hollywood movies and the modern way of life.

The thing is, the growing middle-class and lower-middle-class audiences, and in particular the young audiences, were yearning and dreaming of an ideal female who was pretty, energetic, diligent at work, clever at play, and somehow Westernized, a girl who could work and play through the hard times with them. That is to say, the audience at that time needed a model like Lam Fung to talk to, admire, and emulate, not a sad woman they saw every day or a legendary heroine high up there, but a friend they could reach and understand. Incidentally or deliberately, the films and promotions with Lam Fung were all aimed in that direction.

It is of interest that such a female icon did not emerge from Shaw's Mandarin films of the same period, but from its Cantonese ones. Perhaps this was because the Mandarin directors were still using the actresses of the older generation, actresses who had made their names in China in the 1940s, like Li Lihau, Zhou Menhua, or the Japanese actress Li Xianglan. Newcomers like Linda Lindai and Lucilla You Min were usually typecast in traditional roles: the former as an ancient beauty and the latter as a nice and tender girl of the distinctly weaker sex. Further, they all spoke Mandarin and lived in a reality that the contemporary Hong Kong audience could hardly relate to.

In retrospect, it is Grace Chang (Ge Lan), of MP & GI, who was the most similar to Lam Fung as a modern female icon in the late 1950s and early 1960s. Grace Chang was famous for her singing and dancing ability and her youthful, energetic, cheerful character. Incidentally, the same year that Lam Fung acted in her first film, Chang made her star quality known for the first time in *Mambo Girl* (1957), a film that is remembered for its youthful spirit, trendy songs, dancing numbers, and a story that tells about the search for a Hong Kong identity. At that time, youth film was becoming one of the major genres at MP & GI and was developing in directions similar to Shaw's Cantonese productions, the only major difference being that MP & GI's were more refined and more sophisticated to suit the middle-class taste. As early as 1955, Grace Chang appeared in a Hollywood film, *Soldier of Fortune* (starring Clark Gable), when it had a location shoot in Hong Kong. In 1957, she was invited to sing onstage in the United States and appeared as a guest of honor "from China" on Dinah Shore's TV show. At the same time, Lam Fung was trying to act in a few Mandarin films, but without much success. This might be a good indication of the veracity of Run Run Shaw's belief that the Mandarin language represented the modern nationhood of China and thus was easier to go global with, whereas Cantonese was more regional and represented only the image of Hong Kong.

Conclusion

I would say that the Shaw Brothers Cantonese productions played a significant role in the rejuvenation and modernization of Cantonese cinema in Hong Kong and that the Cantonese section set a good example for Shaw Brothers Studio with its low-budget films and talented new stars that could actually win at the box office. It was not until 1964 that Run Run Shaw fully realized that what SB really needed was new blood. He then seriously recruited more and more talent, gave them good training, and gave them opportunities to act in main roles. And this policy proved to be practical and fruitful.

A majority of the Cantonese films were made by core members of the section, with very limited resources but with high efficiency. The staff members and the actors and actresses worked together closely. In terms of technical capabilities, they were still quite crude; in terms of creativity, they were undergoing a learning process that paralleled Hollywood trends. The writers and directors borrowed characters, plots, and scenes from Hollywood cinema for dramatic use, absorbing some of the new elements in Western popular culture as entertaining gadgetry but not identifying them with Western culture and ideals. Very often the films were critical toward the Western values of freedom, individuality, and, in particular, youthful rebellion. Although the films were full of youthful entertainment, they remained dubious of the idea of modernization and materialization, which seemed to result in making the rich richer and the poor poorer. The films stood with the lower class and lower-middle class and were in general culturally conservative, complying with traditional Chinese family values and Chinese morality. However, these films brought a great deal of youthful elements, energy, and fashionable lifestyle into Hong Kong's cinema that reflected the changes in Hong Kong society and the likes and wants of the younger generation in the late 1950s and early 1960s. In comparison with the Mandarin productions of

Shaw Brothers, we can see that the Mandarin films more or less came out of Run Run Shaw's Chinese imagination, whereas the Cantonese ones reflected more or less the local Hong Kong reality.

Notes

1. *Hong Kong Almanac 1962* (in Chinese) (Hong Kong: Wah Kiu Yat Po, 1963).

2. For more details on the branching out of Shanghai's Tianyi (Unique) Studio to Hong Kong, see Zhou Chengren, "Shanghai's Unique Film Productions and Hong Kong's Early Cinema," in Wong Ain-ling, ed., *The Shaw Screen: A Preliminary Study* (Hong Kong: Hong Kong Film Archive, 2003), pp. 30–34.

3. As estimated from statistics compiled by the Research Section of the Hong Kong Film Archive.

4. Weng Ling-wen, "The Dianmou Film Company: Cantonese Film Group," in Lin Nien-tung, ed., *Cantonese Cinema Retrospective (1950–1959): The 2nd Hong Kong International Film Festival Catalogue* (Hong Kong: The Urban Council, 1978), pp. 58–59.

5. "Cantonese Movies of the Sixties: An Oral History by Chan Wan," collated by Cindy Chan, in Law Kar, *The Restless Breed: Cantonese Stars of the Sixties: The 20th Hong Kong International Film Festival Catalogue* (Hong Kong: The Urban Council, 1996), pp. 114–15.

6. The standard budget for a Mandarin film was HK$160,000, according to independent producer Cheung Kwok-hing (Zhang Guoxing).

7. "Cantonese Movies of the Sixties," p. 115.

8. Poshek Fu, "Going Global: A Cultural History of the Shaw Brothers Studio, 1960–1970," in Law Kar, ed., *Border Crossings in Hong Kong Cinema: The 24th Hong Kong International Film Festival Catalogue* (Hong Kong: The Urban Council, 2000), p. 46.

9. Tau Han-fun, "Making Cantonese Films: Tau Han-fun Remembers," in Wong Ain-ling, ed., *The Cathay Story* (Hong Kong: Hong Kong Film Archive, 2002), pp. 282–83.

3

Embracing Glocalization and
Hong Kong–Made Musical Film

SIU LEUNG LI

The Chinese musical film, in a broad sense—in every which way it has manifested itself and been defined—first emerged in the semicolonial 1930s Shanghai enclave. The Chinese movie musical à la Hollywood came to maturity in the British Crown Colony of Hong Kong some thirty years later. Together with the rise of numerous super singer-actresses and behind-the-scene divas, the Chinese musical film prospered in the post–World War II decades and attracted various Chinese audiences in different overseas Chinese communities, especially in East and Southeast Asia. Somewhat ironic but figuratively as glamorous as the life cycle of the *sakura* blossom, the genre's demise crept up on it during its heyday when the Shaw Brothers Studio churned out Hollywood-style musicals in the genre's full-fledged form in the rapidly Westernizing and modernizing late-1960s Hong Kong. The masculine-macho sword fight and kung fu action genres gradually came on the scene to soon dominate the film industries in Hong Kong and Taiwan, subsequently establishing the Hong Kong action genre and kung fu action choreography as a globally popular form and style of action.

The Chinese movie musicals à la Hollywood were produced at a time (1) when there were decisive economic changes in Hong Kong, East Asia, and Southeast Asia; (2) of consequential social and cultural transformations that were generated in the process of boarding the train of colonial modernity and constituted by an eager acceptance of Euro-American popular cultural forms; (3) of an emerging social awareness of the crisis of identity[1] that was especially complicated and intensified by the sociopolitical unrest spreading to British Hong Kong from Mainland China's turbulent Great Proletarian

Cultural Revolution in the latter half of the 1960s and the colonial government's subsequent political strategies to counter mainland influences by cultivating a local Hong Kong conscious among Hong Kong Chinese. Reexamining the musical film from the perspective of our (post)modern age of global linking and transnational identity politics, it would be most instructive (perhaps even imperative) to situate these 1950s and 1960s musical films in a transnational interpretative framework so as to fully understand the social relevance and cultural significance of this imaginary representation in its own spatial-temporal context and in relation to our own experience of the early twenty-first century.

I

The transnational perspective in studying Hong Kong, Taiwan, and Mainland Chinese cinemas has in a few years yielded inspiring reinterpretations of various aspects of these cinemas.[2] The history of the influential Shaw Brothers Studio since the late 1950s under the leadership of Sir Run Run Shaw (born 1907) has been reread as an ambitious film enterprise aspiring to internationality.[3] Critics have also rediscovered the modern, transnational business vision of Dato Loke Wan-tho (1915–64), head of the Motion Picture and General Investment Film Co. Ltd. (MP & GI)[4] that rivaled the Shaws. These two competing film studios had dominated the Southeast Asian and other overseas Chinese film markets in the 1950s and 1960s. Although MP & GI gradually declined toward the close of the 1960s after the untimely death of Loke, the Shaws' dominating influence stretched into the early 1980s after new studios such as Golden Harvest and Cinema City emerged in the 1970s to challenge and finally overshadow the Shaws. There are two points to note here. For one thing, the formation of these two major film studios (Shaw and MP & GI) was in the beginning border crossing. They were modeled on the Hollywood studio system and were geopolitically not merely "Hong Kong" studios. The two could be understood from today's perspective as transnational enterprises interlocking at least (1) Hong Kong the British Crown Colony, (2) Nanyang (Singapore and Malaysia), and (3) Taiwan, the Republic of China (the People's Republic of China was absent from this scene for its political self-isolation until 1978 after the death of Chairman Mao and the fall of the Gang of Four). These two commercial enterprises virtually constituted a translocal network within an emerging global form of exchange in the capitalist world market that culminated at the turn of the twenty-first century in a new global form of sovereignty known as Empire.[5] Second, the two studios, especially Shaws Brothers, pioneered in experimenting transnational coproduction, collaborating at various stages with Japan, South Korean, and Euro-American film studios.[6] This translocal/transnational structural setup of the Shaws and MP & GI was to bear on the musical imaginary in significant ways, as we shall see.

Competing for success in their translocal network of markets, these studios produced films in a variety of genres, with the Shaws excelling in costume drama and historical epics. There was a peculiar fascination with popular songs (shidaiqu) in the so-called Mandarin films from 1930s Shanghai to 1950s Hong Kong, so that the veteran music critic Wong Kee-chee once stated, "Mandarin films made twenty years ago [i.e., the 1950s] give the impression that every film features at least one song sequence."[7] Later on, Stephen Teo echoed this point, saying that Hong Kong's Mandarin cinema, "in the great majority of its productions, regardless of genres, featured a tune or two," emphasizing that this is an uptake of the "particular Shanghai tradition of sing-song girls,"[8] whereas Wong attributed this further back to the deep-rooted theatrical culture of Chinese opera.[9] The movie musical (loosely defined) apparently carried a special lure in Mandarin films of the 1950s and 60s. During the period, the genre gradually transformed from the less sophisticated format of a romance film (typically with a substantial countryside setting) with added song sequences—as exemplified by the 1956 Songs of the Peach Blossom River (Taohua jiang) produced by the Hsin Hwa Motion Picture Company—to the fully developed, glamorous, wide-screen, color, Hollywood-style movie musical culminating in the productions of the Shaws—arguably best represented by the extravagant 1967 Hong Kong Nocturne (Xiang jiang hua yue ye), directed, scripted, and with music composed by Japanese filmmakers and musicians recruited by Shaw Brothers—which centered on major themes of the urban imaginary in a condition of crisscrossing colonial modernity. By crisscrossing, I refer to the replacing of original Japanese films to the Hong Kong context by Umetsugu Inoue (born 1923) in his self-adaptations for Shaw Brothers.[10] This cultural replacing engendered delicate issues in reading Inoue's Hong Kong movie musicals. Japan's postwar occupation by the United States under Gen. Douglas MacArthur and the accompanying clear and present invasion by U.S. culture rightly places Japan's lived experience in the 1950s and 1960s in a form of colonial modernity.

Equally prevalent from the late 1950s to the late 1960s was another genre that at first sight seems to be everything the opposite of the musical but on closer look would bring forth contrastive yet related underlying meanings to help construct a broader view of the Hong Kong movie musical: the historical epic. It will be revealing to juxtapose the two genres to contextualize the present investigation into the movie musical of its desire for the modern and the international in the shadow of the "nation." Specifically in the case of the Shaw Brothers Studio—which boosted the musical to its peak and very much monopolized the historical epic—these two genres in different manners constituted a complex processing of the positioning of the self in relation to the reimagination and unimagination of the "nation" and the "national" in the larger realm of the emerging transnational condition. Curiously enough, with the rise of an intense local awareness of Hong Kong's cultural (trans) formation and an international attention to Hong Kong cinema throughout the 1990s, the musical film and the historical epic produced in the two decades after World War II have to date been given at best preliminary studies by critics and scholars,[11] in sharp contrast with the tons of studies and fan publications recently produced on Hong Kong action films.

Simultaneously in 1960s Hong Kong cinema, the glossy musicals narrate the romance and anxiety of modern city life, whereas the grand historical epics narrate the dynastic history of the "nation." The musical film points to an emerging complex of desire for and an imagination of modernity, transnationality, and local self-identity; the historical epic demonstrates a reimagining of traditional China that was not only for the consumption of Chinese audiences around the globe but also effective in representing "China" to the world when these films competed and were screened in various international film festivals.[12] Veteran film critic Sek Kei rightly expressed that the Shaw Brothers Studio manufactured predominately "the China dream."[13] One could further argue that the power of this China dream also resided in its being a cultural sign, a semiotic commodity that could circulate and be reimagined across boundaries quickly and with ease.

The Shaws' historical epics, with successful films including *Diau Charn of the Three Kingdoms* (*Diao Chan*; 1958), *The Kingdom and the Beauty* (*Jiangshan meiren*; 1959), *Yang Geifei* (1963), *The Empress Wu* (*Wu Zetian*; 1963), *Lady General Hua Mulan* (*Hua Mulan*; 1964), and *Beyond the Great Wall of China* (*Wang Zhaojun*; 1964), all featuring a female protagonist, be it an empress, a femme fatale, a beauty, a cross-dressed woman warrior (now Americanized by Disney's animated film *Mulan* [1998]), were popular at the time of colonial Hong Kong's beginning to jump on the bandwagon of Euro-American modernity. These films are more than simply products of a nostalgic nationalism in exile after the political takeover of Mainland China by the Chinese Communist Party in 1949. They can be more fruitfully read as complex representations addressing issues of the imaginary homeland of reconstructing "China-home" outside China, reconstructing grand historical narratives for contemporary use, the diasporic desire for a place in the global context, and self-feminization in representing the "I" in an uneven world dominated by the Orientalist gaze. The discourse of these historical epics depends on re-presenting "China" in specific ways of cultural imagination: a visual style of the grand artificiality of studio shooting plus a meticulous attention to historical details, sets, and props (arguably most prominently represented by the work of director Li Hanxiang [1926–96]). The imaginary of the historical epic in this era amounts to a kind of reappearance of "China" as an object of quest already lost in time.

Vis-à-vis the historical epics, the musical films demonstrate an interesting contrastive imagination in relation to the nation and the national. I would like to suggest that these cultural texts effect a veiled motto of "forgetting China." "China" is put under erasure; it is very much invisible, lost in the emerging webs of desire for Westernization and the transnational modern in an age seeing the first rise of the media and the visual in everyday life and an intensification of the commodification of culture. The imaginary of the movie musical insinuates a disappearance of "China"—the nation that is vanishing, if not already vanished in the hilarious quest for youthful pleasure,[14] Euro-American modernity, and local identity in an interlocking network of the worldwide turbulence of the 1960s.

II

The made-in-Hong Kong musical at its summit made contemporary social and cultural traces into an escapist and spectacular entertainment that loomed larger than the form it employed and tactfully negotiated the city's imagination of itself not merely locally but also intranationally in relation to "China" and internationally to the world at large. Stephen Teo once used in passing the term the *made-in-Hong Kong musical* in his inspiring, pioneering work in English on the history of Hong Kong cinema.[15] I shall reappropriate this term here as a vehicle to register this chapter's focus of reading the musical film as produced in and at once constituting the Hong Kong social experience of the late 1950s and 1960s. In this respect, the Shaws' musicals of the 1960s—such as *Love Parade* (*Huatuan jincu;* 1963), *The Dancing Millionairess* (*Wanhua yingchun;* 1964), *The Lark* (*Xiaoyunque;* 1965), *Hong Kong Nocturne* (*Xian jiang hua yue ye;* 1967), *King Drummer* (*Qingchun guwang;* 1967), and *Hong Kong Rhapsody* (*Huayue liangxiao;* 1968), just to name a few important pictures—are perhaps of particular interest. I say that these entertainment films loom larger than the form they make use of in the sense that whereas the musicals are generally perceived as a superficial genre of surface spectacle even within the variety of popular cinemas, I try to make a fuller sense out of them with reference to their semiotic effects in addressing larger patterns of social experiences and cultural concerns in specific temporal-spatial context and interpretive community.[16] In this respect, Inoue's Hong Kong remakes of his Japanese originals might be what Sek Kei called "simulation behind closed doors"[17] and in their inception had little or perhaps even no direct interconnection with Hong Kong's social reality; however, the purity of a consciously thoughtful, high cultural aesthetic and a philosophical intent do not necessarily control or limit the semiotic construction and dissemination of meanings of these cultural texts in interaction with their social context once they are put in circulation.

Before moving farther into Shaws' musicals, let us step a few years back to reconstruct traces of thematic continuities of modernity and identity by way of addressing two big hits from the late 1950s black-and-white musical films of the Hsin Wah Motion Picture Company and MP & GI, respectively. It would be enlightening to read together the trendsetting 1956 *Songs of the Peach Blossom River*[18] (Hsin Hwa) with the now classic 1957 *Mambo Girl* (*Manbo nülang*; MP & GI)[19] in terms of a cultural imagination that negotiates what I would dub the processes of "forgetting Shanghai, leaving China behind, embracing Hong Kong, and catching up with Euro-modernity." Critics have already noticed the "Hong Kong self-positioning" in *Songs of the Peach Blossom River*.[20] The female protagonist, Jin Lirong (Zhong Qing), a farmer's daughter with extraordinary singing talent living in a backward countryside somewhere, presumably China and unmistakably so—although "China" is never spoken of in the film—is to be discovered by the man from modern Hong Kong and repackaged for the urban middle-class audience. She will leave rural China and settle in Hong Kong—a city described by the male protagonist, Li Ming (Loh Wei), as "having a lot of playful things to be enjoyed" (*xianggang haowan de dongxi duodehen*).[21] Li Ming, born in Hong Kong, is the Westernized-modern-techno-middle-class-male-folk-music-culture-collector intruding into the world of the female rural, equipped with his lure and surprise of the technogadgets, such as the open-reel tape recorder and the camera. The film sets up the binary opposition of the urban (Hong Kong) versus the rural (China). Somewhat of a surprise to us looking back from the vantage point of the early twenty-first century, this five-decade-old film already demonstrated one of the first cultural representations signifying Hong Kong's modernity vis-à-vis Mainland China's premodern condition.

Mambo Girl—the melodramatic story of a female middle-class high school teenager in Hong Kong who searches for her biological mother but in the end identifies and stays with her foster parents—is perhaps a political metaphor with the between-the-line message all too obvious in addressing the colonial Hong Kong–homeland China relationship. Law Wai-ming says that "no one seemed to have managed director Yi Wen's open espousal of belonging to Hong Kong as seen in *Mambo Girl*."[22] Sam Ho describes the film as "putting the city (of Hong Kong) on the map."[23] Law Kar states, "[I]t must be noted that it took a long time [almost two decades] for the Hong Kong cinema to break loose from the shadow cast by its Shanghai past."[24] Today, looking back at these 1950s musical films made a half-century ago, we see in the city's cultural imagination the emergence of a Hong Kong identity initiated in an attempt at getting rid of the China shadow and, for better or worse, soon to embrace and celebrate Western modernity from Euro-America that is invariably dubbed the "international" and the "world." *Songs of the Peach Blossom River* poses as a transition leading up to a decisive break with Shanghai/China in *Mambo Girl* made two years later. Hong Kong cinema becoming independent from its Shanghai influence is contrapuntal with the *becoming* of Hong Kong and the Hong Konger (*xianggangren*). A new horizon was soon to appear as the Hong Kong movie musical reached the first full-color and well-defined form à la Hollywood in MP & GI's 1959 *Calendar Girls* (*Longxiang fengwu*), climaxed in the ultimate grand and glamorous spectacles by Shaw Brothers in the late 1960s, all in all contributing to the musical project of chasing Western modernity in an international frame.

III

Poshek Fu's rereading of the 1960s Shaw Brothers enterprise in the vein of the recently thriving study of modern Chinese transnationalism[25] argues that Run Run Shaw manifested a "global vision" in his attempt at "establishing a transnational film empire."[26] Fu's attribution of such "cosmopolitan vision and modern ideals" to the Shaw Brothers Studio at once acknowledges that socially "Hong Kong was to enter a new age of modern values and transnational consciousness."[27] Examining the studio's 1960s productions, specifically the musical film and the historical epic discussed previously, we can see that this very modern project of Shaw Brothers unfolded in a highly complex interplay between the imaginations of the cosmopolitan, the local, and the national. The project of the musical film as part of this quest for modernity demonstrated a strong desire to emulate the West, specifically the Hollywood musical in this context. In a 1964 issue of Shaw Brothers' official magazine, *The Milky Way Pictorial* (*Yinhe huabao*), an article (that reads more like a press release) promoting the "high standard" (*gaoshuizhun*)[28] of the new musical *Dancing Millionairess* expresses a will to contest with foreign musicals in a formulaic, artificial style of publicity discourse. The article quotes from an anonymous film director first admitting that "we [Hong Kong] are lacking of singing and dancing talents, and in comparison our musical films are way beyond that of the U.K. and the U.S."[29] Yet the essence of this speech is in fact an official expression of a business determination to compete with the foreign competitors (with a twist of context, this is not without an affinity to the literary critic Harold Bloom's theorization of "the anxiety of influence" that poetry is a site of struggle between strong poets[30]), "It is only with a resolution to overcome the fear of losing that we could gradually produce musical scenes comparable to that of the British, Americans and Japanese."[31] It is important to note that this publicity utterance stretches the geographic boundary from Europe through North America to East Asia. The global imagination in which Hong Kong is situated in relation to the world is aptly implied. At once, the foregrounding of the subjecthood of the local in this global connection points to a confident, ambitious aspiration that has to incessantly negotiate in the continuum between the global and the local—the glocal. This prototypical global localization positioning might turn out to be the best tactic of sustaining profits. In reality, Shaw Brothers had already employed various Japanese film personalities to boost its production under the cost-effective and time-saving principles of capitalism,[32] a realization of the "time is money" metaphor. This piece of press release betrays a logic of Shaw Brothers' movie musical: that the whole point of making films is to make profit, that moviegoers demand primarily entertainment, and that the best entertainment is the musical:

> I [the writer] . . . discovered that some of the better musical films in the past had very excellent box office records. I have further checked with the film studio and found out that movie musicals are the best business to do; there is no worry of failure in sales and in fact in most cases there have been profits. . . . Why? The ultimate answer lies in the audience. The moviegoer's purpose is to look for entertainment. What would the best entertainment be were it not singing and dancing with vivid sets and attention-holding plots?[33]

The primary principle of entertainment—the necessity of profitability—the spirit of catching up with the foreign, and the self-confidence of "I can do it, too" altogether constituted the logic of a form that is epitomized in the

1960s movie musicals of the Shaw Brothers Studio. Sharing some similarities with today's dot-com entrepreneurial vigor of trading globally without boundaries, Shaw Brothers, apart from employing the very Westernized directors from Shanghai[34] who had worked for MP & GI (e.g., Tao Qing and Yue Feng), also brought in Japanese directors, cinematographers, and composers to tell stories—not without an ironic sense of cultural dislocation—that clearly named (if not really rooted in) Hong Kong as their local context. Thus in the beginning was the designation of Hong Kong in film titles—*Hong Kong Nocturne, Hong Kong Rhapsody,* which figured in the musical tropes of either nocturne or rhapsody, two forms that the incomparably romantic yet nationalistic Chopin so excelled in. Although the made-in-Hong Kong musical from MP & GI to Shaw Brothers may very well be romantic (in the popular sense of the word), it is every way but nationalistic. For example, Chen Ziqing (Peter Chan), the young and tragically short-lived composer in *Hong Kong Nocturne,* spiritedly claims on a rooftop at night that "recently I feel that I am filled with confidence and I wish to create a new form of singing and dancing to express this very beauty of Hong Kong at night"[35] and that his posthumous magnum opus, a musical play entitled *Hong Kong Nocturne,* had its premiere broadcast live on a television show named *Hong Kong Music Lovers* (original) at the station's tenth anniversary at the end of the film. At the same time, the young classical music composer Suen Yiqiang (Yang Fan) in *King Drummer* finally receives from the British Thomas Foundation sponsorship of his "Hong Kong Symphony" and conducts the premiere of this piece by himself with a live television broadcast. At all these moments, the sign and its referent (Hong Kong) are interlocked in a process of defining a social experience, signifying an emergent "structure of feeling" (borrowing from Raymond Williams)[36] that is being constituted by a growing sense of the local and self-identity and a celebration of modernity in which the rise of the mass media and the commodification of culture cannot but hint at a possible future emergence of Guy Debord's society of the spectacle. The key terms employed here require some quick qualification before the further elaborations on the Shaw Brothers musicals. For "identity," it is to be understood as not necessarily a substantiated positional fixation but may be whatever—and in whatever fluid forms—it takes to be continually represented; for the "local," it is neither provincially Hong Kong nor a nationalistic identification with the homeland of China but is imagined in an interrelation with the modern and the global; for "media culture," we see that television, the record industry, the press, and yellow journalism are constitutive structural elements in a number of these musical films; for "the commodification of culture," one question would immediately come to mind: For what would the two "king drummers" be in the first place if not commodities (or even signs) produced by their female boss and star maker in *King Drummer*?

The gist of the film *King Drummer* is better presented by its Chinese title: *Qingchun guwang*, literally "the youthful king drummer." The theme of youth is a recurring motif of the film director, Inoue, in his works from Japan to Hong Kong, although the transplanting of youthfulness from 1950s Japan to late 1960s Hong Kong might have been an embarrassing dislocation of time and culture.[37] In any case, the supposedly rebellious young drummer, Suen Zhiqiang (Ling Yun), is after all a commodity for the consumption of an emerging media age in which television images have begun to disseminate into private and public space. The two rival drummers, the other being Charlie (Chen Honglie), are made by Huang Lizhen (Lily Ho), an artist-manageress who owns an agency, was educated in the United States, and holds a degree in business administration. She is pretty successful everywhere in the music business world. Her passionate love for every "commodity"— first Charlie and then Zhiqiang—she produced seems to suggest that there is a conflation of romantic love and commodity fetishism. Each of her king drummers is nicknamed: "Charlie the Golden Arm" and "Suen Zhiqiang the Thunder Drummer." The commodity/sign relationship in which each reproduces the other has long been a practical rule in show business. Suen Zhiqiang's first appearance in the film (not counting the opening credits in which he and Charlie are presented in a montage sequence) tells us that he originally belongs to the people, to the folk. He is drumming marvelously on empty oil barrels—not on a drum set—with his friends at a pier in a remote countryside in the New Territories. Suen Zhiqiang's friends are making music together with him playing the Chinese *dizi* and the Western guitar. A hybridization of music is in the making. It is popular culture in the sense of culture actually made by people for themselves[38] and is posing a momentary resistance to high and commercial mainstream culture. When the drummer gets to the nightclub and is donning his shiny tuxedo and sitting in front of his glittering drum set while preparing to appear on the live television show, he and his music are immediately transformed into a commodity from the popular. The show business world in *King Drummer* is one in which the ultimate real success is to be on television. The two drummers' competition for the title of the "Youthful King Drummer" on a live television show turns them into a real-time media spectacle that reaches the record company executives in their offices as well as the young spectators on the street who dance to Suen Zhiqiang's song "I Am a Jazz Singer," while gazing at this new, youthful idol on television. Right here, the intercut shots showing the two drummers in the studio between the color scene at the live studio and the black-and-white domestic television screens frame people's imagination of the community; space already began to compress in the 1960s. This contest on television is metaphorically the final duel between the two rival "warriors." It is virtually a mortal combat, only that the spectacle has been moved from the Colosseum to the television studio. In ancient Roman times, one went to the Colosseum, and now the television broadcast comes to you. In *Hong Kong Nocturne,* the airing of the now-dead Chen Ziqing's musical cuts into the living room of his affluent parents, who, tearfully holding Chen's posthumous baby, are watching the show together with their three handmaids, this time around on a color television set. The spectacle/image intrudes to the extent of the very personal of everyday life. Culture and the commodity principle as represented in this 1960s musical are that of a materialization and degeneration of "culture," yet not without a gesture of resistance in collapsing the dichotomy of high and low (pop) culture.

It is probably a long stretch from the musical spectacle (as a remarkable sight and an impressive display) to Debord's society of the spectacle (meaning "the historical moment at which the commodity completes its colonization of social life").[39] But if we agree that Law Kar is right in saying, "The impure amalgams that are *Hong Kong Nocturne* and *The Singing Thief* . . . are signs of the cinema's future development, signaling its entry into an era of spectacles"[40] (read "the musical spectacle"), it at least registers Hong Kong culture's one small but not insignificant step toward postmodern production and consumption of signs. From Grace Chang (Ge Lan; the ultimate movie musical icon in the 1950s and 1960s) to Leon Lai (one of the "four heavenly kings" in Cantopop in the 1990s) is, in a way, capitalist logic along the same line; although almost three decades apart, they are both popular cultural icons, "signs" for consumption. But the fact that one sings marvelously (Chang) and the other could hardly get a sequence of notes in good intonation (Lai) differentiates two modes of economy: one representing a time when a commodity came with both sign and use value, the other an empty sign in the Baudrillardian sense; or, in words of conventional wisdom, Grace Chang is an *artist,* whereas Leon Lai an *artiste.* The transformation of Run Run Shaw from the supreme head of a film enterprise maximizing on the vertical chain of film production (commodities) to the chairman of a transnational corporation in the flexible mode of production—Television Broadcasts Ltd. (TVB) and its worldwide subsidiary companies, TVBI Company Ltd., TVB.COM Ltd.—of largely circulating mass entertainment (signs) in the form of the Internet, television, video, DVD, and pop music is also instructive in this respect.

Being globally connected (including access to cyberspace) has been an obsession since the late twentieth century. In everyday life, the connected and the unconnected represent a division of hierarchical power. The persistent presence of markers of international connection and traces of Westernization in the 1960s Shaw Brothers movie musicals can be seen as a first indicator that a new structure of feeling in Hong Kong society was forming. Although Huang Lizhen, the king drummer maker, is a cosmopolitan, Westernized, "vogue," and "chic" "modern woman,"[41] the stern millionairess Mei Qianru (Le Di) in the 1964 *Dancing Millionairess* (dir. Tao Qin) heads a big corporation and checks the Dow Jones Index the first thing every morning. In this global economy, we see the superstar singer Shi Xiaoyun (Gu Mei) in *The Lark* (dir. Xue Qun) enjoying the status of a translocal celebrity traveling between Southeast Asia, Hong Kong, and Japan. The reality base of this filmic imagination is the fact that the show business enterprise of Shaw Brothers and MP & GI had been developing into a transnational network since the 1950s.

This and other kinds of nonlocal references and foreign linkages are standard occurrences in Shaw Brothers' musical world. The media and record companies in *King Drummer* are international traders with names such as Hong Kong International TV Company Ltd. It is very prominently remarked in the film that Charlie the Golden Arm is of "international standard" and has been invited to perform in Japan. Suen Zhiqiang's younger brother, Yiqiang, who aspires to become a classical music composer, takes lessons from an English music professor and receives an endorsement from a foreign organization in Hong Kong known as the Thomas Foundation. Bilingual signs in Chinese and English are everywhere in the film. The bar that the people frequent is designated in English only—Sharp & Flat Bar—quite in line with the flavor of a musical film. Some characters are known by their English names, including Charlie. The pattern of naming also roughly differentiates the good guys who always have Chinese names from the bad guys who usually have English names (it may not be totally unrelated; in Hollywood, arch villains more often than not speak stylishly with a classy British accent). Having an English name may sound trendily modern, yet it may also summon forth a deep-seated mistrust of Westernization. The clash between traditional values and modern Western values and their respective signifiers is enmeshed in a complex web of sometimes incompatible signifieds.

IV

The primary milieu in the Chinese musical film is often the nightclub (*yezonghui, wuting*). This controlling sign signifies the very nature of Hong Kong as a business city, the nightclub acting as a site for business transactions (the exchange of money) in the midst of auditory and visual pleasures, the sensuality of the body in hilarious singing and dancing (the exchange of sex). In 1997 (the year that Hong Kong changed from a British colony to become part of China), Japanese director Tayayoshi Watanabe made a romantic comedy adventure shot almost entirely in Hong Kong, *Hong Kong Night Club*,[42] featuring pop idol Shingo Katori from the leading pop band SMAP, who later reached up to take the male lead in the 2004 NHK Taiga drama *Shinsen gumi*. From the Hong Kong side is popular actress Anita Yuen, playing a humble amusement park-nightclub entertainer. The conflation of Hong Kong and the nightclub in the narrative of this film seems to have made explicit an underlying metaphor running through the made-in-Hong Kong musical; that is, Hong Kong *is* a nightclub.

Hong Kong nightclubs and cabaret singers had a long and fascinating history in Hong Kong, especially between the 1950s and 1970s; the nightclub world in Hong Kong musical films is not at all unfounded in social reality. This Japanese film *Hong Kong Night Club*, although set in the 1990s, is in many ways a retro imagination by an "other"—Japan of the late 1990s—being nostalgic for "the other"—Hong Kong of the 1960s. The film represents a Hong Kong that does not exist anymore; the golden years of nightclubs and amusement parks have passed. Pan-Asian supericon singer-actress Anita Mui had an upbringing as a child performer at amusement parks and nightclubs in 1960s Hong Kong, and her sudden death in late 2003 sent shockwaves radiating through East and Southeast Asia that symbolically and officially sealed an era of flashiness in the history of Hong Kong popular culture.

Shaw Brothers' *Hong Kong Nocturne*, like many other Hong Kong musical films, is a story centering on the nightclub; one could possibly say that the world of the Hong Kong musical film is very much a world of nightclubs—there is the musical within a musical in *Nocturne*. As a formal feature, it is a pragmatic development that this Hollywood genre often has stories embedded in show business (e.g., *Singin' in the Rain* [1952], *There's No Business Like Show Business* [1954]) in order to conveniently make up occasions to display musical numbers.[43] But it does not mean that the resulting episodic narratives of the musical are merely trivial pretext to provide for song and dance, as many critics have argued.[44] The nightclub in Hong Kong musical films must also be read beyond a formal structural device, for Hong Kong is often embodied in the nightclub and Hong Kong is already show business. "Nothing Is above Entertainment" (*yule zhishang*), as one of the musical numbers in the film proclaims. The Night Pearl Night Club in *Hong Kong Nocturne* is the site where an ahistorical claim of identity and local positioning take place, immersing in the pale trope of the "night pearl" or "pearl of the Orient" that has long been employed without traces of its origin in Hong Kong's cultural discourse of self-fashioning. The sense of local yet modern identity—the musical *Hong Kong Nocturne* in the film *Hong Kong Nocturne* and the symphony "Hong Kong Symphony" in *King Drummer* all dedicated to (construct and hail) Hong Kong—does not seem to have much substance or essence apart from being represented in spectacles, always Westernized, presently trendy, and, above all, hybridized. The "Hong Kong Symphony" is, of course, not really a symphony in musical structure and style (had the film's composer Ryoichi Hattori created the piece in an authentic symphonic style, it would have effected a very postmodern incongruity in this context). High culture here is only a signifier emptied out of its conventional signified; that is, high culture in the film has become an empty sign with no substance. But the high cultural status of the name is needed to denote the seriousness of dedication to Hong Kong.[45] The "Hong Kong Symphony" turns out to be a pastiche of Mandarin pop with a choir, big band jazz, and some Gershwin. Contrasting with Sibelius's nation-building orchestral work *Finlandia* (1900) or Chopin's nationalist *Krakowiak* (1828) and *Fantasia on Polish Airs* (1831), the imaginary "Hong Kong Symphony" within a movie musical reinvents Hong Kong in cultural eclecticism, resulting in a patchwork of hybridization (in the first place, this musical film and many others were made by Japanese director Inoue in collaboration with composer Hattori). Or the ode to Hong Kong is signified in and out of the form of the Hollywood musical with a displacement if its music style by Mandarin pop. The world of *King Drummer* and *Hong Kong Nocturne* sees its present—and only the present is there to be seen and lived—as a nightclub in an ahistorical vacuum of hybrid entertainment business that "registered its historical deficiency by losing itself"[46] in a mishmash of high and low art, serious and pop musical forms. The nation and its tradition are not there for reference.

William Tay, in a long series of 1997 newspaper articles published in Taiwan,[47] puts forward an argument that Hong Kong is the only public space between Taiwan and the mainland that has allowed the emergence of a variety of cultural forms and processes not possible on either side of the strait. As for film, he argues that it is only in Hong Kong that Hollywood-style musical films could be produced, for three reasons: (1) MP & GI as well as Shaw Brothers had full-fledged studios and could thus give hardware support, (2) only those filmmakers who moved from Shanghai to Hong Kong were especially familiar with this unique U.S. genre, and (3) it is only in Hong Kong that the film industry could avoid the "dominant melody of politics" to fully commit to escapist entertainment and going Westernized totally for show business.[48] I would like to pick up the third point and further elaborate that the Hong Kong musical film was a commercial project in public space. It is exactly the opposite of all the state projects in modern China's various modernization attempts. It was a project conceived out of marketing consideration. Shaw Brothers did whatever possible to emulate the other (Hollywood) for the prime consideration to speed up production to increase the rate of capital accumulation. This intention and its subsequent action by Shaw Brothers of "buying"[49] the technique, technology, and operation from Japan's more advanced film industry brought about hybridization through this border crossing, the mixing of genres (*King Drummer* as a mix of the musical, gangster, and domestic drama) and styles (the comparison between Inoue's original Japanese works and his Hong Kong adaptations deserves a separate full-length study). Commercial pragmatism turned into a driving force toward cultural hybridity. This border crossing was further enhanced through the film studio's marketing network in Southeast Asian and other overseas Chinese communities. This initial integration with the global redefined and constituted local (Hong Kong) identity in a complex way. In films such as *Hong Kong Nocturne* and *King Drummer*, we see that the formation of self-identity depends not on the reconstruction of a certain cultural authenticity; instead, there is more of a world of the interplay of differences. Hong Kong's experience of identity and modernity in the 1960s is not simply a look back to some Chinese cultural roots and anticolonialism but a process of Westernization, technologization, and hybridization. The double movement of local awareness/outward looking vision led to the disruption of a unifying monolithic cultural plane. The local awareness was in the making in a flux of alien cultural forms. The world of *Hong Kong Nocturne* and *King Drummer* is not conceived inwardly but transnationally, not in national Chinese terms but in a cultural matrix. The absence of the state in this project of the musical film may further explain one of the major themes of this genre: "the family crisis as the central conflict."[50] The absent father, father as loser, the single parent, the defunct family, all so common in many of these movie musicals, signify the losing of the patriarchal state's grip on society and imagination in what Tay calls the only public space between Taiwan and Mainland China.

Although even in the posthandover era, Hong Kongers still linger on a nostalgia for the 1960s, as exemplified by Radio Television Hong Kong's 2001 documentary series *Remembering Hong Kong—1960s* and Wong Kar-wai's film *In the Mood for Love* (2001), a further reverie of Wong's on the 1960s after his *Days of Being Wild* (1990). Law Wai-ming writes in a short article that he could not help thinking of *Days of Being Wild* while watching *Mambo*

Girl (1958) in terms of self-identification.[51] This comparison of two films made three decades apart reminds us of another significant point regarding representation. Although many people will see a kind of "nostalgia for the present" (borrowing from Fredric Jameson) in Wong Kar-wai, Stanley Kwan, or pop fiction writer Lilian Lee and the like, what we can learn from the musical films from *Mambo Girl* to *Hong Kong Nocturne* is how the period represented itself and negotiated its social experience in a form that is at once so radically alien yet so familiar. Hong Kong's cultural experience through the colonial and postcolonial times is a mélange of Westernization, the emergence of local nonnational identity, the rise of ethnonationalism (especially notable with the rise of Bruce Lee and the kung fu genre in the 1970s and the success of the Chinese launching their first astronaut in 2003 and the lunar exploration satellite *Chang'e No. 1* in 2007), the unconscious self-Orientalization, and the conscious business-is-all-there-is approach. The cultural framing of "Sayonara, Shanghai! Good morning, Hong Kong!" seen in the musical film is not a one-way exit on the high road to Western modernity and cosmopolitanism in Hong Kong's coming to terms with itself, China, and the world. The process is multivalent and incoherent. Although "China" is unimagined in some films, the same object is reimagined in other films in complex ways (as seen in the historical epics of the 1960s). If we believe that the 1950s and 1960s musical genre is an indication that a certain structure of feeling was forming, that structure of feeling—urban Hong Kong culture—had earlier on unveiled a trace of movement from the north (China) to the south (Hong Kong), from the disappearance of Shanghai to the emerging visibility of Hong Kong. Running up to 1997, Stephen Teo wrote that Anita Mui's interpretation of the Shanghai sing-song girl character in the film *Au Revoir, Mon Amour* (*Heri jun zailai;* 1991) "shows how far and how completely Hong Kong had absorbed Shanghai."[52] Yet a couple of years later, Hong Kong cinema in the first years of the twenty-first century is perhaps indicative of the forming of a reverted structure of feeling that is northbound looking. There have been "Hong Kong" films with a contemporary China story, shot on location in China, set against the backdrop of Shanghai, and using mainland actors. From pop idol singer-actor Aaron Kwok's big flop *Para Para Sakura* (*Pala Pala yingzhihua;* dir. Jingle Ma, 2001)—coincidentally a musical film—through Stephen Chow's enormous transnational success *Shaolin Soccer* (*Shaolin zuqiu;* 2001) to Leon Lai and Faye Wong's Shanghai glamorization *Leaving Me, Loving You* (*Dacheng xiaoshi;* dir. Wilson Yip, 2004), the forgotten has returned as a major player in the Beckettian endgame of Hong Kong self-fashioning.

Notes

The author wishes to thank Professor Yung Sai-shing for generously sharing his materials and ideas on the Hong Kong movie musical at a time when the musical films of the Shaw Brothers and MP & GI were not yet available on DVD. The author has also benefited greatly from the conversations with Professor William Tay on this topic.

1. There has been plenty of work on Hong Kong identity politics. To name a few key markers: the earlier anthropological, Hugh Baker, "Life in the Cities: The Emergence of Hong Kong Man," *The China Quarterly* 95 (1983): pp. 469–79; the pre-1997, Matthew Turner and Irene Ngan, eds., *Hong Kong Sixties: Designing Identity* (Hong Kong: Hong Kong Arts Centre, 1995); the post-1997, Alvin So and Ming Chan, eds., *Crisis and Transformation in China's Hong Kong* (New York: M. E. Sharpe, 2002).

2. A latest work is Esther Cheung and Chu Yiu-wai, eds., *Between Home and World: A Reader in Hong Kong Cinema* (Hong Kong: Oxford University Press, 2004); a forthcoming volume is Meaghan Morris, Stephen Chan Ching-kiu, and Siu Leung Li, eds., *Hong Kong Connections: Transnational Imagination in Action Cinema* (Hong Kong: Hong Kong University Press). See also Esther Yau, ed., *At Full Speed: Hong Kong Cinema in a Borderless World* (Minneapolis: University of Minnesota Press, 2001); Bono Lee and Sam Ho, eds., *Border Crossing in Hong Kong Cinema* (Hong Kong: Leisure and Cultural Services Department, 2000); Sheldon H. Lu, ed., *Transnational Chinese Cinemas: Identity, Nationhood, Gender* (Honolulu: University of Hawai'i Press, 1997); Cindy Hing-yuk Wong, "Cities, Cultures and Cassettes: Hong Kong Cinema and Transnational Audiences," *Postscript* 19, no. 1 (1999): pp. 87–106; Anne T. Ciecko and Sheldon H. Lu, "The Heroic Trio: Anita Mui, Maggie Cheung, Michelle Yeoh—Self-Reflexivity and the Globalization of the Hong Kong Action Heroine," *Postscript* 19, no. 1 (1999): pp. 70–86.

3. Poshek Fu, "Going Global: A Cultural History of the Shaw Brothers Studio, 1960–1970," in Lee and Ho, *Border Crossing in Hong Kong Cinema*, pp. 43–51.

4. Stephanie Chung Po-yin, "A Southeast Asian Tycoon and His Movie Dream: Loke Wan Tho and MP & GI," in Wong Ain-ling, ed., *The Cathy Story* (Hong Kong: Hong Kong Film Archive, 2002), pp. 36–51; Poshek Fu, "Hong Kong and Singapore: A History of the Cathay Cinema," in Wong Ain-ling, *The Cathay Story*, pp. 60–75; Yeh Yueh-yu, "Taiwan: The Transnational Battlefield of Cathay and Shaws," in Wong Ain-ling, *The Cathay Story*, pp. 142–49; Shu Kei, "Notes on MP & GI," in Wong Ain-ling, *The Cathay Story*, pp. 86–107.

5. Michael Hardt and Antonio Negri, *Empire* (Cambridge, Mass.: Harvard University Press, 2000).

6. As early as 1955, the Shaw Brothers Studio and Japan's Daiei Company coproduced the film *Princess Yang Kwei Fei* (*Yang Guifei; Yokihi*), the first film to bear the common brand name of a "Hong Kong–Japan co-production." See Kinnia Yau,

"Shaw's Japanese Collaboration and Competition as Seen through the Asian Film Festival Evolution," in Wong Ainling, ed., *The Shaw Screen: A Preliminary Study* (Hong Kong: Hong Kong Film Archive, 2003), p. 282.

7. Wong Kee-chee, "A Song in Every Film," in *Hong Kong Cinema Survey 1946–1968* (Hong Kong: Urban Council, 1979), p. 29.

8. Stephen Teo, *Hong Kong Cinema: The Extra Dimensions* (London: British Film Institute, 1997), p. 29.

9. Wong Kee-chee, "A Song in Every Film," pp. 29–30.

10. "Of the 17 films he made for Shaws, at least six were remakes of his Japanese pictures"; D. W. Davis and Emilie Yeh Yueh-yu, "Inoue at Shaws: The Wellspring of Youth," in Wong Ainling, ed., *The Shaw Screen*, p. 261.

11. A useful collection of historical and critical essays related to the Chinese musical film is Law Kar, ed., *Mandarin Films and Popular Songs: 40s-60s* (Hong Kong: Urban Council, 1993).

12. Poshek Fu briefly commented on Shaw Brothers' historical epics in overseas markets and their awards at international film festivals, saying that "Run Run Shaw invariably expressed his enthusiasm to conquer the land of Hollywood in terms of nationalism"; Fu, "Going Global," p. 47.

13. Sek Kei, "Shaw Movie Town's 'China Dream' and 'Hong Kong Sentiments'," in Wong Ainling, ed., *The Shaw Screen*, pp. 37–47.

14. For studies related to youth culture in Hong Kong in the 1950s and 1960s, see Yung Sai-shing, "The Joy of Youth, Made in Hong Kong: Patricia Lam Fung and Shaws' Cantonese Films," in Wong Ainling, ed., *The Shaw Screen*, pp. 221–35; Yung Sai-shing "'The Song of Youth': Vanishing Nationality in Hong Kong Cantonese Pop in the 1950s" (conference paper delivered at the Fourteenth European Association of Chinese Studies Conference, August 26–28, 2002, Moscow); see also Poshek Fu, "The 1960s: Modernity, Youth Culture, and Hong Kong Cantonese Cinema," in Poshek Fu and David Desser, eds., *The Cinema of Hong Kong: History, Arts, Identity* (Cambridge: Cambridge University Press, 2000), pp. 71–89.

15. Teo, *Hong Kong Cinema*, p. 37.

16. Here I am simultaneously borrowing and deviating from the new historicist critic Stephen Greenblatt's concept and practice of cultural poetics of choosing a few "arresting figures" (such as Thomas More, Christopher Marlowe, and Shakespeare, in his case) from the thousands: "So from the thousands, we seize upon a handful of arresting figures who seem to contain within themselves much of what we need, who both reward intense, individual attention and promise access to larger cultural patterns"; Stephen Greenblatt, *Renaissance Self-Fashioning: From More to Shakespeare* (Chicago: University of Chicago Press, 1980), p. 6. Singling out recognized high cultural elites might not be too unlike focusing on the commercial and popular in cultural research.

17. Sek Kei, "Shaw Movie Town's 'China Dream' and 'Hong Kong Sentiments'," p. 44.

18. Tong Yuejuan recalled that the film was sold out everywhere in Southeast Asia, Taiwan, and Hong Kong. See Tong Yuejuan, "Tong Yuejuan: Xinhua suiyue" (Tong Yuejuan: The Best of Times in Hsin Hwa), in Kwok Ching-li, ed., *Xianggang yingren koushu lishi congshu: nanlai xianggong* (*Monographs of Hong Kong Film Veterans: Hong Kong Here I Come*) (Hong Kong: Hong Kong Film Archive, 2000), p. 34. (This is a Chinese-English bilingual publication, but the lines I drew on are not found in the English translation. The reference here is to the Chinese text.)

19. "In *Mambo Girl* Hong Kong cinema produced its first musical masterpiece"; Stephen Teo, "Oh, Karaoke!—Mandarin Pop and Musicals," in Law Kar, *Mandarin Films and Popular Songs*, p. 35.

20. "Zhong's exile in Hong Kong in the last third of *Peach Blossom River* is a conscious effort to put the city on the map"; Sam Ho, "The Songstress, the Farmer's Daughter, the Mambo Girl and the Songstress Again," in Law Kar, *Mandarin Films and Popular Songs*, p. 64. "By the mid '50s, 'Hong Kong' was actually a line spoken in the dialogue, referred to by its characters as a real city and not seen in the background as a vague urban locality standing in for Shanghai. . . . Hong Kong comes into its own place of both the mind and the heart"; ibid., p. 34.

21. My translation.

22. Law Wai-ming, "Old Images of Two Cities: The Position of Mandarin Cinema in 1950s Hong Kong," in Law Kar, ed., *Cinema of Two Cities: Hong Kong—Shanghai* (Hong Kong: Urban Council, 1994), p. 38.

23. Ho, "The Songstress, the Farmer's Daughter, the Mambo Girl and the Songstress Again," p. 64.

24. Law Kar, "Epilogue: The Beginning and End of an Era," in Law Kar, *Mandarin Films and Popular Songs*, p. 80.

25. For instance, Aihwa Ong and Donald Nonini, eds., *Ungrounded Empires: The Cultural Politics of Modern Chinese Transnationalism* (New York: Routledge, 1997).

26. Fu, "Going Global," p. 43.

27. Ibid.

28. *The Milky Way Pictorial* 71 (February 1964): p. 34. Translations from this article are mine.

29. Ibid.

30. Harold Bloom, *The Anxiety of Influence: A Theory of Poetry* (New York: Oxford University Press, 1973).

31. *The Milky Way Pictorial*, p. 34.

32. "Shaws' top priority at the time of Inoue's recruitment was plainly 'more is better': to produce more films, faster, and more efficiently"; D. W. Davis and Emilie Yeh, "Inoue at Shadows: The Wellspring of Youth," in Wong Ainling, ed., *The Shaw Screen*, p. 256.

33. *The Milky Way Pictorial*, p. 34.

34. William Tay (Zheng Shusen) says that the film workers from Shanghai, namely Tao Qin, Song Qi, and others, were *caizi* (talented scholars) who knew the genre of

the movie musical very well but did not listen to Mandarin pop songs. See William Tay, "Huigu xianggang zai haixia lianganjian de wenhua juese: zaige zaiwu, zhiyou zai xianggang" ("A Review of the Cultural Role of Hong Kong between Taiwan and Mainland China: Singing and Dancing Were Possible Only in Hong Kong"), *Lianhe Bao*, June 20, 1997.

35. My translation.

36. Raymond Williams, "Structures of Feeling," in Raymond Williams, ed., *Marxism and Literature* (Oxford: Oxford University Press, 1977), pp. 128–35.

37. Davis and Yeh, "Inoue at Shadows," pp. 255–71.

38. Raymond Williams, *Keywords: A Vocabulary of Culture and Society* (New York: Oxford University Press, 1976), p. 237.

39. Guy Debord, *The Society of the Spectacle*, trans. Donald Nicholson-Smith (New York: Zone Books, 1994), p. 29.

40. Law Kar, "Epilogue: The Beginning and End of an Era," in Law Kar, *Mandarin Films and Popular Songs*, p. 80.

41. Edward Lam, "Lily Ho of Hong Kong," in Wong Ainling, ed., *The Shaw Screen*, 246.

42. *Hong Kong Night Club* (Amuse Inc./Nippon TV Network Corp., 1997).

43. A similar convention that was long seen in European opera is the not infrequent self-reflexive operatic subplot of singing competitions, such as Richard Wagner's *Tannhäuser* and *Die Meistersinger*, which is also not unlike the frequent feature of martial arts tournaments in the kung fu action genre. Herbert Lindenberger has argued that the "performances-within-performances," "song-within-a-song," and "the opera-within-an-opera" tell about "the nature of performing through the very processes by which performers perform" and demonstrate "the self-referentiality that opera displays"; Herbert Lindenberger, *Opera: The Extravagant Art* (Ithaca, N.Y.: Cornell University Press, 1984), p. 141.

44. For instance, Jane Feuer, *The Hollywood Musical* (Bloomington: Indiana University Press, 1982); Rick Altman, *The American Film Musical* (Bloomington: Indiana University Press, 1987).

45. The film sets up a binary opposition between high and low culture: Suen Zhiqiang the elder brother is pop and jazz, whereas Suen Yiqiang the younger is classical.

46. Fredric Jameson, "Nostalgia for the Present," *Postmodernism; Or, the Cultural Logic of Late Capitalism* (Durham, N.C.: Duke University Press, 1991), p. 296.

47. Zheng Shusen (William Tay), "Huigu xianggang zai haixia lianganjian de wenhua juese" ("A Review of the Cultural Role of Hong Kong between Taiwan and Mainland China," 14 installments, *Lianhe Bao*, June 14–July 1, 1997.

48. Ibid., June 20, 1997.

49. "Umetsugu Inoue has quoted an Asahi Weekly article in his autobiography *Madonoshita ni Yujiro ga ita* (1987). The article had said that in order to raise efficiency, decrease costs and enrich content, Shaw Brothers was keen to buy Japanese

film technology which had a reputation for cost-efficiency. Perhaps because of this factor, the Japanese directors who worked in Hong Kong cinema were either viewed by their colleagues or by themselves as mere technicians and journeymen. This may be why that apart from Umetsugu Inoue, the rest of the Japanese directors working in Hong Kong changed their names"; Kinnia Yau Shuk Ting, "Hong Kong and Japan: Not One Less," trans. Stephen Teo, in Lee and Ho, *Border Crossing in Hong Kong Cinema*, p. 110.

50. Ho, "The Songstress, the Farmer's Daughter, the Mambo Girl and the Songstress Again," p. 66.

51. Law Wai-ming, "Old Images of Two Cities," p. 37.

52. Teo, *Hong Kong Cinema*, p. 38.

4

Three Readings of
Hong Kong Nocturne

PAUL G. PICKOWICZ

Hong Kong Nocturne (*Xiang jiang hua yue ye*), a flashy urban musical produced by Run Run Shaw (Shao Yifu) and released by the Shaw Brothers Studio in late January 1967, was supported by a high-visibility advertising blitz, and screened simultaneously in five theaters. The studio's plan was to cash in on the extreme excitement associated each year with the two-week lunar New Year season. By all accounts, *Hong Kong Nocturne* was a smashing commercial success, not only in Hong Kong but also in several places in Southeast Asia.[1]

Huaqiao ribao, a popular Hong Kong news daily, praised the film in lavish terms, stressing that on the eve of the lunar New Year the broad public wanted to be entertained and to have fun.[2] For three days in a row in late January, the paper published an attractive serialized summary of the plot, complete with captivating photos.[3] With the approach of February 9, New Year's Day, *Huaqiao ribao* offered a glowing review of the music (written by a Japanese composer) as well as the dance numbers (said to have been influenced by the latest in U.S. styles) and applauded the producers of *Hong Kong Nocturne* for casting ten film stars in the production.[4] *Ming bao,* a well-established Hong Kong periodical, also carried a number of positive overviews of the film during the New Year season,[5] though one reviewer, who found that the film's structure was loose and that the characters lacked depth, offered mild criticism.[6]

The response of Hong Kong students was far more critical. In late February 1967, *Zhongguo xuesheng zhoubao* carried two reviews that attacked *Hong Kong Nocturne* in stridently nationalistic terms. One commentator insisted that the whole story was exceedingly artificial and the film's Japanese director

(Inoue Umetsugu) had done a poor job. Another reviewer was shocked by scenes involving seminudity and felt that the music written by the Japanese composer was ineffective.[7]

Of course, there are many ways to evaluate this remarkably popular film, a work that earned HK$310,000 in the first four days.[8] For instance, *Hong Kong Nocturne* can be understood as carrying on the traditions of commercial filmmaking in Shanghai in the late 1920s and early 1930s. That is to say, there are important continuities that link *Hong Kong Nocturne* to the highly successful, if somewhat formulaic, entertainment films produced by the Shaw Brothers and others at such famous Shanghai studios as Tianyi, Mingxing, and Lianhua in the prewar era.[9]

In *Hong Kong Nocturne*, as in popular films of the Nanjing Decade (1927–37), the narrative involves a family-centered melodrama that raises questions about the contemporary relevance of both old-style (Confucian) values and new-style (modern/Western) modes. The field of conflict in such films is almost always the dazzling, but disorienting and vaguely threatening, neon-lit metropolis.[10]

Hong Kong Nocturne tells the story of a troubled family of entertainers who live and work in Hong Kong in the mid-1960s. At the outset, the film reminds us a bit of the 1937 classic *Street Angel* (*Malu tianshi*). In the case of *Hong Kong Nocturne*, the widowed patriarch, Jia Sizhen, a name that can be understood as meaning "fake, but seems real," is a master magician who works in glittering Hong Kong nightclubs. His three attractive and talented adult daughters, Cuicui, Juanjuan, and Tingting, perform glamorous song-and-dance routines during Jia's magic act. In reality, fun-seeking customers are far more interested in the singing and dancing of the sisters than in the shopworn magic routines of the patriarch.

Like many family melodramas of the 1930s, *Hong Kong Nocturne* introduces at the outset themes that resonate with the highly critical May Fourth way of thinking about cultural traditions.[11] In brief, the family is dysfunctional, the daughters feel oppressed, and the patriarch seems to be responsible for their suffering. For instance, though it is the sisters who attract all the customers, the old man always collects their pay packet from the nightclub manager and gives the sisters little if anything of their earnings. To make matters worse, Jia Sizhen is carrying on a sordid liaison with a much younger woman, Xiao Hua, who seems to be a 1960s version of the 1930s screen vamp. Jia turns almost all of his money over to the slick young woman and constantly makes a fool of himself chasing after her in various nightclubs and 1960s-style go-go dance halls. The young woman's goal is to take Jia for everything he is worth.

Under the circumstances, the sisters feel overly dependent and frustrated. Each has a dream about winning individual independence and breaking away from the family and the patriarch to succeed on her own. The elder sister, Cuicui, has a boyfriend named Lin Gaogui who has promised to secure a movie career for her in Japan. The second sister, Juanjuan, wants to join the newly formed Hong Kong Song and Dance Troupe that features the pop music of Chen Ziqing, a Dean Martin look-alike, who is a friend of the sisters. The youngest sister, Tingting, wants to pursue a career in ballet by studying at the New Life Ballet School run by the famous dance teacher Yan Fang, who was permanently handicapped under circumstances that are never explained.

One night, an ugly family confrontation occurs when the old magician fails once again to give his daughters any money because he has turned it all over to the sexy vamp. After a loud fight, the sisters decide to walk out and win their independence: Cuicui will go to Japan, Juanjuan to the Song and Dance Troupe, and Tingting to the ballet school. But Juanjuan, the most filial of the three sisters, has a change of heart and returns almost immediately to the control of old Jia. But the nightclub audience wants three sisters, not one, so the owner tells Jia there is only one way the magician can continue performing at the club: Juanjuan will have to appear nude during the act. The father readily agrees and instructs a distraught Juanjuan to cooperate. At the next performance, the audience is told in advance that Juanjuan's clothes will "disappear" during the show. The plan is for Juanjuan to enter a tall box fully clothed in a fancy stage costume and then, magically, exit stark naked from a second tall box on the other side of the stage. A tearful Juanjuan enters the first box but, to the embarrassment of her father, fails to reappear, after three tries, in the second box. The audience complains and the old magician is fired. Juanjuan, fortunately, is rescued by her love interest, the Dean Martin-like songwriter, Chen Ziqing. The old man protests, but Chen declares that Jia is "not fit" to be Juanjuan's father and takes her away to the safety of the Song and Dance Troupe. Chen then proposes marriage to Juanjuan.

Like the popular films of Shanghai in the early 1930s, including successful musicals, *Hong Kong Nocturne* approaches modernity in two conflicting ways. On the one hand, all urban dwellers understand the allures of modernity and consciously strive to be "modern," fashionable, and up to date in terms of world standards set in the West. On the other hand, everyone seems to be at least partly aware of the dangers of modernity. Thus, a discourse on "spiritual pollution" often surfaces in these types of films and runs counter to and eventually overshadows the May Fourth tradition of cultural criticism. Individual liberation from patriarchal tyrants like Jia Sizhen may seem like a good thing, but modern cities are dangerous places that rip people from their cultural bearings and leave them with no meaningful identity at all.[12]

At this point in the narrative, *Hong Kong Nocturne* follows the pattern of many early 1930s films, including *A Dream in Pink* (*Fenhongse de meng*, 1932), *Queen of Sports* (*Tiyu huanghou*, 1934) and *Little Angel* (*Xiao tianshi*, 1935), in warning vulnerable young people of the pitfalls of modernity. For example, as soon as the old magician loses his daughters, he discovers the young vamp, Xiao Hua, with another, younger man. When she tries to kick Jia out of her apartment (paid for by Jia), he protests, saying, "I've spent so much money on you!" She responds, "You've run out of money, so we are through." At this point, the pitiful Jia is soundly thrashed by the younger man.

Things go much worse for Cuicui, the eldest sister. She flies to Tokyo with Lin Gaogui. She believes they will be married there and that Lin will guide her movie career in Japan. Lin does indeed set up a meeting between Cuicui and a Japanese film director, but the "director" turns out to be a disgusting producer of eight millimeter pornographic films. The lecherous director tells Cuicui that Lin has been supplying him with "stars" for some time. Meanwhile, Lin has stolen all of Cuicui's money and disappeared with the funds paid by the Japanese director for Cuicui's "contract." When the director asks Cuicui to be his mistress, Cuicui slaps him in the face and says, "You're worse than my father!"

Back in Hong Kong, the youngest sister, Tingting, is having a most difficult time at the part-work, part-study ballet school. Yan Fang, the head of the school, seems to think that Tingting is hopeless. Tingting responds by nearly working herself to death.

Juanjuan and Chen Ziqing get married, but they do so over the objections of his rather controlling parents, who want Ziqing to quit songwriting and Juanjuan to give up singing and dancing. They look down upon Juanjuan as the "daughter of a showman." But the couple marry, nonetheless, and are given moral support by their friends in the Song and Dance Troupe. Tingting, still struggling at the ballet school, and Cuicui, back from Japan, show up at the wedding as well.

Declaring, "All men are faithless," Cuicui begins a new career singing degrading and suggestive songs at a sleazy bar. One night, while she sings drunk and out of control, a fight breaks out as men compete for her affection, but Cuicui is spirited away by a dashing young man named Fang Yuntai, who is a talented trumpet player. Fang takes the intoxicated Cuicui back to his apartment, and just when it appears to her that he is about to assault her, he turns out to be a knight in shining armor who merely wanted to rescue Cuicui. He had seen her perform once before and was inspired by her singing. Fang suggests that the two work out a professional partnership and perform in Southeast Asia, where he retreated following a failed marriage in Hong Kong. Cuicui agrees and departs Hong Kong once again.

The final part of *Hong Kong Nocturne* is full of twists and turns that move the narrative farther and farther away from the May Fourth "individual liberation" thrust of its opening section. For instance, not only does the marriage between second sister Juanjuan to Chen Ziqing work out well, Juanjuan discovers she is pregnant (with a son, of course!) and resolves to drop out of the Song and Dance Troupe at precisely the moment the group is approached by a Hong Kong television station to commit to a long-term program that will feature Juanjuan as the star. Juanjuan decides to sacrifice everything for the child. She has found love and happiness and no longer thinks about a career. She will find fulfillment in the home.

Tingting, the youngest sister, works so hard at ballet that she collapses in exhaustion one day. Only at this point is the softer side of the lonely headmaster Yan apparent. He is touched by her dedication and reveals that he was unusually hard on her in the past only because he admired her and thought she would have a bright future if she worked hard. Tingting now blossoms as a ballet dancer and appears to be developing a love interest in the considerably older and physically disabled Yan Fang.

Elder sister Cuicui, off in Southeast Asia with the trumpet player, is also doing well professionally and, not surprisingly, is becoming increasingly fond of her savior. All three sisters seem to be involved in or headed toward a fulfilling domestic life with a kind and sincere mate. The idea of family happiness and harmony (anchored by strong male figures) is now being reconsidered. Indeed, the narrative has come full circle, and it is time to bring the sisters' odious father back into the picture.

Indeed, the great reunion (or *da tuanyuan*), so common in entertainment movies of the 1920s and 1930s, is fully evident by the end of the film. Cuicui, a star now, has a chance encounter with her father, the magician, in Southeast Asia, where the old master is scrounging for any work he can find. A tearful—and virtually instantaneous—reconciliation follows. A letter from Juanjuan and Tingting back in Hong Kong convinces Cuicui and her now mellow and reasonable father to return to Hong Kong to bring everyone together. Cuicui wants to marry Fang Yuntai, the man with the horn, but the melancholy trumpet player has too many bad memories of Hong Kong and, despite his love for Cuicui, decides to remain in Southeast Asia. Life as an artist is too bitter, he says, and it is better for them to part now and be able to cherish the memories of the good times they had together.

As soon as the three sisters and their father reunite in Hong Kong, disaster strikes. Juanjuan's loving husband, Chen Ziqing, dies in a plane crash. The family gathers around to offer comfort and support. Chen's nasty parents show up to apologize for their previous shabby treatment of Juanjuan. They invite Juanjuan to move in to their lavish house, and they show tremendous interest in Juanjuan's son, once he is born. Juanjuan dedicates herself to the care of her son, said to be the spitting image of Ziqing himself. Thus, the "great reunion" format is extended to include Juanjuan's in-laws as well as her own father.

Hong Kong Nocturne ends when all the members of the Song and Dance Troupe come by to see Juanjuan and to announce that the television station wants to do a special tribute program featuring the music of Chen Ziqing. The group wants Juanjuan to participate as a way of honoring her late husband. Indeed, they want all three sisters to participate. Juanjuan hesitates but is pleased when her now reasonable in-laws agree that she should participate in the program and resume her career. They will take care of the boy child.

Tingting decides to quit ballet and join up with Cuicui and Juanjuan. She also openly declares her affection for her ballet teacher, Yan Fang. Yan reluctantly agrees that there is nothing wrong with giving up ballet for song and dance work on television, but he insists that he is too old and impaired to enter into an emotional relationship with Tingting.

In the end, the three sisters are back together with their father. All three sisters have lost the men they love: Fang Yuntai, the trumpet player, remains in Southeast Asia, convinced that he can never know unending love; Chen Ziqing is dead; Yan Fang, too, believes that he is not fated to know love.

The televised tribute to Chen Ziqing features all three sisters and is an enormous success. The theme of the program is the need to move on in life. Put the past behind, they sing. "Begin life over again" because things are pretty good after all. In the past, it seemed like only the "foreign moon" was bright. Now things have changed. We, too, can sing and dance. When all is said and done, Hong Kong is still the best place. No need to be discouraged by all the disappointments and uncertainties of life. No matter how difficult things may seem, it is important to strive to overcome all obstacles.

It is useful to locate *Hong Kong Nocturne* in the context of Chinese filmmaking in the late 1920s and early 1930s and thereby better understand the

From left: Cuicui (Lily Ho), Juanjuan (Cheng Pei-pei), and Tingting (Qin Ping) perform a dance routine in *Hong Kong Nocturne.* (Courtesy of Celestial Pictures Ltd.)

ways in which popular Shaw Brothers productions of the 1960s are linked thematically to earlier Shaw Brothers films produced in Shanghai. This approach to *Hong Kong Nocturne* allows us to see that the narrative deals with intimate personal and family relations that have been complicated by the pushes and pulls of tradition on the one hand and modernity on the other. The conflict between tradition and modernity had been an important feature of Chinese cultural discourse since at least the 1880s. It is in this sense that the *Hong Kong Nocturne* narrative is relatively timeless. That is to say, it could just as easily have been set in the 1880s, the 1910s, or the 1930s. It is a general social and cultural narrative. The concrete politics of the day do not need to be mentioned. They are, in a way, irrelevant to the generalized problem of the tension between tradition and modernity.

And it is certainly the case that *Hong Kong Nocturne* says absolutely nothing about the local, regional, and world politics that were pressing on Hong Kong in 1967, the year the film was released. But what happens when one views the film not in the context of Shanghai filmmaking in the late 1920s and early 1930s (with the May Fourth/counter-May Fourth problematic at the center) but in the radically different context of the everyday political situation in Hong Kong at the time of the film's production and release?

It is not unfair to say that almost nothing in this film alerts the historian to the profound uncertainties and traumas that were shaking political life in Hong Kong in early 1967. One would never know it from watching this playful musical melodrama, but it must have seemed to almost all citizens of Hong Kong that their world was coming to an end in 1967. For one thing, the Vietnam War was raging right next door with no conclusion in sight. Indeed, with the Tet Offensive in spring 1967, it looked like U.S. forces were losing the war. U.S. naval vessels sailed back and forth between Vietnam and Hong Kong on a regular basis. Tens of thousands of U.S. servicemen, many of them disillusioned with the war, visited Hong Kong on rest-and-recreation leaves. Some refused to return to Vietnam at the end of such visits. People in Hong Kong were well aware of the tumultuous conflict in Vietnam.

The U.S. authorities insisted that if Vietnam fell to communist forces, Laos, Cambodia, and perhaps even Thailand would be next. It was pointed out repeatedly that the entirety of Mainland China was ruled by communist revolutionaries, North Korea was still very much in the hands of communist forces after the Korean War, and there were constant reports of communist insurgency in the Philippines. Reports of these developments were carried in Hong Kong newspapers every day, yet *Hong Kong Nocturne*, even though it is set in 1967, made no mention whatsoever of these unsettling events or provided any insights into what local people thought about the troubles and their meanings for Hong Kong.

Though the film makes no explicit references to local history, Hong Kong was, of course, a colony of Great Britain. With anti-imperialist wars of national liberation challenging colonial and neocolonial regimes throughout Asia and in other parts of what was known as the Third World, Hong Kong stuck out like a sore thumb. It was a conspicuous symbol of British colonial power. To Asian revolutionaries, Hong Kong was part of the problem, not part of the solution. For Asian revolutionaries, it was painful to live under the humiliation of colonial domination, with its daily reminders of nineteenth-century debacles. If the British were pushed out of Asia (as the French had been in the 1950s), what would become of colonial Hong Kong?

Many residents of Hong Kong feared the People's Republic of China, but a not insignificant minority, organized in leftist labor unions, schools, industrial units, and cultural organizations, including newspapers and film studios, identified with the People's Republic and its drive to stand up in the wake of foreign aggression and failed Nationalist governance in Mainland China.

To complicate matters even further, in early 1966, at the time *Hong Kong Nocturne* was in production, the Cultural Revolution erupted in Mainland China and the image of the People's Republic took on a new and far more menacing form for many in Hong Kong. Throughout 1966, Hong Kong residents read about uninterrupted chaos and violence in Mainland China. The Communist Party hierarchy was attacked by rebels and Red Guards blessed by Chairman Mao. Throughout China, countless public officials, teachers, intellectuals, cultural workers, and former capitalists were dragged out, humiliated, beaten, and killed.[13] The rebels, backed by the People's Liberation Army, declared that the Soviet Union was not revolutionary enough and that the Chinese model of revolution, not the Soviet model, would inspire the anti-imperialist, anticolonial movement in Asia and the rest of the Third World, including colonial Hong Kong.

In 1967, Hong Kong residents learned that the violence, chaos, and terror associated with anticolonial uprisings in Asia and the Cultural Revolution in Mainland China were much more than worrisome events that were happening elsewhere. In 1967, the Cultural Revolution and the Third World anticolonial uprising came to Hong Kong itself. It all started in the wake of the January Revolution that finally toppled the Communist Party old guard in Shanghai and other major urban centers in Mainland China. The January Revolution was a major victory for the Maoist faction in Mainland China.

In April 1967, within weeks of the January Revolution in Mainland China, the peace and tranquility of Hong Kong was shattered and British power was challenged for the first time since the founding of the People's Republic in 1949. At the outset of the uprising, leftist labor unions were encouraged by Cultural Revolutionaries in Mainland China to rise up in Hong Kong against capitalist owners and the British colonial authorities. It was an effort to get the British to abandon Hong Kong. Tensions escalated almost overnight.

From May 1967 to late December 1967, Hong Kong was in a constant state of turmoil. All organizations under the control of the People's Republic, including labor unions, schools, newspapers, retail enterprises, and cultural organizations, joined in to prove their loyalty to Chairman Mao and the Cultural Revolution. Strikes, transportation disruptions, protest marches, sit-ins, takeovers, and demonstrations occurred almost every day for nine months. In addition to these public displays, many of which pitted Hong Kong Cultural Revolutionaries against colonial police forces, terrorists were quite active behind the scenes manufacturing homemade bombs, planting bombs in public places, setting buildings on fire, and firebombing cars and buses. In the first six months of the tumult alone, the authorities reported 993 bombs, 214 of which exploded and 779 of which were defused by antiterrorist specialists. On May 11, a police specialist died instantly after his arms and legs were blown off while he was trying to defuse a bomb. An additional 4,080 fake bombs, placed in the open to disrupt public order and shake public confidence in British rule, were detected and removed. By the end of October, the police had arrested 4,050 people in connection with the riots, 1,749 of whom were sentenced to prison terms ranging from a few months to ten years. In the same period, the police carried out 253 raids on left-wing schools, unions, retail stores, and residences in an effort to seize weapons and bombs. On nineteen occasions, there were incidents along the border between Hong Kong and the People's Republic, some of which involved deadly pitched battles between Hong Kong forces (including elite Gurkha gunners) and citizens of the People's Republic who charged across the boundary line. Hong Kong residents, including many who had fled the revolution on the mainland years earlier, must have been wondering whether Hong Kong was going to be attacked and occupied by Maoist military units.[14]

By December 19, 1967, the terror rampage ended (presumably on orders from Beijing) just as suddenly as it had started in April. Apparently, the message did not reach everyone. The next day, December 20, just prior to the entry of 2,000 students and visitors, the police discovered and defused bombs that were placed at the Hong Kong Industrial Products Exhibition.[15]

It would not be unreasonable to argue that these events, no matter how disturbing, have no bearing on the production in 1966 and release in 1967 of *Hong Kong Nocturne* and no meaningful connection to the bustling film world of Hong Kong. Sources indicate, however, that the Hong Kong film world was very much caught in the middle of the terror of 1967. As early as May 15, actors, actresses, and staff associated with leftist film studios chanted Maoist slogans and put up big character posters at a demonstration at Government House. Prominent among them was the thirty-one-year-old matinee idol Shi Hui and her actor husband, Fu Qi, both dressed in proletarian garb, waving Chairman Mao's little red book, and wearing a Mao badge. Both of them worked for the left-wing Great Wall Motion Picture Company (Chang cheng dianying gongsi). On July 10, Great Wall film workers were involved in a stone-throwing scuffle with police that led to a number of arrests. Five days later at 2:00 A.M., police searched the home of Shi Hui and Fu Qi and arrested both film stars. Fu Qi was accused of being a leader of one of the key "struggle committees" orchestrating the riots.[16]

Shaw Brothers Studio, widely known as an apolitical popular entertainment enterprise, was also brought into the 1967 conflict. On June 8, the studio was forced to release a statement denying that a struggle committee functioned on its premises. But two weeks later, three Shaw Brothers workers were arrested for posting and distributing literature that promoted rioting and turmoil. On June 25, two more Shaw Brothers workers were arrested. One of them, a man named Li An, died the next day in the hospital prior to a scheduled court appearance. Three Chinese constables were formally charged on October 4 with the murder of Li An. The constables were found guilty on November 6 and sentenced to prison terms from six to eight years. On October 10, National Day in Taiwan, a left-wing screenwriter in Hong Kong by the name of Zhang Sen defected to Taiwan.[17]

The 1967 terror did not spare movie theaters and ordinary film fans. On June 9, the police raided the Silver Capital (Yin du) theater in Kowloon and confiscated riot-related literature. A week later, the police returned to shut down the theater on the grounds that it incited rioting in its programming. On July 17, outside the Oriental Theater (Dongfang xiyuan) in Wanchai, terrorists threw bombs at a police vehicle. On July 30, a bomb was discovered in the men's room of the Hollywood Theater.

Young China scholars in the United States, Europe, and Japan (graduate students and junior faculty) had virtually no firsthand experience with the violence, national independence wars, and revolutions that were sweeping through Asia in the 1960s. But many young Asianists were staunchly opposed to U.S. involvement in the Vietnam War and actively participated in such antiwar organizations as the Committee of Concerned Asian Scholars. At that time, to be critical of the U.S. war effort often involved being critical of single-party systems in places like South Korea, Taiwan, the Philippines, and, for that matter, colonial Hong Kong. Similarly, opposition to the Vietnam War often entailed open sympathy for those in Vietnam, Cambodia, Laos, the Philippines, and elsewhere who seemed to be waging just struggles for national independence and those in China, North Korea, North Vietnam, and elsewhere who seemed to be building egalitarian, postcolonial social systems.

Owing to diplomatic restrictions and complications, no young China schol-ars in the West had actually traveled to Mainland China, but as the Vietnam War continued to expand, curiosity about and sympathy for the People's Republic became increasingly pronounced in graduate student and junior faculty circles in the United States and Europe. Whether one was sympathetic to the Chinese revolution or not, there was a growing sense that although the Soviet Union and its satellites were repressive bureaucratic states, China was an independent and creative force that encouraged mass participation in the revolutionary movement.[18]

Beginning in the mid-1960s, it was no longer politically correct in West-ern academic circles to use Cold War terminology when discussing China. Because of opposition to the Vietnam War, skepticism about Cold War pri-orities, and sympathy for anticolonial movements, the China studies field underwent a transformation. Graduate students of my generation were clearly influenced by John Israel's book on student nationalism in China (1966), Stuart Schram's flattering biography of Mao Zedong (1967), and other works of so-called liberal scholarship.[19] But the most captivating books were by prominent leftist scholars who spoke approvingly of the Chinese revolu-tion: William Hinton's "documentary" of revolution in a North China vil-lage (1966), Franz Schurman's sympathetic magnum opus on ideology and organization in the People's Republic (1967), and Maurice Meisner's powerful study of Li Dazhao and the origins of Chinese Marxism (1967).[20] All these pathbreaking works seemed to be saying the same thing. The study of con-temporary China means the study of the People's Republic and its Cultural Revolution. To understand the People's Republic and the Cultural Revolution, and to appreciate China's uniqueness in the world, it is necessary to study the entire history of the Chinese revolution from the Opium Wars to the present. Studying the Chinese revolution meant studying failed and flawed revolutions prior to 1919. The question was: Why had earlier revolutions failed? Studying the revolution after 1919 meant studying the history of the Communist Party. Why did it succeed where others failed? Those who did not study some aspect of the mainland revolution were marginalized.

This approach, shaped by opposition to the Vietnam War and support for anticolonial movements in Asia, was China-centered and communist revolution–centered. Other approaches seemed irrelevant or anachronistic. The People's Republic and revolution seemed like the realities of the present and future, whereas colonial Hong Kong and Guomindang Taiwan seemed like relics of the past that had no future.

I have not seen any Cultural Revolution–era reviews published in the People's Republic that are critical of *Hong Kong Nocturne*. It may be that there are none. But it is not very difficult to imagine how Cultural Revolutionaries in China or young China scholars in the West, sympathetic to the grand narrative of revolution in Mainland China, might have viewed the film. The film would have been attacked and dismissed in harsh, even contemptuous, terms. Mainland China–centered critics, full of self-righteousness, would have seen *Hong Kong Nocturne* as little more than a trivial and embarrassing vestige of prewar Shanghai-style bourgeois decadence. The film would have been seen as socially and politically irresponsible for failing to connect to and reflect on the burning issues of the day (the Vietnam War, the Cultural Revolution, Third World anticolonial struggles, and tensions in Hong Kong itself).

Moreover, such critics would have said that although *Hong Kong Nocturne* appears on the surface to be a harmless, apolitical, innocent, almost mindless entertainment film in which the characters express no views whatsoever on the crises of the day, in reality it is a highly political film, a veritable "sugar-coated bullet," that numbs the minds of the masses and endorses a myriad of counterrevolutionary and reactionary social and cultural values. By failing to relate to the earthshaking politics of 1967, the film encouraged people to escape from a reality that was, in the end, inescapable.

Mainland China–centered critics would have attacked *Hong Kong Nocturne* for shamelessly aping U.S. pop culture, the culture of the imperialist aggressor that was chiefly responsible for the miseries of oppressed peoples of the Third World. The music of the three sisters is U.S.-style pop music that is preoccupied with frivolous romances and love affairs. The sisters, their father, and all their friends look completely ridiculous jumping around in various U.S.-style go-go dance halls. They seem to have sacrificed their Chineseness, their dignity. Their self-centeredness, even their alien clothing, hairstyles, makeup, and affectations, links them to the capitalist West rather than to their Chinese roots. The film would have been censured for what it supposedly intentionally left out: class polarization in Hong Kong, the racism of the colonial overlords, and the objectification of women (including the three sisters).

Despite the "Broadway musical" form of the film, revolution-centered critics would not have claimed that there is no evidence of Chinese culture in *Hong Kong Nocturne*. Some elements of Chinese culture are indeed present. The problem is that these elements are negative and reactionary facets of feudal culture that progressive Chinese had been seeking to abandon during the course of the revolution. At the beginning of the film, the three sisters are seen in mortal combat with their oppressive father, while Juanjuan and her Dean Martin-like husband, Chen Ziqing, are locked in conflict with his unreasonable parents. But then, suddenly and without explanation at the end of the film, the families are reunited and the patriarchal structure of society is maintained. It is as though the detestable old magician never stole money from his daughters and never ordered Juanjuan to perform in the nude.

More than anything else, perhaps, mid-1960s critics would have condemned the crass materialism of virtually every character who appears in *Hong Kong Nocturne*. Everyone is out for himself or herself, blindly chasing individual fame and fortune. Everyone wants a private career that will bring him or her into the spotlight. The obsession with self and money makes it impossible for the characters to think of the interests or needs of society in general. In this sense, the characters are amazingly superficial. Their main concerns are: Will I find true romantic love, will I achieve fame, will I have lots of money? In a word, they do not seek to "serve the people." From the very first scene of the film to the very last, people appear as commodities that are being marketed. All human relations seem to be defined by cash exchanges. Everything is for sale. Old man Jia steals money from his daughters and gives it to his vamplike would-be mistress. The mistress, Xiao Hua, sells herself every day and seems to think of nothing but money. She rejects old Jia as soon as he "runs out of money." Cuicui's "fiancé," Lin Gaogui, steals her money and sells her in Japan to a "film director" who produces and sells pornographic movies. The old magician tries to make money by forcing his own daughter to take off her clothes in front of a nightclub audience. Cuicui sings for money in a grubby bar full of men who leer at and fondle her. Dean Martin-like Chen Ziqing is constantly trying to sell commercial songs, organize commercial entertainment troupes, and win television and recording contracts.

Thus, from the perspective of a China studies field that was undergoing a significant transformation at the time of the Vietnam War, the Cultural Revolution, the Third World anticolonial movement, and the anti-British movement in Hong Kong, *Hong Kong Nocturne* looks shallow in the extreme and irrelevant to the political and historical forces that seemed to be shaping the ongoing Chinese revolution and Asia itself.

My suspicion is that this film was not even taken seriously enough in China to warrant critical attacks. I do not expect to discover any serious Mainland Chinese critiques of it. It was probably ignored by cultural critics who were preoccupied with the upheavals of 1967.

I recall my own extended visit to Hong Kong about two-and-a-half years after the end of 1967. Like most graduate students at the time (and this would be unthinkable today), I had only seen one Chinese film prior to my arrival in Hong Kong. It was a spectacular, packed-house, late-night screening in spring 1969 at Harvard University of the three-hour Maoist epic *The East Is Red* (*Dongfang hong*). This film was made much earlier (1965) in the People's Republic, but due to the absence of diplomatic relations between the United States and China and extremely tight control of "Red" Chinese cultural imports into the United States, the film made its way into the United States only in the late 1960s. Curiosity about Mao's China was part of the fabric of U.S. counterculture at the time.

Upon arrival in Hong Kong in 1970, I met Leo Ou-fan Lee, a remarkably interesting young assistant professor from Dartmouth College, who was spending a year in "exile" at the Chinese University of Hong Kong, owing to visa problems in the United States. He was (and still is) a very sensible person. On the one hand, he was finishing his *The Romantic Generation of Modern Chinese Writers*, which seemed to me at the time to be a courteous, but firm, departure from the classic Cold War approach to modern Chinese literature and culture pioneered by his mentors, C. T. Hsia and T. A. Hsia.[21] On the other hand, he had informal, nonscholarly, but meaningful connections to King Hu (Hu Jingquan) and the commercial film worlds of Hong Kong and Taiwan. No doubt during that year we spent together in Hong Kong he wisely enjoyed many Shaw Brothers films and may well have given some thought to their meaning. It never occurred to me, however, to see such irrelevant and silly movies produced in the colonial setting.

Instead, swept up by the Chinese revolution paradigm, I seized every opportunity to visit "patriotic" cinemas to attend colorful premieres of the Cultural Revolution film versions of Jiang Qing's model operas (*yangban xi*). These remarkable works seduced me in the same way that *The East Is Red* had in 1969. In fact, the very first essay I ever published on Chinese filmmaking was about my impressions of *Taking Tiger Mountain by Strategy* (*Zhi qu weihu shan*, 1970), which showed in six theaters in Hong Kong and Kowloon in late 1970.[22] Among other "weighty" subjects, my essay talked about the "charm and fantasy" of the film and raised serious questions about the criteria we should use when we "evaluate a work of art." More dismissive than and not as sensible as Leo Lee, it would not have occurred to me at that time to take a film like *Hong Kong Nocturne* very seriously. If I had seen it, and been forced to write about it, I certainly would have ridiculed it.

The two approaches to *Hong Kong Nocturne* discussed so far in this chapter, the 1920s and 1930s Shanghai approach and the 1960s and 1970s Cultural Revolution approach, are certainly quite different. From the perspective of the present day, the first approach still seems viable and reasonable. The Cultural Revolution approach seems shrill and doctrinaire, however. I hasten to add that its harshness and inflexibility did not seem so apparent at the time. Indeed, there was a certain logic to the approach. It was consistent with major political trends ("realities") that appeared to be unfolding at the time and with trends that were becoming dominant in the China studies field itself.

Just as the silliness and irrelevance of *Hong Kong Nocturne* seemed so obvious in the light of the Mainland China–centered Chinese revolution perspective, so, too, has the rigidity and one-dimensionality of the Cultural Revolution approach become more apparent with the passage of time. In the forty years since the release of *Hong Kong Nocturne,* it has become clear that the revolutionary approach to social, economic, and cultural change in Mainland China has failed and that revolutionary uprisings in the Third World have sputtered and fizzled. Very little that seemed to be happening on the revolutionary front in Asia has come to pass. One by one, socialist nations in Asia have abandoned socialism (but not single-party dictatorship), whereas the places that were condemned in the 1960s as colonial or neocolonial backwaters (South Korea, Taiwan, Hong Kong) have developed into economic powerhouses with their own political and cultural identities (which, of course, they had all along). With the collapse of the Soviet Union and the Eastern European socialist camp, the Cold War ended rather abruptly.

Not surprisingly, as the region and the world changed yet again, the Asian studies and China studies fields underwent another transformation of its own, just as it had in the mid-1960s. With the demise of Mao's communist revolution and its self-proclaimed leadership of Third World revolutionary movements, Mainland China and the Chinese revolution seemed much less at the center of modern Chinese history.[23] Indeed, beginning in the late 1980s and throughout the 1990s, scholars have paid less attention to national histories in general and to the national history of China in particular. Moreover, with the rise of popular culture studies, less attention was now given to the study of political elites and ruling parties as more emphasis was placed on non-elites.[24] Instead of talking exclusively about individual national entities, more emphasis was placed on regional and local identities within China on the one hand and on larger transnational and cross-border dynamics beyond Mainland China on the other.[25]

It must be conceded, however, that the new attention to Greater China dynamics that functioned in imperial times and still function today was motivated to a significant degree by Mainland China's own post-Mao desire not only to open up to the world outside the People's Republic but actually to integrate with various East Asian and international systems. Instead of pursuing research agendas that privilege national histories, young scholars are now looking at extremes at both ends of the spectrum, namely, local identities and systems and global identities and systems.[26]

This is a healthy and useful corrective, even though it, too, is the by-product of economic and political trends in East Asia and in the world. Like all scholarly tendencies, including the revolution paradigm of the 1960s and 1970s, the newest one can produce distortions and can be very political.

Thus, one cannot avoid the temptation to ask what *Hong Kong Nocturne* looks like from a third perspective, that is, the perspective of present-day transnational, Greater China, and globalization research. The unavoidable answer is that it is impossible under such circumstances to be dismissive of this film. Indeed, in many ways the film is an example of long-term trans-national and Greater China systems at work long before it was fashionable to say so.

When seen from the Greater China perspective, the values and identities of the people who inhabit the world of *Hong Kong Nocturne* seem remarkably up to date. For one thing, it is misleading to refer to *Hong Kong Nocturne* as a Hong Kong movie at all. It is truly a transnational, regional production. Shaw Brothers Studio produced the film, but its director and screenwriter, Inoue Umetsugu, was Japanese. Many in the production staff were Japanese. The language of the film is Mandarin Chinese (*guo yu*, or *putong hua*), cer-tainly not the language of Hong Kong. *Hong Kong Nocturne* was shown in Hong Kong in the troubled year of 1967, but it was also shown throughout Southeast Asia. Indeed, one strongly suspects that most of its revenues came from audiences outside Hong Kong. Once one understands the film's trans-national nature, then its timelessness and it apolitical entertainment thrust make much more sense. All politics are local politics, thus a film that is de-signed for multiple localities would obviously have to avoid a treatment of particularistic politics.

Even the content of *Hong Kong Nocturne* has a greater East Asian, even global, feel. The characters identify with Hong Kong but are extremely com-fortable coming and going freely between such places as Japan and Southeast Asia. Indeed, they identify more with greater East Asia than they do with Mainland China. Moreover, they take tremendous pride in participating in and consuming global (especially U.S.) popular culture. As noted previ-ously, their family values remain Chinese, but they see no conflict between being Chinese and being modern. They thrive on television culture, they live in modern Western-style homes and apartments that have all the latest consumer goods, they dance to go-go music, they frequent nightclubs, and Tingting even dances in *Swan Lake*. All of these activities are presented as normal and natural.

From the perspective of present-day globalization and commercialization priorities, there is nothing the least bit unusual about the money-mindedness and careerism of the characters in *Hong Kong Nocturne*. They make active use of complicated commercial networks that link Hong Kong to Japan and Southeast Asia in order to earn a living and rise to the top in their careers. The state is never shown stepping in to rescue those who have stumbled in their economic or business life. In fact, one never sees the state or government. There is no welfare net. Everyone, especially the young, seems to accept the fact that people are on their own, competition is intense, and people have to learn to protect themselves against swindlers and cheats. In short, it is a tough world, and each person needs to look out for his or her own interests.

Beginning in late 1970s, Mainland China began to abandon the collective, communist mode, at least in economic and social life, at a rapid clip. Socialism was soon replaced by a system that looks quite like the one featured in *Hong Kong Nocturne*. For enterprising individuals to get rich was now said to be glorious. Condescending critiques of the daily life of overseas Chinese and the polluted ways of Chinese residents of Southeast Asia, Hong Kong, and Taiwan were no longer heard as Mainland China sought to link up to the dynamic economy of East Asia and attract investment funds from Greater China. In the late 1970s, more and more Mainland Chinese sought to immigrate (legally or illegally) to Hong Kong and other parts of Greater China.

In terms of daily life, beginning in the late 1970s more and more Mainland Chinese, profoundly influenced by exposure to Chinese residents of Greater China and access to global culture, actively cultivated modern, up-to-date identities. Although the state was not always satisfied with the breakneck speed of the cultural transformation, young people, especially in the urban sector, saw little conflict between their Chinese and their modern identities when it came to clothing, makeup, hair styles, music, sunglasses, consumer goods, fast-food eating habits, and matters of the heart.[27]

I suspect that *Hong Kong Nocturne* has never been screened publicly in Mainland China. In the 1960s and 1970s, a screening would have been impossible for political reasons. Political barriers have been down for some time, but audiences now prefer new work and would probably not buy tickets to something as dated as *Hong Kong Nocturne*. But surely in terms of content, there is nothing in *Hong Kong Nocturne* that is inconsistent with the culture of commercialization and globalization that is now enthusiastically promoted in Mainland China. It is for this reason that *Hong Kong Nocturne*, a film released in 1967 that had absolutely nothing to do with the daily lives of ordinary people in Mainland China in 1967, explains so much about daily life in Mainland China in 2007. These days, Mainland China is doing much more than joining the thriving regional and global communities of today; it is simultaneously joining a Greater China that was already functioning quite effectively in 1967 and earlier.

Notes

1. *Huaqiao ribao*, January 25, 1967.

2. *Huaqiao ribao*, January 24, 1967.

3. *Huaqiao ribao*, January 28–30, 1967.

4. *Huaqiao ribao*, February 4 and 8, 1967.

5. *Ming bao*, January 30 and February 23, 1967.

6. *Ming bao*, February 11, 1967.

7. *Zhongguo xuesheng zhoubao* (Chinese Student Weekly), no. 762, February 24, 1967.

8. *Huaqiao ribao*, February 14, 1967.

9. For a listing of the films produced by the Tianyi (1925–37), Mingxing (1922–37) and Lianhua (1930–37) studios, see Cheng Jihua, ed., *Zhongguo dianying fazhan shi* (A History of the Development of Chinese Cinemas) (Beijing: Zhongguo dianying chuban she, 1981), vol. 1, pp. 529–50, 565–76, 603–14.

10. For a discussion of the family-centered melodrama of the 1930s, see Paul G. Pickowicz, "Melodramatic Representation and the 'May Fourth' Tradition of Chinese Cinema," in Ellen Widmer and David Der-wei Wang, eds., *From May Fourth to June Fourth: Fiction and Film in Twentieth Century China* (Cambridge, Mass.: Harvard University Press, 1993). For a stimulating treatment of the modern metropolis in China, see Leo Ou-fan Lee, *Shanghai Modern: The Flowering of a New Urban Culture in China, 1930–1945* (Cambridge, Mass.: Harvard University Press, 1999).

11. For a discussion of the impact of the May Fourth intellectual and political legacy on fiction and film of the 1930s, see Yingjin Zhang, *The City in Modern Chinese Literature and Film: Configurations of Space, Time, and Gender* (Stanford, Calif.: Stanford University Press, 1996).

12. See Paul G. Pickowicz, "The Theme of Spiritual Pollution in Chinese Films of the 1930s," *Modern China* 17, no. 1 (January 1991): pp. 38–75.

13. See Joseph W. Esherick, Paul G. Pickowicz, and Andrew G. Walder, eds., *The Chinese Cultural Revolution as History* (Stanford, Calif.: Stanford University Press, 2006), especially chapter 3.

14. Ma Ming, ed., *Xianggang dongluan hua shi (A Pictorial History of the Hong Kong Riots)* (Hong Kong: Sky Horse, 1967), p. 163.

15. Ibid., p. 166.

16. Ibid., pp. 23–82.

17. Ibid., pp. 56–57, 66–67, 130, 135.

18. For an example of Vietnam-era scholarship on Asia, see Edward Friedman and Mark Selden, eds., *America's Asia* (New York: Vintage, 1971).

19. John Israel, *Student Nationalism in China, 1927–1937* (Stanford, Calif.: Stanford University Press, 1966); Stuart Schram, *Mao Tse-tung* (New York: Simon and Schuster, 1967).

20. William Hinton, *Fanshen: A Documentary of Revolution in a Chinese Village* (New York: Vintage, 1966); Franz Schurman, *Ideology and Organization in Communist China* (Berkeley and Los Angeles: University of California Press, 1967); Maurice Meisner, *Li Ta-chao and the Origins of Chinese Marxism* (Cambridge, Mass.: Harvard University Press, 1967).

21. Leo Ou-fan Lee, *The Romantic Generation of Modern Chinese Writers* (Cambridge, Mass.: Harvard University Press, 1973).

22. Paul G. Pickowicz, "The Modern Revolutionary Peking Opera 'Taking Tiger Mountain by Strategy': An American's View," *Eastern Horizon* 10, no. 4 (1971): pp. 31–34.

23. For an example of recent scholarship on the first half of the twentieth century that seeks to de-center the story of the Chinese Communist Party, see Wen-hsin Yeh, ed., *Becoming Chinese: Passages to Modernity and Beyond* (Berkeley and Los Angeles: University of California Press, 2000).

24. See Perry Link, Richard Madsen, and Paul G. Pickowicz, eds., *Unofficial China: Popular Culture and Thought in the People's Republic* (Boulder, Colo.: Westview Press, 1989).

25. See Sheldon Hsiao-peng Lu, ed., *Transnational Chinese Cinemas: Identity, Nationhood, Gender* (Honolulu: University of Hawai'i Press, 1997); Nick Browne, Paul G. Pickowicz, Vivian Sobchack, and Esther Yau, eds., *New Chinese Cinemas: Forms, Identities, Politics* (Cambridge: Cambridge University Press, 1994).

26. Poshek Fu and David Desser, eds., *The Cinema of Hong Kong: History, Arts, Identity* (Cambridge: Cambridge University Press, 2000).

27. See Perry Link, Richard Madsen, and Paul G. Pickowicz, eds., *Popular China: Unofficial Culture in a Globalizing Society* (New York: Rowman and Littlefield, 2002).

5

The Black-and-White
Wenyi Films of Shaws

WONG AIN-LING

Is Shaws all about the glamour of gold and jade, the allure of red and purple? Not necessarily. It actually had a period of unadorned simplicity. If anything, it has made quite a lot of *wenyi* films,[1] the most interesting of which should be its black-and-white productions made in the 1950s and early 1960s. Perhaps I am jumping to a conclusion, because precious little of the black-and-white *wenyi* films are available. Yet with the few I have managed to see, and from reading old magazines that have been so fortunately preserved, I feel emboldened to make this claim. And, yes, there is yet another consideration: The golden age of Hong Kong melodrama is the 1950s, possibly stretching as far as the early 1960s. Also, is not Motion Picture and General Investment Co. Ltd. (Dianmao, hereinafter called MP & GI), Shaws' major rival of the time, known for its black-and-white *wenyi* films of the 1950s and 1960s? There is ample reason to believe that there should be much to be discovered among Shaws' *wenyi* films of the same period.

Tianyi Film Productions and Nanyang, the Shaw studio's predecessors, made only Cantonese films, targeted for the Hong Kong and Southeast Asian markets in the 1930s and 1940s. Runde Shaw (Shao Cunren) renamed Nanyang as Shaw Studio and set up Shaw and Sons Ltd. in 1950 and shifted its production from Cantonese to Mandarin films and primarily *wenyi* films set in contemporary times. Between 1952 and 1958, the only costume films produced by Shaws were *Beyond the Grave* (*Ren gui lian*, 1954), *Princess Yang Kwei Fei* (*Yang Guifei*, 1955, a coproduction with Japan, directed by Mizoguchi Kenji), *Chin Ping Mei* (*Jing Ping Mei*, 1955), and *Diau Charn* (*Diao Chan*, 1958). What accounted for the studio's total switch to Mandarin films when the Mandarin-speaking mainland market had totally collapsed after the establishment of the People's Republic of China in 1949?[2] And why the preference for contemporary films over costume films? Many believed that Shaw and Sons, under the control of Runde Shaw, focused on contemporary films because of the low production cost. Taiwan film historian Du Yunzhi commented on Runde Shaw: "Runde Shaw's principle is to use as little resources as possible. He is extremely calculating in financial terms. Because of tight budgeting, productions of the time are usually humble in scale, meaning no extravagant sets, no big name directors and stars, thus resulting in works of low artistic quality."[3] Whether other factors contributed to this production policy is yet unknown. All these are issues that warrant further study. Cai Guorong has devoted a chapter to the Shaws' *wenyi* films in his work *Zhongguo Jindai Wenyi Dianying Yanjiu (A Study of Modern Chinese Wenyi Cinema)*, which aptly offers an overview on the genre. This chapter is only a preliminary examination of Shaws' *wenyi* films.

Unforgettable Homesickness

The major works made in the Shaw and Sons era are mostly directed by Wang Yin, Tu Guangqi, Doe Ching (Tao Qin), and Li Han-hsiang (Li Hanxiang). Among them, Wang and Tu were the most experienced, both already active since 1930s Shanghai. Wang was the studio's top director, his work covering a variety of genres, including light comedies (*Midsummer Night's Romance*, or *Zhongxiaye zhi lian*, 1953), romantic family melodramas (*Little Couple*, or *Xiao fuqi*, 1954), costume films (*Chin Ping Mei*), and a remake of the Hollywood classic *Gone with the Wind*, titled *Beauty in the Maelstrom* (*Luanshi yao ji*, 1956) and set in the Early Republican period, the latter two major productions of the Shaw and Sons era. Tu also made a lot of films with romantic or family melodramatic stories, such as *Meal Time* (*Guifang le*, 1953), *Love and Duty* (*Lian'ai yu yiwu*, 1955), and *The Mortal Wind* (*Feng xiaoxiao*, 1954), based on the novel by Xu Xu. But time marched on, and those who hesitated, even just slightly, were left behind. Wang scaled down his directorial work in the mid-1950s, focusing instead on acting. He shuttled between MP & GI and Shaws, leaving on celluloid a number of memorable performances. Compared to Wang, Tu Guangqi was not so lucky; his output suffering a steady drop in the late 1950s. On the other hand, the writer and screenwriter-turned-director Doe Ching, though one year Tu's junior, became an important figure of the studio in the 1950s, with works like *A Song to Remember* (*Han chan qu*, 1953), *The Third Life* (*Cansheng*, 1954), *A Lonely Heart*

(*Ling yan*, 1956), and *A Married Woman's Secret* (*Shaonainai de mimi*, 1956). He reached a new height in his career after jumping ship to MP & GI in 1956, helping to define the house style of the studio with such films as *Our Sister Hedy* (*Si qianjin*, 1957) and *Calendar Girl* (*Longxiang fengwu*, 1959). He later returned to Shaw Brothers, continuing to serve as the studio's main creative force in *wenyi* films. As for Li Han-hsiang, he joined Shaw and Sons in the mid-1950s, making several *wenyi* films, such as *Beyond the Blue Horizon* (*Shuixian*, 1956), *A Mellow Spring* (*Chun guang wuxian hao*, 1957), and *Dan Feng Street* (*Danfeng jie*, 1958). His most important act, however, was convincing Runde Shaw to let him make the costume film *Diau Charn*, which was not only a turning point in his career but also steered the studio in a brand new direction. This is a familiar story, and I will not get into it here.

Cantonese cinema of the 1950s was more closely related to local life in comparison with its Mandarin counterpart, the latter often imbued with nostalgia for the homeland owing largely to a creative force that came from Shanghai and other mainland areas. This is especially true of the Shaw productions, not only in its Shaw and Sons period but also stretching as far as the glamorous Shaw Brothers era. Hong Kong critic Sek Kei's observations on the Chineseness of Shaws' vintage films are highly revealing.[4] Films from the Shaw and Sons era are largely unavailable; here, I will cite three films as examples.

Destroy! (*Huimie*) was made in 1952 and scripted by Doe Ching, directed by Richard Poh (Bu Wancang), and starring Bai Guang and Wang Hao. We had not been able to find information about the film's release, although a friend had recorded a copy of it from a late-night television broadcast. According to film researcher Yu Mo-wan (Yu Muyun), a small production company made the film with investment from Shaw and Sons before the latter went into production. Other films produced in a similar manner include *Tears of Songstress* (*Genü hong lingyan*, 1953) and *Closed Chamber* (*Xin xixiang ji*, 1953), produced by Far East Motion Picture Company. In *Destroy!* Bai plays a dance hall girl, who is forced into the trade after falling for the wrong man and bearing a girl for him before he disappears. But she is no typical, hapless woman who raises her child through humiliation. Instead, she pursues her own happiness, caring little even if that happiness is built on relationships of which society disapproves. She is obstinate, for no other reason than the fact that she is Bai Guang.[5] To put it plainly, this is her personal style. Her body oozes a Shanghai aura; no matter where she is, she brings with her the decadence and excesses of the Bund. In a chance meeting, she has her eyes on a respectable, controlled married man, Wang Hao. Notice that it is she who has her eyes on him, not the other way round. Also, she "has her eyes" on him, not "falls in love" with him, like a ferocious beast training its gaze on its prey. And so the man falls, step by bigger step, into a whirlpool of desire, abandoning his wife and daughter for the bewitching Bai and running away from the calm and quiet of Qingdao to the glorious nightlife of Shanghai. He ends up in jail, his face disfigured, his future ruined. But *she* lives on. The entire story takes place in Qingdao and Shanghai, with no connection at all to Hong Kong.

The conclusion of *Destroy!* is the beginning of *My Darling Dear* (*Bi yun tian*, 1952). Across the courtroom hangs a banner: "Uncorrupted Justice." Presiding is a judge played by Wang Hao, in a case against the madwoman played by Li Lihua. The film constitutes two flashbacks. The first is the judge's, when he meets with the head of the mental asylum and recounts his past experience with a woman. She is the madwoman, five years ago. Back then, she was at the prime of her beauty, passionately in love with the young master Huang He. Despite the vehement objections of his father, they got married and a son was born. Huang made a living selling paintings on the street, later losing his sight due to sickness. Li took up responsibility for the family and waited tables at a coffee shop. There, she met Wang Hao, who, before leaving Hong Kong to go overseas, gave her a sum of money to buy a sewing machine as a way to make a living. The second flashback is that of Li at the asylum, remembering what happened to her after Wang left. Feeling inferior, her husband, Huang, left home. Meanwhile, Li lost her money, plunging her life into desperation. A thug cheated her into prostitution, and when she resisted, she killed him accidentally. Li receives a light sentence and, on her release, is greeted at the door by Huang and their son, ending the film with a happy reunion. In the film, the only signs of Hong Kong are the handbills on the walls, advertising for herbal doctors and Chinese medicines. Half a century later, when Wong Kar-wai (Wang Jiawei) re-creates 1960s Hong Kong in *In the Mood for Love* (*Huayang nianhua*, 2000), Chinese medicine ads on the walls of the narrow alleys are again used as emblems of the time. Look a little closer, and we can see that Wang Yin's Hong Kong is a schizophrenic one. In one corner of that Hong Kong, we see neighborhood stores with ads for Westernized drinks like Coca-Cola.

In another corner, when Li is at the end of the road, she is forced to move into a shabby inn. Near its entrance are ruins that remind us of the desolation of the postwar years. It is located at the end of an alley with an arched doorway, the street name carved on top with standard calligraphy, almost taking us back to the Shanghai of *Street Angel* (*Malu tianshi*, 1937). Taken together, these films give us an impression that, although these filmmakers

My Darling Dear, directed by Wang Yin. (Courtesy of Shaw Brothers (HK) Ltd.)

are in Hong Kong, their spirits still linger in the lanes, streets, and passages of yesteryear.

If Richard Poh's style is stately and relaxed and Wang Yin's is sturdy and plain, then Li Han-hsiang's is light and nimble. His *A Mellow Spring* was made in 1957, with a script by Cheng Gang. Set during a stormy night, the story takes place in an old building. Living in it are the young professional Linda Lin Dai; three friends who are active in theater, Yang Zhiqing, Chao Lei (Zhao Lei), and Wu Jiaxiang; the five-member family headed by the unemployed Mr. Zhao (Hao lüren); and the kindhearted landlady, Zhuang Yuanyong, and the stingy landlord, Hong Bo. In the film, Hong says to his wife, "You must have seen too many mean landladies in movies, so you want to be a good one." In Cantonese films, characters are presented in ready stereotypes, one of the most cherished is the mean landlady played by To Sam-ku (Tu Sangu). An inside joke on Cantonese films, this line of dialogue must have come from scriptwriter Cheng Gang, who was one of those rare filmmakers who straddled both the Mandarin and Cantonese sides of Hong Kong cinema. In Cantonese films with similar settings, such as *In the Face of*

Demolition (*Weilou chunxiao*, 1953), *Typhoon Signal No. 10* (*Shi hao fengbo*, 1959), and *Father Is Back* (*Huoku you lan*, 1960), the tenants sharing the crowded quarters usually bring a healthy mix of backgrounds, unlike those in *A Mellow Spring*, all of whom hail from the mainland (mostly Shanghai) and are mostly educated members of the intelligentsia. In Chao and Wu's room, their graduation photo is hung on the wall.

Even Wang Lai, whom Linda Lin Dai mistakes for her trustworthy friend, is also from Shanghai: "These film and theater people are so snobbish. But back in Shanghai, he [Zhao Lei] was trying to court me!" Zhao plays a care-free actor, who frequently gets into arguments with Wu over the conflicting merits of art and livelihood, arguments that sometimes end in fisticuffs. Wu teases Zhao for his snobbishness and thinks that his idea of art for art's sake is unrealistic, for theater cannot find an audience in Hong Kong and films hold no promise for the future. But Zhao takes pride in his straitened circumstances, not finding any problems with putting his feet into a pair of worn-out shoes. "As long as there are no holes in my soul," he declares.

Li Hanxiang's *A Mellow Spring*. (Courtesy of Shaw Brothers (HK) Ltd.)

Rarely in Hong Kong films can such a direct portrayal be found of film-makers or theater artists who had moved south. Scriptwriter Cheng Gang is said to have quite an artist's temper, and the story may be something of a personal statement.

Li manages to turn a script with a strong theatrical overtone into a film with a touch of both cinema and stage. The film begins with several outdoor scenes in the spring, followed by a street scene at night. The lights have been turned on in the building. It is a two-story structure, with a wooden staircase one can vaguely see, linking the small community upstairs with the large community on the streets. The store on the corner is still open, a few passersby hurrying in front. The wind is blowing hard, and everyone is trying to get home. A high-angle shot introduces the entire set, like staring out from the second floor, looking at the tube of swirling blue, red, and white outside the barbershop. The camera pulls back to display a room, as Linda Lin Dai enters from the right, running over to close the window. The camera moves slowly as Yang Zhiqing enters through the door. We get a glimpse of the

A scene from *A Mellow Spring*. (Courtesy of Shaw Brothers (HK) Ltd.)

single bed; folded on it is a blanket, which is wrapped inside a silk bedsheet, the way it is done south of the Yangtze area.

Lin asks Yang, "Brother Zhu, is it easy to get an entry visa here?" This is 1950s Hong Kong, where a group of mainlanders live. The exiles are starting to feel that their stay would not be a matter of only one or two years. Lin is therefore planning to send for her mother, who has been stranded in Singapore. Li's camera moves along the narrow hallway, between the doorways and the window frames, capturing the humanity trapped inside this tight space. In the scene in which Zhao eavesdrops on Lin and Wang, he is standing at the right foreground, watching through the glass windows at the hallway. The deep-focus photography is simple yet layered, and the audience, like Zhao, is hiding backstage to watch the performance onstage with a perfect view. What about the world outside? The Coca-Cola sign in the store once again signals that this is 1950s Hong Kong, where Western materialistic culture is washing on shore. Lo Wei (Luo Wei) is the spokesman for this money-driven evil society, and Wang Lai is the "moral purchaser" of that transition period. After an entire night of commotion, Mrs. Zhao gives birth to a baby. The exiles from the north have finally established a blood tie with the new land. Watching this film of half a century ago is like returning to the space and time of my parents, and I can almost smell the fragrance of the newly washed sheets.

The Settled Generation

In the 1960s, Shaw Brothers (Hong Kong) Ltd. had already entered the color era. But in 1963 and 1964, *wenyi* films were still mostly shot in black and white. Doe Ching was one of the studio's key directors, specializing in *wenyi* films in both the Shaw and Sons phase and the Shaw Brothers period. He made only one costume film, *Beyond the Grave,* and one *wuxia* film, *Twin Blades of Doom* (*Yinyang dao,* 1969), which was also his last. Watching Doe's *Love without End* (*Bu liao qing,* 1961) and *The Golden Trumpet* (*Jin laba,* 1961) again is an interesting experience. Both films are set against the nightlife of Hong Kong, the former centered around the songstress Linda Lin Dai, the latter focusing on the trumpeter Paul Chang Chung (Zhang Chong).

Lin in *Love without End* is an orphan girl. Unlike the Mandarin films of the early and mid-1950s, characters in the film are no longer preoccupied with Shanghai or the mainland, instead hastily establishing that they are "from elsewhere." The film starts with a wide shot of the Tsim Sha Tsui train station, where a young girl wearing a plain cotton *qipao* and carrying a rattan basket alights from the train. One would guess she is from the mainland. Regardless, she does not arrive by plane and is brimming with earthiness, very unlike the Julie Yeh Feng (Ye Feng) who flies in from Singapore at the beginning of MP & GI's *It's Always Spring* (*Taoli zhengchun*, 1962). Her worried face is superimposed on the typical nightscape of Hong Kong, with one nightclub neon sign followed by another, reminding us of the Shanghai of the 1930s and 1940s. When the male and female protagonists first meet, Kwan Shan (Guan Shan) mistakenly thinks Lin is trying to kill herself. She explains: "I come here to look for life, not death." Ironically, she dies in the end, and the man she loves has survived because of her sacrifice. A consummate genre film, *Love without End* makes no effort to be realistic. Lin is a star from the very beginning, with thick lashes, heavy eyeliner, and a trendy hairstyle, nothing like a girl from the mainland. Coincidences are chained together like a pearl necklace, and the audience entering the theater looking for dreams is perfectly happy to accept such arrangements. The first time Lin sings on stage, the camera captures her inexperience through a giant glass frame, bringing us into the realm of life as a spectacle. Hong Kong *wenyi* films mostly feature actresses as lead characters, and *Love without End* is a prime example.

Much of the drama in *The Golden Trumpet* is carried by the relatively unknown Paul Chang Chung and child star Fei Li. This is unusual for that period of feminine screen dominance. Chang plays a professional trumpeter who performs in nightclubs. To raise money to care for his pregnant wife, he resorts to gambling, is tricked by a social butterfly, and beaten up by a gangster, even verges on the edge of committing a crime as he tries to keep the money he finds. When he has finally raised the money, he is robbed. In the span of two days and one night, he leads his son to look for the crook. They traverse all over Hong Kong, going from commercial skyscrapers to roadside food stalls, capturing a large amount of real-life street scenery that was rare for 1960s Shaws productions. A friend comments that this is a Hong Kong version of *The Bicycle Thief* (1948), which is quite correct, although the backdrop is no longer the ruinous postwar 1950s but an increasingly modern city. Chang is no longer a newcomer but someone who has his roots here, complete with family and career. Looking at it today, the film seems to act as a test of male morality. Yes, male, a very important point. When women sing on the stage, they are selling themselves. It is supposed to be temporary, terminating when the mission is accomplished, like Lin in *Love without End*, or most actresses in the Hong Kong film industry, who seldom consider performing as a lifetime career. Men regard their job skills with dignity, and the film begins with Chang playing the trumpet onstage and ends with the same situation. At the end, band members redeem the trumpet that Chang had pawned. His son takes the instrument out and everyone is silent. Chang takes his trumpet, walks to the middle of the nightclub, and plays by himself, losing himself in his music. The camera pans across the empty seats, followed by a shot of a packed house, as jazz music swims through the smoke-filled room. The father plays on the stage as the son listens backstage. Their gazes meet, and the familial order of father and son is reestablished after a series of tests. The man, after passing a series of tests, is finally able to settle in this booby-trapped city.

Several years later, *Song of Tomorrow* (*Mingri zhi ge*, 1967), also written and directed by Doe Ching, is no longer as free-flowing as *The Golden Trumpet* and *Love without End*. The use of color is unnatural and exaggerated, completely losing the texture of the black-and-white films. The film focuses on a drummer played by Chiao Chuang (Qiao Zhuang), who is a talented musician but not as confident as Chang in *The Golden Trumpet*. To overcome his stage fright, he takes to drugs and becomes addicted. He is thus a fragile man in a violent era. Chang in *Love without End* finds affirmation of his moral integrity while raising money for his pregnant wife, but Chiao's maturity comes at the expense of his wife's, Ivy Ling Bo's, selfless sacrifices. The man in *Love without End* is someone who fulfils his career through the sacrifice of his woman, but this is only because of his ignorance, the ignorance of a man too self-centered and spoiled. But Chiao in *Song of Tomorrow* is a man whose will has been eroded by a harsh environment, a defeated rooster. I indulge in a one-sided thought that perhaps Doe Ching is using Chiao's fear and restlessness to lament his own life as a filmmaker. At the time, Shaws has already entered the violent *wuxia* era. Even Yue Feng, the most experienced director on the back lot, had to take up arms and join the ranks of the martial arts world in addition to making *wenyi*, *huangmei diao* opera films, and costume epics. The same year, Yue directed *The Dragon Creek* (*Longhu gou*, 1967) and *Rape of the Sword* (*Dao jian*, 1967). Although Doe is the most skilled among the Shaws directors of *wenyi* films and the most persistent in the genre, he must have felt the pressure around him. In spring 1968, he made *Twin Blades of Doom* while suffering from illness. The next year, he died of stomach cancer at the age of 54.[6] The same year, Chun Kim (Qin Jian), who switched from directing Cantonese films to Mandarin films after joining Shaws, hanged himself inside the Shaw quarters. Life is like a bubble of dreams, the intricacies involved are certainly too complex to sum up in a few words, but factors of the grand scheme cannot be ignored.

In a 1969 interview, veteran director Yue Feng severely criticized "*wuxia* films that emphasise brutality."[7] Although he did not name names, it was obvious he was referring to Chang Cheh (Zhang Che) and Shaws' production direction at the time. He also mentioned that, among his own work, his favorites are MP & GI's *Golden Lotus* (*Jin lianhua*, 1957) and Shaws' *Bitter Sweet* (*Wei shui xinku wei shui mang*, 1962). The former is about the determined pursuit of love by youths, and the latter is an expression of an older generation's (and Yue's) disappointment in the younger generation. I had a chance to see another family melodrama of his, *The Younger Generation* (*Ernü shi women de*, 1970), although it was difficult to sit through. A year later, he remade *Bitter Sweet,* casting Chen Yanyan in the role of the mother and naming it *Sons and Daughters* (*Qianwan renjia*, 1971). Only history did not repeat itself this time, and in the 1970s Shaw Brothers had entirely lost interest in romance and *wenyi* films. Yuan Qiufeng, who filled Raymond Chow's void as production manager at the studio, once mentioned in an interview that to meet market demands, Shaws would concentrate on *wuxia* films, though *wenyi* films would still be made. He handed in his resignation two years later, finally leaving Shaws in 1973.[8] In those two or three years, the number of *wenyi* films produced by Shaws was meager. In an interview, Yuan expressed his displeasure: "This kind of situation cannot be reversed only with my effort. . . . Before, when people addressed me as Director Yuan, I would be happy. Now, if people call me that, I would blush with embarrassment."[9]

Evolution of Wenyi Films and the Remake of Ma Xu Weibang's Classics

Mentioning Yuan Qiufeng, his mentor Ma Xu Weibang springs to mind. Ma Xu in fact can be related to Shaws. He was a noted director in the 1930s and 1940s, and his consistent thematic concerns and stylistic uniqueness were peerless in Chinese cinema.[10] He came to Hong Kong in 1949, and although his career suffered a setback, he continued making several Mandarin films in the 1950s and eventually directed only Amoy-dialect films. Before directing Mandarin films, Yuan served as his assistant director. Later, Yuan joined Shaws, and his first Mandarin film was a remake of Ma Xu's Shanghai masterpiece *Singing at Midnight* (*Yeban gesheng,* 1937). Lo Chen (Luo Zhen), another *wenyi* director at Shaws, also served an apprenticeship under Ma Xu. After the *wenyi* films entered the color phase, he remade Ma Xu's classic *The Story of Qiu Hai Tang* (*Qiu Hai Tang,* 1943). Looking at these two remakes, perhaps we can trace the qualitative changes of the Shaw Brothers era.

Yuan remade *Singing at Midnight* into *The Mid-Nightmare* (*Yeban gesheng*, 1962–63, in two parts) in 1961. On February 14 of that year, Ma Xu died in an accident.[11] In Ma Xu's *Singing at Midnight*, his sympathy for outcasts and his mastery of light and shadow are affected by the influence of German Expressionism. The film begins on a night with a full moon. A deserted theater is about to be demolished, a notice pasted on its door. As the night deepens, families hurriedly close their window and doors. Appearing on the screen is the huge shadow of the male protagonist, Song, followed by the female protagonist, Li, who, in her long gown, walks through the long, quiet corridor like a ghost, pushing open a window and directing her gaze into the darkness outside. This reminds us of F. W. Murnau's *Nosferatu, eine Symphonie des Grauens* (1922). Yuan's version remains faithful to Ma Xu's, also with two installments and giving original script credit to his mentor. Indeed, certain passages feel like Yuan was directing the film with Ma Xu's script, although the changes in the new version reveal changes in time and industry. The treatment of the second female lead, Green Butterfly, is a ready example. In the original, Green Butterfly is the star of the theater troupe and the lover of the actor Sun. She is young and beautiful, yet she has no fear of the villain Tang but for her dignity as an artist. In the Shaw Brothers version, Green Butterfly is played by Fanny Fan Lai (Fan Li), who has always played the role of "sensuous star" in Shaws productions. In the remake, she dutifully serves her role with obligatory seductiveness, turning an impetuous character into a stereotyped actress who indulges in vanity and jealousy. On the other hand, Yuan expresses through the words of his male lead, Song (Zhao Lei), his "artistic manifesto." In the film, Song says to Sun (Paul Chang Chung), "Theater does not just provide entertainment, it's a tool that reflects time, and that's why people still go to the theater during times of turbulence. But they want to see new themes and new stories." Like Doe Ching and Lo Chen, Yuan also was once a writer, having worked as a war journalist, and *The Mid-Nightmare* reflects the compromises and contradictions he had to endure at Shaws. In the 1960s, there was still some creative room at Shaws, but by the 1970s it was a totally different situation.

Four years later, Lo Chen, Ma Xu's other student, embarks on the remake of *The Story of Qiu Hai Tang*, the title of which was changed to *Vermilion Door* (*Hong Ling Lei*, 1965). Leafing through the pages of Shaws' official publication *Southern Screen* (*Nanguo Dianying*), it only briefly mentioned that the film is based on a novel of the same title. The name of the author, Qin Shou'ou, is not even listed, not to mention Ma Xu Weibang. Perhaps that name had been forgotten and no longer served any publicity purposes. Ma Xu's version is focused on the male lead, Lü Yukun, who is well versed in Peking and *kunqu* operas. He also appears onstage in female impersonation roles, a practice that has almost disappeared. During that time, Li Lihua, only seventeen or eighteen, plays both the role of the student Luo and the daughter Meibao, showing her budding talent. More than twenty years later, Li miraculously remains the focus of the camera, reinforcing her title of "evergreen actress." Only this time, she no longer plays the innocent young student but an actress who shares the stage with Qiu Hai Tang. I believe the reason for shifting the dramatic focus from Qiu Hai Tang to the actress played by Li is because in the entire Shaws studio of the 1960s, an actor of Lü's caliber simply could not be found. Also, the *wenyi* films of the 1960s usually have a female star taking center stage, so it was natural to focus on the Peking opera–trained Li. The film starts with an interior shot of a theater, the stage flooded in a sea of red as an opera highlight unfolds on stage. Li, in a full theatrical costume with feathers and headdress, mesmerizes the audience (including, of course, Warlord Yuan Baofan) with her skillful moves and suggestive gazes. In regular clothes and out of her costumes, Li seems a little too old for her character; however, such an accomplished actress who could express so fully the heart and mind of the theatrical world in the film's time would be second to none. Director Lo Chen managed to make *Vermilion Door* into a tight drama, merging two chapters into one, and the film rushes through like a roller coaster, not allowing any slow moments.

From the two versions of *The Story of Qiu Hai Tang*, we can see two kinds of sentiments and two types of films. Ma Xu Weibang's film starts with a series of still photographs, of front doors and landmarks that represent an aging Chinese culture. The camera then slides down the hanging lamp in an interior hallway, moving slowly into a courtyard, where the faint cries of a Beijing *erhu* (a string instrument) and the sounds of children can be heard. A teacher, brandishing his cane, is yelling commands at a boy who is pirouetting on one leg. To one side, seven or eight shirtless boys are also practicing. The camera strolls into the inside chamber, stopping at Lü Yukun, who is sitting idly in front of a window. He plays the melancholic Wu Yuqin, stage named Qiu Hai Tang. Not wasting any words, Ma Xu has captured the background of his lead character and the environment he grew up in. The camera then pans from Lü to the entrance of the room, through which his stage brother enters, telling Lü that the troupe leader has accepted an offer to play at the Guang He Theatre. The film immediately switches to the stage of the theater, where Lü, in character, is sorrowfully sighing about the sufferings of his life. Sitting in the audience and loudly expressing his praise is none other than

Yuan Baofan, the warlord who rules the land. For those who play and those who watch, the men and the women (or the men who play women), the seeds of tragedy have already been sown in the deeply entrenched views of society. Qiu Hai Tang's most celebrated play is *Su San, the Convict on Her Way*, a tragedy. But offstage, he is most fond of singing "Luo Cheng Calls at the Gate," a masculine number. In them are buried humiliations that cannot be fully disclosed.

Ma Xu Weibang is in no hurry to push the narrative forward, instead lingering on the development of emotions, such as when Qiu sees Luo again at the warlord's mansion. The feelings between the characters are subtly expressed. Luo is like a mirror that reflects the talents of Qiu Hai Tang, whereas he finds in her loving devotion his true audience. After he is disfigured, Ma Xu patiently photographs his face, contorted by pain. Audiences today may find this excessive, but revisiting this film recently, I feel that Ma Xu is making this film with the style and techniques of silent films, his use of close-ups reminding us of Carl Dreyer. Finally, he lets Qiu Hai Tang jump down from the building, ending his life in the same way Song plunges into the ocean in *Singing at Midnight*. In the 1960s, that sense of extreme self-pity and dignity turns into one of sorrow, when Qiu Hai Tang dies of hard work, breathing his last in the tender arms of his love. Ma Xu Weibang seems to be emptying out what is inside, but in the dream factory of Shaw Brothers, the concern is how to make it entertaining, and, if necessary, what is inside can well be discarded.

Conclusion

Hong Kong cinema is a general term. In it are various entities, such as the distinct realms of Cantonese and Mandarin films, although there were also infiltrations and influences between them. For Mandarin films, researchers cannot divert their attentions from MP & GI and Shaws, often consciously or subconsciously comparing the two. In terms of the length of its activities, the number of productions, and the diversity of genres, MP & GI cannot measure up to Shaws. Yet most researchers feel that the *wenyi* films of MP & GI are superior to those of Shaws. But it is too early to really make an extensive comparison. It is impossible even to draw a conclusive evaluation on the films of Shaws alone. The reason is simply that we are still unable to see most films, especially the early productions. Under these limitations, this chapter is therefore only an attempt to offer some initial observations based on a few *wenyi* films of the 1950s and 1960s. It is interesting that even in such a preliminary study, the direction and development of Shaws' films can be glimpsed.

Take the films *Destroy!*, *My Poor Darling*, and *A Mellow Spring* discussed previously. They all have a strong mainland sensibility. Although set in contemporary times, their sense of the time is weaker than the more Westernized films of MP & GI, though we can hardly say that the Shaws films do not reflect their time. After the establishment of Shaw Brothers, the direction of *wenyi* films became closer to that of MP & GI, perhaps due to market considerations, such as Doe Ching's *Darling Daughter* (*Qian jin xiaojie*, 1959), Yue Feng's *Spring Frolic* (*Xi chun tu*, 1959), and Richard Poh's *Eve of the Wedding* (*Daijia chun xin*, 1960). Just looking at the films' stories, one has a feeling that by swapping the logo at the beginning, they could be passed off as MP & GI productions. We must not forget that both Doe Ching and Yue Feng were raided from MP & GI. In the early 1960s work of Doe Ching, such as *Love without End* and *The Golden Trumpet*, although the backgrounds of the characters are played down, the city of Hong Kong becomes more defined. In fact, Shaws' *wenyi* films of the time are drawn from a rich variety of topics, including social realism (*Street Boys* [*Jietong*, 1960], *The Pistol* [*Shouqiang*, 1961]), family melodrama (*Back Door* [*Houmen*, 1960], *Bitter Sweet*), and psychological drama (*Flames of Passion* [*Yuhuo fenshen*, 1960], *The Deformed* [*Jiren yanfu*, 1960]). But in the remake of two Ma Xu Weibang films, we can detect some basic changes in the genre, obviously driven by the production policies of Shaws. It is worthy to note that as Shaws' *wenyi* films evolve from black and white to color, the sense of everyday life is drained, and they become vacuous and lost. From Chun Kim's *Pink Tears* (*Chiqing lei*, 1965) and *Farewell, My Love* (*Chuncan*, 1969) to Lo Chen's *Swan Song* (*Chuisi tiane*, 1967) and *The Rainbow* (*Hong*, 1968), the *wenyi* genre is plunged into an abyss of emptiness. This coincided with the fact that Hong Kong as the center of *wenyi* productions was replaced by Taiwan from the mid-1960s onward.[12] At the same time, propelled by the market, the *wuxia* genre became more and more energetic, eventually taking over the *wenyi* genre entirely. From this perspective, Chor Yuen's (Chu Yuan's) sword films of the 1970s stand out as a rather unique fusion of the *wenyi* and *wuxia* genres, especially *Intimate Confessions of a Chinese Courtesan* (*Ainu*, 1971) and his better works in the Gulong series, such as *Killer Clans* (*Liuxing, hudie, jian*, 1976), *The Magic Blade* (*Tianya, mingyue, dao*, 1976), *Clans of Intrigue* (*Chu liuxiang*, 1977), and so forth.[13] This topic certainly deserves more in-depth study. Wong Kar-wai's enigmatic *Ashes of Time* (*Dong xie xi du*, 1994), for example, could make very interesting reading seen in the light of Chor Yuen's works of this period.

Coming back to Shaws, the studio went from the simplicity of black and white to the glorious world of color and from standard ratio to the glamorous Scope. The romance and morality of the middle class gives way to the sex, violence, and energy of the grassroots. In a short twenty years, we witnessed the fall of the *wenyi* genre, resulting in a totally different outlook of Hong Kong cinema. Shaws is a solid organization with many resources. To study Hong Kong cinema, especially Mandarin cinema, one cannot ignore it. Whether one likes it or not, the Hong Kong cinema of today was to a large degree molded by Shaws, and the jury is still out on the studio's accomplishments. Because most of Shaws' *wenyi* films are still unavailable, especially the early black-and-white productions, the observations made in this chapter are regrettably incomplete. Let us hope that more films will be made available in the future, allowing us to study them on a more reasonable basis.

Notes

Translated by Sam Ho. First published in Wong Ain-Ling, ed., *The Shaw Screen: A Preliminary Study* (Hong Kong: Hong Kong Film Archive, 2003); revised on May 14, 2004.

1. *Wenyi* film is a broad and hard-to-define genre. *Wenyi* could literally be translated as literature and art. Cai Guorong, in his book *Zhongguo Jindai Wenyi Dianying Yanjiu* (*A Study of Modern Chinese Wenyi Cinema*) (Taipei, Taiwan: ROC Film Library, 1985), defined *wenyi* films as "works set in contemporary times or the late Qing/early Republican period in which the focus of dramatic attention is on the depiction of human feelings and family relationships." According to him, *wenyi* films that deal with family relationships and ethics can be traced back to *Gu'er jiu zu ji* (*How the Orphan Rescued His Grandparents*, 1924, scripted by Zheng Zhengqiu and directed by Zhang Shichuan), whereas the earliest work of the romance type dates back to Dan Duyu's *Haishi* (*Pledge of Love*, 1921). In Hong Kong, the first comprehensive study on the *wenyi* genre is *Cantonese Melodrama*, the Tenth Hong Kong International Film Festival retrospective catalog edited by Li Cheuk-to (Hong Kong: Urban Council, 1986). In his introduction, Li explained that *wenyipian* is quite similar to melodrama in the West, seen by many as a so-called phantom genre because it includes works that are difficult to categorize, and most of them share the specificities of melodrama: highly schematic characters, plots punctuated by fortuities and coincidences, extreme emotions and conflicts. For convenience's sake, he has thus chosen to name the Chinese title of the retrospective *wenyipian*, and the English melodrama, fully aware that the two terms are not strictly identical. "While *wenyipian* is mainly delimited by its subject-matter or theme, melodrama is essentially a kind of dramatic convention, applicable to films of various subject-matters or themes."

2. Some believe that Runde devoted Shaws to the production of Mandarin films because they would create a bigger market and secure better overseas prices and were

boosted by the postwar influx of southbound filmmakers from Shanghai; Stephanie Chung Po-yin, "The Industrial Evolution of a Fraternal Enterprise: The Shaw Brothers and the Shaw Organisation," in Wong Ain-ling, ed., *The Shaw Screen: A Preliminary Study* (Hong Kong: Hong Kong Film Archive, 2003), p. 6.

3. Du Yunzhi, *Shaoshi dianying wangguo mixin (Inside Story of the Shaw Film Empire)* (Taipei, Taiwan: Li Wo Ta Film Magazine, 1979), pp. 51–52.

4. "In the past, Shaw productions were thought of as Hong Kong films, as opposed to mainland Chinese and Taiwanese films. Their strong Chinese roots rarely came to mind. Although it is common knowledge that Hong Kong cinema is an integral part of Chinese cinema and that Cantonese and Mandarin films produced in the territory have close links with Chinese traditions, there has been a kind of amnesia regarding the China connection due, understandably, to the emergence of an increasingly distinct 'Hong Kong style' in local cinema and other aspects of society over the last 20 years or so. When re-watching the old films, one is astounded at their strong Chineseness, and one comes to realize that the sense of country and nation has eluded the films of today"; Sek Kei, "Shaw Movie Town's *China Dream* and *Hong Kong Sentiments*," in Wong Ain-ling, *The Shaw Screen*.

MP & GI, Shaws' rival company of the time, steered a different course, and its products were often infused with an urban air. This could be largely explained by the background of MP & GI's director, Loke Wan-tho. Loke grew up in Southeast Asia and received a very exclusive British education. Thus, his key executives were also people with Westernized lifestyles and outlooks. For details, see Law Kar, "A Glimpse of MP & GI's Creative/Production Situation: Some Speculations, Some Doubts," and Shu Kei, "Notes on MP & GI," in Wong Ain-ling, ed., *The Cathay Story* (Hong Kong: Hong Kong Film Archive, 2002).

5. Bai Guang (1920–99) is a legendary singer and actress of the 1940s and 1950s. She was famous for her femme fatale persona and was as unconventional in her real life as on the big screen. If we have to draw a comparison with the West, then we could probably place her in the line of Arletty and Marlene Dietrich, fondly cherished even today both for her bewitching charm and sensuous songs.

6. According to "Mourning Director Tao Chin [Doe Ching]," *Hong Kong Movie News*, no. 43 (July 1969), Doe fell ill in midwinter 1967. Believing himself to be better, he started the shooting of *Twin Blades of Doom* in spring 1968, but in the midst of shooting, his illness recurred, and he was replaced by Yue Feng. Despite treatment in Taiwan and Hong Kong, his body succumbed and he died on May 16, 1969.

7. He Sen, "Yuanlao Daoyan Yue Feng Fangwen Ji" (Veteran Director Yue Feng), *Southern Screen*, no. 132 (February 1969): pp. 42–43.

8. "Fang Shaoshi Xinren Zhipian Jingli: He Yuan Qiufeng Yi Xi Hua" ("A Talk with Yuan Qiufeng: The New Shaws Production Manager"), *Hong Kong Movie News*, no. 54 (June 1970): pp. 18–19; "A Succession of Personnel Changes for Shaws," *The Milky Way Pictorial*, no. 184 (July 1973): pp. 56–57.

9. See Yan Nanxiang, "Yuan Qiufeng Jingli Guo Yiduan Zui Jiannan de Daoyan

shengya" ("Yuan Qiufeng's Most Difficult Period as a Director"), *Cinemart,* no. 44 (August 1973): p. 43.

10. For Ma Xu Weibang's films, see Chen Huiyang's insightful piece, "Ziwo zhi shanghen: lun Ma Xu Weibang" ("Self Wounds: On Ma Xu Weibang"), *Meng ying ji: Zhongguo dianying yinxiang* (*Dreams and Shadows: Chinese Cinema Impressions*) (Taipei, Taiwan: Asian Culture, 1990).

11. "It was the Chinese New Year Eve, [Ma Xu Weibang], on his way to pick some fruit after his dinner at his girlfriend's place in North Point, was knocked down and killed by a reckless bus in a hurry"; Gongsun Lu, *Zhongguo dianying shihua* (*Anecdotes of Chinese Film History*) (Hong Kong: Nantian Shu Ye Gongsi, 1961), p. 209.

12. In *A Study of Modern Chinese Wenyi Cinema*, Cai Guorong stated that from the top ten box office hits lists of the 1950s and 1960s, it is obvious that the majority of Hong Kong productions on the list before 1960 were *wenyi* films. During the years from 1963 to 1965, the *huangmei diao* singing films were most popular, whereas Taiwan *wenyi* films began to pick up momentum in the mid-1960s, a trend that lasted until the mid-1980s. For details, see pp. 46–47.

13. Chor Yuen is a prolific and highly versatile director, and his career has spanned some thirty years, covering genres as varied as *wenyi* and swordplay, realistic and fantastic, costume and contemporary, comic and tragic, and often creating new trends without consciously willing it. He is also one of the few who successfully crossed over from Cantonese to Mandarin cinema in the early 1970s when Cantonese cinema literally died out, joining big studios such as Cathay and Shaw Brothers. Swordplay novelist Gu Long's surrealistic world of the swordsmen provides Chor Yuen with the ideal playground for his romantic imagination.

6

Territorialization and the Entertainment Industry of the Shaw Brothers in Southeast Asia

SAI-SHING YUNG

Shaw Brothers Limited (Incorporated in the Straits
Settlements), 116, Robinson Road, Singapore. Office
and agencies throughout Malaya, Indo-China, Batavia,
Bangkok etc. Studios in Hong Kong. Control over 60
theatres all over Malaya.

—Translation of an advertisement in the
Nanyang Yearbook, Singapore, 1939

Operated by the Shaw Brothers Ltd., the New World
Amusement Park at Penang will officially launch this
month: [In the park] there will be three theaters. One
will show first-run Chinese and Western movies. One
will stage Bangsawan. One will perform Cantonese
and Teochew operas on an alternate basis.

—*Screen Voice* (Singapore), December 1, 1939

Introduction

Shaw Brothers is a complex cultural institution that has produced a wide
range of multicultural entertainments across diverse historical periods and
regional settings. Since the 1930s, the nature of the Shaw Brothers industry
has been cross-regional (Shanghai, Hong Kong, Singapore, Malaya), cross-
genre (opera, cinema, popular song), cross-language (Cantonese, Hokkien,
Teochew, Mandarin), and multiethnic (Chinese, Malay, Indian). From a
Malayan-Singaporean perspective, besides thinking and going global, Shaw
Brothers was always acting and, more important, selling local.

This chapter outlines the history of Shaw Brothers entertainment in Southeast Asia. Special attention is paid to how the company wove a network of amusement parks and movie houses on the Malay Peninsula, thus serving to territorialize their entertainment industry in the region. The term *territorialization* is used to signify the company's strategic commercial action that defined and expanded its spatial boundaries. Such spatial expansion or encroachment sometimes provoked resistance and competition, in turn. An obvious example was the decades-long competition between the Shaw Brothers and Cathay Keris. Closely connected to this web of theaters were the production and supply of local entertainment for local consumption. In this chapter, I use the term *localization* to denote the practice and process of cultural productions of the Shaw Brothers, which endeavored to tap into the unique local demand of the Malayan-Singaporean market. Whether a cultural form is local or not is a relative question, but as defined here, local entertainment refers to such productions as dialect/ethnic movies, regional operas, folk music, and dance. Some examples that will be touched on in this chapter are Cantonese opera, Cantonese cinema, Hokkien opera, Amoy cinema, Bangsawan, and Malay cinema. Moreover, such expression of localism was also embodied in the filmmaking domain through productions that, for instance, adapted local legends or popular tales, exhibited local music and dance, foregrounded local scenes, or exhibited local customs and costumes. I shall address this issue in the final section of the chapter.

The Arrival of Sound, the Emergence of a New Market: Chinese Dialect Cinema in Malaya-Singapore

The marriage between the Shaw Brothers and Chinese dialect cinema dates back to 1932, when Runje Shaw decided to shoot their first Cantonese opera film, *Baijin long* (*White Golden Dragon*). The great success of this Cantonese movie deeply influenced the market strategies of the Shaw Brothers and reshaped their direction of filmmaking up through the mid-1940s.

Before the 1930s, the market for Chinese films in Singapore was dominated by silent films. The first Chinese feature film screened in Singapore was *Orphan Rescues His Grandfather* (*Ming Xing*, 1923). A silent film from Shanghai, it was shown in the Marlborough Theatre, a venue that generally screened only first-run Western movies. This film created a great sensation in the Chinese community and marked a new stage in the history of Chinese cinema in Malaya-Singapore.[1] At about the same time, the Shaw brothers started exploring business opportunities on the Malay Peninsula. Runme Shaw arrived in Singapore in 1924 and later incorporated the Hai Hsin Company.

In modest collaboration with a local film distributor, the Shaw Brothers ran movies in the Empire Theatre (Hua Ying Theatre) located in Tanjong Pagar.[2] Promotional materials of the company indicate that in the late 1920s the Hai Hsin Company imported and distributed silent films produced by Shanghai film companies. Needless to say, the Shanghai Tianyi Company (also known as Unique Film Productions), owned by the Shaw Brothers, was one of the major film distribution sources. In 1927, the Empire screened a series of Tianyi productions, including the sequels of *The Romance of the Three Kingdoms* and *Journey to the West, Goddess of Mercy Attains Transcendence*, and the *Half Pound of Flesh*, which is a Chinese film version of the Shakespearean play *Merchant of Venice*.[3]

The arrival of the talkies changed the marketing and production direction of the Tianyi Company. The invention of sound movies brought about the emergence of a new cinematic genre that made full use of the new acoustic technology in filmmaking. Probably inspired by the success of the Hollywood's film musical *The Jazz Singer* (Warner Brothers, 1927), Shanghai filmmakers began to produce Chinese opera movies that could fully exploit the acoustic quality of this new medium of entertainment.[4] In fact, the 1930s saw a new movement among the Shanghai film studios to capture Chinese opera on film. For instance, in 1933 the Ming Xing Company shot the Peking opera movie *Er Jin Gong* (*Entering the Palace Twice*), whereas the Tianyi shot the *Silang Tan Wu* (*Silang Visits His Mother*).[5] In the same year, Tianyi produced the first Cantonese opera movie in the history of Chinese cinema: *Baijin long, White Golden Dragon*.

In its original production, *Baijin long* was a masterpiece of Cantonese opera performed by the eminent opera actor Sit Kok Sin (Xue Juexian, 1904–56). An adaptation of the Hollywood movie *The Grand Duchess and the Waiter* (1926), the play was tailor-made for Sit by the Cantonese playwright Liang Jintong.[6] The title of the play—*Baijin long*—was taken from the name of the protagonist, a character who was himself named to promote a brand of cigarette in 1930.[7] At that time, *Baijin long* was known as a typical Western dress-style play (*xizhuang xi*) and belonged to one of the modern subgenres of Cantonese opera that began to appear in the late 1920s. Probably a response to the competition from Hollywood, such productions were usually set in an imagined Western country and displayed exotic costumes, foreign lifestyles, and fancy scenery on the traditional Chinese opera stage. *Baijin long* was first presented in Hong Kong in 1930 and was a huge box office success. It proved to be equally successful when Sit Kok Sin and his troupe toured the production in Southeast Asia.[8]

In 1932, Sit Kok Sin was introduced to Runje Shaw in Shanghai, a business meeting that proved to be historic. The result was to change the business strategy of the Tianyi Company. It subsequently adopted a two-pronged policy to produce both Mandarin and Cantonese movies. The company also relocated their studio to Hong Kong and sought to intensify their development of the Southeast Asian market.

In a joint venture with Sit Kok Sin's Nanfang Film Company, Runje Shaw decided to put *Baijin long* on the silver screen. The film was shot in the Tianyi studio at Shanghai and was directed by Runje Shaw himself. Zhou Shilu, who headed the Cantonese Movie Group of Shaw Brothers in the mid-1950s, was the cinematographer.[9] Even before the film premiered in October 1933, film critics in Shanghai already foresaw that this dialect movie would reap huge profits for the Shaw Brothers from the markets of South China and Southeast Asia.[10] The prediction proved to be true. *Baijin long* stormed the box office throughout Cantonese-speaking regions, including Guangzhou, Hong Kong, Macao, and cities in Southeast Asia. In Guangzhou it grossed more than US$85,000, and in Hong Kong the movie played for one whole month and was seen by ten thousand.[11]

As pointed out by film historians, the success of *Baijin long* drew the attention of the Shaw Brothers to the market for dialect cinema in Southeast Asia. Riding the crest of *Baijin long*, the Shaw Brothers invited top Cantonese opera actors to star in subsequent Shaw studio productions that went on to become masterpieces. These included *Mourning of the Chaste Tree Flower* (1934) by Bai Jurong (1892–1974), *Nocturnal Mourning* (1935) by Gui Mingyang (1909–58), *The General of the Dragon City* (1938) by Ma Shizeng (1900–64), and *The Filial Son and the Unworthy Mother* (1939) by Xin Ma Shizeng (1916–97). Moreover, after *Baijin long*, Sit Kok Sin took the leading role in two well-known Cantonese opera movies—*Romance of the Opera* (1934) and *The Deadly Rose* (1937)—for the Shaw Brothers.[12]

Besides opera movies, Shaw Brothers continued to produce nonmusical Cantonese movies at a rapid pace during this period. From 1933 to 1947, Shaw Brothers Studio filmed more than a hundred Cantonese movies.[13] Obviously, one of their target markets was the overseas Chinese. In the late 1930s, the demand for Cantonese cinema in Southeast Asia surged. A reporter for *Screen Voice*, the official magazine of the Shaw Brothers, depicted the prosperous market of Cantonese cinema in Singapore as follows:

> Singapore has a long history of screening Chinese cinema. After the talkies appeared, Cantonese movies enjoyed a uniquely rising popularity in the region. Benefiting from the local audience's associations with their dialect, the market for Cantonese movies expanded to the point where demand for

the films even surpassed their Mandarin counterparts. The burgeoning film companies in Hong Kong that were the major suppliers of Chinese films to Singapore grew prosperous. In addition, their strategies of production also catered to the tastes of the Singapore market.[14]

The rise of such a new market was intimately tied to the familiarity of the dialect made possible by the talkies. The local dialect and familiar stories on the silver screen served as a temporary balm to soothe the homesickness of Chinese immigrants who went to movie houses. Realizing the potential of such a profitable market, the Shaw Brothers established a branch studio in Hong Kong in 1934, namely the Unique Film Production Hong Kong Studio (also known as Tianyi Gangchang), which specialized in the production of Cantonese cinema. The first film produced by the new company was another masterpiece of Cantonese opera, *Mourning of the Chaste Tree Flower*.[15] In 1937, the Hong Kong studio was renamed Nanyang Studio. It continued to supply Cantonese films to Southeast Asian markets after the Tianyi studio at Shanghai had been destroyed when the Japanese invaded Shanghai in the same year.

Strategies of Territorialization

While the Shaw brothers were relocating their film studio to Hong Kong, their entertainment kingdom in Southeast Asia was also taking shape. In 1937, Shaw Brothers Limited was incorporated in the Straits Settlement.[16] Two years later, in a piece of advertising in the *Nanyang Yearbook* published in Singapore, the Shaw Brothers clarified both the geographic and commercial scope of their entertainment industry.[17] The six main business activities itemized in the advertisement were as follows:

1. Developing movie markets in Southeast Asia.
2. Setting up film studios to produce Chinese sound movies.
3. Managing more than sixty theaters in different locations (in Malaya).
4. Operating amusement parks.
5. Selling equipment and accessories for sound movies.
6. Purchasing and distributing Western and Indian cinema.[18]

I have translated item 1 loosely as "film markets in Southeast Asia." In fact, the original expression in Chinese is "film markets in Nanyang *geshu*," literally "various dependent territories in South Seas." Traditionally, Chinese uses the term *South Seas* (Nanyang) to denote Southeast Asia. Nanyang *geshu*, more often known as Nanyang *sishu*, refers to the "four dependent territories in Nanyang," namely British-ruled Malaya-Singapore, Dutch-ruled Indonesia, French-ruled Vietnam, and Thailand.[19]

From this advertisement, we learn that in the 1930s Shaw Brothers set up offices and agencies "throughout Malaya, Indo-China, Batavia, and Bangkok" to oversee their business in these four territories. At least until the outbreak of the Pacific War, the company was able to dominate all the major markets there for Chinese film distribution. In the same era, returns from Cantonese movies screened in these regions covered 50 percent of their production cost.[20] Apparently, Shaw Brothers perceived these four disparate areas as a regional totality, one that constituted the biggest market for entertainment outside of China to be explored and developed.

Hand in hand with such commercial expansion were the construction and consolidation of a network of theaters. Since its formative period in the late 1920s, Shaw Brothers has persistently built up its network of theaters and amusement parks in the region. It is no exaggeration to say that the history of Shaw Brothers between the 1920s and 1960s was in fact a history of movie house construction and acquisition. From its earliest publicity to its most recent Web site (*The Shaw Story*), Shaw Brothers promotional materials consistently highlight its new acquisitions alongside the total number of theaters in different locations in order to emphasize the size and vitality of the Shaw kingdom. As reported in *Screen Voice*, in 1938, the Shaw Brothers acquired the famous Alhambra and Marlborough Theatres of Singapore, each of which was located at Beach Road. The former became the first air-conditioned theater to screen first-run Hollywood movies, whereas the latter specialized in Chinese and Indian cinema.[21]

Theater acquisition and construction projects were not confined to these elegant modern movie houses located in big cities such as Singapore, Penang, Ipoh, and Kuala Lumpur. In the smaller towns and kampongs (rural villages), one could also find more simple theaters with crude wooden benches and ceiling fans. Some of these minor theaters were originally Malay opera houses, retrofitted by the Shaws in joint ventures with the local owners.[22]

As mentioned previously, by 1939 Shaw Brothers controlled more than sixty theaters on the Malay Peninsula. Two years later, in an advertisement in *Sin Chew Jit Poh* (*The Singapore Daily*), published on January 1, 1941, Shaw Brothers presented the list of movies screened in their theater circuit during the New Year. As shown in this advertisement, their network in the early 1940s consisted of sixty-nine theaters positioned in urban and town centers in peninsular Malaya. They included Singapore (eight theaters), Penang (six), Kuala Lumpur (four), Malacca (three), Ipoh (six), Seremban (three), Johore

Bahru, Muar, Kluang, Taiping (two), Telok Anson, Sungei Patani (two), Batu Pahat (two), Kuala Ketil, Kulim, and others in Port Swettenham, Kuantan, and so on.[23] The genres of film that were shown included Chinese, Western, Malay, and Indian. The geographic distribution of the theaters is represented in map 6.1.

After World War II, acquisition efforts accelerated, and by the 1950s the number of theaters totaled more than a hundred. During the Korean War, prices escalated for Malayan-produced rubber and tin. The Singapore-Malaya economy benefited from such a sudden demand, and the entertainment in-

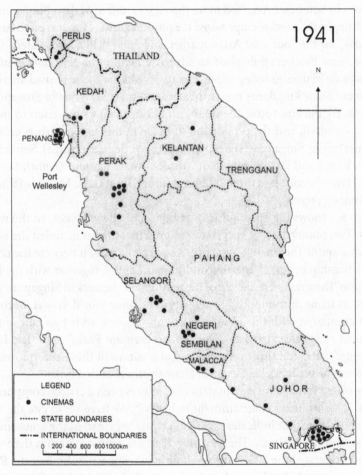

Shaw theater circuit in 1941.

dustry boomed. In the newly launched movie magazine *Southern Screen,* one article gives an update on recent developments in the Shaw Brothers empire: "[In 1958, the Shaw Brothers,] operating more than 100 theaters in Malaya, Singapore, North Borneo, Vietnam, Thailand, Hong Kong, and Taiwan, connected with 200 to 300 theaters. Producing films through studios in Hong Kong and Singapore, shooting Mandarin, Cantonese, and movies of other dialects prevailing in Southeast Asia."[24] In that decade, the company initiated a theater-a-month expansion project. Using S$1.5 million, they established twenty-two theaters within two years before 1958.[25] The number of new theaters totaled 124 in 1959, after completion of the famous Globe Theatre in the Great World Amusement Park in Singapore.[26] It was reported that this entertainment network in Southeast Asia "fed more than 4,500 staff in Malaya/Singapore."[27] Interestingly, the passage emphasized the production of "Cantonese and Amoy cinemas" for the Southeast Asian market, an issue I shall address later.

The Shaw Brothers published an advertisement in the *New Born Malaya* to celebrate Malaysia's independence in 1957.[28] Similar to the 1941 ad, this one noted the Shaw kingdom's major theaters and their locations in Singapore-Malaya. By the late 1950s, the total number of theaters has risen to more than a hundred, and the proportion of those in the region's urban centers was increasing: Singapore (sixteen), Muar (two), Segamat (three), Seremban (two), Klang and Port Swettenham (three), Kuala Lumpur (eight), Sungei Patani (two), Alor Star (three), Taiping (four), Ipoh (six), Malacca (three), and Penang (seven).

Map 6.2 shows the geographic distribution of Shaw theaters in the mid-1950s. Two points deserve special attention. First, the list included the well-known Capitol Theatre of Singapore. Acquired in 1946, it became the company's flagship theater.[29] The air-conditioned Capitol, together with the Rex and Lido Theatres, were the three best-equipped theaters in Singapore and served as icons of modernity in the city-state after World War II. Second, when compared with the ad of 1941, the 1957 notice adds two new entertainment categories, listed as "The Ten Amusement Parks" and "The Four Cabarets." Such additions reflect the vital position of these entertainment locales in the business landscape of Shaw Brothers at that time.

The operation of amusement parks has always been a crucial component of the Shaw Brothers entertainment industry.[30] We have yet to cite the historical evidence that indicates when Shaw Brothers started the amusement park side of the business. The *Nanyang Yearbook* from 1938 notes the Shaw Brothers operated the following entertainment venues: "Bukit Bintang Park at Kuala Lumpur, Jubilee Park at Ipoh, City Park at Malacca, Coronation

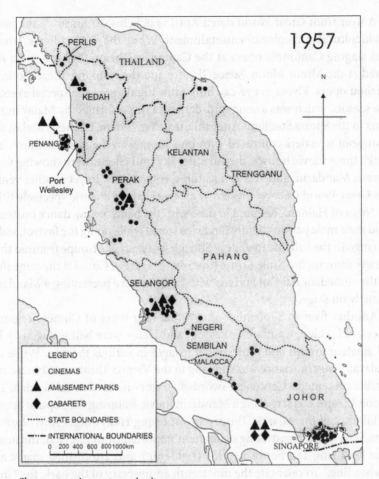

Shaw entertainment empire in 1957.

Park at Taiping, Grand Amusement Park at Alor Star and New World Park at Singapore in conjunction with Mr. Ong Peng Hock."[31] In 1940, Shaw Brothers acquired the Great World Amusement Park in Singapore, after which it held control of the country's two key amusement parks up through the 1980s.

These amusement parks remain a significant part of Singaporeans' collective memory of leisure and entertainment from their time growing up. Since the 1920s, the parks have provided the local population a wide range of entertainment, including vernacular operas, storytelling, dancing, music, magic shows, revues, movies, cabarets, game booths, mechanical games, and even gambling stalls.

A flyer from Great World dated April 1948 helps demonstrate the park's multicultural and colorful entertainment. While the Valiant Eagle Troupe was staging Cantonese opera at the Cantonese Theatre, Peking opera featured at the Minor Moon Palace Theatre and the Nanking Theatre offered Fuzhou opera. Flyers in eye-catching fonts highlighted the special event of the season, which was a song-and-dance revue performed by Malay movie stars in the Sports Stadium. After this, teams of Indian, Chinese, Malay, and European wrestlers competed with one another in the same stadium. The park's three movie houses, the Atlantic, Sky, and Globe, were showing Cantonese, Mandarin, and Western features, respectively. In yet another venue, the Great World Cabaret presented an exotic and romantic spectacle titled "A Night of Hainan." Keeping in time with the band, young dance hostesses held their male patrons tightly (and vice versa) while doing the foxtrot, waltz, or tango in the hall. Meanwhile, a Shanghai-style revue troupe featured their variety show on the Xinle Ko-tai (the Song Terrace of Ciros) at the same time as the comedian Bai Yan and his wife Ye Qing were presenting a Mandarin comedy on stage.

Another flyer in September shows that four types of Chinese regional opera—Hokkien, Cantonese, Peking, and Han—were being staged by local amateur groups and professional troupes in various theaters. While the Malayan *ronggeng* dance was showing in the Vienna Theatre, a Chinese storyteller presented a Cantonese swordsman story in the Central Garden. The Globe Theatre was screening a Mandarin movie featuring the popular actress Li Lihua, and the Atlantic Theatre was showing Hollywood's *Adventures of Tom Sawyer*. Demonstrating equipment imported from England, the magician Dr. Liang Tan performed his frightening and astonishing magic act, "Beheading." To celebrate the nineteenth anniversary of the park, the Great World Cabaret held special parties in which "all the musicians of the dance band will play extravagantly; all the dance hostesses will dance wildly; the whole atmosphere will be extremely hot; the guests will be entertained unrestrainedly."[32]

The Shaw Brothers amusement parks in Singapore-Malaya were where a wide range of local entertainment and native art forms could be exhibited and viewed. These local art forms were juxtaposed with other more Westernized amusements, such as Hollywood movies, ballroom dancing, and revue shows. In other words, the amusement parks were the cultural space in which local/global, regional/transnational, and native/Western entertainments converged and influenced one another. Shaw Brothers served as the cultural-business institution that brought these multicultural amusements together. Furthermore, at least since the 1930s, Shaw Brothers has financed a constant stream of popular movie stars and opera actors and actresses from Hong Kong to tour or give single-location performances in their amusement parks across Singapore-Malaya. In addition, theater audiences in the amusement parks were fed an unending diet of Mandarin and Cantonese movies that Shaw Brothers produced in their Shanghai and Hong Kong studios. In such a way, the whole circuit of amusement parks and theaters on the peninsula were further linked to the Shaw Brothers network in Shanghai and Hong Kong.

As mentioned previously, Shaw Brothers was the major institution backing local entertainment in the amusement parks. Not only did they play a significant role in providing the venues, organizing the programs, and promoting the events, they also provided financial subsidies for the local artists to form and maintain their troupes. According to the research of Tan Sooi Beng, since the 1930s Shaw Brothers has offered financial support to the troupes of Bangsawan. For example, Menah Yem, a Bangsawan actor in the 1930s, received a loan of $5,000 from Shaw Brothers to start his troupe. In return, he was asked to sign a contract with the company to perform in all the Shaw Brothers' amusement parks throughout Malaya. The rental of halls, printing of tickets and posters, and housing for performers were all taken care of by the company.[33]

In order to provide a constant supply of new faces and fresh entertainment to the chain of amusement parks, local artists and their troupes were absorbed into the company. They were either acquired or subsidized by Shaw Brothers to tour in the big cities on the Malay Peninsula, moving from stage to stage along the company's circuit of amusement parks and theaters. I cite another example to illustrate this commercial practice of internalization.

Mr. Gwee Bock Huat has been the manager of the famous Singapore Hokkien opera troupe—Sin Sai Hong Troupe—since the 1940s. In an interview, Mr. Gwee told me that after World War II his troupe was hired by Shaw Brothers to tour Hokkien opera in peninsular Malaya. From 1946 to 1953, they traveled throughout major cities, including Singapore, Kuala Lumpur, Malacca, Penang, Alor Star, Ipoh, Taiping, and Klang, performing at the parks operated by Shaw Brothers. Besides covering travel expenses, Shaw Brothers subsidized them to a certain extent. Each park would have had a Hokkien troupe stationed there for two to three weeks, but Cantonese opera troupes usually stayed for much longer, anywhere up to three to six months.[34] In other words, not only did the Shaw Brothers acquire the so-called hardware—amusement parks and theaters—they also internalized the so-called software related to their entertainment industry, the most important being the talented local performers and performing troupes that received Shaw Brothers sponsorship.[35]

Once absorbed, or internalized, into the corporate family, these local artists, besides performing their specialized art forms in the amusement parks, were invited to play a part in the mainstream filmmaking business of Shaw Brothers. For example, the Malayan actors of Bangsawan were recruited by Malay Film Production of Shaw Brothers to star in Malay movies, whereas the Bangsawan dancers and musical accompanists were employed as choreographers, musicians, composers, and performers in the productions.[36] Meanwhile, the Mandarin-speaking actors belonging to the Chinese revues were recruited into Mandarin cinema productions. For example, two performers from the Golden Star Revue, Ma Jun and Ye Qing (Mrs. Bai Yan), were featured in the first Mandarin movie produced by Shaw Brothers in Singapore after World War II, namely *The Song of Singapore* (*Singapura di Waktu Malam*, 1947).

Localism after World War II: From The Song of Singapore to The Merdeka Bridge

The Song of Singapore and *My Second Homeland* (*Di'er guxiang*) were two Mandarin movies guest-directed by Wu Cun, a director from Mainland China, shortly after the end of the Pacific War. As recalled by Ye Qing, a revue actress who participated in the filming of *The Song of Singapore,* the movie was shot in a Singapore studio meant for Malay film productions.[37] Such a studio would most likely have been the Malay Film Production located at 8 Jalan Ampas. This is also the studio where the first Malay film of the Shaw Brothers, *Singapore at Night* (*Singapura di Waktu Malam*), was made after the war.[38] Interestingly, this studio managed to make two movies simultaneously, one in Mandarin and one in Malay, and both of their story settings were related to Singapore.

The narrative of *The Song of Singapore* begins on the eve of the Pacific War in 1941. It tells the stories of three women of very different personalities by portraying their experiences during the Japanese occupation. The film captures Singapore's Dark Ages during World War II and depicts the courageous deeds of the protagonists in the anti-Japanese campaign. At that time, the major selling points of the movie were that it conveyed a "totally Nanyang style" and a "fully Nanyang atmosphere." The promotional materials highlighted it as "An epitome of the dreadful history of Singapore during the Japanese Occupation" and "The portrayal of the heroic deeds of the anti-Japanese army of Malaya."[39] In this postwar movie, local style, local flavor, and local character were foregrounded and emphasized. Due to limited source materials, the plot of *My Second Homeland* cannot be summarized here, but judging from the title of the film, the background would have likely also been set in Singapore-Malaya.

Regarding the localism of *The Song of Singapore*, two points are worth noting. Although the film highlights Nanyang style and Nanyang atmosphere, the identity of being a Chinese national was still predominant in the movie. This was apparent in the promotional material's claim, "Elevating the cultural standard of *huaqiao*" and "Consolidating the film industry of *huaqiao*." The term *huaqiao* denotes the Chinese overseas, with the connotative meaning that they are currently "residing guests" in a foreign country and will ultimately return to their homeland in China. The title of the second movie, *My Second Homeland*, evokes this mentality and identity even more directly. Singapore was known as the second homeland of these "guest-residents" from China. (Needless to say, their first homeland was China.) Such a sense of identity among the Chinese in Singapore began to change in the mid-1950s.

Second, as was mentioned earlier, Cantonese cinema had occupied a significant market in Southeast Asia before World War II. The first Chinese movie produced in the Singapore studio was not a Cantonese film, however, but a Mandarin one. In fact, from 1945 to 1950, the Nanyang Studio in Hong Kong filmed fewer than ten Cantonese movies. From 1950 onward, Shaw Brothers produced no Cantonese films, until they made *The Opera Boat in Singapore* in 1955.[40] After the war, the output of Cantonese cinema dropped substantially. This shift of production direction was related to changes in the Southeast Asian market.

This new market development was mentioned in an article, titled "The Production Direction of the Shaw Brothers." Published in *Screen Voice* in 1947, the article reveals the Shaw Brothers' assessment of the postwar market for Cantonese cinema:

> Before World War II, the profit return yielded from the Southeast Asia (the Four Dependent Territories in Nanyang) was enough to cover 50 percent of the production cost. Now the situation has changed. Because of wars and unstable situations, the markets in Indonesia and Vietnam have shrunk. Moreover, Singapore and Thailand have suffered from a sluggish economy, experiencing a high unemployment rate. Moreover, today most of the Chinese in Singapore-Malaya can understand Mandarin. Their support to the Cantonese cinema is not as wholehearted as before. Therefore, the sale price of the Cantonese cinema can only cover 25 percent [of the production cost]. . . . Nowadays, the only profitable market of Cantonese cinema is Hong Kong.[41]

These new political and economic conditions brought about the decline of the Cantonese film market in Southeast Asia. Besides, Mandarin had started to become more popular in the region. These factors contributed to the stagnation of Cantonese film production in the Shaw studios. In the late 1940s, the Shaw Brothers revised their earlier two-pronged policy and concentrated primarily on the making of Mandarin films. Nonetheless, the industry faced yet more changes in the mid-1950s.

In 1955, the Shaw Brothers Studio in Singapore filmed their first Cantonese movie, *The Opera Boat in Singapore* (*Xingdao hongchuan*). After a hiatus of almost ten years, Cantonese cinema now started to return to the Shaw studios. Starring three young Cantonese opera artists from Hong Kong, Li Wensuo, Li Baoying, and Zhong Lirong, the film was shot on location in Singapore and mostly completed in local studios. The original Chinese title of the film literally means "Red Boat of Singapore." In the past, Cantonese opera troupes traveled along rivers to perform in the Guangdong region of China, and traditionally the whole troupe lived together on a red boat. The "red boat" thus became a symbol of Cantonese opera culture. Judging from its title, the story content of the movie must have revolved around Cantonese opera troupes in Singapore. Interestingly, in 1933 the Shaw Brothers had successfully expanded the market for Cantonese film in Southeast Asia with their Cantonese opera film *Baijin long*. After more than twenty years, they were to repeat the same market strategy, using the same cinematic genre— Cantonese opera film—to spearhead the revival.

It is no accident that *The Opera Boat in Singapore* was made during this particular period, nor was its production a unique occurrence. The mid-1950s witnessed a trend toward localization in the Shaw studios: presenting and selling native cultures, local dialects, and regional scenery in their filmmaking. Such an emphasis on cinematic localism was embodied in different domains of production. *The Opera Boat in Singapore* was only one manifestation of this prevailing trend. I cite more cases to illustrate this new wave of localism that took place in the mid-1950.

In 1955, the same year *The Opera Boat in Singapore* premiered, the Shaw Brothers established their Cantonese Movie Group in Hong Kong. Headed by Zhou Shilu, this new unit specialized in the filming of Cantonese cinema. Their first work, *Pearl of the Island,* was produced in 1957 and starred Pearl Au Ka-wei.[42] The following year, the Shaw Brothers shot their first Amoy movie in Singapore, which initiated a new production line to make Amoy cinema.[43] The target audiences for this dialect-based cinema were the Hokkien Chinese of Southeast Asia. Moreover, in 1959 the Cantonese Movie

Group in Hong Kong produced three Cantonese movies that were all shot on location in Singapore at the same time. These were *The Merdeka Bridge* (*Duliqiao zhi lian*), *When Durians Bloom* (*Liulian piao xiang*), and *Bride from Other Town* (*Guobu xinniang*). All featured Patricia Lam Fung, the most popular Cantonese movie star in the company.

When Durians Bloom narrates a love story between a native Nyonya and a Chinese male. Needless to say, the movie's leading Nyonya role was portrayed by Lam Fung. Sporting a stylish *kebaya*, she performs a lively Malayan folk dance at the beginning of the movie that was taught to her especially by a Malay instructor in Singapore.[44] As an aside, in the same scene she sings the theme song of the movie, "When Durians Bloom," which went on to become a classic in the history of Cantonese popular song.[45] In *Bride from Other Town*, Lam Fung features as a Chinese girl from Hong Kong who falls in love with a trishaw driver. The film was shot on location in the Great World Amusement Park in Singapore. The actress, this time dressed in her plain Cantonese-styled *sam-fu*, sells cigarettes from a stand outside the park. Another famous scenic spot in Singapore—the Merdeka Bridge—is captured in the third movie of the same title. It narrates the romance between a sing-song girl and a painter, the latter played by Cheung Ying Choy. Partly influenced by Hollywood's *Waterloo Bridge* (Warner Brothers, 1940), the final scene shows Lam Fung's attempt to commit suicide by jumping into the sea. Unlike the tragic death of Vivien Leigh in the Hollywood version, however, Lam Fung is rescued and thereafter lives happily with her lover.

The Merdeka Bridge was titled after a newly completed construction project in Singapore of the same name and was redolent with political and cultural meaning in the era of the 1950s. In Malay, *merdeka* means "independence." The bridge was built to commemorate the political struggle in Malaya in the 1950s that led to the country's eventual independence from Britain in 1957. It served to represent the triumph of the Singapore-Malaya people over the forces of Western colonialism and imperialism. The outcome of the struggle gave birth to a new national identity and inspired pride among members of this newly independent nation in regard to the local and ethnic cultures that constituted it. Thus, the emergence of localism in Shaw Brothers productions of the mid-1950s should be read in the context of this newly emerged cultural identity and national pride.

Such local sensibilities are also manifested in the domain of Mandarin cinema of the time. From 1956 to 1960, Shaw Brothers Studios shot at least five Mandarin movies set in Singapore-Malaya, including *A Lonely Heart* (1956, starring Chao Lei and Lucilla You Min), *An Affair in Malaya* (1958, with Tang Dan, Paul Chang Chung, and Zaiton), *Black Gold* (1959, with Paul Chang Chung and Shi Ying), *Rendezvous in the South Seas* (1960, with Peter Chan Ho, Ting Ning, and Paul Chang Chung), and *Malayan Affair* (1960, with Paul Chang Chung, Betty Loh Ti, and Margaret Tu Chuan).[46] As mentioned previously, the Shaw Brothers' business orientation was that "locality sells." Thus, most of these movies were shot on location in Singapore-Malaya. For example, *Black Gold,* made by the Filipino American director Rolf Bayer, was shot in Hong Kong and Singapore as well as in Malaya's Cameron Highlands and capitol city, Kuala Lumpur.[47]

Moreover, *An Affair in Malaya* serves as an interesting example of the cross-regional and multiethnic character of filmmaking in the Shaw studios. The screenplay was written by the Chinese writer Chua Boon Hean. Featuring both Chinese and Malayan movie stars, the movie narrates the triangular relationships of two women—one Malay and one Chinese—and a Chinese male, all of whom reside in a Malayan village. The Indian director, Phani Majumdar, originally a director of Malay films, was invited to direct this Chinese movie, for which he assumed the Chinese name Ma Chundai. Previously Majumdar had directed a Malay film titled *Masharakat Pinchang* (*Crippled Society*), which was an adaptation of the Chinese novel *Jiaofeng Yeyu* and was also written by Chua Boon Hean. It seems that *An Affair in Malaya* was never screened in Hong Kong. This could be explained by its Singapore-Malaya setting and casting, which would not have attracted moviegoers in Hong Kong.[48]

A promotional article for *An Affair in Malaya* in *Southern Screen* magazine at the time of the film's release details the latest developments of Shaw Brothers. Reading between the lines, we can detect some of the political and cultural factors contributing to the emphasis on localism in their filmmaking. The passage reads, "Because of the latest changes of situation in Singapore-Malaya, in 1958 [Shaw Brothers] has worked out a plan of development. First, we expand the studio in Singapore. Second, we establish a large and modernized studio in Hong Kong. . . . We have shot two Mandarin movies— *The Black Gold* and *An Affair in Malaya*—in the Singapore studio, which has planned to film Mandarin cinema since the end of last year."[49] During the Cold War era, politics was generally taboo in Hong Kong's mass media, and this was especially true for entertainment magazines such as *Southern Screen.* Thus, the author of the article had to make his points in a subtle manner by toning down the independent movement of Singapore-Malaya into "changes of situation." Still, from this passage we notice two points. First, the new wave of producing "local" in the Shaw studios was closely connected to the political and social movements taking place on the Malay Peninsula in the mid-1950s. As mentioned before, the birth of a new nation had brought about new cultural pride and local consciousness. Second, in order to feed such a newly emerged "local" market, Shaw Brothers expanded its studios in Singapore and Hong Kong. Formerly, location shots filmed in Singapore had to be sent back to Hong Kong for processing and editing. Now, with the completion of Shaw's ultramodern and well-quipped processing unit in Singapore, this work could be done locally.[50]

The ethnic film genre that was most intimately connected to issues of nationalism and local identity was Malay cinema.[51] The 1950s to the early 1960s were known as the golden era of Malay cinema, during which time more than 250 Malay movies were released. Shaw Brothers and Cathay-Keris were the two key sponsors of this substantial repertoire of Malay films. Before 1939, Shaw Brothers' Malay productions were mainly shot in their Hong Kong studio.[52] In 1939, they set up the Malay Film Production unit in Singapore to produce Malay cinema for the Southeast Asian market. Promoted as "A Solid Fort of Malayan Cultural Enterprise," by 1958 the studio had produced more than a hundred Malayan movies. It had also made one Cantonese and five Mandarin features, besides providing Malay dialogue for scores of foreign films from places such as Egypt, India, and the Philippines. The films thus produced were supplied not only to several hundred of Shaw's theaters in Malaya but also to the much more widespread markets of Indonesia.[53] Malay films during this period represented a newly discovered form of expression, one that was tied to oral storytelling traditions of the past while also creating a new, modern identity. The iconic hero of the genre, actor P. Ramlee, saw himself as a social reformer who was using the developing art form of film to promote social ideas of modernity and independence.

Conclusion

Shaw Brothers has become an object of contemporary interest for scholars of Asian cinema and popular culture, who have focused, by far, mainly on the company's Mandarin cinema. At least two areas have been thus neglected: Malay cinema and Chinese-dialect cinema, the latter including both Cantonese and Amoy movies. These understudied cinematic genres had two golden eras during the 1930s and 1950s. Moreover, they shared the same regional market in Southeast Asia.

For the multiethnic populations of the Malayan Peninsula, the variety of entertainment supplied by Shaw Brothers went far beyond Mandarin movies.

Since the 1930s, Shaw Brothers has fundamentally shaped inhabitants' recreational and leisure life in the region. Drawing upon evidence from various source materials, this chapter has surveyed the history of the Shaw Brothers as they developed their entertainment industry in Southeast Asia. I have focused on two interrelated aspects in my analysis: (1) how the Shaw Brothers territorialized their enterprise through strategic positioning, first by steadily weaving, and then spatially expanding, a network of amusement parks and movie houses in the region; and (2) how they produced and exhibited different forms of local entertainment for the consumption of local markets. I have delineated the historical profile—rise and fall, wax and wane—of Cantonese cinema in Shaw Brothers studios. I have also addressed the multicultural range of entertainment exhibited in the amusement parks and the expressions of cinematic localism after World War II. As I have emphasized, these strategies and features of production have been driven by market forces. Shaw Brothers has been ever alert to changing conditions so as to readily adjust to emerging political situations, changing economic conditions, and new cultural value orientations of the region.

Notes

This chapter was partly funded by the Academic Research Fund, FASS, NUS for my project "Chinese Opera in Singapore (1887–1937): Perspectives from Social History and Ethnomusicology" (R-102-000-010-107). I have benefited from discussions with colleagues, including Henry Yeung, Lily Kong, and Timothy Barnard. I would like to thank Law Kar, Wong Ainling, and Monique Shiu for helping me access the collections of movie magazines at the Hong Kong Film Archive. I also thank Miss Lee Li Kheng, Yap Wee Cheng, Jessie Yak, and Yee Sok Kiang for providing assistance at various stages of the research.

Unless otherwise stated, all Chinese-English translations are my own.

1. Yu Shukun, ed., *Nanyang Nianjian* (*Nanyang Yearbook*) (Singapore: Nanyang Siang Pau, 1951), section 2 "Singapore," chapter 16, *yi*, p. 199.

2. *Hai Hsin* 1 (1927), 9 (1927).

3. *Hai Hsin* 1 (1927), 9 (1927).

4. *The Jazz Singer* was shown in Singapore in 1929. See *The Shaw Story*, p. 2.

5. *Ling Lung* (*Lin Loon*) 82 (January 18, 1933), p. 92.

6. Interestingly, this Hollywood movie is also an adaptation of a play of the same title performed in the Lyceum Theater, New York, in 1925; see Basil Rathbone: Master of Stage and Screen, *The Grand Duchess and the Waiter*, available at http://www .basilrathbone.net/theater/grandduchess.htm. Here, we can see a history of adaptation and remake of the same story from a Broadway play to a Hollywood movie and then localized to Cantonese opera and Cantonese opera film.

7. Part of the promotion project of the Nanyang Brother Tobacco Company was to use Cantonese opera to advertise its brands. On the first night of staging *Baijin long*, the company distributed Bai Jin Long cigarettes for free outside the theater. See Lai Bojiang, *Xue Juexian yiyuan chunqiu* (*A History of Sit Kok Sin's Artistic Life*) (Shanghai: Shanghai Wenhua chubanshe, 1993), pp. 70–74. Under the brand Jin Long (Gold Dragon), there were two types of packaging, Bai Jin Long and Hong Jin Long, which literally meant "Gold Dragon brand of white pack" and "Gold Dragon brand of red pack." The Bai Jin Long brand had ten cigarettes in each pack, and the Hong Jin Long brand had twelve. These two cigarette brands were sold in the market at least until the 1950s.

8. Lai Bojiang, *Xue Juexian yiyuan chunqiu*, pp. 97–98.

9. According to recollections of Tang Xiaodan, who was the set designer of *Baijin long*, Runje Shaw was supposed to direct. Runje fell ill at the last minute, however, and Tang was assigned to direct this Cantonese opera film instead. Quoted from Zhou Chengren, "Shanghai's Unique Film Production and Hong Kong's Early Cinema," trans. Stephen Teo, in Wong Ainling, ed., *The Shaw Screen: A Preliminary Study* (Hong Kong: Hong Kong Film Archive, 2003), p. 32.

10. *Ling Lung* 80 (December 28, 1932), p. 1434. The film premiered in Shanghai during the Mid-Autumn Festival of 1933. It was not well received in Shanghai and was ranked at a grade of "C+," which was the second lowest position on the list of "A Ranking List of Chinese and Western Movies in These Two Weeks." *Ling Lung* 116 (October 18, 1933), p. 1983.

11. *The Shaw Story*, p. 2. Yu Mo-wan, *Xianggang dianying bashi nian* (*Eighty Years of Hong Kong Cinema*) (Hong Kong: Regional Council, Hong Kong, 1994), p. 17.

12. Yu Mo-wan, Angel Shing, and Lee Chun Wai, "The Shaw Filmography," in Wong Ainling, *The Shaw Screen*, pp. 346–52.

13. Ibid.

14. *Screen Voice* 60, January 1940. *Screen Voice* (Singapore) was launched in the late 1930s and was edited by Chua Boon Hean. The Shaw Brothers launched *Screen Voice* (Hong Kong) in the 1950s. In this chapter, all the references to *Screen Voice* (hereafter abbreviated as *SV*) are cited from *Screen Voice* (Singapore).

15. Yu Mo-wan et al., "The Shaw Filmography," p. 346.

16. Yu Shukun, *Nanyang Nianjian*, section 2 "Singapore," chapter 16, *yi*, p. 199.

17. Fu Wumen, ed., *Nanyang Nianjian* (*Nanyang Yearbook*) (Singapore: Nanyang Siang Pau, 1939), appendix, p. 80.

18. Ibid.

19. Another version is Malaya-Singapore, Indonesia, Vietnam, and the U.S.-ruled Philippines.

20. *SV* 119, March 15, 1947.

21. *SV* 19, April 16, 1938.

22. *The Shaw Story*, p. 6.

23. I am indebted to my research assistant, Ms. Wee Tong Bao, in drawing my attention to this piece of source material.

24. *Southern Screen* (hereafter referred to as *SS*) 2, January 1958, p. 3.

25. *SS* 10, December 1958, p. 9.

26. *SS* 13, March 1959.

27. *SS* 2, January 1958, p. 3.

28. Chen Jimou, Song Yunzheng, et al., eds., *Malaiya xinzhi* (*New Born Malaya*) (Kuala Lumpur: Zhongguo Bao, 1957).

29. *The Shaw Story*, p. 9.

30. For a study of the history of amusement parks in Singapore, refer to Jurgen Rudolph, "Amusements in the Three 'Worlds'," in Sanjay Krishnan, ed., *Looking at Culture* (Singapore, 1996), pp. 21–33; Yung Sai-shing, Chan Kwok Bun, "Leisure, Pleasure and Consumption: Ways of Entertaining Oneself," in Chan Kwok Bun and Tong Chee Kiong, eds., *Past Times: A Social History of Singapore* (Singapore: Times Editions, 2003), pp. 153–81; *The Shaw Story*, p. 4.

31. Fu Wumen, *Nanyang Nianjian*, appendix, p. 80.

32. I thank Mr. Bai Yan in providing me with these two pieces of source material.

33. Tan Sooi Beng, *Bangsawan: A Social and Stylistic History of Popular Malay Opera* (Singapore: Oxford University Press, 1993), p. 31.

34. Personal interview, July 24, 2003.

35. The two flyers I have analyzed were produced by the Shaw Brothers printing house. The company formed its own publishing concern to print tickets, handbills, flyers, and pamphlets and to publish newspapers, movie story booklets, and movie magazines. Examples of the latter include *Amusement, Screen Voice*, and *Southern Screen*. This is another example of business internalization.

36. Tan Sooi Beng, *Bangsawan*, p. 167.

37. A series of interviews conducted with Mr. Bai Yan and Ye Qing (Mrs. Bai Yan) between 1997 and 1998.

38. Jan Uhde and Yvonne Ng Uhde, *Latent Images: Film in Singapore* (Oxford: Oxford University Press, 2000), p. 6.

39. *SV* 117 (special issue on *The Song of Singapore*), January 15, 1947.

40. Yu Mo-wan et al., "The Shaw Filmography," p. 352–54.

41. "The Production Direction of the Shaw Brothers," *SV* 119, March 15, 1947.

42. Yu Mo-wan et al., "The Shaw Filmography," p. 355.

43. *SS* 6, May 1958, p. 31.

44. *SS* 15, May 1959, p. 72.

45. For a discussion of the production of Cantonese popular song and the "image of youth" of Lam Fung in the Shaws' Cantonese films, see Yung Sai-shing, "The Joy of Youth, Made in Hong Kong: Patricia Lam Fung and Shaws' Cantonese Films," in Wong Ain-ling, *The Shaw Screen*, pp. 211–35.

46. Based on *Southern Screen* and Yu Mo-wan et al., "The Shaw Filmography," pp. 355–60.

47. *SS* 4, March 1958, p. 23.

48. Another Mandarin movie titled *Malayan Affair* was produced in the Hong Kong studios. Directed by Ho Meng-hua in 1960, the film is an adaptation of Leo Tolstoy's Anna Karenina. Featuring Betty Loh Ti and Margaret Tu Chuan, this Hong Kong version was also shot on location in Singapore. See *The Great Wall Pictorial* (*Changcheng huabao*) 104 (May 1960). I am indebted to Wong Ainling, of the Hong Kong Film Archive, in providing me with this reference.

49. *SS* 5, April 1958, p. 21.

50. *SS* 13, March 1959, p. 64.

51. For a study of Malay cinema, see William van der Heide, *Malaysian Cinema, Asian Film: Border Crossings and National Culture* (Amsterdam, Netherlands: University of Amsterdam Press, 2002); Jan Uhde and Yvonne Ng Uhde, *Latent Images: Film in Singapore* (Singapore: Oxford University Press, 2000); Rohayati Paseng Barnard and Timothy P. Barnard, "The Ambivalence of P. Ramlee: *Penarek Beca* and *Bujang Lapok* in Perspective," *Asian Cinema* 13, no. 2 (2002): pp. 9–23.

52. *SV* 55, October 16, 1939.

53. *SS* 7, June 1958, p. 3.

7

The Shaw Brothers'
Malay Films

TIMOTHY P. BARNARD

From the late 1940s until the mid-1960s, Shaw Brothers was a dominant force in Malay cinema. With a studio in Singapore and a vast network of movie houses in Malaya, Shaw Brothers executives oversaw the production of films that bear little resemblance to the product for which they are best known around the world. The more than 150 films the studio produced had little or no martial arts, and only a handful were based on tales from China. In contrast, the Malay films produced in Singapore, as well as a few shot in Hong Kong, reflected Southeast Asian cultural conventions as well as interactions with the other major film-producing society in Asia: India. The initial relationship Malay writers and actors had with Indian directors led to a "golden age of Malay cinema" but also led to an increased advocacy among Malay participants in the filmmaking process that reflected growing nationalistic sentiments. Although these films are mostly forgotten in the story of the Shaw Brothers' influence on Asian cinema, they are remembered with great fondness in the Malay community, holding a place of significance within its social memory. The films from this fertile period are still discussed on a daily basis among Malays in Singapore and Malaysia, are constantly shown on television, and even the stars of the films—many quietly living in retirement—are still revered.[1] Shaw Brothers' Malay films may have been an attempt to sell local product to local audiences, but they also reflected larger events and cultural influences that the region experienced in the period following World War II.

It is doubtful that Runme Shaw planned on producing Malay films when he arrived in Singapore in 1924. Focusing his efforts on the importation and distribution of Chinese films, he slowly built up a network of cinemas that was centered on the Malay Peninsula. Runme Shaw concentrated on the administrative and financial side of the business, whereas his brother Run Run, who arrived in the late 1920s, was more interested in film production. The two brothers were able to parlay the growing popularity of Cantonese films in Southeast Asia in the 1930s into an entertainment empire that included not only movie houses but also amusement parks that featured live orchestras and theater performances as well as movies. Shaw Brothers Limited was incorporated in the Straits Settlements in 1937, and by the 1950s it operated more than a hundred cinemas throughout Southeast Asia, with the Capitol Theatre in Singapore being its flagship.[2]

Despite the focus on film distribution to their cinemas in cities with large Chinese populations, Shaw Brothers also owned movie houses in areas where many Malay speakers lived. To provide product for these cinemas, as well as for more portable cloth screens and projectors on the back of trucks that provided entertainment in kampongs (villages), Shaw Brothers founded Malay Film Productions (MFP) in 1939. Prior to World War II, MFP produced eight films. The films were based on Bangsawan, or popular Malay theater, which was a new form of entertainment that had arisen in the late nineteenth century throughout Malaya. Heavily influenced by Parsi theater, Bangsawan performers in the late nineteenth century quickly replaced the original Hindustani language featured in the productions with Malay-language songs, and its popularity grew. By the early twentieth century, Bangsawan attracted a multiethnic audience in urban centers. By the 1930s, many Bangsawan troops performed in Shaw-owned amusement parks, thus the filming of their performances was easily arranged.[3]

Little is known about the prewar productions of Shaw Brothers' MFP studio, beyond their titles and a few general impressions from those who viewed the films. For example, it is known that a Chinese man and woman, named "Miss Yen" and Wan Hai Ling, directed all eight films.[4] According to Jamil Sulong, a well-known director and writer whose career began in the 1950s, these films were simple "household dramas" (*drama rumahtangga*) that involved both love stories and plenty of scares. The rarity of seeing Malay-language dramas through the modern medium of film drew large crowds, although the technical quality of the product was limited. The films were apparently shot on a small stage with little movement from the actors and the camera and no use of close ups.[5] World War II brought this early era of Malay-language film to a close. Although these eight films were of limited influence, from these early efforts the Shaw Brothers were to develop a studio that transformed Malay film and reflected the political, social, and cultural changes that Singapore and Malaysia would undergo in the postwar period.

Indian Influence in a Chinese Studio

The first postwar Malay film, *Seruan Merdeka* (*Cry of Freedom*), was released in 1946. The producer of the film was K. R. S. Kristy, an Indian businessman who owned Malay Arts Film Productions. The film starred Salleh Ghani, a star of MFP's prewar films and a well-known Bangsawan performer. Little is known about the film, but it reintroduced an influential figure to Malay film, B. S. Rajhans. Born in Calcutta, Rajhans first came to Singapore in the early 1930s when he directed the first Malay-language film, *Laila Majnun,* in 1934.[6] Rajhans returned to India shortly thereafter and worked in the Bombay film industry until 1946. Following the release of *Seruan Merdeka,* Shaw Brothers hired Rajhans to direct films for MFP and oversee production at the newly emerging studio. In 1947, MFP released *Singapura Waktu Malam* (*Singapore at Night*), beginning a tumultuous period of filmmaking that often paralleled the movement of Malaya toward greater autonomy and independence.

Although Shaw Brothers initially employed Indian directors for their Malay films, they also used a number of Chinese technicians from their Hong Kong studios. The two earliest cameramen were Chou Cheng Kok and Tong Chye. Cheng in particular was remembered fondly because he brought years of experience to MFP, having been a cameraman since the silent era. The sound technicians were also from Hong Kong. The only Malay of any position in the early days of MFP was the art director, Haniff, who is best known as the father of one of the great Malay directors of the early 1960s, Hussein Haniff. When Haniff (the elder) died in the early 1950s, two Indians took his place.[7] Thus, although MFP was a multiethnic studio, there were clear-cut roles for different ethnic groups. Under the leadership of Indian directors, Chinese and Indian technicians shot and recorded Malay actors and singers performing stories that were initially written by the directors. The result was direct translations of popular Indian film plots, along with the songs that were both a combination of Indian cinema and Bangsawan traditions, performed in Malay.

The MFP studio was located at 8 Jalan (meaning "road") Ampas, a small street off Balestier Road to the north of downtown Singapore. The studio originally consisted of two buildings, with the first being a soundstage. The second building at Jalan Ampas was for pre- and postproduction work. On the top floor of this building were a dance studio, executive offices, as well as editing and film-processing facilities. On the ground floor there was a screen for viewing rushes and a sound studio mainly used to record the songs that were a ubiquitous feature of Malay films at the time. The equipment in the studio was quite old. The cameras, as well as most sound recording equipment, had been shipped from Shaw Brothers' central facilities in Hong Kong, where they had been replaced with newer equipment. Most of the non-Singaporean employees lived in company housing at nearby Boon Teck Road. Managing these facilities in the 1950s was Vee Ing Shaw, the son of Runde Shaw. Vee Ing's wife, Daisy, also played an important role as his assistant. She is remembered as being in charge of paying salaries and daily expense requests.[8]

By 1951, MFP was producing more than ten Malay-language films a year and reached its peak of productivity, at thirteen, in 1952. This increased activity eventually led to an expansion of the studio. New buildings were constructed—technically at Number 9—including three stages and additional room for backdrops, props, dresses, and rehearsal space. The original Number 8 studio was demolished and a new structure was built with expanded offices for personnel. MFP eventually developed two film units, A and B. When one unit was using the Jalan Ampas studio, the other would shoot outdoors. Each film was budgeted at Malayan $30,000 (approximately U.S.$10,000) and was usually conceived, shot, edited, and in the cinemas within three months. The facilities for processing the film were also at Jalan Ampas.[9]

Although Indian directors such as Rajhans brought a certain amount of technical knowledge to early Malay film, there were still cultural boundaries that were difficult to cross. One of the most common complaints in the memoirs and oral histories of participants of the time was the inability of Indian directors to communicate in Malay. Scripts and advice to actors usually had to undergo a laborious process of translation from various Indian dialects into English and then into Malay and back again.[10] Beyond such difficulties, there was also the larger issue of cultural differences. Although there are cultural similarities between South and Southeast Asia, and a long history of interaction that stretches across two millennia, the direct translation of style, plots, and dialogue from Indian films created conflict.[11] One prominent example is in the film *Putus Harapan* (*Lost Hope*, 1953), in which a character carries the dead body of a woman away from her home. This scene offended Malay Muslim sensibilities because the body was taken away from her family and was carried in a fairly haphazard manner.[12]

Realizing that he needed to expand the workforce for his films, instead of relying solely on Bangsawan performers, as well as needing to develop local talent, Rajhans traveled throughout the Malay Peninsula and Singapore in search of musicians, actors, and writers in the late 1940s. These efforts resulted in the recruitment of a number of new faces who would transform Malay film in the 1950s. For example, among the earliest writers to find employment in the film industry were Jamil Sulong and Omar Rojik, who began working as a script writer and common laborer, respectively, in 1950 at MFP. Jamil and Omar had been young journalists in the hothouse atmosphere of the postwar publishing industry in Singapore, which was highly nationalistic and modern. They understood that film was an avenue for reaching a mass audience, however, and thus shifted their talents over to the film studio, where they became influential screenwriters and directors. Like many others who joined the organization under Rajhans, they blossomed during the 1950s and made their biggest contribution to the film industry by promoting modern ideals that reflected a desire for an independent nation.

On one of his scouting trips in 1948, Rajhans saw a performance by a young musician who would become the key figure in the transformation of Malay film as a tool of both entertainment as well as edification. This young musician was named P. Ramlee. Although he was not a conventionally attractive man, being skinny with acne scars on his face, Ramlee had charisma and a musical ability that led Rajhans to invite him to Singapore for a screen test. Ramlee was quickly hired to lead the studio orchestra, and because practically every Malay film of the period featured songs, he was also to appear before the cameras either leading the orchestra or singing a musical number. Ramlee first appeared in Rajhans's 1948 film *Chinta* (*Love*), in which he sang five songs. He soon moved away from the orchestra pit and took increasingly larger speaking roles. By 1950, Ramlee starred in *Bakti* (*Faith*), and for the next twenty years he would dominate all aspects of the Malay film industry as an actor, writer, and director.

Although Rajhans was the most influential figure in the early development of Malay film, directing the first seven postwar MFP productions from 1947 to 1949, Shaw Brothers hired more Indian directors to film their growing slate of MFP productions. Among these directors was B. N. Rao, who was hired following a successful career as a director in South Asia, where he had made a number of films in the Tamil film industry. Rao arrived in Singapore in 1952 on a three-year contract, having been lured away from India during a period in which Tamil cinema was in the doldrums. Another director who reflected a subtle shift that would allow for a more sensitive approach to Malay customs and culture in the early 1950s was L. Krishnan, the director of *Bakti*. Krishnan was born in Madras, grew up in Penang, was multilingual, and had worked in Sumatra during the Japanese occupation. After 1945, he returned to India, where he founded the Youth Movement of the Indian Congress and became an influential figure in the Madras film industry. In 1949, Shaw Brothers recruited Krishnan to direct Malay films, mainly due to his ability to speak Malay. Krishnan directed eight films while at MFP, and Rao directed six, before both moved over to the rival Cathay Keris studio in 1954 and 1956, respectively.[13]

Another Indian director who was more sensitive to local interests was S. Ramanathan, the son of a Tamil immigrant who had worked for the colonial railway company in Malaya. Ramanathan was born and raised in Kuala Lumpur but moved to India as a teenager following his father's retirement. Much like Krishnan, Ramanathan was able to speak Malay, a talent that convinced Shaw Brothers' executives to hire him as a director and writer for their burgeoning local film industry.[14] Ramanathan appealed to both the Malay talent and Chinese businessmen who oversaw MFP. He shot his films very quickly, thus saving the studio money, and was open to suggestions from the Malay actors, as well as the growing number of Malay assistant directors and writers, such as Jamil Sulong and Omar Rojik, to infuse the films with story lines that were more appealing to a Malay audience. The result was a series of films that are the best-remembered Malay films of the early 1950s, particularly *Juwita* (1951), *Ibu* (*Mother*, 1953), and *Panggilan Pulau* (*Call of the Islands*, 1954).[15] The first two films are especially important in that they solidified P. Ramlee's status as the leading male star of the Malay film industry.

Phani Majumdar also pushed Malay film in new directions, making him another influential Indian director by the mid-1950s. An activist in the Bengal film industry, Majumdar arrived in Singapore in 1955 and directed only seven films before returning to India. Shaw Brothers originally hired Majumdar to replace B. N. Rao and reorganize the studio, which he accomplished by promoting Malays who had been working behind the scenes as assistant directors, cameramen, and editors to increasingly important positions, while also supporting new story lines and ideas. Majumdar wanted to introduce some of the activism he advocated in India into the Malay film industry by encouraging innovation. For example, he went beyond the confines of the studio to film in Borneo (*Rumah Panjang,* or *The Long House,* 1957), thus pushing the technical limits of filmmaking and storytelling at MFP at the time.[16] Although he would eventually infuse MFP with new skills and confidence on behalf of the Malay workers, his first task was to film a classic Malay story. Alongside the increasing power and status of P. Ramlee, they were to make one of the most important films in Malay cinema and in the process moved Malay film away from its Indian origins to one that was more centered in Malay concerns of the time.

Hang Tuah and Malay Activism at MFP

Hikayat Hang Tuah (*The Story of Hang Tuah*) is one of the most influential texts in the Malay world. Originally recorded sometime in the sixteenth century, it tells the story of a loyal warrior who serves the ruler of the powerful fifteenth-century Malay port city of Melaka. The *hikayat*, a traditional form of history and literature in the region, consists of a series of tales that recount Hang Tuah's adventures and plays an important role in the development of the Malay heroic archetype due to the title character's bravery, intelligence, and undying loyalty to the ruler. The most famous tale in the *hikayat* describes Hang Tuah's murder of Hang Jebat, who, although he is Hang Tuah's best friend, must be killed for insulting the sultan and questioning his ability to rule. In an attempt to push the Malay film industry to new heights, and to counter attempts by Cathay Keris to capture the Malay market, Shaw Brothers approved a budget that has been estimated at $1 million to film this classic tale in color.[17]

Majumdar wrote the screenplay for *Hang Tuah* with the assistance of Jamil Sulong and Mubin Sheppard, a British civil servant and historian who eventually stayed in Malaya following its independence in 1957. In addition, Majumdar asked for input from Mahmud Ahmad, Abdullah Hussain, and Haji Buyong Adil, all of whom were leading writers or cultural activists at the time. The result was one of the first films to incorporate traditional sayings (*gurindam*) and poetry (*pantun*) as integral parts of the plot and dialogue of a classic story. Shaw Brothers' executives' high hopes for the film pushed Majumdar to complete the film so that it could qualify for competition in the Asian Film Festival circuit in 1955. Postproduction, which involved flying the film to London for processing, however, took too long. The film was finally released in 1956, and it went on to win prizes at film festivals in Hong Kong and was shown in Indonesia, Thailand, and the Middle East as well as at the Berlin Film Festival, all firsts in the Malay film industry.[18]

Despite such success, the film received harsh criticism from the Malay activist community, becoming a focus of all complaints that artists had at the time toward both MFP and Cathay Keris as well as British rule of the region. *Hikayat Hang Tuah* is a complicated text filled with subtleties that allow for numerous interpretations. The film reduced many of these complexities to an account of four of the most famous tales in the text. This simplification, and the inclusion of two songs in the film, led to criticism of the film as being "too Indian." Although the "singing Hang Tuah" would be the focus of criticism for many Malay activists, who were becoming more vocal in their demands as negotiations for Malayan independence neared, their main point of contention seemed to be the difficulty of accepting an Indian director for such an important Malay story as well as the participation of Sheppard.[19]

The criticisms directed toward *Hang Tuah* were made in a context of increased social and cultural activism that was related to growing nationalistic feelings. One of the most influential organizations at that time was a group of Malay artists and writers known as the ASAS 50 (an acronym for Angkatan Sasterawan 50, or Generation of the Writers of the 1950s), which promoted the ideal of "art for society." Although best known for their novels or short stories, many ASAS 50 members also worked in the film industry. Influential members of the organization included S. Roomai Noor, an early MFP actor who had moved to Cathay Keris in 1954, and Jamil Sulong. As the representative of the film community, Roomai Noor made a passionate plea at a key ASAS 50 meeting in 1956 for Malays to gain control over the content of their films so they would reflect Malay cultural values and correct Malay-language usage. This also reflected the desire of many in the Malay film industry to use film as a vehicle for their ideals.[20] One of their common complaints at the time was that the films did not reflect the concerns of the Malay community, for which the Indian directors were harshly criticized. Majumdar provided greater opportunities for Malay input into the filmmaking process, however, with *Hang Tuah* being the first step. The social activism Majumdar encouraged, as well as attempts—all overseen by many of the activists—to incorporate Malay dances and customs into the film, led to a new era in Malay filmmaking.

While *Hang Tuah* was being edited and prepared for release, P. Ramlee directed a film he had written with the assistance of Jamil Sulong and Abdullah Hussain that would combine the growing influence of Malay artists with the activism that Majumdar brought to the industry. The film was *Penarek Beca* (*The Trishaw Puller*), which was released in 1955. *Penarek Beca* focused on the tribulations of a bicycle rickshaw driver, played by Ramlee, in modern Singapore. A well-to-do young woman hires the rickshaw driver and falls in love with him, while constantly encouraging him to look beyond class differences and to take a more active role in trying to better his life. The film represents the beginning of a new era in Malay filmmaking in which social and historical concerns of the time were presented in an entertaining fashion on the screen.[21] The financial and artistic success of *Penarek Beca* allowed for greater participation of Malay writers and directors in the filmmaking process and a reduction in Indian influence. As long as the films made money, Shaw Brothers could actively ignore this small branch in their larger entertainment empire.

The popularity of *Penarek Beca*, combined with the release of *Hang Tuah*, opened the door for a greater activism at MFP headquarters at Jalan Ampas. This also occurred in the context of impending Malayan independence, which was achieved in 1957. As the date for independence, and the form that the government would take, was being debated in London, Kuala Lumpur, and Singapore, Malays were becoming increasingly involved in political and labor disputes. A film workers union, PERSAMA (Persatuan Artis Malaya, or Malayan Artists Union), had been founded in 1954 with P. Ramlee as the first president and Salleh Ghani and Jamil Sulong as the other main officers. The goals of PERSAMA were common to most trade unions at the time. Their activities, however, were often more public due to the industry in which they worked. In addition there were often clashes among the membership over the focus of the trade union. Some members of PERSAMA pushed for social and artistic goals, leading to disputes between the "artistic talent" and the more technical workers, such as cameramen and carpenters, who were more interested in wages and work hours.[22]

By February 1957, PERSAMA was organized well enough to approach Shaw Brothers' executives to ask for an increase in wages. The approximately 150 Malay employees at MFP, with the exception of P. Ramlee, received a wage of less than M$300 a month.[23] Although MFP employees received bonuses for each film they completed, and many lived in the Shaw Brothers–owned housing complex on Boon Teck Road, they received no raises once the initial salary had been agreed upon. Thus, there were employees who had been receiving the same salary for as long as ten years. Under these circumstances, PERSAMA representatives made four basic demands: an agreed salary scale for all MFP employees, bigger bonuses for each completed picture, prompt payment of overtime, and one-half day off on Saturdays and a full day off on Sundays.[24]

The reply to these demands was received on March 3, 1957: three PERSAMA members were fired from MFP. The three were Musalmah, Omar Rojik, and H. M. Rohaizad. Musalmah was an actress whose home on Tembeling Road served as PERSAMA headquarters. Rojik had been a journalist in the late 1940s, had worked his way up to assistant director and supporting actor, and in the early 1960s would become one of the leading directors of dramatic political films at MFP. During the strike, he was described as a "villain" in Malay films. The third person fired, Rohaizad, was an assistant director and prominent PERSAMA member. When protests continued, two of the most vocal agitators, S. Kadarisman and Syed Hassan Safi, who worked as assistant directors, were also fired on March 5.[25]

The firings shifted the focus of the dispute. PERSAMA members approached leading Malay politicians and cultural figures, asking them to issue statements of support. Shortly thereafter, the Malay rulers announced that they would not take sides in the dispute. Protests were planned. With Shaw Brothers refusing to negotiate, claiming that the five were fired due to "non-cooperation and lackness," a strike began on March 16, 1957. More than 120 MFP employees picketed the Jalan Ampas studios. In addition, film stars were seen picketing Queens Cinema in Geylang, including Ahmad Mahmud, whose own film was being shown there.[26] In an attempt to gain support, further mass protests occurred at Happy World amusement park, Pulau Berani, and Al-Islamiah Madrasah on Pasir Panjang Road, all public places that were popular gathering places for the Malay community.[27] In the midst of the strike and demonstrations, Shaw Brothers appealed to the government to provide subsidies for the local film industry. The company claimed that MFP was overstaffed and needed only around sixty employees to run the studio. Shaw Brothers' management had supposedly issued warning of retrenchment as early as 1955, and the firing of the five employees was necessary to make ends meet.[28] During this period, the salary demands that had prompted the firings were not mentioned.

Such strikes and protests were not limited to the film industry in early 1957. Both workers and employees throughout the Malay Peninsula and Singapore were in a state of anxiety over the form of the new nation that was to be created later in the year. With the final details of the structure of an independent Malaya being negotiated in London in the first few months of 1957, trade union strikes were rampant amid fears that foreign employers would leave without the security the British had provided and uncertainty over the status of Chinese and Indian immigrants in the new nation.[29] Against a background of strong trade union activism, the Malay film industry reflected larger anxieties of the time. The convergence of labor issues and artistic control were coming to a head. As the protests outside Shaw Brothers' cinemas continued throughout March 1957, the future financial stability of the studio was at stake.

Perspective was brought to the dispute between Shaw Brothers and its employees with the publication of a letter to the editor in the *Straits Times* on March 22, 1957. The writer, "Realist" in Kuala Lumpur, was sympathetic to Shaw Brothers and claimed that PERSAMA members' cry of "art and culture" was simplistic considering the financial state of Malay film. The writer claimed that out of one hundred filmgoers in the federation (which would not include Singapore), forty-two paid to see Chinese films, twenty-seven watched English-language films, nineteen went to Indian films, and only twelve wanted to view a Malay film. Although these numbers may have fluctuated during the 1950s, it is doubtful that the letter writer exaggerated the figures when considering what was shown at cinemas during the period. In Singapore, for example, from a network of sixteen Shaw Brothers cinemas, only one or two periodically showed Malay films, and both of these cinemas were located in predominately Malay areas of the city. "Realist" then explained that Malay films produced only $3 million in ticket sales a year. Because $1 million went to the government as an entertainment tax, and $1 million went to the cinemas (albeit owned by the company that produced the films), there was only $1 million dollars left to produce the sixteen films that MFP and Cathay Keris made in 1956.[30]

As the strike continued, leading Malay politicians finally got involved. Tunku Abdul Rahman, who five months later was to become the first prime minister of the federation, sent one of his senior aides, Senu Abdul Rahman, to act as a mediator between the two parties. Following two days of negotiations, the strike was resolved on April 7, 1957. Run Run Shaw, who was "very cooperative and sincere," rehired the five fired employees, and the PERSAMA representatives agreed to drop demands for payment of overtime. How the other issues were resolved was not mentioned.[31]

A not-so-subtle critique of Shaw Brothers' management during the strike appeared on screen later that year in the film *Mogok* (*Strike*). Written by Jamil Sulong, the film tells the story of factory workers who are exploited by a manager—ironically, played by S. Kadarisman—who is working with the greedy daughter of their kind, but distant, employer. The film intersperses the day-to-day toils of the factory workers with monologues in which Omar Rojik and several other workers discuss the importance of union representation. After a series of accidents, including the factory owner's daughter hitting an employee with a car, the manager burns down the house of a suffering female employee. Just as the workers are about to riot, the kindly factory owner arrives. He fires the manager, disowns his daughter, and embraces the workers and their union as vital components of a prosperous future for all.

The 1957 strike was a turning point in the Malay film industry. Although Malay films were in a brief period of both artistic and financial success, looming issues of profitability and worker rights clashed, ironically leading to the long decline of Shaw Brothers' MFP studio. The tensions between Shaw Brothers and its employees had been settled temporarily, but MFP's rival in Malay filmmaking, Cathay Keris, used the opportunity to take advantage of the situation. Since its founding in 1953, Cathay Keris executives had mined the tension at MFP to lure actors, directors, and technicians to their studios in eastern Singapore. The early stars of Cathay Keris, particularly S. Roomai Noor and Maria Menado, had been enticed with larger contracts and the right to have greater control over the creative process after they had begun their careers at MFP. During the 1957 strike, Ho Ah Loke, the chief executive at Cathay Keris, sent supplies such as rice as well as notes of encouragement to the strikers. This strategy was successful. After 1957, the shift in employees over to Cathay Keris, whose higher salaries and more modern equipment and facilities were quite attractive, was even more noticeable.[32]

The movement of employees from MFP to Cathay Keris was not the only battle that the Shaw Brothers' rivals won in 1957. Cathay Keris had been a distant second in the Malay film industry since its founding, mainly due to the superior network of Shaw Brothers–owned cinemas and the presence of the ever-popular P. Ramlee at MFP. Three weeks after the strike was over, however, Cathay Keris released a film that would transform the industry. *Pontianak* (*Vampire*) premiered on May 1, 1957, the Islamic holiday of Aidul Fitri that year, at the main Cathay cinema at Dhoby Ghaut in Singapore and ran for a number of weeks. The film attracted crowds—including Chinese and Indians—a phenomenon never seen before in Malay film. The film starred Maria Menado and was directed by B. N. Rao, the influential early director at MFP. The success of the film symbolized the arrival of Cathay Keris as a formidable rival in the Malay film industry. Maria Menado now became a star and producer who would rival P. Ramlee in status within the community. In addition, Malay activists such as Hamzah Hussin, Hussein Haniff, and Roomai Noor were given control over the films they produced and wrote, leading to a period during which Malay consciousness and intellectual debates that represented the vibrant joy of a newly independent nation were presented to mass audiences in a modern medium.[33]

Although the Shaw Brothers did not stop making Malay-language films for many years, and only in 1961 did Cathay Keris make more Malay-language films than MFP, the slow withdrawal from Malay filmmaking had begun. In 1957, Run Run Shaw returned to Hong Kong to take over the management of the family business. Shaw Brothers faced a period of turmoil and family disputes, which eventually resulted in Run Run and Runme Shaw gaining control over the entertainment empire. Although he had originally allied with his uncle, Vee Ing Shaw resigned from the company shortly thereafter.[34] These events meant that new management oversaw the already troubled studios at Jalan Ampas. A series of managers—recalled only by family names Lui, Kwek, and Hsu—tried to run the studio but faced criticism among the Malay workers for being too bureaucratic and unfriendly. Eventually, MFP employees signed petitions to have them replaced. Although the final manager, Lee Tun Koo, brought some temporary stability to the situation, the atmosphere of a newly independent nation, labor activism, and limited financial returns were proving too much to overcome for a Chinese business empire that was shifting its focus back to Hong Kong.[35]

Southeast Asian (Nanyang) Audience

With Run Run Shaw in Hong Kong about to oversee the studio's greatest period of success as a producer of Chinese films, the number and quality of MFP's Malay-language productions went into decline as budgets were slashed. The official creative head of the studio, Phani Majumdar, was busy filming in Borneo as well as making films that would supposedly appeal to the Southeast Asian Chinese (*nanyang*) audience. To accommodate this new direction, Run Run Shaw transferred some actors and technicians to Singapore. Among the films made during this period were *Masyarakat Pinchang* (*Crippled Society*, 1958), which was a remake of a Chinese novel, and *Sri Menanti* (1958), an interracial love story.[36] *Sri Menanti* starred Zaiton, a leading female star at MFP, and Paul Chang Chung and Tang Dan, stars of Shaw Brothers productions in Hong Kong. Although Paul Chang Chung became a mainstay of the five Shaw Brothers Chinese films made in Singapore and Malaya, Malay participants mainly recall the difficulties of filming with such a diverse group of actors and technicians. Phani Majumdar's assistant on both films was Jamil Sulong, who remembers that Tang Dan did not know English, thus making it difficult to direct her. Each actor also delivered lines in his or her own language, which led to problems with pacing because each performer had to anticipate when the other actor would stop talking. In a bizarre twist, S. Kadarishman, the union activist, was hired to play Tang Dan's father in *Sri Menanti*.[37] Ultimately, none of these collaborations was very successful. *Sri Menanti* was not even released in Hong Kong, and *Masyarakat Pinchang* was lost amid a short-lived fad for horror films following the success of Cathay Keris's *Pontianak*.[38]

Despite the conclusion of the 1957 strike, the attempts to tap all of the resources at the Shaw Brothers' disposal seemed to have led to further anxieties

and tensions among the Malay staff. In addition, resentment over labor issues remained at MFP. Over the next five years, there were numerous strikes,
work slowdowns, and protests. P. Ramlee returned as the head of PERSAMA
in 1959; however, within the union there was little unity. The financial situation was unstable, and there was a great amount of tension between the
technicians and the artists over the role of culture and politics in Malay film.
Ramlee tried to get members to be more active in paying their dues and more
accepting in matters of negotiations with studio executives, but this led many
of his fellow unionists to criticize him vigorously, particularly because of his
high salary.[39] Ultimately, P. Ramlee had to resign from PERSAMA, and his
unique status at the studio led to resentment and tension on the lot.

The new leader of the union was Jins Shamsudin, a popular dramatic actor,
who had just entered the film business at the time of the 1957 strike. As the
older Malay artists were focusing on artistic and social issues, Jins Shamsudin
had become affiliated with a diverse group of artists' associations and unions
around Singapore that was more political. Under his leadership, as well as
that of H. M. Rohaizad, a new organization for MFP employees arose in the
form of the Singapore Association of Trade Unions (SATU), which was considered to be radical and aggressive. Many of the MFP employees who were
active in SATU had been hired since 1955 and did not agree with PERSAMA's
tactics, which they perceived as too accommodating. SATU members were
particularly distressed at the limitations in their contracts, which forbade
interaction with Cathay Keris artists—a difficult proposition considering the
small numbers in the Malay filmmaking community in Singapore—and had
strict morality clauses. The split between PERSAMA and SATU supporters
led to great animosity at the studio. Between November 1961 and May 1962,
there were a series of protests in support of a carpenters' strike at MFP, and
eventually the artists themselves went on strike for fifty-six days, shutting
down several productions.[40]

By this time, Run Run Shaw had reached the limit of his patience with
the money-losing studio and its labor problems. In 1961, Shaw purchased
Merdeka Studios from Ho Ah Loke, who had left Cathay Keris in 1958 in an
attempt to transfer production to Kuala Lumpur, where costs would be less
than in the volatile labor market of Singapore. In 1963, most of Shaw Brothers' Malay-language film production was transferred to Kuala Lumpur, where
Malay film eventually severed all ties with Shaw Brothers. Nevertheless, Run
Run Shaw tried to lure P. Ramlee, the one guaranteed profitable star at MFP,
to Hong Kong to make a film. Shaw promised the film—*Seniwati* (*Female
Artist*)—would be made in CinemaScope to entice Ramlee. Before he could

leave, however, Ramlee faced vocal protests from Jins Shamsudin, who feared that the film would lack any cultural resonance among Malays and do little to help develop the Malay film industry. Eventually, a lack of funding and the protests led to cancellation of the production.[41] With few films being produced, and their quality clearly diminishing, Ramlee moved to Kuala Lumpur in April 1964 with the blessings of Shaw Brothers. This signaled an initial end of Shaw Brothers' efforts to make Malay-language films in Singapore, and MFP studios were closed in 1965.

To counter criticism that they were abandoning the market and to please the political leadership of Malaysia, Shaw Brothers agreed to reopen MFP in a last-gasp effort to make a spectacular Malay-language film. The film was *Raja Bersiong* (*The King with Fangs,* 1968), an epic in the style of Hollywood productions of the late 1950s and early 1960s. It was filmed in Shawscope, in color, and with thousands of extras. In addition to being an epic, *Raja Bersiong* was also a political film, as it was the idea of Tunku Abdul Rahman, the first prime minister of Malaysia and an important figure in the independence movement. The Tunku, as he is invariably known, took a personal interest in the film by offering advice on the script and possible locations for the filmmakers. He often showed up to watch the filming in Singapore, at the newly reopened MFP studios, or on location in Alor Star in northern Malaysia. In addition, Run Run Shaw came to Singapore to oversee the film and to placate the Tunku's concerns. To handle the technical aspects of filming in color and CinemaScope, Shaw Brothers hired Japanese cameramen and directors to assist Jamil Sulong, who officially wrote the screenplay and was the director. These Japanese filmmakers quickly took over the production, apparently with the Tunku's approval. In addition, dancers were brought in from Bangkok, government workers were forced upon the production to fill minor roles, and the Malaysian army was used for battle scenes. The result was a costly, bloated epic that would never recoup its costs at the box office. More important, although it involved technical skills rarely seen in Malay film, it ironically had little of the nationalistic and artistic content that many of the films since 1955 had displayed. The initial efforts of Run Run Shaw to sell local product to Malays in Singapore and the Malay Peninsula had now become an expensive proposition with leading politicians dictating the content and style of films.[42]

The idea of making Malay-language films at the Shaw Brothers' main headquarters in Hong Kong, however, continued. After *Raja Bersiong* had become a box office bomb, Run Run Shaw approached Jins Shamsudin about making several films in Hong Kong. They were to be the sequels to the popular Jefri

Zain series of films. Tapping into the worldwide popularity of James Bond in the mid-1960s, MFP had made a film entitled *Jefri Zain dalam Gerak Kilat* (*Jefri Zain in Operation Lightning*, 1966). It was a rare success for MFP at the time, receiving publicity not only for its plot and action but also for a "realistic" kiss between Jins Shamsudin and the Malay actress Sarimah. The sequel, *Jebak Maut* (*Death Trap*, 1967), costarred Rosy Wong and Susan Chua and continued the formula of beautiful women and dangerous situations for the Jefri Zain character. The success of the first two Jefri Zain films led the Shaw Brothers to propose that a spin-off, titled *Nora Zain Agen Wanita 001* (*Nora Zain, Female Agent 001*, 1968), as well as two other Jefri Zain films be made in Hong Kong. Although he had opposed the making of a P. Ramlee film in Hong Kong in 1964, Jins Shamsudin relented because he had seen MFP releases dwindle to barely one a year, and he was offered the position of assistant director and access to the more modern equipment available at the Shaw Brothers' studio in Hong Kong.[43]

The three Malay secret agent films made in Hong Kong in 1967 and 1968 were made under the direction of Wei Lo, the well-known Chinese director of films that included Bruce Lee's *The Big Boss* (1971), with a Chinese crew. *Nora Zain* starred well-known star Sarimah as well as two Malay actors. The two Jefri Zain films, of course, featured Jins Shamsudin and were titled *Bayangan Ajal* (*Shadow of Death*, 1968) and *Jurang Bahaya* (*Danger Valley*, 1969).[44] The films were made alongside Chinese versions, with the Malay actors and actresses being substituted into the action in already-filmed scenes from the Chinese version. For example, *Nora Zain Agen Wanita 001* is the Malay version of *Angel with an Iron Fist*, the 1967 film starring Lily Hong. The same Chinese actors appeared in all three films, with starring roles given to Landi Chang and Malaysian-born Fanny Fan. All three films were in color, made using Shawscope, and dubbed into English, Cantonese, and Malay so they would appeal to different markets. With each film, Jins Shamsudin oversaw the Malay-language dubbing and used Rosnani Jamil for the various female voices.[45]

Although these last three Shaw Brothers Malay-language films were made in Hong Kong, they still contained subtle nods toward Malay nationalism in a modern world, qualities that often can be found in the films made after 1955. In each of these films, Jefri Zain, debonair as always, must negotiate his way through a Chinese society while retaining his Malay identity. Scenes in which he outwits a nightclub strongman and subsequently offers his apologies for doing so, as well as his ability to seduce women in the service of his government, hark back to the ultimate Malay icon Hang Tuah. To this day, it is difficult for the Malay public to separate the actor Jins Shamsudin from the character Jefri Zain, as he is often identified by his fans. The resulting series of films blended elements of modernity and identity until they had a much clearer resonance in Malay consciousness than *Raja Bersiong*, a politically motivated Malay legend on film that was pushed onto the Malay public and roundly rejected. Despite the fond memories and box office success of the Jefri Zain series, Shaw Brothers abandoned efforts to sell a local product in Malaysia and Singapore. They closed the studios at Jalan Ampas in 1967, and *Jurang Bahaya* was their last Malay-language release.[46]

The Shaw Brothers were originally looking for a cheap product to sell locally. In the process, they introduced Indian filmmakers to Bangsawan traditions. In the fertile ground of a modernizing Malaya, it led to the development of a new medium of expression for Malay writers, directors, and actors. In Malay communities, however, these films are not easily forgotten. They are symbolic of the transition from an oral-based storytelling tradition to a modern, technologically sophisticated, and independent society. Through film, they were able to promote a nationalistic agenda of pride in Malay culture and history that was also reflected in increasingly tense labor relations at the studio. More than 150 Malay-language films—more than 250 if the films produced at Cathay Keris are included—were produced in Singapore over a twenty-year period between 1947 and 1967. However, these efforts have been largely overlooked in the scholarship of Asian cinema. They are even marginalized within the Shaw Brothers' empire. This is understandable considering the impact the Shaw Brothers made on Chinese cinema and business. Despite being overshadowed in the larger history of Chinese businessmen in Southeast Asia, it reflects the power that such shadows can have not only on the movie screen but also in the story of the society they encompass.

Notes

I would like to thank Sai-shing Yung, as well as Jamil Sulong, Rosnani Jamil, and Jins Shamsudin, for the conversations that helped shape much of what appears in this chapter. Any mistakes, of course, are the author's alone.

1. I attended a conference in December 2003 in Kuching, Malaysia, in which many of the stars from the 1950s also were present. It was difficult to hold conversations in public areas of the hotel due to the large number of guests, many in their teens, requesting autographs and photographs. Most of these fans had happened upon the elderly stars by chance because there had been no formal announcement of their presence.

2. See Sai-shing Yung's contribution to this collection. Stephanie Chung Po-yin, "The Industrial Evolution of a Fraternal Enterprise: The Shaw Brothers and the Shaw Organisation," in Wong Ain-ling, ed., *The Shaw Screen: A Preliminary Study* (Hong Kong: Hong Kong Film Archive, 2003), pp. 1–17.

3. Tan Sooi Beng, *Bangsawan: A Social and Stylistic History of Popular Malay Opera* (Singapore: Oxford University Press, 1993), pp. 16–18.

4. Jan Uhde and Yvonne Ng Uhde, *Latent Images: Film in Singapore* (Singapore: Oxford University Press, 2000), p. 224.

5. Jamil Sulong, *Kaca Permata: Memoir Seorang Pengarah* (Kuala Lumpur: Dewan Bahasa dan Pustaka, 1993), p. 9.

6. Tan, *Bangsawan*, pp. 10–11. An Indian company, Motilal Chemical, produced *Laila Majnun*.

7. Ibid., pp. 31, 35; James Harding and Ahmad Sarji, *P. Ramlee: The Bright Star* (Petaling Jaya: Pelanduk, 2002), p. 151.

8. Jamil Sulong, *Kaca Permata*, pp. 31, 35, 54, 59.

9. Ibid., pp. 35, 59. The exchange rate was pegged at U.S.$1 = M$2.12 in 1946. In September 1949, this rate grew worse when the British pound devalued against the U.S. dollar, making U.S.$1 worth approximately M$2.80. Thus, most films were made for around U.S.$10,000.

10. Jamil Sulong, *Kaca Permata*, pp. 24, 47, 50–51.

11. The focus on the similarities is at the heart of Bill van der Heide, "Malaysian Movies: The Shaw Brothers Meet the Pandava Brothers in the Land below the Winds," in Bruce Bennett, Jeff Doyle, and Satendra Nandan, eds., *Crossing Cultures: Essays on Literature and Culture of the Asia-Pacific* (London: Skoob Books, 1997), pp. 101–10. I would like to caution attempts at stressing such similarities, particularly when it was a central point of contention among many Malay participants in the filmmaking process at the time.

12. Ahmad Sarji, *P. Ramlee: Erti yang Sakti* (Petaling Jaya: Pelanduk, 1999), p. 300; Hamzah Hussin, *Memoir Hamzah Hussin: Dari Keris Film ke Studio Merdeka* (Bangi: University Kebangsaan Malaysia, 1997), pp. 82–83; Adeline Siaw-Hui Kueh, "The Filmic Representations of Malayan Women: An Analysis of Malayan Films from the 1950s and 1960s" (unpublished masters thesis, Murdoch University, 1997), pp. 5–6.

13. Harding and Sarji, *P. Ramlee: The Bright Star*, p. 60; Prem K Prasha, *The Krishnan Odyssey: A Pictorial Biography of Dato' L. Krishnan* (Kuala Lumpur: Nasarre, 2003). Cathay Keris was the other main producer of Malay films at the time. For a study of their contributions to Malay film, see Timothy P. Barnard, "Vampires, Heroes, and Jesters: A History of Cathay Keris," in Wong Ain-ling, ed., *The Cathay Story* (Hong Kong: Hong Kong Film Archive, 2002), pp. 124–41.

14. Jamil Sulong, however, writes that Ramanathan's Malay-language ability was limited, at least in the early phases of his career. In addition, the filmmaking experience of many of these early Indian directors, except for Rajhans and Rao, seems to have been suspect at best. Jamil describes Krishnan as a "clapper-boy" in the Indian

film industry, whereas Ramanathan was a "studio assistant" and extra in Indian films prior to his return to Malaya. Harding and Sarji, *P. Ramlee: The Bright Star,* p. 50; Jamil Sulong, *Kaca Permata,* pp. 19, 51.

15. Harding and Sarji, *P. Ramlee: The Bright Star,* p. 50; Timothy P. Barnard, "Sedih sampai Buta: Blindness, Modernity and Tradition in Malay Films of the 1950s and 1960s," *Bijdragen tot de Taal-, Land- en Volkenkunde* 161, no. 4 (2005): pp. 433–53; Sarji, *P. Ramlee: Erti yang Sakti,* pp. 315–16.

16. Jamil Sulong, *Kaca Permata,* pp. 86, 94.

17. Although color film would be more expensive, and the film clearly had a higher budget than previous MFP productions, it is doubtful that it cost $1 million, as claimed by Harding and Sarji, particularly because the average Malay film at the time was made for approximately $30,000; Harding and Sarji, *P. Ramlee: The Bright Star,* p. 67.

18. Ibid., p. 72; Sarji, *P. Ramlee: Erti yang Sakti,* pp. 80–81; Jamil Sulong, *Kaca Permata,* p. 86. *Hang Tuah,* however, was not the first Malay film made in color. This honor goes to the Cathay-produced *Buluh Perindu* (*Bamboo of Yearning,* 1953); Timothy P. Barnard, "Vampires, Heroes, and Jesters," pp. 126–27.

19. Harding and Sarji, *P. Ramlee: The Bright Star,* p. 72.

20. Abdullah Hussain and Nik Safiah Karim, eds., *Memoranda Angkatan Sastrawan '50,* 2nd ed. (Petaling Jaya: Fajar Bakti, 1987), pp. 156–64.

21. For more information on *Penarek Beca* and its social and historical context, see Rohayati P. Barnard and Timothy P. Barnard, "The Ambivalence of P. Ramlee: *Penarek Beca* and *Bujang Lapok* in Perspective," *Asian Cinema* 13, no. 2 (2002): pp. 9–23.

22. Jamil Sulong, *Kaca Permata,* pp. 118–19; Hamzah Hussin, *Memoir Hamzah Hussin,* pp. 51–54.

23. Jamil Sulong, *Kaca Permata,* p. 130. The majority made less than M$200. Ramlee made around M$600 per month, which was on par with the imported technical personnel from Hong Kong and India. Ramlee, however, received huge bonuses in the thousands of dollars for each completed film. The exchange rate was U.S.$1 = M$2.80.

24. "Film Stars Demand—'No News,'" *The Straits Times* (hereafter *ST*), February 28, 1957, p. 4.

25. "Film Star Union Seeks Support," *ST,* March 4, 1957, p. 4; Ahmad Sarji, *P. Ramlee: Erti yang Sakti,* pp. 190–91, 216, 326–27; Jamil Sulong, *Kaca Permata,* p. 130; "Two More Film Men Sacked," *ST,* March 6, 1957, p. 5.

26. Harding and Sarji, *P. Ramlee: The Bright Star,* p. 137; Jamil Sulong, *Kaca Permata,* pp. 130–32; "Film Stars, Union Seek Support," *ST,* March 4, 1957, p. 4; "Stars Plea to Mentris," *ST,* April 6, 1957, p. 7.

27. Zamberi A. Malek, *Suria Kencana: Biografi Jins Shamsudin* (Bangi: Universiti Kebangsaan Malaysia, 1998), p. 232.

28. "Film Magnates Want Subsidy," *ST,* March 21, 1957, p. 8.

29. For more information on such labor issues and the context, see T. N. Harper, *The End of Empire and the Making of Malaya* (Cambridge: Cambridge University Press, 1999).

30. Realist, letter to the editor, *ST,* March 22, 1957, p. 6. The two studios actually made only thirteen films in 1956 and fifteen in 1955.

31. "Film Workers Strike Over," *ST,* April 8, 1957, p. 4. Lee Kuan Yew, as a leading figure in the Workers Union and a member of the Lee and Lee law firm, helped draw up some of the initial documents that PERSAMA presented to the studio. Some of the letters and documents related to the strike can be found in Jamil Sulong, *Kaca Permata,* pp. 130–31.

32. Barnard, "Vampires, Heroes, and Jesters," pp. 124–41; Hamzah Hussin, *Memoir Hamzah Hussin,* p. 51; Jamil Sulong, *Kaca Permata,* pp. 151, 167, 170.

33. Barnard, "Vampires, Heroes, and Jesters"; Hamzah Hussin, *Memoir Hamzah Hussin,* p. 41.

34. I. C. Jarvie, *Window on Hong Kong: A Sociological Study of the Hong Kong Film Industry and Its Audience* (Hong Kong: University of Hong Kong Press, 1977), p. 45; Chung, "The Industrial Evolution of a Fraternal Enterprise," pp. 6–7.

35. Jamil Sulong, *Kaca Permata,* p. 170.

36. The common English translation for the film is *An Affair in Malaya.* The title in Malay refers to someone's name or title. See Sai-shing Yung's contribution to this collection for more information on how this production is viewed within Chinese film circles.

37. Jamil Sulong, *Kaca Permata,* p. 94.

38. Seven of the twenty Malay-language films released in 1958 were horror films.

39. Harding and Sarji, *P. Ramlee: The Bright Star,* pp. 136–38; Mohd. Zamberi, *Suria Kencana,* pp. 232–34. By this time, Ramlee's films were the only profitable product coming out of MFP. For each completed production, he supposedly received $30,000.

40. Mohd. Zamberi, *Suria Kencana,* pp. 232–37; Jamil Sulong, *Kaca Permata,* p. 125; Hamzah Hussin, *Memoir Hamzah Hussin,* p. 52.

41. Harding and Sarji, *P. Ramlee: The Bright Star,* pp. 185–86.

42. Jamil Sulong, *Kaca Permata,* pp. 198–208; Uhde and Uhde, *Latent Images,* p. 27; Mohd. Zamberi, *Suria Kencana,* pp. 237–40.

43. Jamil Sulong, *Kaca Permata,* pp. 196–98; Mohd. Zamberi, *Suria Kencana,* pp. 62–64.

44. *Bayangan Ajal* was released as *Jefri Zain in Hong Kong.*

45. Mohd. Zamberi, *Suria Kencana,* pp. 64–68.

46. Jins Shamsudin believes that the filming in Hong Kong was useful for Shaw Brothers because it distanced the increasingly radical figure from his fellow actors as the studio was being closed. Before going to Hong Kong, he had been visited by various security officials and warned about his political and labor activities, which were considered particularly volatile because he was a Malaysian citizen working in newly independent Singapore; Mohd. Zamberi, *Suria Kencana,* pp. 89, 237–41.

8

Bridging the Pacific
with *Love Eterne*

RAMONA CURRY

During the second half of the twentieth century, Hong Kong emerged as a leading source and sign of popular cultural forms that have enjoyed tremendous success throughout East and Southeast Asia and to an extent in other regions of the globe. Most international media historians and others attentive to the transnational flow of commercial entertainment would concur with that assertion, as well as agree that aspects of Hong Kong–produced (and related Chinese-produced) media have in recent decades attained crossover status in the United States, regularly reaching consumers who have no ethnic Chinese or other close cultural associations with Hong Kong. Observers do not as readily agree about the significance of the U.S. crossover markets for Hong Kong–produced films nor indeed about how securely those films are culturally or economically rooted in Asia, given the rise of an amalgamated trans-Pacific popular culture as much marked—and globally marketed by—"Hollywood" as "Hong Kong." However contested the present or likely future state of the Hong Kong–Hollywood nexus, the history of how Hong Kong–associated film genres and performers first managed to penetrate the largely insular popular U.S. media markets appears self-evident: It was Hong Kong martial arts style films that achieved the so-called breakthrough into New York and other U.S. urban media distribution and exhibition networks in the early 1970s.

This chapter seeks not to counter the many well-grounded analyses of that historical moment but rather to offer a preliminary prehistory to that singular founding tale of Hong Kong cinema's crossover reception in the United States. My research thus shifts attention to the international media's economic and cultural practices of the 1950s and 1960s, when several Hong Kong media producers—Shaw Brothers foremost among them—undertook to expand their North American markets beyond their long-established followings among Chinese urban immigrant populations in and around the Chinatowns of San Francisco, New York, Los Angeles, Vancouver, and Toronto. Film archival and newspaper records indicate that the early 1970s U.S. breakthrough for Hong Kong martial arts films—usually portrayed as an explosive, climactic moment—in fact built on a full decade of patient U.S. market exploration and long-term investments in exhibition that centrally involved the work of many individuals on the margins of both Hollywood and Hong Kong. I will thus offer a less dramatic but more gradual and multifocal, if still partial, supplemental account of how Hong Kong (-related) films managed over the second half of the twentieth century to develop—however sporadically or incompletely—a crossover market in the United States.

The gender connotations of my descriptive terms are, of course, purposive. Examining Hong Kong film exhibition in the United States before 1970 necessarily foregrounds the film genre of musical costume historical drama, coded, as we shall see, as feminine by both Chinese and U.S. writers, in contrast to the more widely discussed (masculine) martial arts films. Further, the film reviews and other archival records that yield this alternative tale exude a preoccupation with gender concerns as well as a focus on national culture. Thus critical approaches to gender, genre, and (trans)national culture will structure my alternative history, which in its brief form here departs from a delimited case study: the distinctive reception in the United States, compared to its impact in Asia, of a 1963 Hong Kong–produced Shaw Brothers production entitled *Love Eterne* (*Liang Shanbo yu Zhu Yingtai*).[1]

The research leading to this chapter initially aimed to situate *Love Eterne* in relation to Shaw Brothers' innovative aesthetic and business practices of the early 1960s, a time when the company sought to secure and extend its dominance across a Pan-Chinese film distribution network. Unexpectedly, the exploration led to the discovery of an unsung, even forgotten, and yet crucial figure in the so-called Shaw Story and the broader history of cross-Pacific media exchanges: an enterprising U.S.-born civic leader in San Francisco's Chinatown named Frank Lee, who in business cooperation with Run Run Shaw in the 1960s systematically worked to build opportunities for crossover Hong Kong film distribution in major U.S. and Canadian cities. Thus the chapter's corollary goal is to begin to restore to film's historical record the important contributions of Frank Lee Sr. to fostering subsequent U.S. exhibition and distribution of Hong Kong films. Besides Sir Run Run

Shaw, three well-known media historical figures play major roles in this restoration: *New York Times* critic Bosley Crowther and two filmmakers who share Lee's surname: the director of *Love Eterne* and that of *Crouching Tiger, Hidden Dragon.*

Pan-Chinese Film Heritage: From *Love Eterne* to *Crouching Tiger*

The Chinese (Mandarin) title of *Love Eterne, Liang Shanbo yu Zhu Yingtai,* refers to a folk opera from Southeast China based on a centuries-old popular legend sometimes known in English as "The Butterfly Lovers." The tale has appeared in manifold forms over the past fifty years: on stage as an opera and more recently a ballet as well as the inspiration for a widely performed violin concerto that was composed in Shanghai in the 1950s, a novelization also written in Shanghai in the 1950s, and in multiple versions on Pan-Chinese cinema and television screens, including an animated feature released to cinemas in early 2004 by Taiwanese producers under the English title *Butterfly Lovers: Leon and Jo.*[2] The story, in short: A young woman in Confucian China, Zhu Yingtai, is able to study only by dressing as a man. Setting off to school in that disguise, she becomes fast friends with a fellow student, Liang Shanbo, who does not see through her masquerade, even as they fall mutually in love. Eventually, she reveals her gender, and the pair aims to marry, but the young woman's father has betrothed her to a powerful local landlord, and she must yield to his decision. The romantic tragedy ends, inviting comparisons to *Romeo and Juliet,* with the lovers united in death, as they escape the tomb as a pair of butterflies.

Li Han-hsiang (Li Hanxiang; 1926–96) had already made a name for himself at Shaw Brothers, beginning with *Diau Charn/Diao Chan* (1958), for directing commercially successful historical costume dramas that developed a cinematic adaptation of the popular *huangmei diao* (yellow plum melody) opera style. Thought to have initially developed out of girls' tea-picking songs along the lower stretches of the Yangtze River, the *huangmei diao* popular folk theatrical tradition had evolved in early twentieth-century Shanghai into a melodic and emotionally expressive mode incorporating a range of Chinese and Western instruments and deftly integrating dance, song, and vernacular dialogue.[3] In its female-centered casting (with actress Ivy Ling Po/Ling Bo playing the male lead alongside Shaw Brothers' star Betty Loh Ti/Le Di as the female student) and the exceptional artistry of its mise-en-scène, poetic allusions, and musical realization, *Love Eterne* positively exceeded expectations for a contemporary screen version of that central work in the repertoire of Southeast Chinese regional operas.[4] The film set astounding new box office records upon its April 1963 release in Hong Kong, Taiwan, and elsewhere throughout Shaw Brothers' established distribution circuit in East and Southeast Asia.[5] Indeed, the film's reception rapidly developed, particularly in Taiwan, into an unprecedented cultural phenomenon that critics have characterized as a craze and frenzy, with thousands of middle-aged women as well as many men demonstrating an intense cult worship of Ling Bo, the actress who played the male lead. Film critic Peggy Chiao Hsiung-ping recalls that in Taiwan *Love Eterne* initiated the practice of going to the cinema repeatedly to see a popular film, with many returning to rewatch it twenty or more times. "[T]the audience would sing along with the stars. . . . [H]ousewives, young women, and children memorized the lyrics and knew the plot by heart. Regardless, they all had handkerchiefs ready for the tragic . . . scenes." She compares the experience of participation and community generated among *Love Eterne* audiences to the audience involvement in *Rocky Horror Picture Show* (Jim Sharman, 1975) that she witnessed years later in the United States.[6]

Chiao proposes several reasons for the film's remarkable popular impact in Taiwan in the 1960s. She argues that especially female audiences of the period were receptive to the film's thoroughly sympathetic depiction of a young woman struggling against the oppression of traditional female roles, behaviors, and values.[7] Chiao goes on to suggest that, possibly like some audiences for the all-female Japanese Takarazuka Revue, Ling Bo's fans may have seen their idol as an understanding and unthreatening surrogate male, with whom they could fantasize a "spiritual extramarital affair," which provided a safe means of their expressing desires that repressive marital morality otherwise disallowed. She further points to director Li's artistry in deploying rich visual imagery and making "economic but comprehensive" use of familiar poetic metaphors and visually symbolic tropes that satisfyingly evoked "the Chinese cultural landscape."[8] The skillful cinematic presentation of traditionally valued symbols and forms, including arched bridges and pavilions, fluent calligraphy and scroll paintings, and luxuriant costumes and set decorations, served to extend *Love Eterne*'s appeal to a broad cross-class and cross-gender viewership. Chiao asserts that the experience of *Love Eterne* may have fostered narcissistic projection particularly among the literati, evoking an intense nostalgia for an idealized prelapsarian China, particularly those in (self-imposed) exile from the homeland. However, Chiao also rather off-handedly points to an additional, explicitly political economic explanation for *Love Eterne*'s success: the ancillary saturation of limited media outlets, for "[B]efore and after [*Love Eterne*'s] release, the *huangmei diao* theme song had exploded in the world of radio and records," at a time when, she points out, radio and cinema were "the two most favoured entertainment media," for very few people in Taiwan could then afford television sets.[9]

Chiao's recollections and analyses have particular value for being one of the few English-language critical sources that seriously explore *Love Eterne*'s phenomenal Asian reception and possible sociocultural significance. But it was Chiao's compatriot, Ang Lee, who first alerted contemporary U.S. media consumers to *Love Eterne*'s iconographic cultural status and, indeed, very existence, for few Americans without direct ties to Asia or good knowledge of Chinese had likely ever heard of that film until Lee spoke about it in a *New York Times* feature in March 2001.[10] In that subsequently much-cited profile piece, one in a series of interviews that *Times* writer Rick Lyman conducted with contemporary (all male, mostly U.S.-based) film directors about a single film that had strongly influenced their own work, Lee praises *Love Eterne* as the pinnacle of the feminine melodramatic style that he says dominated Chinese filmmaking prior to the rise of the masculine martial arts genre. Lee explains that he sought to blend those two strands of (Hong Kong) film culture in making *Crouching Tiger, Hidden Dragon*, which, at the time the *New York Times* interview appeared, had been running for three months in U.S. theaters and nominated for ten Academy Awards, four of which it subsequently won.

Lee speaks at length in the interview about *Love Eterne*'s emotional impact on him as a child, when he saw the film repeatedly and each time cried copiously. Lee also remembers being able as a nine-year-old to recite *Love Eterne*'s entire dialogue weeks before seeing the film, thanks to the island-wide marketing of a four-record soundtrack simultaneous to the film's release in Taipei, Taiwan. Like Chiao, Lee asserts that the film was immensely popular with everyone in Taiwan, especially housewives, intellectuals, and children like himself. Lee attributes the film's power particularly to the capacity of its skillful cinematography and editing to elicit sympathy for the unconventionally characterized female lead and to glorify classical Chinese culture and geography. While briefly addressing factors underlying *Love Eterne*'s initial reception in Taiwan, Lee emphasizes the profound enduring effect that film has on him personally, without directly asserting its indisputable status as a national treasure for millions of Chinese.

By contrast, Chiao's essay, published two years later, concludes by noting *Love Eterne*'s revitalized popularity in Taiwan. She reports that "A new generation of film fans bore witness to the grand sing-along inside the cinema" at revival screenings of *Love Eterne* in Taipei in December 2002. Scheduled as the inaugural feature in a festival of six newly remastered Shaw Brothers films, *Love Eterne* had attracted packed houses, as did an associated concert performance that the now sixty-three-year-old Canadian resident Ling Bo had returned to deliver.[11] The English-language *Taipei Times* had helped publicize the gala events with advance reports under headlines like "Revisiting the Classics" and "Butterfly Lovers Still Crazy after 40 Years."[12] *The Taipei Times* incorporated Ang Lee's comments to the New York newspaper (without noting the source) as key evidence for *Love Eterne*'s continuing emotional power and cultural significance for a range of viewers, male as well as female. Thereby, the Taipei newspaper rallied interest in the revival as an occasion for national historical remembrance, clearly casting the experience of viewing *Love Eterne* as a metaphor for being, if not essentially Chinese, then Chinese Taiwanese, even if—as for Ang Lee—only from the far shores of the United States. The report does not make as explicit the likely connection between Lee's having publicly expressed his personal memories and high regard for *Love Eterne* in the internationally influential U.S. "newspaper of record" and the movie being highlighted in a commercial media event in his homeland eighteen months later.

Several younger Chinese film and cultural scholars who have grown up hearing about *Love Eterne*, like Siu Leung Li, Tan See Kam, and Annette Aw, have also recently addressed in print what value(s) and cultural meanings contemporary media consumers in Hong Kong and elsewhere in Asia may find in the film, particularly due to its complex cross-gender play.[13] Their analyses often compare the construction of *Love Eterne* to that of other *huangmei diaopian* or more recent cinematic retellings of *Liang Shanbo yu Zhu Yingtai* that through straight casting and narrative reshaping attempt to "unqueer" the 1963 film's thoroughly embedded gender bending, such as the 1991 Cantonese version directed by Tsui Hark (Xu Ke) in Hong Kong and circulated under the English title *The Lovers*.[14] However, these elucidating critical reconsiderations do not seek to the same extent as Chiao's or even Ang Lee's to document or analyze *Love Eterne*'s initial historical impact with audiences in Asia and among Chinese populations elsewhere. Extending Chiao and Lee's accounts, I would argue that *Love Eterne*'s power with audiences at the time of its release arose from three facets of its construction and experience: its artfully realizing (and subtly modernizing) a mixture of popular cultural styles of representation, its engaging in mid-twentieth-century debates about changing familial and gender roles, and its eliciting catharsis about recent political trauma.

In *Love Eterne,* two actresses appear as the "butterfly lovers" in a prelapsarian China: *center,* Betty Loh Ti, as Zhu Yingtai in the male disguise that has enabled her to pursue formal study; *right,* Ivy Ling Po, playing her classmate and "sworn brother" Liang Shanbo. In this "eighteen-mile escorting" scene, Shanbo remains humorously oblivious to Yingtai's persistent attempts before their parting to reveal her gender through poetic song. (Courtesy of Celestial Pictures Ltd.)

To Pan-Chinese audiences in the early 1960s, part of *Love Eterne*'s appeal inhered in its realizing the well-loved story afresh in the quite distinctive *huangmei diao* cinematic style that built on a popular tradition of Cantonese opera films that Shaw Brothers and other Hong Kong studios had elaborated for the modern screen beginning in the late 1950s. These purportedly feminine costume film melodramas very fluently integrated stylized traditional Chinese cultural forms (drawing not only from popular opera but also from an amalgam of classical and vernacular architecture, painting, poetry, and legend) with more naturalistic and contemporary cinematic representational techniques, including Hollywood-style camerawork and continuity editing. *Love Eterne*'s synthesis of those elements seems particularly and consistently fluent, due to its almost constantly tracking camera and character movement, its luxuriant and colorful set design laden with cultural symbols, Loh and Ling's passionate yet graceful performances, and the subtle segues between melodic musical interludes and the familiar dialogue, spoken in (dubbed) vernacular Mandarin, the official language of both the People's Republic and Taiwan. Such multifaceted formal fluency surely brought great aesthetic pleasure to many viewers then, as now, especially in Taiwan and among recent emigrants elsewhere from the mainland who could appreciate the film's literal fluency in their mother tongue.

As Ang Lee, Chiao, and others have argued, Li Han-hsiang's adaptation (and Betty Loh Ti's performance) presents Yingtai as an emergent contemporary woman who struggles against restraints on her personal freedom and desires and even actively resists the powerful overarching code of filial piety. From the opening scene, Yingtai agitates to attend school like a young man, and on first meeting with Shanbo fifteen minutes into the film explicitly advocates equality between the sexes from within her male disguise; indeed, as Chiao points out, Yingtai falls in love with Shanbo *because* he defends women's rights.[15] This version's unusual emphasis on the central female character (to say nothing of its complex engagement with gender relations through its cross-dressed same-sex casting, however conventional those encodings within Chinese opera) was likely another factor in its initial appeal, along with its humor (as a cross-dressing comedy) and the overall sense of modernity (often, as here, within a classical guise) that Shaw Brothers productions encoded. For example, the bright, colorful look and playful exchanges through the film's first three-quarters (before the lovers must perforce part and die) create a light tone that evokes an operetta in the Western tradition or even a 1930s Hollywood screwball comedy as much as a tragic time-honored Chinese tale.[16] *Love Eterne* thereby adeptly evades Paul Fonoroff's characterization of Hong Kong *huangmei diao* musicals as a "decidedly traditional mode" of movies, to which, he notes, "at a time . . . [of] rapid modernization and Westernization both Cantonese and Mandarin cinema audiences flocked."[17]

Nonetheless, the remarkably broad Pan-Chinese response to this particular Shaw production points to its capacity to deeply engage viewers at a fundamentally conservative level, that of national cultural identity, even as the film served metaphorically to bridge national difference for and within its audience.[18] Shaw Brothers' Mandarin *huangmei diao* films of the late 1950s and early 1960s (sometimes dubbed or subtitled in Chinese script to extend distribution) filled a market niche that their own and other producers' Cantonese opera films of the 1930s to 1950s had served in Hong Kong and among overseas Chinese film audiences elsewhere.[19] Law Kar's argument that the internationally popular Cantonese opera companies that toured widely during the 1920s and 1930s brought "community feeling and cultural nourishment from the homeland to Chinese communities abroad"[20] would seem to pertain to costume drama films of the 1950s and 1960s in either spoken dialect. But it is clear that especially Mandarin-speaking refugees and residents in Taiwan and elsewhere, struggling in the 1960s to remain politically and culturally fully Chinese—that is, to establish an alternative Chinese national identity in the rapidly modernizing world away from the mainland—were especially responsive to *Love Eterne*'s idyllic rendering of the now Forbidden Country. Besides through the implicitly contemporary performance of the lovers' roles and its gender complexities, the film appears in the 1960s to have attracted fervent responses from many precisely through the regressively nostalgic respite it offered from the cold facts of recent emigration. Indeed, that appeal itself seems a strong, enduring basis for *Love Eterne*'s impressive economic as well as its emotional impact: its offering millions of Chinese, displaced or otherwise recently affected by war, revolution, and poverty, a beguilingly colorful, melodic experience of a particularly nostalgically envisioned homeland.

Crossing the Pacific:
From Li Han-hsiang to Frank Lee Sr.

Among the Shaw family's many contributions over their decades-long development of a Pan-Chinese entertainment circuit, film historians have well documented especially Run Run Shaw's innovations in producing and distributing the Hong Kong–based Mandarin-language films produced after he relocated from Singapore and with Runme organized Shaw Brothers (HK) Ltd. in 1958. Policies that gave that company a competitive edge in Asia included, in Poshek Fu's words, "professionalism, lavishness, rational management, advanced technology, and aggressive marketing"; "[Run Run] Shaw understood the importance of promotion and marketing in a mass consumer economy."[21] By the mid-1960s, these practices had helped Shaw Brothers attain a dominant position in the Hong Kong and established Southeast Asian circuits and gain an increased share of the lucrative film market in Taiwan. Notably, Run Run Shaw's strategy of introducing films internationally through festivals had succeeded handsomely: Shaw films and stars had been a visible presence and frequent winners at the Asian Film Festival since its founding in Japan in 1954, and the whole company had gained prestige through visibility gained at that and other film events in the Pacific region. *Love Eterne* further augmented Shaw Brothers reputation for distinctive, quality productions when the film swept the awards at the second annual Taipei Golden Horse Film Festival.

Apparently seeking also to gain broader access to North American and European audiences (or, at minimum, further enhance the company's reputation in Asia), Shaw Brothers (HK) Ltd. began submitting its prestige productions to film festivals in Europe and the United States immediately upon undertaking Mandarin-language film production in Hong Kong in 1958. Three Shaw films played at the Cannes International Film Festival between 1960 and 1963: *The Enchanting Shadow* (*Qiannü Youhun*, 1960), starring Betty Loh Ti; *The Magnificent Concubine* (*Yang Kwei Fei*, 1962); and *Empress Wu* (*Wu Tse-tien*, 1963), both starring Li Lihua. Li Han-hsiang directed all three titles. *Magnificent Concubine* won a special Grand Prix for cinematography at the Cannes Film Festival, and *Empress Wu* played at the 1963 Berlin International Film Festival as well as at Cannes. By the close of that year, appropriately dubbed versions of both films had opened for commercial runs in London and Paris, with *Empress Wu* reportedly becoming "the then widest released Chinese film in history."[22]

Movies produced by the Shaw family companies and other major film companies based in East and Southeast Asia (and sometimes in the United States itself) had long enjoyed successful runs in U.S. Chinatown theaters, especially in Honolulu, San Francisco, and New York City.[23] In the early 1960s, however, Shaw Brothers began actively to cultivate opportunities for crossover exhibition of their Mandarin films in North America. Thus Run Run Shaw traveled to the U.S. West Coast (including to the Seattle World's Fair) in 1962 and the next year sent his daughter Vivian to the Honolulu opening of *Love Eterne*.[24] Several years prior to making those personal appearances and prior even to gaining exposure for Li-directed films through European festivals, however, Shaw Brothers had steadily begun submitting its prizewinning productions to the first international film festival in the Western hemisphere, in San Francisco.

The founder, in 1957, and force for a number of years behind the San Francisco International Film Festival was Irving Levin. Levin operated a number of San Francisco movie theaters that he had inherited, some of which played foreign films throughout the 1950s. The festival design bespoke Levin's and the cosponsoring city art commission's combined art and commercial goals.[25] During those initial years, scheduled to run for about two weeks in late October and early November, the festival generally featured a single film (most in their North American premieres) from each of a dozen or so countries, each shown once or twice in an English-subtitled original-language version in evening or weekend matinee screenings. The festival venue was a large downtown Levin-owned first-run theater (initially the Metro) that remained open to the public.

Between 1958 and 1964, seven "Chinese" films played at the San Francisco festival, five of them Shaw Brothers productions, along with two titles by other Hong Kong–based producers: in 1958 *Nobody's Child* (*Kuer Liulang Ji*, 1958), directed by Bu Wancang (with production attributed to Tang Wei/Guofeng), and the following year *Tragedy of Love* (*Tian Chang Di Jiu*, 1959), directed by Doe Ching (Tao Qin) and produced by MP & GI (Cathay), Shaw Brothers' primary competitor. Given the concerted rivalry between the two companies during that period, it is no surprise to find that the Shaw Brothers also had its first entry at the San Francisco International Film Festival that year: *Kingdom and the Beauty* (*Jiang Shan Mei Ren*, 1959), directed by Li Han-hsiang. Shaw Brothers appears subsequently to have won a kind of monopoly as a representative for films from Hong Kong, Taiwan, Formosa, or "China," as festival records and newspaper reviews describe the sources of the subsequent Shaw entries. Li's *Enchanting Shadow*, an evocative ghost story, played in 1960 (as it had at Cannes five months earlier), followed in 1961 by the contemporary drama *The Golden Trumpet* (*Jin La Ba*, 1961), directed by Doe Ching, who had joined Shaw Brothers. After a year's interlude came *Love Eterne* in 1963 and the next year *Between Tears and Smiles* (*Yu Lou Sanfeng*, 1964), directed by Lo Chen and starring Li Lihua and Ivy Ling Po (Ling Bo).[26] Subsequent to the 1964 event, the San Francisco International Film Festival included no further feature films from China (of whatever geographical attribution) until 1971, when it presented *Red Detachment of Women* from the People's Republic.[27]

Although the Hollywood establishment generally ignored the festival in its early years, the industry trade journal *Variety* carried short reviews of most features, including Shaw's submissions. *The San Francisco Chronicle* also printed a fairly substantial review of most festival features, again including the Shaw films. But those reviews generally appeared only a few days after each Chinese film's single screening, in contrast to the next-day reviews that *The Chronicle* ran on most European and other entries, which appeared in time to attract audiences to second showings of those titles.

Like Shaw entries in other years, *Love Eterne* played in the festival theater on a Sunday afternoon, outside the prime evening screening times but presumably convenient for families of Chinese or other backgrounds who might want to attend. Two days following the November 10, 1963, screening, *The San Francisco Chronicle* ran a review (on the festival's closing day) by John Wasserman under the headline, "An Exquisite Chinese Film." After noting that the film was "Formosa's entry" (a categorical attribution enabling the film to represent the then U.S. trade-worthy "China"), Wasserman praised the "extraordinarily beautiful" settings and cinematography and suggested that the film might win the best photography prize (which it did not). Wasserman also showed appreciation for the film's humor and remarked that it offers "an interesting look at upper class customs in old China" but complained that "endless repetition" of the musical theme becomes tedious.[28] Judy Stone's review the next day in *Variety* expressed the same emphases: the poetic tale of doomed love in Fourth Century China has much humor and charm and the film is visually superb, but it lacks commercial appeal for Western audiences.[29]

I have not yet been able to locate other indications of the film's immediate reception in its first venue playing outside Chinatowns in the United States: what the size and ethnic or language composition of the audience at Levin's Metro theater was or whether viewers sang along or shed tears of national cultural sentiment or otherwise. Short of that information, we can seek to position the film at least tentatively within a historically detailed local cultural and political landscape. Certainly, the local and national context in November 1963 is quite distinctive and memorable, especially for those who experienced it: Within two weeks after *Love Eterne* played at the festival, President John F. Kennedy was assassinated. News and analysis of that event and its aftermath supplanted the *Chronicle*'s usual coverage of the art and entertainment scene for a period. However, its advertisements for feature film showings indicate that cinema fare otherwise playing in San Francisco diverged rather markedly from the style, not to say the national cultural derivation, of *Love Eterne*. Following the festival, Levin's and other Bay Area first-run movie houses were playing titles like *Cleopatra*, *Lilies of the Field*, *How the West Was Won*, and *55 Days at Peking* (a dramatic depiction of the defeat of the Boxer Rebellion, directed by Nicholas Ray and featuring an all-star cast, including Charlton Heston and Ava Gardner). Meanwhile, second-run or smaller theaters showed films like *The Birds*, *Touch of Evil*, and a few foreign "art films" (often European sex comedies or existentialist New Wave films).

Such parallel occurrences to *Love Eterne*'s screening might suggest little hope of Shaw Brothers Ltd. gaining U.S. distribution or even any further crossover play dates for that or any titles the company had submitted to the San Francisco festival, however varied their styles and period settings. Indeed, most international entries (and independently produced U.S. entries) in those years at the San Francisco Festival, even those that won top prizes, never achieved wide (if any) circulation or lasting recognition in the United States. Less than a year later, however, *Love Eterne* did, quite exceptionally, have a six-week run at a newly opened art cinema in San Francisco in fall

1964 and a few months later opened for a month-long run in New York City at the 55th Street Playhouse, a 250-seat Midtown cinema that had long programmed international films and Hollywood art film revivals.[30]

In both cities, *Love Eterne* appeared in movie houses that had recently adopted policies of programming exclusively Mandarin films with English and Chinese subtitles and, in fact, of showing only Shaw Brothers' Mandarin films, primarily its spectacular costume dramas. In San Francisco, the previously shuttered Bella Union Theater reopened in May 1964 with daily screenings for eight weeks of the Asian prizewinning film *The Lady General* (*Hua Mulan*, Yueh Feng, 1964), starring Ivy Ling Po as Mulan. A succession of titles directed by Li Han-hsiang followed, including *Love Eterne,* which played twice daily from early September to mid-October in a double bill with Doe Ching's *Love without End* (*Bu Liao Qing*, 1961), starring Lin Dai.[31] In New York City, *Love Eterne* ran from mid-January to mid-February 1965 as the second entry in an extensive series of Shaw titles at the 55th Street Playhouse that had begun the previous month, starting with *The Last Woman of Shang* (*Da Ji*, Yueh Feng, 1964, starring Lin Dai), which played for a month over the holidays. *The Lady General* immediately followed *Love Eterne*, also for a four-week run. Among other Shaw Brothers titles that played in the first year of that theater's exclusive programming of Mandarin-language films were *The Empress Wu, The Shepherd Girl* (*Shan Ge Lian*, Law Chun, 1964), and *The Grand Substitution* (*Wan Gu Liu Fang*, Yan Jun, 1965), another *huangmei*-style film starring Ivy Ling Po and Li Lihua.

As surprising as the phenomenon is of Shaw's 1960s Mandarin-language costume dramas running one after the other, multiple times daily, through the mid-1960s in U.S. cities outside Chinatowns—especially notably in Midtown Manhattan, those bookings of course did not yet constitute a breakthrough into the broader U.S. film distribution and exhibition market. Both the reopened Bella Union and the 55th Street Playhouse targeted an art house clientele, including moviegoers with Chinese associations who might patronize theaters outside ethnically segregated residential and business areas.[32] Nonetheless, within the U.S. social and film industrial contexts of that period (as even now, despite changes that have occurred), the very fact of such regular screenings being set up and persisting, as newspaper records reveal, for several years running, is a remarkable film historical moment worthy of closer investigation. Given their almost identical programming policies, it is also no surprise to discover that a single operator had leased both theaters: a San Francisco native named Frank Lee Sr. It is not yet clear how the agreement between Lee and Shaw Brothers initially came about, whether Lee approached Shaw Brothers or the Hong Kong company somehow identified Lee as a possible in-country exhibitor/distributor through other channels. Certainly, substantial backing from Shaw Brothers or other investors had to be involved. Born in California of parents who had emigrated from Guangdong, Lee was educated in both the United States and China and worked for a number of years in San Francisco as an engineer. Lee also became a civic leader in San Francisco's Chinatown, and in the mid-1950s he and his wife founded and for a number of years produced and directed the radio program *Voice of Chinatown*.[33] Lee eventually resigned his engineering position at the Presidio (an outpost of the U.S. Department of Defense) to concentrate on exhibiting and distributing Chinese-language films in a number of cities in North America.[34]

Reports in *The Chronicle* and *New York Times* about the local theater conversion to a Mandarin movie house, as well as the reviews of the opening films, both emphasize Lee's link to Shaw Brothers and the company's important status in Asia and allow Lee to articulate Shaw's transcultural business aims. In a June 1964 *Chronicle* interview, Lee explains, "I want to expose the American public to good Chinese films that appeal to both Caucasian and Oriental audiences . . . [to] expose the Caucasian and the American Chinese to the history and culture of China."[35] An early December 1964 piece by *New York Times* movie reporter and critic Howard Thompson notes Shaw Brothers' business plan for expansion into the U.S. film market: "The local response to the films . . . will help shape plans for showings in other major cities." The article further cites Lee:

> We have very carefully chosen New York as a springboard for our operation for good reasons. The four Chinese film theaters operating here in Chinatown show only movies in Cantonese dialect that are geared for mass Chinese audiences. In Greater New York alone, we estimate 30,000 people have a familiarity with Mandarin dialect. We feel that this is the right place and time, culturally and commercially, for a large scale introduction of our best films, on an art-house level, to American audiences.[36]

Subsequent developments suggest that the joint Shaw/Lee endeavor had a rather mixed outcome, at least in the short term. The San Francisco and New York venues apparently enjoyed sufficient success not only to continue showing Shaw Mandarin titles continuously for several years but also to encourage Lee to expand the programming to a Los Angeles art house.[37] Within three years, by spring 1967, however, the profile of the films running at the 55th Street Playhouse had shifted, as Lee's programming began to introduce

Japanese samurai films starring Tatsuya Nakadai and Toshiro Mifune.[38] New York art house popularity of Japanese historical action dramas, which had followed in part upon their garnering festival prizes and critical acclaim in Europe and elsewhere, formed an important context for the reception of Hong Kong–produced films in the United States and certainly warrants further research, as do Shaw Brothers' and other Chinese producers' relations to Japanese movie production.[39] Questions of cinematic artistry, established cultural and economic exchange, and Cold War imperatives all doubtless figured into the circumscribed reception or, in the limited instance of the trajectory of Lee's programming at the 55th Street Playhouse, direct displacement of Chinese by Japanese period films. But at least in the present case focused on Frank Lee's experiences, this programming shift appears to have had less to do with national origin than with gender, as—judging from successive program listings and advertisements in *The New York Times*—the "feminine" Hong Kong (in Ang Lee's terms) musical costume dramas gradually ceded the 55th Street Playhouse screen to masculine martial arts action films.

Such explicitly engendered genre associations clearly emerge in the New York film critics' initial response to the new programming, beginning particularly with *Love Eterne,* the second film Lee ran at the 55th Street Playhouse. Again, as for the San Francisco film festival screening, film reviews offer the limited available record of viewer response to *Love Eterne* and the other Shaw titles that Lee promoted. But those reviews are extraordinarily vivid and telling and likely substantially influenced Caucasian and other non-Chinese readers' potential movie attendance and reactions, especially at the commercially crucial New York venue. Longtime *New York Times* lead film critic Bosley Crowther reviewed three of the first four films Frank Lee booked at the Playhouse, including *Love Eterne;* especially his responses likely had an immediate impact, for his stature and emphatic voice set a distinctive tone. All three reviews are essentially pans, overall dismissing the films with what from forty years' remove seems inexcusable cultural and linguistic ignorance and rude condescension. Like the West Coast festival reviewers, Crowther praises *Love Eterne*'s cinematography and settings and costumes, even to a point of hyperbole: "[T]he silken intricacy of the things the characters wear and the superb ingenuity of the hair styles continue to cause astonishment and delight." He also finds the leading players "fascinating," noting that "Betty Loh Tih [*sic*] . . . is nice to look at" and that "Ivy Ling Po, who in the traditional fashion, plays the man, does a rather amusing impersonation, aided somewhat by her Clark Gable ears."[40]

Crowther otherwise jokes at length about *Love Eterne*'s being "appropriately named," for, he exclaims, "it inclines to a characteristic signified by the name of Mr. Shaw. It runs on and on—it seems forever . . . the separate scenes are extended to interminable lengths. The characters . . . continue their exchanges as though there were no one to tell them when to stop . . . even a fascinated viewer is likely to become thoroughly wearied before the end." His remarks about the singing and dialogue, which so entranced Chinese viewers far and wide, are even more dismissive: "[T]he dialogue is exchanged in reedy, screechy sing-song voices" and, however much the film may rely on "the conventions and the lore of the Chinese theater," of which he flatly professes ignorance, "it's all quite tedious, by occidental comparisons."

Crowther adopts a marginally less arrogant tone in addressing the matter of language in response to "readers who hastened to correct a mistake I made." In his review the previous month of *The Last Woman of Shang*, he had commented, "A feature of this and other Shaw productions is that the dialogue is spoken in Mandarin, the pure ancient language of China, as distinct from the latter-day dialects, which indicate that even our local dialect speakers will have to read what is being said."[41] He concludes his *Love Eterne* review by dutifully (and more correctly) explaining the need for both Chinese and English subtitles, but signs off rather flippantly: "You pay your money and you take your pick."

Possibly in response to reader (or Lee's own?) complaints about the tone or effect of Crowther's scathing pan, a backup critic named Howard Thompson reviewed Lee's next Shaw release, *The Lady General*. Thompson's generally positive short review makes a point of noting that "[t]he English titles are easy enough to follow on the screen,"[42] and in the many reviews he wrote in the coming years of films running at the 55th Street Playhouse appears altogether more open-minded and cosmopolitan than Crowther. Indeed, a week following the appearance of Crowther's *Love Eterne* review, a report by Thompson appeared on the subject of ethnic movie theaters, which began, "Foreign-language films without subtitles are a flourishing entertainment fixture in the metropolitan area."[43]

The following month, Crowther wrote the review of *Empress Wu*, the last he would give of a Shaw Brothers film, and used the occasion to continue his campaign against subtitling. Indeed, Crowther focuses quite evident antagonism toward the film, besides on star Li Lihua (whom he says, "plays the supposedly volatile empress with virtuous vapidity"), on the necessity of reading subtitles: "[The dialogue] may be euphonious and eloquent to those whose ears are tuned to the meanings and accent of the Mandarin dialect . . . [b]ut for those of us who have to pick it out of the Chinese or English subtitles that glitter like strings of winking sequins at the bottom of the frame, it is dismally infelicitous and hard to follow. . . . It is also excruciatingly painful and punishing on the eyes."[44] Crowther (who became critic emeritus in late 1967 and fully retired in 1969) had earlier in his long career become known both for encouraging attendance at international films that were "strikingly different in content and technique from American productions" and for leading "the movement that popularized dubbing for non-art house patrons."[45] And even Howard Thompson, for all his comparative "lack of contempt" (to cite a posthumous profile of the critic), did subsequently complain in his Shaw film reviews about the discomfort of reading "tiny, rather squatty English titles" at the bottom of the screen.[46]

These New York critics' reactions to subtitling were likely a crucial factor in the mid-1960s reception of *Love Eterne* and other Shaw films' reception in the United States, even among those film writers and art film exhibitors and patrons who otherwise readily tolerated or even sought out subtitled original-language versions of international films—at least if the language were Indo-European or the film at least stylishly modernist. The trial run with the 55th Street Playhouse showings appears gradually to have convinced Frank Lee and Shaw Brothers that they could not reach substantial crossover audiences or even engage supposedly urbane film critics in the United States with subtitled Mandarin productions, however artistic their cinematic style or classical their literary source. Further research may reveal whether these critical discourses in 1964 and 1965 had direct bearing on subsequent business decisions in favor of the practice of reediting and dubbing martial arts films for broader U.S. release (an issue of ongoing industry concern resulting in the delayed U.S. release—or Hollywood-instigated shelving—of Chinese films). Lee's New York experiences in any case indicated that even Shaw's very best historical costume dramas, which had won numerous prestigious prizes in Asia, could not bridge what the influential 1960s film critics in the United States implied was—and thereby helped to perpetuate—a vast cultural divide. Thereby, I would argue that the critics' plaints about dim subtitles for the unfamiliar language functioned largely synecdochically: It was not only the films' spoken and sung language that they found incomprehensible, but also their use of genre conventions, their national/cultural signification, and even their inscription of gender.

Those three terms provide a concluding basis for assessing the overall disappointing reception of *Love Eterne* in the United States in the mid-1960s, compared to its huge popularity in East and Southeast Asia. First, beyond admiring the film's beguiling use of texture and color and camera (thereby largely addressing its formal visual construction), critics on both U.S. coasts situated *Love Eterne* largely in relation to traditional Chinese opera, however little they themselves knew of those traditions. In arguing that the film's purported genre conventions—such as extended, apparently repetitive musical sequences and stylized body movements—threw up a barrier to Western audiences, the reviewers lost in their translation for readers the film's combinations of styles and conventions—the modernizing of the traditional—that some U.S. audiences might have (as now) discerned and enjoyed, even without having linguistic access to *Love Eterne*'s realization of poetic language in dialogue and song that so enthralled audiences in Taiwan and elsewhere. Nor could they themselves grasp the subtle signification of the actors' gestures or details in the mise-en-scène that so had gratified audiences educated in classical Chinese culture. The U.S. critics also had no knowledge of the genealogy or cultural significance of "The Butterfly Lovers" tale and so could not position the film as an adaptation nor otherwise enrich their readers' contexts for approaching its narrative or characters.

The "fascinating" and "charming" performances of the leads seemed to offer more crossover appeal, at least for the duration of the viewing, but that was not supported by any established star personae circulating outside the cinema. Quite notably, the refreshing revision of conventional gender and generational behavior patterns that the film evidently suggested to many Chinese viewers elicited no comment in the U.S. reviews: The "Feminine Mystique" appears still to have held sway over Crowther, certainly, but even the evidently more progressive critics did not respond explicitly to Yingtai's (contextually unusual) depiction, perhaps because the character seemed so much like a familiar Western type: a modern young woman. Even the single aspect of the film that usually first catches a contemporary U.S. viewer's attention and possible interest—the obvious cross-gender masquerade—went all but unremarked in San Francisco and New York.[47] Yet especially Crowther—who praised Ivy Ling Po's "amusing" masquerade—seemed provoked by the overall feminine gendering of the film: its nuance in framing and editing, its slower pacing, its building narratively from indirectly conveyed emotions to impassioned melodramatic expression. Thus, *Love Eterne*'s inscription of gender, like that of genre, proved more of a barrier than a basis for connection, particularly, I would suggest, given the primary masculine gender of the critics at that time—and of the dominant U.S. art-film audience of the period.

Finally, the facet of *Love Eterne* that I have argued may have lent its particular power for Taiwanese and other diasporic Chinese at the historical moment of its release—its appealing for a depoliticized Pan-Chinese cultural unity through its idyllic depictions of a pleasantly modernized premodern China—would also not have registered for many potential non-Chinese viewers, who most likely framed the issues of the "two Chinas" in relation to the mid-1960s public discourse about which country should have United Nations membership.[48] Although *Love Eterne* did no doubt signify "China" to those in the United States who saw the film (if not to those who heard only the title), it was to a China of a distant time and imagined space, possibly, like the subtitles, too distant for ease of comprehension. Thus the production and reception of *Love Eterne* in Asia did not manage successfully to bridge the film economic and cultural divide of the Pacific beyond the ongoing interflow into and out of diasporic Chinese communities or on their peripheries, where bicultural Chinese Americans like Frank Lee resided.

Conclusion: From Lee Sr. to Lee Jr. and Ang Lee

Four decades later, the same major newspaper that had invited Frank Lee to speak of his media crossover ambitions (before Crowther's reviews sharply undercut their realization) cited Ang Lee's aims for his Asia-produced, Mandarin-language genre, gender, and cultural crossover film *Crouching Tiger, Hidden Dragon*: "I wanted to appeal to the Asian audiences and to the Western art-house audience. I had no idea of it crossing over to the Western mainstream, as it has."[49] The similarity of the two Mr. Lees' statements is striking, as is the very different outcome of their goals: Frank Lee voices his hopes; Ang Lee modestly downplays having already surpassed his. The circumstances allowing for a more visible, if not necessarily more balanced and continuous, Asian-U.S. media interflow had clearly changed somewhat in the intervening thirty-five years, in complex ways and for reasons that many scholars have addressed.

Although *Crouching Tiger, Hidden Dragon* is not a Hong Kong production (however much producers there might retroactively have wished it were), it certainly arose out of the same mode of cultural and generic hybridity that Hong Kong cinema realized as thoroughly forty years ago as presently. Indeed, Ang Lee himself points out that he shaped his film consciously as a hybrid largely of two forty-year-old "Chinese" film genres (without noting their initial Hong Kong rooting.) Both of those genres made surface claims (e.g., through nostalgic, somewhat culturally essentialist representations as in *Love Eterne*) of being Pan-Chinese and harbored commercial aims of achieving that audience and more. Although both genres (and their realization in *Crouching Tiger*) succeeded stupendously in the Asian region, only the "masculine" martial arts films of the 1960s and 1970s managed a crossover into the North American market—and that is arguably the generic strand of *Crouching Tiger, Hidden Dragon* that bore Lee into the upper echelons of global filmmakers.[50] And yet that breakthrough was of course not sudden nor, for that matter, enduring, neither for Ang Lee nor for another even more revered cinema star named Lee active in late 1960s and early 1970s that I have not mentioned.

Returning in summary to the period preceding the ostensible climactic moment: The forgotten historical record I have pointed to previously reveals that the more successful 1970s crossover distribution of "masculine" Hong Kong martial arts films in New York City and elsewhere in the United States (which occurred to some extent also under Frank Lee's sponsorship) clearly built on the extensive and persistent U.S. market exploration and exhibition efforts that that individual U.S. entrepreneur had undertaken with the Shaw Brothers' "feminine" prestige pictures. However modest or unprofitable their initial joint efforts to reach a crossover U.S. audience, Lee's and Shaw Brothers' attempts to exhibit to U.S. urban dwellers the musical costume films that were so popular in Asia garnered important business experiences and cross-cultural insights that laid the groundwork for future export strategies not only for Shaw Brothers but also for Raymond Chow, who took the knowledge thus gleaned as he founded Golden Harvest in 1970. Ultimately, one must thus recognize Ang Lee's debt not only to the Li who directed the younger Lee's much-loved film *Love Eterne* but also to his heretofore unsung predecessor in crossover cultural bridge building, Frank Lee (and, all right, also to Frank Lee's fellow San Francisco–born Chinese American Bruce).

Frank Lee's promotion of crossover reception of Chinese films outside segregated U.S. Chinese communities continues fluently in the work of Frank Lee Jr., who owns and operates San Francisco's Four Star Theater, where he sometimes shows the Shaw prints his recently deceased father accumulated along with many other Asian and independent U.S. films to an ethnically and culturally mixed audience. Lee Jr. also founded an annual Asian Film Festival in 1997 and has since 2004 operated another movie theater, the Presidio, which he rescued from threat of demolition and developed into a four-screen cinema venue at which he programs both first-run releases and independent and international film fare.[51] The film *Love Eterne* would likely not attract the sing-along local audiences in Frank Lee Jr.'s cinema locales that it did in Taipei in 2002—although it might well gain a playful crossover gender-bending following at theaters like the Castro in San Francisco and in other U.S. urban centers. The Bella Union, 55th Street Playhouse, Canal, and other cinemas where Lee's father showed *Love Eterne* for weeks on end in the mid-1960s have since mostly been demolished, but a would-be crossover viewer need no longer, as Rick Lyman advised in 2001, hope to be the lucky consumer who might "stumble across a copy from abroad in some out-of-the-way video shop."[52] Hong Kong–based Celestial's clearly subtitled, well-produced, and fully legal DVD and VCD copies of *Love Eterne* and most of the other titles mentioned in this chapter are now (or soon will be) available in the United States via the Internet from enterprising vendors on both coasts who carry on, in a new technological mode, the important cross-cultural distribution of Hong Kong cinema initiated by Frank Lee Sr.

Notes

For research and other assistance and conceptual input into this ongoing project, I thank Nancy Abelmann, Gene Bild, David Bordwell, Anne Burkus-Chasson, Chan Wing Hang, Jing Jing Chang, David Desser, Poshek Fu, Han Mei, Linn Haynes, Hoover Hu Jingzhen, Jennifer Law, Law Kar, Frank Lee, Nicole Lee, Emilie Yeh Yueh-Yu, Yung Sai-Shing, and Gary Xu Gang, as well as the staff of the University of Illinois Library. I also thank the U.S. Fulbright Association and the David C. Lam Institute for East West Studies (LEWI) for the opportunity to develop and present the material to Hong Kong–based audiences during a research semester in spring 2004.

1. Direction and screenplay by Li Hanxiang (Li Han-hsiang); produced by Zhao Yifu (Run Run Shaw); assistant directors Hu Jinquan (King Hu), Song Cunshou, and Zhu Mu; cinematography by Nishimoto Tadashi (He Lanshan); art direction by Chen Qirui; music composition by Zhou Lanping, edited by Jiang Xinglong; with Le Di (Betty Loh Ti), Ling Bo (Ivy Ling Po), Ren Jie, and Li Kun.

2. *Leon and Jo,* dir. Tsai Ming Ching, with voices by Rene Liu, Elva Hsiao, and Jacky Wu, 2004. In his recent book *Cross-Dressing in Chinese Opera* (Hong Kong: HKU Press, 2003), Siu Leung Li mentions several Chinese anthologies that comprehensively list the legend's multiple manifestations, including "a three-volume monumental collection published by the esteemed Zhonghua Press in Beijing in 1999" (p. 110).

3. Siu Wang-Ngai, *Chinese Opera: Images and Stories,* with Peter Lovrick (Vancouver: University of British Columbia Press, 1997), pp. 22–23. On the *huangmei diao* film style, see Paul Fonoroff's essay "Hong Kong Cinema," in Yingjin Zhang and Zhiwei Xiao, eds., *Encyclopedia of Chinese Film* (London: Routledge, 1998), p. 39.

4. See Li, *Cross-Dressing in Chinese Opera,* p. 112, and, for the images of the operatic costuming conventions, Siu, *Chinese Opera,* pp. 33–35.

5. That circuit did not include the Chinese mainland, as that territory was politically closed to Shaw's films; on this point, see Fonoroff, "Hong Kong Cinema," p. 37. For box office reports, see Jiao Xiongping (Peggy Chiao Hsiung-ping), *Gai bian lishi*

di wunian: Guo lian dianying yanjiu (*Five Years that Changed History: Studies on the Guolian Studio*) (Taipei, Taiwan: Wanxiang, 1993), pp. 16–18. For a brief account in the official Shaw company history, see "About Shaw," available at http://www.shaw.sg/sw_about.aspx.

6. Peggy Chiao Hsiung-ping, "The Female Consciousness, the World of Signification and Safe Extramarital Affairs: A 40th Year Tribute to *The Love Eterne*," in *The Shaw Screen: A Preliminary Study* (Hong Kong: Hong Kong Film Archive, 2003), pp. 76–77.

7. Ibid., pp. 79, 84.

8. Ibid., p. 83.

9. Ibid., p. 75.

10. Rick Lyman, "Watching Movies with Ang Lee," *New York Times*, March 9, 2001. In fact, Lyman does not provide readers with accurate information to identify and locate the film, for, probably due to a fact-checker's relying too heavily on the Internet Movie Database or other online source, information at the article's end falsely identifies the Chinese title of the film he watched with Lee as *Qi Cai Hu Bu Gui*. The English title of *that* film is, in fact, *Eternal Love*, but it is a Cantonese film directed by Li Tie (Lee Tit) in 1966. The information in Lyman's article confuses things further by listing that film's release date as 1963 and giving a combination of the production credits from the two films.

11. Chiao, "The Female Consciousness," p. 85. Hong Kong–based Celestial Pictures had organized the event to herald its release of the first of 760 Shaw feature films to appear on DVD, all of which should be released over the next few years.

12. Yu Sen-Lun, "Revisiting the Classics," *Taipei Times*, December 6, 2002; Yu Sen-Lun, "Butterfly Lovers Still Crazy after 40 Years," *Taipei Times*, December 13, 2002.

13. Li, *Cross-Dressing in Chinese Opera*, especially chapter 5, pp. 109–34; Tan See Kam and Annette Aw, "Love Eterne: Almost a (Heterosexual) Love Story," in Chris Berry, ed., *Chinese Films in Focus: 25 New Takes* (London: British Film Institute, 2003), pp. 137–43.

14. Li, *Cross-Dressing in Chinese Opera*, pp. 127–31.

15. Chiao, "The Female Consciousness," p. 79

16. For readings of the film's use of opera conventions, see Tan and Aw, "Love Eterne"; Li, *Cross-Dressing in Chinese Opera*, pp. 110–33. The latter argues that the casting of an actress (Ling Po) in the role of Liang Shanbo was fully in keeping with the practices of Yueju opera (to which *huangmei diaopian* is most closely related), which Li calls "an (almost) all-female theatre" (p. 112).

17. Fonoroff, "Hong Kong Cinema," p. 39.

18. Chiao, "The Female Consciousness," p. 76, remarks on the Ling Bo idolatry as helping transcend cultural divisions between the Taiwanese born on the island (*bensheng*) and postwar migrants from mainland China (*waisheng*).

19. "About Shaw," available at http://www.shaw.sg/sw_about.aspx.

20. Law Kar, "The American Connection in Early Hong Kong Cinema," in Poshek

Fu and David Desser, eds., *The Cinema of Hong Kong: History, Arts, Identity* (New York: Cambridge University Press, 2000) 59.

21. Poshek Fu, "The 1960s: Modernity, Youth Culture, and Hong Kong Cantonese Cinema," in Fu and Desser, *The Cinema of Hong Kong*, p. 79.

22. "About Shaw," available at http://www.shaw.sg/sw_about.aspx.

23. Law Kar, "The American Connection," in Fu and Desser, *The Cinema of Hong Kong*, pp. 44–70.

24. "About Shaw," available at http://www.shaw.sg/sw_about.aspx.

25. Paine Knickerbocker, "The growth of a Festival and Its Dedicated Director," *San Francisco Sunday Chronicle Datebook*, October 11, 1964, p. 3; Traude Gomez, "How the San Francisco International Film Festival Started," in the Levine Archive of the San Francisco International Film Festival, available at http://history.sffs.org/our_history/how_sfiff_started.php.

26. This information was gleaned from a thorough search of the Levin Archive of the San Francisco International Film Festival, available at http://history.sffs.org/films/.

27. The falloff in Shaw submissions has many possible explanations, including the festival's short-term fiscal losses and decline in local critical support after the 1964 San Francisco festival, possibly even due to the 1964 airplane death in Asia of Loke Wantho (Lu Yuntao), the head of Shaw's chief rival MP & GI (Cathay), along with other senior personnel, and Cathay's subsequent diminishment as a competitor in the Asian regional markets.

28. John Wasserman, "*Love Eterne*: An Exquisite Chinese Film," *San Francisco Chronicle*, November 12, 1963.

29. Judy, "The Love Eterne," *Variety*, November 13, 1963, p. 17. Judy Stone was a longtime film critic and author in the Bay Area, including, later, for the *San Francisco Chronicle*.

30. Monique Benoit, "He's a Girl Chaser," in *San Francisco Chronicle*, June 23, 1964; Howard Thompson, "Mandarin Films to Be Seen Here, 55th St. Theater to House Chinese Art Movies," *New York Times*, December 9, 1964.

31. Other films directed by Li Han-hsiang that played the Bella Union's first Mandarin season included *Empress Wu* (eight weeks), *The Coin* (*Yi Mao Qian*, 1964), and *Kingdom and the Beauty* (*Jiang Shan Mei Ren*, 1959).

32. Thompson, "Mandarin Films." The San Francisco Bella Union, a converted mid-nineteenth-century theater located at Washington and Kearny Streets (on property now part of a Buddhist temple), was understood according to Frank Lee Jr. as standing in "Manila Town," on the edges of Chinatown; personal telephone interview on January 3, 2004.

33. Norman K. Dorn, "Movies," in *San Francisco Sunday Chronicle Datebook*, May 3, 1964, p. 9; Benoit, "He's a Girl Chaser"; Thompson, "Mandarin Films"; Cheryl Eddy, "Local Heroes: Frank Lee," *San Francisco Bay Guardian* (2002), available at http://www.bestofthebay.com/2002/localheroes5.html, accessed September 23, 2003; Frank Lee Jr., personal communication.

34. Frank Lee Jr., personal communication. For information on Frank Lee Jr. as well as on his father, see also Francesca Dinglasan, "San Francisco's Four Star: Frank Lee's Independent Art-House Brings Asian Pics to the City by the Bay," *Independent Theatre Showcase*, December 1999, available at http://www.boxoff.com/issues/dec99/asia2.html.

35. Benoit, "He's a Girl Chaser."

36. Thompson, "Mandarin Films."

37. Frank Lee Jr., personal communication. In the mid-1960s, Lee Sr. began booking the same films into what is now the New Beverly (then called The Europe) in the Farmer's Market area of Los Angeles, as well as into a Chinatown theater there. Lee also acquired a business interest in the Canal Theatre in New York's Chinatown around 1967 and in the 1970s developed networks as a distributor of Taiwan-produced films to Toronto and Vancouver.

38. Newspaper reviews and playbill listings for the 55th Street Playhouse reveal that it played exclusively Chinese films in Mandarin from December 1964 to April 1967, when *Sword of Doom* ran, the first Japanese-produced title Lee played. More action-oriented Chinese-language films subsequently returned, such as *Sons of the Good Earth* (*Dadi Ernü*, dir. King Hu, 1965), and occasionally what appear to be Japanese-made films dubbed into Mandarin.

39. David Desser has conducted some work on the latter issue; Cindy Wong Hing-Yuk, "Distant Screen: Film Festivals and the Global Projection of Hong Kong Cinema," in Gina Marchetti and Tan See Kam, eds., *Hong Kong Film, Hollywood and New Global Cinema: No Film Is an Island* (London: Routledge, 2006).

40. Bosley Crowther, "Screen: Run Run Shaw's No. 2 Here: 'Love Eterne' Arrives from Hong Kong," *New York Times*, January 16, 1965.

41. Bosley Crowther, "Screen: Hong Kong's Run Run Shaw: 'Last Woman of Shang' Bows at 55th Street," *New York Times*, December 15, 1964.

42. Howard Thompson, "'The Lady General,' a Chinese Movie," *New York Times*, February 12, 1965.

43. Howard Thompson, "Untranslated Foreign Films Popular," *New York Times*, January 23, 1965.

44. Bosley Crowther, "Screen: 'Empress Wu' Opens at 55th St.: Color Used Lavishingly in Hong Kong Film," *New York Times*, March 16, 1965. Crowther also complains that even the "lengthy synopsis of the story provided by the theater" did not help him grasp the arcane narrative. The New York Times all-around cultural critic (and editor for a time) Richard F. Shepard took quite a different tone in his single review of a Shaw film, *The Shepherd Girl*, on September 2, 1965. He opines, "The subtitles, in ideographs for Cantonese in the audience and in English for outsiders, are faithful to the Mandarin sound track."

45. Arthur Mayer, letter to editor in "Movie Mailbag" feature, "A Critic for All Seasons," *New York Times*, December 10, 1967.

46. Bret McCabe, "Droll Economy," *Baltimore City Paper*, January 1, 2003, available at http://www.metrotimes.com/editorial/story.asp?id=4444, gives a short critical and

biographical sketch of Thompson (1920–2002), who began his journalism career after World War II as a clerk under Crowther. The comment about the squatty subtitles comes from Thompson's April 1967 *New York Times* review of *Sword of Doom*.

47. Los Angeles film critic Kevin Thomas offered an exception. His review of *Love Eterne* begins pointedly: "What's going on here, anyway? Of the four Chinese films Hong Kong's Shaw Bros. have shown at the Europa since taking it over, three have dealt with females disguised as males. Is this, perhaps, another fetish of the Far East like footbinding? . . . *Love Eterne* is the latest [and] also the strongest, for whether or not the effect is intentional, it ends in an explosion of naked lesbian passion of an intensity rarely seen on the screen." Kevin Thomas, "Hong Kong Film Naive and Strange," *Los Angeles Times,* September 2, 1966.

48. "16,000,000 Overseas Chinese Speak Out: Overseas Chinese Oppose Admission of Peiping into U.N.," advertisement in *The New York Times,* November 5, 1965.

49. Lyman, "Watching Movies with Ang Lee."

50. Notwithstanding the criticism that especially (Pan-)Chinese critics have directed toward *Crouching Tiger, Hidden Dragon,* the movie performed very well in its initial run at the box office. See, for example, Stephen Teo, "'We Kicked Jackie Chan's Ass!' An Interview with James Schamus," *Senses of Cinema Journal,* March-April 2001, available at http://www.sensesofcinema.com/contents/01/13/schamus .html. *Crouching Tiger* also garnered nominations for Golden Horse prizes at the 2001 Taipei International Film Festival in thirteen separate categories and won in six.

51. Dinglasan, "San Francisco's Four Star"; Cheryl Eddy, "Local Heroes"; "Script Doctor: Enter the Festival, Notes on the Four Star's Four Star Asian Film Festival," *San Francisco Bay Guardian,* June 25, 2003, available at http://www.sfbg.com/37/45/x_ script_doctor.html.

52. Lyman, "Watching Movies with Ang Lee."

9

Black Audiences, Blaxploitation and Kung Fu Films, and Challenges to White Celluloid Masculinity

SUNDIATA KEITA CHA-JUA

Introduction

African American interest in the martial arts is ubiquitous in the contemporary United States. It can be seen in the burgeoning numbers of black youth enrolled in self-defense classes and in hip-hop culture. African Americans' fascination with the martial arts cuts across artistic genres. The Wu Tang Clan, the rap group most responsible for bringing kung fu to the hip-hop community, markets classic films from Kung Fu Theater. The RZA, the hip-hop group's founder, for example, wrote the scores for Jim Jarmusch's crime drama *Ghost Dog: The Way of the Samurai* (1999) and Quentin Tarantino's homage to Hong Kong kung fu films, *Kill Bill, Vol. 1* (2003) and *Kill Bill, Vol. 2* (2004). Perhaps most illustrative of African Americans' attraction to Chinese martial arts is Black Belt, an art exhibition that appeared at Harlem's Studio Museum during fall 2003. Curator Christine Kim presented forty-four pieces by a racially diverse group of nineteen artists that explored "the black urban fascination with Eastern martial arts and philosophy." The double meaning embodied in the exhibit's title, Black Belt, illustrates the complex relationship at the crux of the black-Asian connection. On the one hand, *a* black belt symbolizes excellence in the martial arts, rendering it the embodiment of "Asianness," according to Mosi Secret. On the other hand, *the* black belt refers to African American ghettos. Ironically, currently it is in the black belt that pursuit of a black belt finds its most ardent following.[1]

African Americans' interest in the martial arts began with a fascination with kung fu films during the early 1970s. The roots of this attraction lay both in Hong Kong and in the United States. In the mid-1960s, Shaw Brothers, soon to become the major Hong Kong movie studio, reconceptualized the martial arts movie, moving it from mysticism toward more realistic and more brutal action. The *wuxia pian* films of the mid-1960s, particularly Shaw Brothers' productions of King Hu's *Come Drink with Me* (1966), Zhang Cheh's *Du bei dao* or *The One-Armed Swordsman* (1966), and his *Dragon Gate Inn* (1967), initiated the transformation. The Shaws' production of Cheh's *Vengeance* and Wang Yu's *Longhu Dou* or *The Chinese Boxer* in 1970 completed the transformation by creating the formula for the kung fu or unarmed combat film. The winning formula called for an explosion of rage and retribution by a long-suffering protagonist who finally embarks on a journey of revenge against a vicious amoral antagonist. Shaw's *Tianxia diyi Quan* or *Five Fingers of Death,* one of the first kung fu classics and the first to play at mainstream U.S. movie houses, launched the kung fu invasion. Shaw Brothers and Warner Brothers, its U.S. distributor, launched the kung fu invasion while Hollywood was in the midst of a financial crisis. Viewed as B-action movies, U.S. distributors were attracted to the genre because its low cost reaped huge profits.[2]

According to film scholar David Desser, African Americans' interest in kung fu films "was a major factor in keeping the kung fu craze alive." The martial arts film audience, like the general action film's, is classed, gendered, and generational. The U.S. action film audience consists largely of young, white, working-class males. The black martial arts audience, however, complicates, if not transcends, the class, gender, and generational limitations of action films' traditional spectators. A broader cross-section of the black community is attracted to this film genre. Why have African Americans been so attracted to martial arts films, especially Hong Kong kung fu films? The simplest and most common answer comes from Desser. He advances two interconnected arguments: First, besides blaxploitation, kung fu films were the only films with nonwhite heroes and heroines; second, they concerned an "underdog of color, often fighting against the colonialist enemies, white culture, or the Japanese." Desser's answer is correct, but he does not provide an explanation. Following Desser's logic, I locate the genesis of African Americans' attraction to kung fu movies in the social relations of domination and resistance, specifically in the dialectical relationship between black racial oppression and the Black Freedom movement. To adequately answer the question, we need to interrogate four interrelated factors. First, we have to account for how the particularities and peculiarities of African American Pan-African nationalist political thought conditioned the black community's receptivity for kung fu films. Second, we should locate African Americans' engagement with Hong Kong cinema—martial arts genre films—in the early 1970s, the sociohistorical context in which they first encountered them. Third, we should interrogate the dominant themes and tropes in blaxploitation films and investigate the multiple ways they articulated with the dominant narrative structures in kung fu films. Fourth, we should take stock of how the Shaw Brothers' reconceptualization of the martial arts movie was perfected by Bruce Lee, the kung fu films' first superstar. Through his dynamic personality, extraordinary martial arts skills, unique polycultural philosophy, and populist pro-working-class film vision, Lee anchored the kung fu formula developed at Shaw Brothers in even greater realism, Chinese nationalism, and a populist working sentiment.[3]

Derived Ideology: Pan-Africanist and Black Internationalist Antecedents

The roots of African Americans' attraction to kung fu films are deeply embedded in their sociohistorical experiences. Simply put, it is a product of blacks' political and cultural resistance to racial oppression. Although "repression breeds resistance," opposing oppression is never simple; it is always varied and complex. Resistance is as likely to include cross-cutting strategies and discourses as mutually reinforcing ones. Two different but overlapping ideological discourses, Pan-Africanism and Black Internationalism, help explain African Americans' fascination with kung fu films. Pan-Africanists view the diverse dispersed peoples of African descent as one family. And perhaps, more importantly, they locate black unity in similar, if not common, national experiences of racial domination, discrimination, and degradation. Pan-Africanists believe that until African-descended people coordinate their resources to create a United States of Africa, they will never experience freedom, justice, and self-determination. Black Internationalism is also a direct outgrowth of African Americans' meditation on and engagement in world affairs. According to Marc Gallicchio, "black internationalists believed that, as victims of racism and imperialism, the world's darker races, a term they employed to describe the non-European world, shared a common interest in overthrowing white supremacy and creating an international order based on racial equality." Although different in emphasis, both Pan-Africanism and Black Internationalism have their roots in Black Nationalist opposition to racial oppression.[4]

Black Nationalism is a complicated and multifarious ideology, which contemporary scholars have treated as a unitary dogma devoid of internal differentiation and contestation. This misguided, narrow, and antagonistic approach toward Black Nationalism has been especially acute among cultural studies scholars. Consequently, Black Internationalism's and especially Pan-Africanism's influence on blacks' receptivity toward Hong Kong martial arts films has been obscured or maligned.[5]

Here I want to highlight three different instances in which Black Internationalist and/or Pan-Africanist activist intellectuals articulated African American and Asian solidarity. The first concerns W. E. B. DuBois, the seminal African American radical scholar-activist. The Nation of Islam, particularly the militant Malcolm X, represents the second. The brilliant, organic, intellectual Huey P. Newton and the Black Panther Party (BPP) constitute the third instance. DuBois, Malcolm X, and Newton came from different classes or class strata, and they reached political maturity during fundamentally different historical moments. By 1934, DuBois was undergoing his final political transformation, remaking himself into a race-conscious Pan-African Marxist. In his last year, 1965, Malcolm would sharply break with the racist millenarian ideology intrinsic to Elijah Muhammad's Nation of Islam. Twenty-one years after DuBois's articulation of a distinctive race-conscious Marxism, Malcolm, too, would reject capitalism, although by his death he had not yet embraced socialism. In the late 1960s, Newton and the BPP would reweave the radical threads left by DuBois, Malcolm X, and others who traversed the black radical tradition into a new Black Internationalism. By 1970, the BPP articulated a Black Internationalist policy that supported revolutionary movements around the world, not just in Africa. The ideas of DuBois, Malcolm X, and Huey P. Newton are united by a common antiracist, anti-imperialist, and anticolonialist policy.

Considered the "father of Pan-Africanism," DuBois was also a Black Internationalist, a humanist, and a committed socialist, who believed race and color made up the international fault line that divided the oppressed from the oppressor. He saw China, Japan, and Asia as part of the world majority of oppressed darker races. His famous 1903 statement on the color line expressed his basic interpretation, "The problem of the twentieth century is the problem of the color line,—the relation of the darker to the lighter races of men in Asia and Africa, in America and the islands of the seas." DuBois expressed political solidarity with China in multiple literary modes: prose, fiction, and poetry. For DuBois, however, the connection between China and people of African descent was not simply rhetorical. He visited China three times, in 1936, in 1958–59, and a year before his death in 1962. During Japan's invasion, Michael T. Martin and Lamont H. Yeakley note that he "contributed to several Chinese organizations" and in 1948 became "an honorary member" of Madam Sun Yat-sen's China Welfare Fund. In his address to the All-African People's Conference, DuBois told the delegates, "Your nearest friends and neighbors are the colored people of China and India, the rest of Asia, the Middle East and the sea Isles. . . . Your bond is not mere color of skin but the deeper experience of wage slavery and contempt." China held a special place in DuBois's heart; he saw China mainly through the ideological prisms of Pan-Africanism and Black Internationalism.[6]

Although not a race-conscious Marxist, or even a Black Internationalist of the DuBoisian variety, Malcolm X, too, articulated a worldview that linked the darker peoples in a common political struggle against white supremacy. Unlike DuBois, whose perspective was grounded in history and political economy, Malcolm's initial understanding of Pan-Africanism and Black Internationalism was rooted in the Nation of Islam's (NOI's) mythology and millenarianism. Malcolm learned the NOI's theology, which claimed African Americans were "the original Asiatic blackman," "descendants of the Asian black nation and of the tribe of Shabazz" and whites were "created devils." NOI eschatology asserted that Allah would destroy the world by unleashing the "Mother ship," which W. D. Fard, the NOI's founder, claimed was built by the Japanese during the 1930s! This is obviously not rational, but in the fiction of the Mother ship, the NOI combined a respect for modern technology and science fiction with biblical prophecy to suggest that Japan, a nation of "the darker peoples" was doing Allah's work![7]

Malcolm X skillfully recast the racial and religious conceptions in NOI mythology. In a late 1950s speech, he argued, "The God of Peace and Righteousness is about to set up his Kingdom of Peace and Righteousness here on this earth. Knowing that God is about to establish his righteous government, Mr. Muhammad is trying to clean up our morals and qualify us to enter into this new Righteous nation of God." Here, Malcolm quickly shifts from religious metaphors to political analysis. Continuing, he argued, "The whole *dark* world wants peace. When I was in Africa last year I was deeply impressed by the desire of our African brothers for peace, but even they agree that there can be no peace without freedom from colonialism, foreign domination, oppression and exploitation." Knowledgeable of world affairs, especially the struggle against colonialism, Malcolm transformed Fard's and Muhammad's religious mythologies into an anticolonial political analysis, thus giving the NOI's theology a facade of relevance.[8]

Perhaps the most sophisticated articulation of Black Internationalism came from Huey P. Newton. As the BPP's leading theorist, Newton struggled to adapt the Panther's ideology to the dynamic global situation unfolding during the last third of the twentieth century. Anticipating the rise of global capitalism, Newton developed a political theory to challenge transnational capital and the U.S. empire. Newton's conception of revolutionary internationalism and, ultimately, revolutionary intercommunalism conformed to the main outlines of DuBois's and Malcolm X's articulations of Black Internationalism, with four exceptions. First, he eschewed an explicit racial analysis preferring to substitute the so-called Third World for racial designations. Second, Newton considered African Americans part of the colonized world. As a colonized people, blacks had a "moral right to nationhood," but according to Newton historical circumstances had conspired to negate that claim. Third, because enslavement eliminated that option, internationalism was African Americans' only viable political position. Newton contended, "We feel that Black people in America have a moral right to claim nationhood because we are a colonized people. But history won't allow us to claim nationhood, because it has bestowed an obligation upon us; to take socialist development to its final stage, to rid the world of the imperialist threat, the threat of the capitalist and the warmonger." This interpretation was not unique to Newton and the Panthers; Max Stanford/Ahmad Muhammad and the Revolutionary Action Movement, who were greatly influenced by Mao Zedong, also shared aspects of it. Finally, Newton argued the United States was not a nation-state but an empire! An empire whose world domination undermined other countries' independence, reducing them to oppressed communities. This formulation was at the crux of the Panther's shift from revolutionary internationalism to revolutionary intercommunalism. As Floyd W. Hayes III and Francis A. Kiene III contend, the move from revolutionary internationalism to revolutionary intercommunalism "was more of a change in emphasis rather than a complete departure from or break from the Party's earlier internationalist position." His commitment to revolutionary solidarity explains Newton's offer of support to the National Liberation Front of South Vietnam in its struggle against United States imperialism.[9]

Although largely derived ideologies—that is, coherent sets of ideas—which were produced by identifiable theorists, Black Internationalist and Pan-Africanist ideas were widely distributed in the African American popular press. Significantly, the three activist intellectuals discussed here all had access to widely read black newspapers and journals. From 1910 to 1934, DuBois edited *Crisis*, the organ of the National Association of Colored People, and from 1940 to 1944, he edited *Phylon*, at that time the premier U.S. social science journal on race at that time. Malcolm X was perhaps the most popular activist intellectual of his time. A popular lecturer in the African American community, Malcolm was also a fixture on national and local radio and television talk shows and on the college lecture circuit. In addition, he founded and was the first editor of *Muhammad Speaks,* the NOI's newspaper. According to historian Claude Andrew Clegg, *Muhammad Speaks* "became the best selling black newspaper in the country," with a circulation of 600,000. In addition, Newton, the BPP's cofounder, had a regular column in the *Black Panther,* the party's influential newspaper, which, according to Charles Jones and Judson Jefferies, between 1968 and 1972 sold an average of 100,000 copies a week between 1968 and 1972. Black Internationalism and Pan-Africanism claimed a significant number of twentieth-century African American academics, activists, and artists as adherents. Included among this group were Hubert Harrison, A. Phillip Randolph, Cyril V. Briggs and the African Blood Brotherhood, Marcus Garvey, Amy Jacques Garvey, George Schuyler, C. L. R. James, Claudia Jones, Langston Hughes, Abram Harris, Rayford Logan, Ralph Bunche, Richard Wright, Paul Robeson and the Council on African Affairs, Lorraine Hansberry, Stokely Carmichael/Kwame Ture, Amiri Baraka, the League of Revolutionary Black Workers, and Assata Shakur.[10]

Corporate Liberalism and Judicious Repression: 1967–1975

The transformation from a movement for civil rights to a struggle for Black Power had contradictory effects. It produced a period that was simultaneously liberating and repressive. Black Power unleashed a previously latent black-nationalist consciousness. Under the influence of Black Power nationalism, African Americans constructed what philosopher Eddie Glaude Jr. called a "politics of transvaluation." Reassessing the meaning of "blackness," African Americans literally remade themselves from "Negroes" into "black people," a transformation that unleashed an unprecedented wave of creativity, desire, and assertiveness. The dominant tendency during the civil rights phase of the Black Freedom movement (BFM) had conformed to the strictures of U.S. liberal pluralism, but after 1966 the previously subordinated nationalist and radical tendencies gained the initiative and transformed the BFM from a struggle for civil rights into a battle for power—Black Power and Peoples' Power. Collectively, the Black Power nationalists, black radicals, and a radicalized Martin Luther King Jr. returned the BFM's concern with international affairs, which the Cold War had pushed to the periphery of African Americans' political agenda. The renewed emphasis on African liberation and support for national liberation movements in the Third World, particularly in Vietnam, established the ideological and discursive contexts dominant in black communities during this period. Yet, on the other hand, the successes of the civil rights and Black Power phases of the BFM engendered a virulent racist backlash.[11]

The government reacted to King's radicalization, the transformation of the BFM, and the urban rebellions in three ways: Contain the uprisings, crush the militants and radicals, and incorporate the liberals and moderates. Federal policy was mainly driven by the need to quell the urban rebellions that scorched more than 300 U.S. cities between the mid-1960s and 1970s. These annual conflagrations involved an estimated 500,000 blacks, destroyed tens of millions of dollars of property, and resulted in 250 deaths, 8,000 injuries, and 50,000 arrests. U.S. Army troops and national guardsmen occupied eight cities. In the two pivotal years, 1967 and 1968, 384 rebellions exploded in 298 cities. After the 1967 Detroit Rebellion, the Lyndon Johnson administration adopted a policy of containment toward the urban uprisings. Containment, similar to the international anticommunist policy from which it derived its name, sought to confine the uprisings to urban ghettos.[12]

According to *Newsweek* reporter Samuel F. Yette, the Richard Nixon administration used the uprisings to "usher in a substantial police state," which was used to *crush* the Black militants and radicals. Under the Omnibus Crime Control and Safe Streets Act, "preventive detention," "no-knock search and seizure" provision, and wiretapping with a court order were authorized. This paved the way for the FBI to unleash a massive campaign of terror on what they termed "black nationalist hate-type groups." The purpose of the Counter Intelligence Program (COINTELPRO) initiative was "to expose, disrupt, misdirect, discredit, or otherwise neutralize the activities" of militant and radical African American individuals and organizations. The move toward a police state, the widespread policing of the black community, and the savage assault on black radicals are best understood as judicious repression. Judicious in that the repression was targeted, aimed at militants and radicals, rather than indiscriminate random violence. Repression of the radicals facilitated the success of the other policies.[13]

Great Society initiatives were a consequence of two decades of militant mass direct action and civil disobedience campaigns, urban rebellions, and the white American elite's stratagem of corporate liberalism, a policy that aimed at incorporating aspiring blacks into the lower and middle rungs of the U.S. political and economic structure. President Johnson's Great Society emphasized political incorporation, education, and job creation. By spring

1975, more than 3,500 blacks held elective office, up from 104 in 1964, a year before the passage of the Voting Rights Act. In four years, from 1969 to 1973, the percentage of African Americans enrolled in college rose 370 percent. The percentage of blacks in white-collar occupations doubled from 13 percent in 1960 to 26 percent in the early 1970s. The median income of black families had also doubled between 1964 and 1974. Education, employment, and electoral politics became the vehicles by which a select few blacks were incorporated in the U.S. capitalist system under the Democratic Party.[14]

In addition to unleashing massive repression against militants and radicals, President Nixon radically shifted federal policy. He did not abandon incorporative strategies, however, rather he shifted the emphasis toward economic incorporation. The Nixon administration established the Office of Minority Business Enterprise (OMBE), which offered low-cost loans for minority entrepreneurial ventures. Between 1969 and 1976, minority businesses quadrupled from 300,000 to 1.2 million and their sales increased from $50 million in 1969 to $12 billion in 1972. Meanwhile, it more than doubled the amount of grants, loans, and guarantees to minority enterprises from $200 million to $472 million. Not surprisingly, John Sibley Butler discovered that 47 percent of African American enterprises listed in Black Enterprise's top 100 black businesses in 1987 were started in the 1970s! Black capitalism was the incorporative, or carrot, aspect of Nixon's combined strategy of corporate liberalism and judicious repression.[15]

In the wake of systematic repression and co-optation, the Black Power nationalists shifted their focus from the United States toward Africa and the Third World. Articles focusing on Africa, Pan-Africanism, and the Third World dominated the movement's leading journals, the Black Scholar and Black World, during the early 1970s. The two distinctive features of 1970s Pan-Africanism were its mass base and the reversal of the transnational circuit of ideas. From the emigration movements of the nineteenth century through the World War II era, the development of Pan-Africanism had been dominated by ideas originating among Africans in the diaspora. This diaspora-centered perspective characterized DuBois's position before 1945. After the first wave of African independence, the circuit was quickly reversed. Heretofore, the ideas of African leaders had very little impact on the thinking of African American activists, but during the 1970s the political thought of African theorists such as Kwame Nkrumah, Frantz Fanon, Julius Nyerere, and Amilcar Cabral began to influence the thinking of militant and radical African American intellectual activists.[16]

Black Internationalism and Pan-Africanism reappeared simultaneously.

And similarly to the new Pan-Africanism, 1970s Black Internationalism was shaped by the ideas of Third World revolutionary theorists. With the possible exception of Marx and Lenin, no nonblack theorist influenced black radicals as much as Mao Zedong. Mao's ideas played a major role in shaping the intellectual development of black radicals, particularly the members of the BPP and the Revolutionary Action Movement, later the African Peoples Party.[17]

Blaxploitation and the Contradictions of Cinematic Masculinist Militancy

It was in the sociohistorical context of massive urban rebellions, the transition from Black Power nationalism to Pan-Africanism and Black Internationalism, and the government's Machiavellian response—corporate liberalism and judicious repression, the dialectical strategy of political repression and economic incorporation—that African Americans first encountered both blaxploitation and kung fu films. As a genre, blaxploitation films were constructed to appeal to the new nationalist consciousness surging through the black community. Blaxploitation films utilized Black Nationalist tropes and codes to appeal to the militant sentiment permeating black communities. The National Politics Study, the most comprehensive public opinion survey of African Americans' political attitudes, contains several items that tap into Black Nationalist ideologies. Many of these themes were incorporated into the narrative and visual structure of blaxploitation films. For instance: (1) the desire for black unity; (2) community service, especially support for youth programs; (3) support for black businesses; (4) participation in all-black organizations; (5) knowledge and practice of African and African American culture; and (6) support for efforts by blacks to gain governance of black communities.[18]

Violence, especially its different usages by protagonists and antagonists, was a central plot device in blaxploitation films. Specifically, white racist characters often engaged in torture, random murder, and other morally reprehensible acts, to which black heroes and heroines responded with defensive or justifiable retaliatory acts. Black violence in blaxploitation films acquired its justification from the sociohistorical context. Filmmakers played on the long history of racist violence against African Americans. The pervasiveness of racist violence is one of the defining characteristics of the black experience in the United States. Closer to the time period, black audiences were keenly aware of the unprovoked violence unleashed upon civil rights demonstrators. They were also cognizant of governmental violence to contain the urban insurrections and the repression of Black Power militants and radicals. Moreover, police brutality was routine in black communities. Finally, Malcolm X, Robert Williams, the Deacons for the Defense, and the BPP, among others, had legitimized black peoples' right to armed self-defense. The use of defensive or retaliatory violence reflected beliefs and practices that were endemic to Black Power nationalism, and as a central plot device in blaxploitation films it not only bequeathed morality to black protagonists' actions but also served to differentiate the new black films and their protagonists from the Sambo and mammy images of the cinematic past.[19]

Film scholar Ed Guerrero identified several developmental phases in the blaxploitation genre, all of which were "predicated on shifts in African American consciousness, politics, and the rising expectations of the black audience." Although he places the origin of blaxploitation films in 1967, Guerrero views Melvin Van Peebles's pioneering *Sweet Sweetback's Baadasssss Song* (1971) as defining the genre's formula. The plot concerns an unlikely, and not wholly sympathetic, character, Sweetback, who works as a stud in a South Central Los Angeles brothel. Responding to unsolved murders, two police officers convince Beatle, Sweetback's boss, to let them arrest Sweetback to pacify their boss and an anxious public. In the course of taking Sweetback to the police station, the racist cops arrest and brutalize a young militant named Moo-Moo. The assault on Moo-Moo enrages Sweetback, who, overwhelmed by feelings of humiliation from years of abuse, explodes and literally hacks the cops to death with their own handcuffs. This is perhaps the most powerful scene in the film. It is the beginning of Sweetback's self-transformation. It is a case of using the master's tools to undo the master. That is, Van Peebles has Sweetback transform handcuffs, the modern symbol of slave chains, into a weapon for escape, if not liberation. Sweetback's action on behalf of the young revolutionary symbolizes self-defense but also black unity. His baptism in blood sets Sweetback on his journey, not only to escape arrest and certain death but also toward what proves to be an incomplete self-transformation. Along the way, Sweetback is aided and supported by large segments of the black community. In one scene, working-class and lumpen blacks burn a police car, enabling his escape. Weaponless, except, ironically, with a knife, Sweetback manages to escape across the Mexican border, mainly by exploiting his sexual prowess.[20]

Explaining the significance of *Sweetback*, Van Peebles claimed, "All the films about black people up to now have been told through the eyes of the Anglo-Saxon majority. . . . In my film, the black audience finally gets a chance to see some their own fantasies acted out—about rising out of the mud and kicking some ass." Van Peebles's film began and ended with potent political messages. The title card stated, "This film is dedicated to all the Brothers and Sisters who have had enough of The Man," and the final frame declared, "A BAADASSSSS NIGGER IS COMING BACK TO COLLECT SOME DUES." In a review that encompassed an entire issue of *Black Panther*, Newton declared *Sweetback* "the first truly revolutionary Black film." *Sweetback's* success—Van Peebles made *Sweetback* for $500,000, but it grossed $10 million—convinced Hollywood executives that huge profits could be made by targeting similar films at the African American community.[21]

The sentiments expressed by Van Peebles or what the Godfather of Soul, James Brown, called "the Big Payback" became the dominant formula for blaxploitation films, but with a significant twist: The explicit antisystem themes would be muted, but not wholly eliminated. Following *Sweetback*, the blaxploitation formula usually presented a simple plot in which white antagonists—usually organized crime figures, corrupt police, and/or mendacious politicians, literarily the personification of the forces of exploitation and occupation—perform a heinous act against one of the hero's or heroine's significant others, thus forcing a reluctant black protagonist to take revenge and thereby symbolically gain retribution for the entire community. Directors inserted superfluous displays of flesh, sex, and drugs, which combined with extreme violence and exaggerated portrayals of whites roused interest in otherwise stale formulaic stories.

Blaxploitation films are greatly misunderstood. Most scholars have misread the class background of protagonists in blaxploitation films. First, they were drawn from a broader class array than is normally recognized. Film scholar Jon Kraszewski contended, "Class became a major way to sell blaxploitation to its audience." Kraszewski was concerned with how class was used to market blaxploitation to its intended audience. According to Kraszewski, this was done mainly through two devices: the class background of the heroes and heroines and the anxiety engendered by increasing class stratification throughout the black community. Although much of his argument is problematic, Kraszewski does provide occasional insights, which are useful for this discussion. First, he is wrong about the protagonists often being "lower-class," if by lower class he means lumpen (e.g., pimps, hustlers, and drug dealers). Lumpen characters are the protagonists in very few blaxploitation films. Whereas after Bruce Lee's intervention, the protagonists in kung fu films were generally working-class figures, the protagonists in blaxploitation films are about evenly divided between working-class and lower-middle-class characters.[22]

Four types of protagonists appeared in blaxploitation films. Unfortunately, the characters that have attracted the most critical attention and are seen as synonymous with the genre were the lumpen characters that initially preyed on the community, such as the protagonists in *The Mack* (1973), *Superfly* (1972), and *Willie Dynamite* (1973). In these films, the narrative involves a lumpen character, who for murky reasons has become ambivalent toward his criminal lifestyle. The protagonist's efforts to quit the "game" are usually opposed by "the Man," the major white criminal with whom they are in business. The second type of antihero featured in blaxploitation films were apparently working-class Vietnam War veterans, such as the protagonists in *The Bus Is Coming* (1971), *Gordon's War* (1973), *Slaughter* (1972), and its sequel, *Slaughter's Big Rip Off* (1973). Vietnam veterans also appear as secondary characters in several other blaxploitation films, often as members of militant nationalist organizations. The story line normally involves the central character returning home from the war to find his community overrun with drugs. The death of a relative, friend, or love interest via drug overdose or murder usually supplies the motivation to clean up the community. Another type of hero/heroine was the person with a working-class background who had risen into a middle-class occupation but whose friendship or kinship relations pull them into a conflict with malevolent white characters who are exploiting the black community. Jim Brown's nightclub owner in *Black Gunn* (1972), Pam Grier's nurse in *Coffy* (1973), or Calvin Lockhart's disc jockey in *Melinda* (1973) represent this character type. A variation of this type of middle-class protagonist is the black police officer or federal agent. Tamara Dobson's title character in *Cleopatra Jones* (1973) and *Cleopatra Jones and the Casino of Gold* (1975; note that it was a joint Warner Brothers and Shaw Brothers production) or Jim Kelly's in *Black Belt Jones* (1974) comes to mind. Often these characters were located in tension-filled, in-between positions, on the one side facing intense racism on the job while encountering skepticism, if not outright hostility, from sectors of the black community; for instance, Yaphet Kotto's detective in *Across 110th Street* (1972).

Despite the diversity of class backgrounds, all four types of protagonists represented middle-class values. This partly explains why, except the *Spook Who Sat by the Door* (1973), few blaxploitation films were revolutionary; that is, advocated fundamental social transformation. Blaxploitation protagonists exhibited self-reliance and African American cultural practices via their dress, handshakes, language, mannerism, and defiant attitude, which were coded to reflect Black Nationalist values. Pluralist protonationalism animated the categories and values articulated in blaxploitation films, not class. They often moved between different classes and class strata, functioning as mediators whose negotiation of an increasingly class-differentiated intraracial landscape demonstrated the continued viability of black unity. *Shaft* is of course the quintessential example, but the same applies to Jim Brown's *Gunn* or Tamara Dobson's *Cleopatra Jones*. The role these characters played was to vitiate class tension in the black community.[23]

Not only was the class background of blaxploitation's protagonists more diverse than generally acknowledged, but the characters also operated within a more collectivist framework than is commonly recognized. The lone avenging super stud hero is overstated. Many of these films drew on the communal elements in African American political culture in constructing their heroes and heroines. For instance, neither hero nor heroine in *Gunn, Melinda,* or *Cleopatra Jones* is capable of defeating their antagonists alone. Even *Shaft* had to recruit nationalist "soldiers"! What is interesting here is that blaxploitation film protagonists reflected mainstream ideals but had to recruit support from the only source then available in the black community: militant nationalist organizations. In *Gunn,* it is the Black Action Group, militant Vietnam veterans led by the protagonist's brother; in *Melinda,* Lockhart turns to his martial arts academy, led by Jim Kelly, which recalls the schools operated by the nationalist Black Karate Association; and *Cleopatra Jones* appealed to Mama Johnson's boys and her love interest, played by Bernie Casey. The sociohistorical context and African American cultural values pushed blaxploitation films to subtly challenge the individual superhero/heroine motif endemic in U.S. action and Hong Kong kung fu films. Even so, blaxploitation films could not jettison U.S. action film conventions, thus they substituted a small body of armed men for broad-based community organizing.

In blaxploitation films, the major villains were white. These characters were explicitly racist, the living embodiment of evil, the "created devils" of NOI mythology. As such, they were usually cardboard characters that were overacted, thus making them cartoonish as well. Although the main villains were white, most of the minor antagonists were black. For instance, drugs provided by an African American dealer, a junior partner of the main white antagonist, killed Coffy's brother. These lumpen characters represented the internal forces of betrayal and were often pimps and hustlers. In their depiction of the complex relationships between the major white villain and the black community, between the major white villain and black underlings, and between the black junior partner and the black community, these films approximated the racial class hierarchies articulated in internal colonial theory.

Blaxploitation films were sensitive to black politics in other ways as well.

Historian Manning Marable reported, "In 1972–73, the popularity of Pan-Africanism among broad segments of the black population was manifested in the activities of the nationalist African Liberation Support Committee (ALSC)." In an effort to appeal to its audience's Pan-African consciousness, both *Shaft* and *Superfly* created African-themed sequels. *Shaft in Africa* (1973) presented the contemporary plight of African migrant workers in Europe as analogous to the Atlantic slave trade. *Superfly T.N.T* (1973) presented Priest as a confused, lost soul searching for the meaning of life. The opportunity to deliver weapons to a struggling African liberation movement is the plot device that snaps him out of his malaise.[24]

Blaxploitation films were uneven, individually and as a genre. Most were poorly made, and several degraded women and glorified drug dealing, pimping, and other criminal behaviors. Nevertheless, despite poor craftsmanship, a significant minority, even in the action subgenre, often aspired toward something higher. The conversation in *Gunn* between the title character and the leaders of BAG is paradigmatic. Gunn comments, "Someone fingered my brother," and an anonymous militant replies, "It was probably a pimp, hustler, or drug pusher; yeah, it was probably a pusher." The dialogue is clear: Pimps, hustlers, and pushers were enemies of the black community. In some films, the visual imagery probably undermined the narrative interpretation, but with few exceptions the genre's formula called for the death of the drug dealer or addict. Like Freddy in *Superfly* or Doodlebug in *Cleopatra Jones*, drug-addicted characters met a gruesome fate, usually murdered by white partners.[25]

Like most U.S. actions films, the blaxploitation action subgenre focused on the immediate and obvious: mobsters, corrupt cops, and shady politicians. These characters, although important at the level of immediate experience, were not the major forces dominating and exploiting black communities. What was lacking in these films was a depiction of the structures of racial oppression. None of the films, except perhaps the *Spook Who Sat by the Door*, attempted to grapple with the more complex elements of racial oppression. In that sense, then, blaxploitation films were cathartic but eschewed a more complex analysis of racial oppression, self-transformation, and the politics of black liberation. Although overstated, some of the critique leveled against *wuxia pian* films can be applied to blaxploitation films. Of the *wuxia pian* genre, one critique argued, "the fantastic martial arts film emphasizes individual grievances in order to obscure the contradictions between the classes; it propagates . . . belief in retribution in order to dull the peoples' determination to resist . . . to deflect the people from the path of struggle in reality."[26]

The Black Nationalist tropes and codes, resistance to oppression, and vio-

lent retribution themes embedded in blaxploitation films helped precondi-
tion the African American audience for the coming of what Desser called
"the kung fu craze." Not only did the kung fu craze not come out of nowhere,
but its core audience, African Americans, were predisposed toward its narrative themes by a long history of Pan-Africanist and Black Internationalist
discourses, a repressive sociohistorical moment, and the core themes of self-
reliance and resistance, which were central to blaxploitation films.[27]

Enter the Dragon: Bruce Lee
and the Allure of Kung Fu Films

> My nomination for the greatest blaxploitation hero of all time
> starred in the *Chinese Connection.*
>
> —Darius James, *That's Blaxploitation: Roots of the Baadasssss 'Tude*

It is no secret that kung fu films overlapped with and then replaced blaxploitation films at inner-city theaters. Film scholar Stuart M. Kaminsky observed,
"The strength of Kung Fu films for black urban audiences is clear in the choice
of theaters in which the films are shown . . . show dates in 1973 indicate that
kung fu films are consistently strong box office in the overwhelmingly black
downtown audience theaters in Chicago."[28] In an analysis of movies shown at
the International Theater an inner-city venue in New Brunswick, New Jersey,
Demetrius Cope discovered that between June 12, 1974, and May 13, 1975,
thirty-two blaxploitation and twenty-seven martial arts films were shown.
Racial segregation, the dominant spatial pattern in U.S. metropolitan areas,
greatly contributed to this pattern. By 1967, African Americans composed a
third of the moviegoing public. This was also a period of white flight from
U.S. cities, and huge cineplexes were being built in suburban areas to accommodate white filmgoers.[29]

Moreover, Desser noted that after 1973, Warner Brothers, which was extremely active in the distribution of both blaxploitation and kung fu films,
began to double book blaxploitation and kung fu features at inner-city locations. In 1975, Warner Brothers and Shaw Brothers attempted to directly
exploit this connection through the vehicle of a single film. With blaxploitation nearing its end, Warner Brothers and Shaw Brothers collaborated in
producing *Cleopatra Jones and the Casino of Gold.* The film teamed Tamara
Dobson's title character, an African American federal agent, with Mi Ling,
who played an undercover Hong Kong police officer. The black and Chinese
female team combined their martial arts skills to defeat the Dragon Lady, a
white female drug lord played by Stella Stevens.[30]

That movie distributors targeted martial arts films toward African Americans is clear from their placement in inner-city theaters. That does not explain why the audience responded favorably, however. As I have argued throughout this chapter, ideological discourses, sociohistorical context, and the similarities in the narrative structures of blaxploitation and kung fu films predisposed African Americans toward Hong Kong martial arts films. Strangely, although Shaw Brothers dominated the production of kung fu films and launched the U. S. kung fu craze, it was not Shaw Brothers films that captured African Americans' imagination. Rather it was films by Golden Harvest Productions, the new company started by Raymond Chow and Leonard Ho, two former Shaw Brothers executives. Golden Harvest was built by luring away Shaw Brothers' most talented directors and actors: King Hu, Wang Yu, and Lo Wei. It was also built by rectifying Run Run Shaw's mistakes, especially his unwillingness to offer Bruce Lee a contract worthy of his immense talent. Yet, more than any other factor, African American moviegoers were attracted to kung fu films by Bruce Lee's personal attributes.[31]

Four factors made Lee appealing to African American audiences. What differentiated Lee from the other cinematic martial artists were his exceptional athletic abilities and fighting skills. Second, the nationalist politics embedded in his films paralleled dominant trends in African American political culture and were a central theme in blaxploitation movies. Lee's third attribute that endeared him to African American audiences was his open, multiracial, and polycultural cultural politics. Fourth, his class politics also broadly mirrored a major theme in blaxploitation films.

As with Jet Li and Wesley Snipes today, speed was Bruce Lee's most impressive martial arts ability. Even by today's standards, Lee's speed was extraordinary. Bordwell described him as "preternaturally fast." During his screen test for the role of Kato in the *Green Hornet* the camera revealed that he could throw a punch in an eighth of a second! Lee was trained in Wing Chung, a southern style developed by Yin Win Chung, a Buddhist nun. Designed for women and small men, Wing Chung emphasized speed rather strength, it encouraged the use of series of rapid punches, not unlike combinations or flurries in boxing. The boxing analogy is apt partly because of Lee's eclectic approach to self-defense, but perhaps more germane to our purposes because of his study of Muhammad Ali's techniques. Lee devotes three pages to "Speed" in the *Tao of Jeet Kune Do*; he discusses five types of speed and exercises to increase it. African Americans, like other enthusiasts were attracted by his fighting skills, especially his speed.[32]

In contrast to Wang Yu, the star of Shaw Brothers' the *Chinese Boxer* and the *One-Armed Swordsman*, Lee was a martial artist who could act, rather than an actor performing martial arts; thus, the camera tricks and slick editing necessary when using actors who lacked real fighting skills were unnecessary with Lee. His skills allowed him to push the genre further toward realism. During the 1960s, a compromise referred to as *credible exaggeration* supplanted the mystical and unbelievable fight scenes prevalent in the *wuxia pian* tradition but retained elements of "weightless" combat techniques. This tradition can be found even in some 1970s films such as *Five Fingers of Death* (1972). Not often, but occasionally, and I must add only for brief moments, the combatants take flight. Lee pushed beyond the "credible exaggeration" of Shaw Brothers films and created Golden Harvest Productions' "believable kung fu." According to Raymond Chow, Bruce Lee's popularity was rooted in the realism his martial arts talents conveyed on screen.[33]

Lee was a renegade and a revolutionary martial artist who was dedicated to movement, growth, and flexibility. His dedication to flexibility led him to reject traditional martial arts styles as rigid and confining. Lee claimed, "In martial arts cultivation, there must be a sense of freedom. A conditioned mind is never a free mind. Conditioning limits a person within the framework of a particular system." His quest for flexibility culminated in the creation of Jeet Kune Do, a synthesis of Wing Chun, Japanese jujitsu, and African American boxing. He trained with boxing equipment, and both the footwork and punches in Jeet Kune Do were based on boxing techniques. The origins, philosophy, and techniques of Jeet Kune Do reveal Lee's preference for eclectic polycultural mixtures. According to Lee, "Jeet Kune Do favors formlessness so that it can assume all forms and since Jeet Kune Do has no style, it can fit in with all styles. As a result, utilizes all ways and is bound by none and, likewise, uses any techniques or means which serve its end." Jeet Kune Do was not just a martial arts philosophy; for Lee, it was a philosophy of life. Lee's openness and polycultural approach was not limited to the martial arts.[34]

Lee's innovations transcended the physical, that is, his martial arts skills; he also transformed the narrative of kung fu films. He introduced themes of racial oppression and class exploitation. Chiao remarked, "The thematic emphases on race and class in Lee's films also mark a departure from the martial arts films that preceded him." Lee's protagonists were working-class, transnational migrants. In one sense, they represented the particularities of working-class Chinese diasporic experiences; however, the labor migration backdrop served to universalize these experiences beyond the Chinese diaspora. By setting his characters outside of China and Hong Kong and in the aftermath of Japan's Twenty-one Demands, Lee heightened the racial aspects of the conflicts his characters encountered. Lee's films demonstrated how the particular can reflect the universal.[35]

Herein lies the real key to understanding Bruce Lee's importance in the African American imagination. The nationalism of his films resonated beyond his Chinese audience; it appealed to African Americans and other racially oppressed peoples. The *Chinese Connection* (1971) is perhaps the best expression of Lee's cinematic nationalism, but it is also a dominant theme in *Fists of Fury* (1972) and *Return of the Dragon* (1972). It is important to note that Lee's nationalism was neither simple nor reactionary; it is not the nationalism of the bourgeoisie. His nationalism was anti-imperialist and was imbricated with racial and class consciousness. The intense nationalism of his films resonated beyond the Chinese and filmic contexts to recall the Asian and African national liberation movements fighting against real-world imperialism and white supremacy. *Return of the Dragon* readily comes to mind. Here, Lee's opponents are Italian gangsters and U.S. and Japanese mercenaries. The anti-imperialist character of his nationalism obtains a "formlessness" that allows it to "assume all forms," thus his anti-imperialist nationalism transcends Chinese particularity and speaks directly to African Americans, articulating with the Pan-Africanist and Black Internationalist discourses prevalent in the black community. The scene that most poignantly demonstrates the universal appeal of Lee's anti-imperialist nationalism occurs in the *Chinese Connection*. Set in Shanghai in the 1920s or 1930s, the film depicts the racism and viciousness of Japanese occupation. Lee's character, Chen, is prevented from entering a park by a police officer, who explains that he cannot enter by pointing to an overhanging sign that reads, "No dogs, or Chinese." Enraged, Chen leaps into the air and kicks and breaks the sign. The racial conflict expressed in this scene is signified throughout Lee's filmography via the race of his antagonists.[36]

I began this section with a quote by Darius James, who considers Bruce Lee "the greatest blaxploitation hero." James may be right. After Bruce Lee's debut, the narrative structure of kung fu films mirrored blaxploitation's: Driven by the heinous violence of racial oppressors, often embodied by gangsters, protagonists are compelled to commit equally vicious acts of revenge and retribution, but the protagonist's actions are invested with moral righteousness by both the specificity of the murderous acts and the general context of racial oppression. As Chiao commented, Lee's films were "overtly political," as were many, if not most, blaxploitation films. More importantly, Lee and the formula he established for kung fu films were political in much the same way as blaxploitation films; that is, they were nationalist visions of self-defense or retaliatory violence against racial oppression, albeit fueled by individual grievances. The narrative of retribution and the use of anti-imperialist nationalist tropes and codes still register a deep emotional feeling and ideological perspective among blacks, even removed from the sociohistorical context of the 1970s. After all, what does the current groundswell for reparations represent, if not a desire for retribution? But more than politics explains African Americans' passion for Bruce Lee's reworking of the Shaw Brothers' violent revenge sagas. There is an aesthetic appeal; his consummate skill as a martial artist, his style, and his attitude combine with the realism of his fight scenes to give him a unique place among black martial arts film aficionados. In one way, however, Bruce Lee and the heroes and heroines in kung fu films differ from those in blaxploitation films. Lee embodied the traditional lone hero, albeit, as Chiao maintained, acting on behalf of the people. As previously argued, the protagonists in blaxploitation films were more communal; they led a group, even if it was an unstable and tenuous coalition of circumstance. Blaxploitation films still required group action.

Conclusion

Kung fu films arrived in the United States in the early 1970s at an important and paradoxical historical moment. In *Black and Red: W. E. B. Du Bois and the Afro-American Response to the Cold War, 1944–1963,* historian Gerald Horne described the black community of the 1940s as "a militant anti-colonialist and anti-imperialist community." This was even truer during the late 1960s and early 1970s, when Pan-Africanist and Black Internationalist ideas were never more popular among African Americans. A broad sector of blacks not only opposed the Vietnam War but also wished for a Vietnamese victory. China and things Chinese were very popular in Afro-America. The little red book circulated widely along with Mao Zedong's two statements on the Black Freedom movement, in 1963 and 1968, respectively. More than anything, this was a time of struggle, perhaps even the term *war* is not inappropriate; after all, urban rebellions shook more than three hundred cities between 1963 and 1973. President Richard M. Nixon combined the policies of ghetto containment, crushing the militants and radicals, and co-optation into a strategy of judicious repression and corporate liberalism. The National Guard, U.S. Army, and local police forces cordoned off the black ghetto in many cities, often for as long as a week. Richard Nixon released the FBI on black militants and radicals. Using unconstitutional tactics, through COINTELPRO the FBI crushed the militant and radicals and thus broke the back of the black insurrection. At the same time, Nixon initiated a program of co-optation organized around the economic incorporation of a minute but strategically positioned minority of African American aspiring capitalists. Collectively, the strategy of judicious repression and corporate liberalism transformed the social-political and ideological landscape of Afro-America.[37]

Blaxploitation films more or less played out this drama on the screen, although in muted and distorted ways. Oversimplification, especially the substitution of heroic vigilantes for sustained community organizing, the collapsing of oppositional culture into criminal activity via occasional glorification of drug use, the exploitation of women, and ultimately the rehabilitation of the agents of repression, the police, and federal agents all served to not only weaken blaxploitation but also to make it at best a diversion and at worst a reactionary genre. Nevertheless, through its use of African American nationalist tropes and codes, blaxploitation did allude to real grievances and the need for individual and social transformation. Finally, the narrative structure of blaxploitation was so similar to that of kung fu films that it preconditioned African Americans for violent tales of retribution, especially the violent racial and class-based revenge sagas pioneered by Shaw Brothers but perfected by Bruce Lee at Golden Harvest.

Lee, his martial skills, especially speed, and his life philosophy and political vision were the final pieces that explain African Americans' attraction to kung fu films. Although his films were, as Ciao has stated, "blatant" exultations of Chinese nationalism, it was not a reactionary nationalism. Lee's polycultural politics subverted the extreme nationalism of his cinematic image, granting the films an anti-imperialist subtext, which was foreground in the African American imagination. The racial context of his films justified his nationalism and his violence, which merged wonderfully with the prevailing sentiment in black communities. His working-class persona also resonated with African Americans, a population which was 77.7 percent working class in 1970. Although black martial artist Jim Kelly had already appeared in *Melinda* (1972), it was his role as Williams in *Enter the Dragon* (1973) that propelled him into the pantheon of black cinematic heroes and heroines. Lee's promotion of Kelly and basketball superstar Kareem Abdul-Jabbar further endeared him to the black community. Finally, it is the transformation of the kung fu genre film's narrative to include race and class themes, a transformation attributed to Bruce Lee, that explains the underlying basis for African Americans attraction to Hong Kong kung fu films.[38]

Notes

1. Inspired by Sun Tzu's classic military text, *The Art of War*, the plotline for Wesley Snipes's similarly named film is structured around deception, which is central to Sun Tzu's war manual. *Ghost Dog*, however, has a different relationship to Yama-

moto Tsunetomo's *Hagakure: A Code for Samurai*. Jim Jarmusch's film is not simply inspired by the *Hagakure*, it incorporates the text into the film's narrative by boldly presenting transcriptions directly on the screen.

2. According to David Bordwell, the thirty-eight kung fu films U.S. distributors purchased during 1973 grossed $11 million dollars by the end of 1974; David Bordwell, *Planet Hong Kong: Popular Cinema and the art of Entertainment* (Cambridge, Mass.: Harvard University Press, 2000), p. 84.

3. Desser also implicates the African American film audience for the genre's quick demise; see David Desser, "The Kung Fu Craze: Hong Kong Cinema's First American Reception," in Poshek Fu and David Desser, eds., *The Cinema of Hong Kong: History, Arts, Identity* (Cambridge: Cambridge University Press, 2000), pp. 25, 38.

4. Marc Gallicchio, *The African American Encounter with Japan and China: Black Internationalism in Asia, 1895–1945* (Chapel Hill: University of North Carolina Press, 2000), p. 2. For a discussion of African American ideologies, see Michael Dawson, *Black Visions: The Roots of Contemporary African-American Political Ideologies* (Chicago: University of Chicago Press, 2001).

5. Darren W. Davis and Ronald Brown, "The Antipathy of Black Nationalism: Behavioral and Attitudinal Implications of an African American Ideology," *American Journal of Political Science* 46, no. 2 (2002): pp. 239–53; Robert A. Brown and Todd C. Shaw, "Separate Nations: Two Attitudinal Dimensions of Black Nationalism," *Journal of Politics* 64, no. 1 (2003): pp. 22–44; Stuart M. Kaminsky, "Kung Fu Film as Ghetto Myth," *Journal of Popular Film* 3, no. 2 (Spring 1974): pp. 129–38; Jon Kraszewski, "Recontextualizing the Historical Reception of Blaxploitation: Articulations of Class, Black Nationalism, and Anxiety in the Genre's Advertisements," *Velvet Light Trap* (Fall 2002): pp. 48–62. For an excellent critique of the postmodernist attack on Black Nationalism, see Madhu Dubey, "Postmodernism as Postnationalism? Racial Representation in U.S. Black Cultural Studies," *Black Scholar* 33, no. 1 (Spring 2003): pp. 2–18.

6. W. E. B. DuBois's April 30, 1957, speech commemorating the second anniversary of the Bandung Conference, reprinted as "The American Negro and the Darker World," in Esther Cooper Jackson with Constance Pohl, eds., *The Freedomways Reader: Prophets in Their Own Country* (Boulder, Colo.: Westview Press, 2000), pp. 11–18; it originally appeared in *Freedomways*, no. 3 (1968). See also W. E. B. DuBois, *The Souls of Black Folk* (New York: Modern Library, 1996), p. 15; W. E. B. DuBois, *Dusk to Dawn: An Essay toward An Autobiography of a Race Concept* (New Brunswick, N.J.: Transition, 1995), p. 117. For works on DuBois and China and Japan, see David Levering Lewis, "Racism in the Service of Civil Rights: Du Bois in Germany, China, and Japan, 1936–37," *Black Renaissance Noire* 4, no. 1 (Spring 2002): pp. 8–25; Michael T. Martin and Lamont H. Yeakey, "Pan-American Asian Solidarity: A Central Theme in Du Bois' Conception of Racial Stratification and Struggle," *Phylon* 43, no. 3 (3rd Quarter, 1982): pp. 210, 216.

7. Elijah Muhammad, *The Supreme Wisdom*, vol. 2 (Newport News, Va.: United

Brothers Communications Systems, 1957), pp. 15, 30, 66. For critiques of the NOI's conception of the "Asiatic Blackman," see Claude Andrew Clegg III, *An Original Man: The Life of Elijah Muhammad* (New York: St. Martin's Press, 1997), especially pp. 41–73; Nathaniel Deutsch, "'The Asiatic Black Man': An African American Orientalism?" *Journal of Asian American Studies* 4, no. 3 (2001): pp. 193–208.

8. Louis E. Lomax, *When the Word Is Given . . . : A Report on Elijah Muhammad, Malcolm X, and the Black Muslim World* (New York: Signet Books, New American Library of World Literature, 1964), pp. 130–31.

9. Huey P. Newton, *The Black Panther*, January 16, 1971, p. 10; quoted in Floyd W. Hayes III and Francis A. Kiene III, "'All Power to the People': The Political Thought of Huey P. Newton and the Black Panther Party," in Charles E. Jones, ed., *The Black Panther Party Reconsidered* (Baltimore: Black Classic Press, 1998), pp. 169–70. See also Huey P. Newton, *To Die for the People: Selected Writings and Speeches* (New York: Writers and Readers, 1995; New York: Random House, 1972), pp. 171, 178–81, 207–14; Judson Jeffries, *Huey P. Newton: The Radical Theorist* (Jackson: University Press of Mississippi, 2002), especially pp. 74–82.

10. Clegg estimated that perhaps only half or 600,000 of *Muhammad Speaks* newspapers were actually in circulation. Nevertheless, a circulation of 300,000 biweekly newspapers provided a large audience for Malcolm and the NOI. See Clegg, *An Original Man*, pp. 160, 320, note 23. Francis Njubi Nesbitt discusses the prevalence of anticolonial and anti-imperialist rhetoric in African American newspapers before the Cold War; see Francis Njubi Nesbitt, *Race for Sanctions: African Americans against Apartheid, 1946–1994* (Bloomington: Indiana University Press, 2004), p. 11.

11. Kraszewski, "Recontextualizing the Historical Reception of Blaxploitation," p. 51; Eddie Glaude Jr., *Is It Nation Time?: Contemporary Essays on Black Power and Black Nationalism (Chicago: University of Chicago Press, 2002), p. 5.

12. Ed Guerrero, *Framing Blackness: The African American Image in Film* (Philadelphia: Temple University Press, 1993), p. 71; Steven F. Lawson, *Running for Freedom: Civil Rights and Black Politics in America since 1941*, 2nd ed. (New York: McGraw-Hill, 1997), p. 127.

13. Samuel F. Yette, *The Choice: The Issue of Black Survival in America* (Silver Springs, Md.: Cottage Books; New York: Putnam, 1971), pp. 187, 266–72; Richard Quinney, *Class, State and Crime: On the Theory and Practice of Criminal Justice* (New York: McKay, 1977), pp. 109–13; Ward Churchill and Jim Vander Wall, *The COINTELPRO Papers: Documents from the FBI's Secret War against Domestic Dissent* (Boston: South End Press, 1990), p. 124. See also Kenneth O'Reilly, *"Racial Matters": The FBI's Secret File on Black America, 1960–1972* (New York: Free Press, 1989), pp. 254–56, 258.

14. Manning Marable, *Race, Reform and Rebellion: The Second Reconstruction in America*, 2nd ed. (Jackson: University of Missouri Press, 1991), p. 119; Kraszewski, "Recontextualizing the Historical Reception of Blaxploitation," pp. 51–53; Sundiata Keita Cha-Jua and Clarence Lang, "Providence, Patriarchy, Pathology: The Rise and Decline of Louis Farrakhan," *New Politics* 8 (Winter 1997): pp. 55–71.

15. Quoted in Robert E. Weems Jr. and Lewis A. Randolph, "The Ideological Origins of Richard M. Nixon's 'Black Capitalism' Initiative," *The Review of Black Political Economy* 29, no. 1 (Summer 2001): p. 53. See also Dean Kotlowski, "Black Power Nixon-Style: The Nixon Administration and Minority Business Enterprise," *Business History Review* 72 (1998): pp. 409–45.

16. Nesbitt, *Race for Sanctions*, p. 4.

17. Robin Kelly, *Freedom Dreams: The Black Radical Imagination* (Boston: Beacon Press, 2003), pp. 93–109.

18. The National Politics Study seeks to determine and analyze African Americans' "group identity, consciousness, ideological beliefs, policy preferences, and candidate evaluations"; see the 2004 National Politics Study, http://sitemaker.umich.edu/nps. See also Davis and Brown, "The Antipathy of Black Nationalism," p. 242.

19. Donald Bogle, *Toms, Coons, Mulattoes, Mammies, and Bucks: An Interpretive History of Blacks in American Films* (New York: Continuum), pp. 194–266; Guerrero, *Framing Blackness*, pp. 69–110; Lisa M. Anderson, *Mammies No More: The Changing Image of Black Women on Stage and Screen* (Lanham, Md.: Rowman and Littlefield, 1997), pp. 116–31.

20. Guerrero, *Framing Blackness*, pp. 70–71.

21. James Robert Parish and George H. Hill, eds., *Black Action Films: Plots, Critiques, Cast and Credits for 235 Theatrical and Made-for-Television Releases* (Jefferson, N.C.: McFarland, 1989), pp. 296–97; Bogle, *Toms, Coons, Mulattoes, Mammies, and Bucks*, p. 253. Huey P. Newton endorses the hypermasculinist vision central to the film's plot. See Newton, "He Won't Bleed Me: A Revolutionary Analysis of 'Sweet Sweetback's Baadasssss Song,'" in *To Die for the People*, p. 113; originally in *Black Panther* 6 (January 19, 1971). For a critique of *Sweetback*, see Lerone Bennett, "The Emancipation Orgasm: Sweetback in Wonderland," *Ebony* 26 (September 1971): pp. 106–16. See also the movie *Baadasssss*, directed by Mario Van Peebles (2004).

22. Kraszewski, "Recontextualizing the Historical Reception of Blaxploitation," p. 54.

23. In 2004, Obsidian Home Entertainment released a thirtieth anniversary edition of the movie *The Spook Who Sat by the Door*, directed by Ivan Dixon (2004).

24. Marable, *Race, Reform and Rebellion*, p. 134.

25. *Black Gunn*, directed by Robert Hartford-Davis (2004).

26. Lau Shing-Hon, "Introduction," in *A Study of the Martial Arts Film*" (Hong Kong: Urban Council, 1980), p. 3.

27. Desser, "The Kung Fu Craze," p. 19.

28. Kaminsky, "Kung Fu Film as Ghetto Myth," p. 30.

29. Twenty-seven general films were also shown during the period of Cope's investigation. Desser, "The Kung Fu Craze," p. 25; Demetrius Cope, "Anatomy of a Blaxploitation Theatre," *Jump Cut: A Review of Contemporary Cinema* no. 9 (October–December 1975): p. 22; Jacqueline Bobo, "'The Subject Is Money': Reconsidering the

Black Film Audience as Theoretical Paradigm," *Black American Literature Forum* 25, no. 2, Black Film Issue (Summer 1991): p. 425.

30. Amy Abugo Ongiri, "'He Wanted to Be Just Like Bruce Lee': African Americans, Kung Fu Theater and Cultural Exchange at the Margins," *Journal of Asian American Studies* 5, no. 1 (2002): pp. 31–40; Kaminsky, "Kung Fu Film as Ghetto Myth," p. 130.

31. As a martial artist, Chow could appreciate Lee's skill, so, unlike Run Run Shaw, he was willing to remunerate him fairly for his skills. Golden Harvest eventually surpassed Shaw Brothers and by 1986 pushed them from movies into mainly television production. See Fredric Dannen and Barry Long, *Hong Kong Babylon: An Insider's Guide to the Hollywood of the East* (New York: Hyperion and Miramax Books, 1997), p. 12; David Bordwell, *Planet Hong Kong: Popular Cinema and the Art of Entertainment* (Cambridge, Mass.: Harvard University Press, 2000), p. 68.

32. Hsiung-Ping Chiao, "Bruce Lee: His Influence on the Evolution of the Kung Fu Genre," *Journal of Popular Film and Television* 9 (Spring 1981): p. 33; Bordwell, *Planet Hong Kong*, pp. 52, 53; Bruce Lee, *Tao of Jeet Kune Do* (Santa Clara, Calif.: Ohara, 1975), pp. 56–59; Richard Meyers, Amy Harlib, Bill Palmer, and Karen Palmer, *From Bruce Lee to the Ninjas: Martial Arts Movies* (New York: Citadel Press, 1991), p. 65.

33. It is interesting that *Crouching Tiger, Hidden Dragon* (2000), Ang Lee's homage to *wuxia pian* films, won four Academy Awards and drew massive crowds. Urban Council, *A Study of the Martial Arts Film* (Hong Kong: Urban Council, 1980), p. 31; Chiao, "Bruce Lee," p. 32.

34. Lee, *Tao of Jeet Kune Do*, pp. 12, 16.

35. Chiao, "Bruce Lee," p. 37.

36. The titles to the *Chinese Connection* and *Fist of Fury* were switched when the films were transported to the United States, so what Hong Kong and Asian audiences know as *Fist of Fury*, we in the United States refer to as *The Chinese Connection*.

37. See Robin D. G. Kelly, "'Roaring from the East': Third World Dreaming," in *Freedom Dreams: The Black Radical Imagination* (Boston: Beacon Press, 2002), pp. 60–109; Gerald Horne, *Black and Red: W. E. B. Du Bois and the Afro-American Response to the Cold War, 1944–1963* (Albany: State University of New York Press, 1986), p. 19.

38. Haywood Derrick Horton, Beverlyn Lundy Allen, Cedric Herring, and Melvin E. Thomas, "Lost in the Storm: The Sociology of the Black Working Class, 1850 to 1990," *American Sociological Review* 65, no. 1 (February 2000), table 1, p. 131.

10

Shaw Brothers Cinema and the Hip-Hop Imagination

FANON CHE WILKINS

> It's not about kicks and flips, like since you understand the lyrics really well, you should sit down and watch some of these movies because it is hard for some people to grasp where we are coming from if they haven't seen these movies.
>
> —Wu-Tang Clan

I was four years old when Bruce Lee died in summer 1973. It seems, however, that I only discovered this fact as an adult. To my recollection, Bruce Lee was alive for much of my childhood. Sitting in a drive-in movie theater with my grandmother (who was just as excited to see Lee as I was) watching *Enter the Dragon* on a larger-than-life movie screen made Bruce Lee a reality for me. It did not help that my Uncle Billy, who was a teenage martial artist at the time (and now a thirty-plus-year black belt veteran of aikido), plastered his room with posters of Lee and often described the Dragon's prowess in slow poetic cadences and hushed whispers as if he was revealing old secrets to an eager young pupil. When talking to me about Lee, my Uncle Billy displayed great humility and took on the persona of a devout student only wishing to bestow honor and respect to a man he knew only through movies.[1] In my later years, I, too, desperately wanted to believe the urban legend that the Dragon would return from an unspecified mountain retreat in China, where he had lived in isolation with peasants, and grace us with his superhuman physicality.

Somewhere between *Enter the Dragon*, the *Game of Death*, and the umpteen Bruce Lee look-alike films, the Dragon became my generation's Tupac

Shakur. We believed, like many present-day fans of the slain rapper, that Bruce Lee's larger-than-life persona guaranteed his immortality and ensured that his physical reemergence was immanent.[2]

For many of my generation, Bruce Lee was our foray into martial arts films. As an adolescent, I was not familiar with the cinematic artistry of King Hu or the carefully choreographed fight scenes of Lau Kar-leung. Although many in my community would venture into dingy movie houses in search of the latest kung fu flick, my most extensive viewing of the chop-socky variety occurred at home.[3] Indeed, I, like so many of my contemporaries, spent many Saturday afternoons—Los Angeles KCOP Channel 13 at 3:00 P.M. to be exact—watching *Kung Fu Theatre* and marveling at the death-defying sword skill of Li Ching, the stoic heroism of Gordon Liu, and the humor and unsurpassed acrobatics of Jackie Chan.[4] Although the fight scenes were carefully choreographed and the plots of revenge and redemption fairly simple, we watched these films nonetheless.

In spite of the telegraphed plot lines, the grainy film quality with the unevenly pitched sound, and the poorly dubbed English voice-overs, there was something very alluring and thrilling about these films. As self-styled aficionados, we coveted the substandard film quality (including the choppy editing) and developed our own aesthetic criteria for evaluating a film's value and worth for our rugged band of neighborhood experts. In comparison to the technically sophisticated films emanating from Hollywood, the grainy qualities of a typical kung fu film produced by Shaw Brothers Studio became a marker of authenticity, much like many current disc jockeys' preference for records on wax as opposed to the supposedly superior sound of a digital compact disc.[5]

By college my interest in kung fu films became insatiable. Those of us with a cultish recall of our favorite Shaw Brothers film frequently gathered at Obe's (pronounced "Oh-bay"), a smug and precocious Brooklynite who had a penchant for collecting bootlegged martial arts films from New York City street vendors who often sold you three tapes for $10 or five tapes for $20 on 125th Street in Harlem or along Flatbush Avenue in Brooklyn.[6] Needless to say, Obe's collection was extensive and by far the largest within our community of martial arts lovers. Moreover, his discerning eye and dogged knack for finding the most sought-after cult classics made his apartment the place to be. And, like true fans of the genre, we did not just passively watch these movies; we studied them and provided our own philosophical analysis of their purpose and value, which, more often than not, revered the metaphysical intelligence of old sages and the timeless wisdom of the ancients, a wisdom that we regarded as crucial to our own internal development as self-styled practitioners of holistic health who had embraced a vegetarian diet and had our lifestyle changes reinforced by hip-hop icons such, as KRS-ONE and the Jungle Brothers.[7] We were never just preoccupied with the fight scenes or the tumbling theatrics. On more than one occasion, those in our midst who only showed an interest in the inevitable showdowns between two warring masters were playfully chastised for their simplicity and urged to recognize the deeper philosophical lessons within the film. As active viewers, we always acknowledged that something else was at stake beyond the fight.

Recognizing that African American youth devise their own aesthetic criteria for analyzing martial arts movies and other forms of popular media, this chapter seeks to discern and elucidate what it is African American youth find appealing in kung fu films. With the understanding that hip-hop music has always been about more than just spine-tingling guitar riffs, thumping bass lines, and innovative rhyme schemes, this chapter aims to explore why some hip-hop artists appropriate kung fu film dialogue, performance, and philosophy into their aural sound scapes and musical production. In this respect, the music and culture of contemporary black youth serve as a portal into understanding how meaning is made and remade through artistic participation and practice.

Hip-hop serves as a cultural storehouse that provides a critical window into the interstices of black life, particularly of African American youth. As an art form borne out of the confluence of national deindustrialization, federal cutbacks in social services for the poor in every area of civil society, and the creation of new electronic technologies, hip-hop provides commentary and insight into how African Americans, particularly the young, make meaning out of the material and imagined resources of the popular world and contribute to the creation of a global popular culture that is geographically boundless and reflexively open to new ideas and innovation from communities outside its various points of origin.[8]

This chapter sits at the intersection of recent scholarship in cinema and hip-hop studies and argues, through a specific analysis of the music, lyrics, and aural sound scapes created by hip-hop artists such as the Wu-Tang Clan and Jeru the Damaja, that beyond the physicality of two warring masters, kung fu films—particularly those of the Shaw Brothers variety produced in the 1970s and early 1980s—offer eager viewers insight into spiritual development and mental mastery as necessary prerequisites to a disciplined body capable of developing expertise in various martial arts techniques. This study will proceed by (1) briefly examining the Wu-Tang Clan's interest in the Lau

Kar-leung's classic *The 36th Chamber of Shaolin*, (2) exploring the spiritual significance of the film in relation to Taoism and Chan Buddhism, (3) closely analyzing the spiritual tropes and motifs presented in *The 36th Chamber of Shaolin*, and (4) demonstrating how and why the Wu-Tang Clan and Jeru the Damaja appropriate these motifs into their aural sound scapes. Fundamentally, this chapter suggests that the metaphysical dimensions of kung fu films provide psychic and spiritual resources for aggrieved communities existentially dogged by poverty and powerlessness yet in relentless search for alternative ideas and practices that can contribute to transforming one's life and creating a more sustainable world for human regeneration. Moreover, the physical dimensions of kung fu, which place a premium on self-defense as opposed to violent aggression, conform with the corporeal experiences of African Americans, who, from the time of the transatlantic slave trade, were forced to respond to, and defend against, external violence and oppression that sought to negate the agency and humanity of African peoples globally.[9]

Hip-Hop and the Screen

Historian and cultural critic George Lipsitz has noted that part of hip-hop's genius lies in the fact that through the process of musical creation, "digital sampling in rap music turns consumers into producers, tapping consumer memories of parts of old songs and redeploying them in the present." As an art form that grew out of the cross-fertilization of African American, Afro-Caribbean, and Latino youth agency and culture in one of the most aggrieved sections of the U.S. landscape (the South Bronx), "hip hop calls into question Western notions of cultural production as property through its evocation, quotation, and outright theft of socially shared musical memories."[10] Moreover, cultural critic and musician Greg Tate argues, "[H]ip hop music is recorded to evoke visual and mental imaging in the manner of radio plays and virtual displays. The best MCs, such as Rakim and the late Biggie Smalls, concocted their rhymes with the intention of extending their poetry and their narrative reach beyond the auditory and into the veritable nervous system." As a collective consciousness that has consistently transformed objects into subjects, hip-hop, according to Tate, "is conceived not just with music lovers and dancers in mind but as a full-blown assault on the sensorium of book addicts, wine tasters, auto drivers, filmgoers, art lovers and mystics." For Tate, "a great hip hop album is a multimedia production on silicon, effortlessly joining narrative tropes and consumer groups."[11] Lipsitz's and Tate's interpretations of what hip-hop actually does serve as a foray into understanding why and how hip-hop artists such as the Wu-Tang Clan sample the grunts, kicks, dialogues, and mystical soliloquies showcased in martial arts films.

Recent works by scholars of cinema have noted that the kung fu craze of the early 1970s, which coincided with the birth of hip-hop culture, was enlivened and ultimately sustained by the deliberate marketing schemes of film conglomerates such as Warner Brothers Pictures. In particular, David Desser has underscored the point that "through pairing kung fu films with blaxploitation movies in inner city movie houses, black and brown audiences were disproportionately exposed to the latest offerings from Shaw Brothers and Golden Harvest."[12] These audiences would develop an affinity for these films largely because the action genre "operated around an axis of power and powerlessness," according to cinema scholar Yvonne Tasker.[13] For Desser, "kung fu films offered the only nonwhite heroes, men and women, to audiences alienated by mainstream culture." These were films that revolved around an underdog, a lone rebel facing tremendous odds against a colonial enemy, "white culture, or the Japanese." Indeed, "fighting a foe with greater economic clout who represented the status quo provides an obvious but nonetheless real connection between kung fu films and black audiences," writes Desser.[14]

Yet beyond the admittedly obvious connections outlined by Desser and others, this chapter is concerned with the nonphysical dimensions of martial arts films that interest ethnic audiences, specifically African American youth. Thus, Shaw Brothers' propensity for setting their movies "in an unspecified mythological past" in which the enemy was often represented "as a threat from outside" resonated with African American audiences that saw striking parallels with a kind of populist Afrocentrism that revered antiquity as a time when black people were free and in control of large-scale societies and civilizations. As Robin Kelley has noted, this Afrocentric impulse grew out of a desire to "look back in search of a better future" free of poverty, police brutality, miseducation, and "arrogant white people questioning [black] intelligence." Scholars who dismiss this thinking as essentialist and myth making miss the point that the imagined world of antiquity (with its obvious shortcomings with regard "to slave labor, class hierarchies, and women's oppression") was evoked simply out of a desire to be free and imbue the present with hope and the promise of a better world.[15]

Enter the 36th Chamber:
The Wu-Tang Clan and the Reign of Shaolin

Founded in the early 1990s, the Wu-Tang Clan burst onto the music scene in 1993 with the multiplatinum album *Enter the Wu-Tang 36 Chamber* on Loud Records. Critics hailed the album an instant classic and shortly thereafter declared the Wu-Tang Clan one of the greatest rap groups in music history and set in motion a string of hit records that would dominate the airwaves and compact disc players of hip-hoppers for much of the 1990s. Marked by an uncanny social realism that toured listeners through the impoverished streets of New York's forgotten borough Staten Island (renamed Shaolin Island by the Clan), the Wu-Tang Clan innovatively sampled the kicks, grunts, and screams of martial arts films in narrating the daunting challenges offered by the modern U.S. ghetto. With an unprecedented record deal that allowed the entire nine-member crew to pursue solo projects beyond group efforts, subsequent Wu-Tang member albums featured what Greg Tate refers to as an "opaque Orientalist Blackness that extol[led] military discipline, skills, and strategy over thuggish brutality."[16]

Robert Diggs (the RZA; pronounced "Ri-zah"), Dennis Coles (Ghostface Killer), and Gary Grice (the GZA; pronounced "Gi-zah") founded the Wu-Tang Clan. Both Diggs and Grice had unsuccessful recording experiences in the late 1980s and decided to assemble the best talent in their neighborhood. They aimed for the underground market with the idea of developing a strong subterranean fan base and using their name recognition to land a record contract for the group and solo deals for each member of the Clan. From its inception, the Wu-Tang Clan was conceptualized as a base and launching pad for the solo careers of its members and a brand that would evolve into a multimillion-dollar entrepreneurial empire that sold everything from clothes to video games.[17] As Clan members declared on their debut album, "we not just to trying to hop in and hop out" of the music business but, instead, are working to build a financial empire that is worldwide.[18] In the spirit of hip-hop appropriation, the Clan's debut album, *Enter the Wu-Tang 36 Chambers*, adapted its title from the 1978 Lau Kar-leung film *The 36th Chamber of Shaolin*, also known as *Master Killer*. (One Clan member took the name Masta Killa as his moniker of choice and in 2004 released his first solo album since the Wu-Tang emerged more than a decade ago.) The Wu-Tang's distinct use of martial arts dialogue in their music immediately gained the ear of the hip-hop community because it tapped the "shared memories" of the youth who instantly recognized the eerie soliloquies of kung fu masters and the poorly dubbed grunts and sound effects that endowed kung fu films with a rebellious outsider status within the film world as a whole.

Among self-styled aficionados and scholars of martial arts cinema alike, *The 36th Chamber of Shaolin* (*Master Killer*) ranks as one of the all-time classics of Asian martial arts films and was at the forefront of a new form of martial arts moviemaking that showcased the skill and practice of Shaolin kung fu. In an interesting skit preceding the fourth song on the Wu-Tang's debut album, "Wu-Tang: 7th Chamber," Clan member Method Man is repeatedly asked by Raekwon the Chef, "[Y]o Meth where is my *Killah* tape at God." Method Man responds by stating that he does not know where the tape is and proceeds to explain that the video mysteriously disappeared after "niggas came over with forties and blunts." Raekwon, unsatisfied with Method Man's explanation, continues his complaint about the lost tape before being interrupted by several abrupt knocks at the door by an anonymous partner of the Clan who tells them that one of their homeboys was just killed (minutes before he arrived) in a drive-by shooting in their neighborhood. The skit device, employed by Clan producer the RZA, serves to draw the audience into the everyday life of the Clan in which a seemingly frivolous exchange over a kung fu video is juxtaposed to the death of a friend in the neighborhood. More telling, however, is the lack of shock among Clan members after hearing the news. As the skit proceeds, the lost video remains the primary concern of both Raekwon and Method Man, an interesting juxtaposition of the search for pleasure (the video) and the hardening realities of the streets (the homicide), two central motifs in the Wu-Tang Clan's music. Humorously, the Clan's penchant for "keeping it real" demands that listeners recognize that Raekwon's lost *Killah* tape is just as serious as death in the streets. And, of course, this was no ordinary video. Raekwon's insistence on his *Killah* tape was insider shorthand for *The 36th Chamber of Shaolin*, also known as *Master Killer*.[19]

Lau Kar-leung directed *The 36th Chamber of Shaolin* after a string of movies in the mid-1970s intended to ride the wave of so-called authentic kung fu filmmaking after Bruce Lee's international success in the early years of the decade. Raised in a family of kung fu practitioners (both his parents were kung fu experts), Lau got his start in the film industry as a martial arts actor and later as a choreographer. As an assistant to director Chang Cheh, master of the *wuxia* sword films of the 1960s, Lau effectively integrated southern-style Chinese kung fu with Japanese sword fighting in Cheh's later films before striking out on his own as a director contracted by the Shaw Brothers in the mid-1970s. Cheh would later work for a Shaw Brothers subsidiary in Taiwan and continue making films, whereas Lau began to experiment with Shaolin motifs and humor in his quest to authenticate the kung fu action movie by developing stories that revolved around more realistic heroes and showcased kung fu as it was practiced in everyday life across time and space.[20]

Though it has been argued that *The 36th Chamber of Shaolin* was not Lau's most important work, it certainly became his signature piece that made the Shaolin Temple a household word for audiences captivated by authentic kung fu. Lau recalled that in the early days of his career, most of the martial arts films employed actors with no real martial arts training and rarely hit people in films. As a practitioner, Lau became a part of new wave of martial artists who brought true fighting skills to film and successfully explored the spiritual and philosophical dimensions of Chan Buddhism that endowed many of their protagonists with a sense of moral cause and ethical justice, a device used to good effect in *The 36th Chamber of Shaolin*.[21]

The film featured the heroics of a revengeful monk who had to overcome a series of physical tests in order to advance through each chamber of a Buddhist monastery. On the surface, the monk's physical challenges seem to be the spine of the of the story, which ultimately leads to San Te's (the main character played by Gordon Liu) return to the outside world to spread the teachings of Shaolin to the common people and defeat the film's antagonists, the Manchus. Liu's aquiline facial features and trademark bald head are accented by concentrated camera close-ups during the training sequences in the film and evoke a deep sense of mental and spiritual concentration. As the challenges mount, we see the beads of sweat dribbling down his forehead. During each physical test, Liu's face exhibits extreme anguish and despair. As Liu moves through each chamber carrying buckets of water, gonging a bell with a weighted stick, and practicing his newly learned kung fu techniques on various esteemed masters in the monastery, time is cinematically collapsed and Liu's mastery of each test is effortlessly melded and integrated into a mastery of self.

As Liu develops physically through a series of grueling exercises that test his stamina, strength, and concentration, he gradually begins to project a sense of inner calmness that is characteristic of the most spiritually evolved monks in the monastery. Here again, Liu's upright and relaxed gate, his frequent invocations of the blessings of Buddha, his pronounced presence of mind, his acquired humility toward his teachers and peers all become representative of a higher sense of spiritual consciousness. Although he had come to the monastery to acquire the famed techniques of Shaolin kung fu and increase his physical prowess, Liu's character emerges as a more spiritually refined human being capable of utilizing his newfound enlightenment in the service of his physical skills. Thus Liu's character not only becomes a master killer through his mastery of Shaolin kung fu, but, more important, he emerges as an archetype representative of the core teachings of Chan Buddhism that recognize spiritual refinement as foundational to physical development.

Cinema scholar Stephen Teo suggests that the transcendentalism and spiritual dimensions of kung fu were pronounced features in the works of Shaw Brothers pioneer King Hu. A predecessor of Lau Kar-leung, Teo notes that Hu's Buddhism is an "explicit cultural element, which allows Chinese culture to exist on a less nationalistic and more metaphysical plane, insofar as Buddhism is an integral part of Chinese culture." Thus, Hu's Buddhist motifs are strategically used "to emphasize the spiritual side of life" that are a part of a "supernatural universe haunted by ghost-spirits and a mystical force capable of giving human beings inhuman strengths and abilities."[22] Yet to understand Lar's cinematic meditations on the centrality of Buddhism in *The 36th Chamber of Shaolin,* I want to suggest that a more detailed analysis of Chan Buddhism is in order for purposes of distinguishing Lar's motifs from Hu's, which I argue provides a critical link for understanding the Wu-Tang Clan's attraction to Shaolin as a distinct form of Chinese martial arts and spiritual practice.

Shaolin literally translates as "youthful forest" and combines a complex mixture of Taoist and Buddhist philosophical principles known as Chan that make up a nonsecular branch of the Buddhist tradition that is essentially atheistic. Taoism, the fifth-century ideas and teachings of Lao-tzu, insisted that the world that human beings inhabited is a knowable universe composed of a duality of opposites—also known as dialectics—in the physical (hot/cold), moral (good/bad), and biological (male/female) realms of existence. These opposites are exemplified by yin and yang, symbolically represented as two fish encapsulated in a circle matched at each end to form a whole. The Taoist believed that keen observations of nature held the keys to understanding the harmony of life and concentrated a great deal of their efforts on examining the difference and "intrinsic nature of Yiness and Yangness." In this regard, Shaolin kung fu's propensity for mimicking the movement and forms of animals is rooted in the Taoist tradition of playing close attention to the natural world.[23]

Where the Taoist saw difference and distinction in the natural world, Buddhists concentrated on the harmony of duality and even argued that there was a neutral position that did not always translate into neat binaries of two.

Bodhidharma, known in Chinese as Tamo, was an Indian Buddhist who introduced the Chinese to what is commonly referred to as Chan Buddhism (Zen Buddhism in Japanese) somewhere around 500 A.D. In addition to stressing the Four Noble Truths and the Eightfold Path, the foundational principles embraced by all Buddhist sects, Tamo "placed the burden of obtaining spiritual enlightenment on the individual" and advocated that seekers of the dharma (the way) be self-motivated and practice self-awareness and self-recognition in their daily lives. Challenging what he believed to be the overtextualization of the Buddhist tradition by religious zealots and idiosyncratic intellectuals, Tamo professed that you are what you do and "left his disciples considerable latitude in how to live." To be a Chan Buddhist practitioner, one did not have to be a celibate monk or engage in an ascetic lifestyle, although many practiced such activity. Indeed, the human condition demanded that spiritual pursuits begin with where a person was in life and proceed down a variety of paths that were distinct to each individual practitioner who had come to understand his or her existence through experiencing life "in all its glory and despair." What united each seeker of the way, according to Tamo, was recognition and practice. There were many roads to enlightenment, and each person was to be his or her "own light" and refuge in their pursuit of the dharma. Moreover, it was standard pedagogical practice among Chan masters "to never tell too plainly" out of an interest of encouraging students to come to their own realization of the value and lesson of a particular idea or experience.[24]

According to the Shaolin Gung Fu Institute, one of the prevailing myths about the development and the evolution of Shaolin is that its primary focus evolved around the pursuit of kung fu martial arts. Well before Shaolin, martial arts existed in a variety of forms throughout Southeast Asia, however, and Shaolin kung fu grew out of the yoga-based movement exercises practiced by Tamo during his teachings in the monasteries. Tamo developed these exercises to assist the monks in coping with the deceptively difficult rigors of daily meditation. These practices, in keeping with Taoist sensibilities, were modeled after eighteen animals in Indo-Chinese iconography. Shaolin practitioners at the Shaolin Gung Fu Institute suggest that the martial dimension of the physical practice of kung fu most likely developed out of a need for self-defense and engaged in violence precisely "to better understand violence" and consequently to avoid violence altogether. A popular Shaolin axiom exclaimed, "One who engages in combat has already lost the battle." Moreover, it was believed that "if a person studied Shaolin and learned little more than kung fu, he was not Shaolin. All the arts of the temple were aimed at leading one close to enlightenment by providing tools to making a whole person."[25]

When Lau Kar-leung set out to try his hand as a director for Shaw Brothers, he insisted that he wanted to make movies that portrayed realistic heroes and showcased a style of kung fu that was actually practiced by Shaolin masters. *The 36th Chamber of Shaolin* was Lau's attempt to authenticate the martial arts film through a detailed cinematic exploration of everyday life in a Shaolin Temple.[26] Chan Buddhist motifs drive the main story line of the film and structure the development of the central character, San Te.

In the first act of *The 36th Chamber of Shaolin,* Lau introduces the audience to San Te by chronicling his involvement with a southern Chinese Ming resistance movement engaged in a guerilla war against Manchu incursion from the north. When Manchu warlords in search of guerilla rebels like himself massacre San Te's family and close friends, San Te decides to search for the nearest Shaolin monastery to learn kung fu. San Te's interest in Shaolin is cinematically represented through his admiration of a simple hand chop of a fellow rebel who informed him that he learned his kung fu at Shaolin. This scene is important because early on we learn that it is possible for Shaolin kung fu to be acquired by ordinary people, including rebels fighting the evil Manchus. Second, when San Te inquires about Shaolin kung fu, this offers Teacher Ho (San Te's schoolteacher and leader in the resistance movement) the opportunity to openly ponder how great it would be if Shaolin kung fu could be taught to the common person as a means for self-defense against the Manchus. Teacher Ho, who later commits suicide before being captured by Manchu rebels, provides a vision that would eventually become the mission of San Te.

Throughout the first act, the camera close-ups reveal San Te's boyish curiosity, naïveté, courage, and determination. All of these qualities come to make up the raw ingredients of his character that will be refined through a deep immersion into the everyday life of the Shaolin monastery. Yet before arriving at the monastery, Lau skillfully sets up another point of dramatic tension when San Te is told by one of his classmates that everyone in the community, including San Te's family, was killed by the Manchus in pursuit of the rebels. In a full-out rage, San Te's friend laments the fact that all that they studied in school was ethics, whereas they should have been studying kung fu. San Te tells his friend that ethics "teach us what is right," yet his friend retorts that ethics have no place when you are dealing with "Manchu killers." This exchange fuels the desire of the protagonist while simultaneously introducing the audience to a philosophical tension that is concerned with the moral and ethical dimensions of revenge and the acquisition of kung fu.

When San Te arrives at the Shaolin monastery, Lau provides an aerial shot of the temple and pans the interior showcasing the work and activity of the monks engaged in the day-to-day activities that enable the community to thrive and develop. Immediately, we recognize that there is no idleness in the monastery and that the monks are involved in a wide range of activities that vary from sweeping and hauling firewood to sewing and tending gardens. Lau skillfully introduces the audience to the monastery without showcasing any kung fu. Instead, we see dedicated monks preoccupied with building the community and refining their self-development through mundane chores and the practice of arts and crafts. Thus, Shaolin appears to be more like a university engaged in nurturing the whole human being, rather than a spawning ground for kung fu pugilists.

Within the Chan Buddhist tradition, meditation is to be practiced at all times and does not require formal exercises or postures to be done effectively.[27] After one year within the monastery, San Te complained that all he had done since arriving at Shaolin was sweep and clean doors, not yet understanding that his work was part of his practice and integral to the kung fu that he would eventually learn. When he inquired of one of the senior monks about learning kung fu so that he could teach it to people within his community for purposes of self-defense against the Manchu's, San Te was admonished by the senior monk for revealing such desire and was then told that their were thirty-five chambers for training within the monastery and that to master Shaolin kung fu one had to successfully complete each chamber. The senior monk then asked San Te where he wanted to begin, and San Te naively chose the thirty-fifth chamber, where a gauntlet of monks sat along a pathway and were instructed by an elderly monk to chant sutra (classic Buddhist text) while rhythmically striking wooden gourds. San Te approached the elderly monk and declared his desire to learn kung fu and was instantly knocked to the ground by a force emitted from the monk's hands that did not require physical touch. San Te cringed in pain and quickly learned that his training had to begin in the first chamber.

Within all Buddhist traditions, the second and the third of the Four Noble Truths declare that desire for things leads to suffering and that extinction of desire ceases pain and suffering, respectively. When San Te revealed his desire to teach Shaolin kung fu to the outside world, he was quickly admonished and told to dispense with such thinking. Yet the senior monk did not disallow San Te to pursue learning kung fu. Recognizing San Te's ambition and inexperience, the senior monk wisely permitted him to choose his chamber of choice to begin his practice and then allowed the negative experience to teach him an additional spiritual lesson. Visually, Lau placed the culture of the monastery at the forefront of each scene, whereas the dialogue and the action elaborated the Chanist sensibilities that undergirded San Te's progress through each chamber. This was especially put to good effect when San Te, in his desperate attempts to learn how to walk across a series of floating logs, awoke from his sleep in the middle of the night and began to practice the delicate integration of speed, balance, and weight to successfully cross the waterway leading to the dining quarters. In keeping with the Chan Buddhist tradition of self-realization, Lau successfully captures this nocturnal epiphany through a shadowy scene that effectively contrasts San Te's sharply lit body with a rich, dark evening, evoking a sense of new awareness and consciousness. Cinematically, San Te's mastery of the floating logs is represented through slow motion and concentrated shots on the lower body.

When San Te initially came to the monastery after secretly stowing away in a food basket pulled on a large rickshaw by several monks from the temple, he spent ten days recovering from a coma before being told by a senior monk that once his health was in order he would have to leave Shaolin Temple immediately. The chief abbot intervened on San Te's behalf, however, and declared that because San Te was able to successfully make the journey to the monastery and recover from his coma, Buddha favored his cause, and this was enough to grant him entry into the temple. After completing all of the thirty-five chambers in record fashion, San Te declared to the abbot that he wanted to create a thirty-sixth chamber that would entail teaching Shaolin kung fu to the outside world. Again, the abbot did not agree with this desire; however, as a punishment for such request, he banished San Te to the outside world, effectively allowing him to pursue his path of creating a thirty-sixth chamber. Indeed, his path had been determined as part of a plot device of revenge; however, in keeping with Chan Buddhism, San Te is allowed to be his own light and his own refuge, gaining spiritual insight through experiencing life as it is.

Mastery of the spirit necessarily leads to a mastery of the self, a veritable obsession of Wu-Tang Clan members who subscribe to the teachings of the Five Percent Nation of Islam (also referred to as the Nation of Gods and Earths), a renegade sect of the Nation of Islam founded by Clarence 13X in 1964. According to the teachings of 13X, also known as Father Allah, the Five Percenters represent 5 percent of the population who are unlike the 85 percent majority, whom they regard as "deaf, dumb, and blind." The additional 10 percent are just as aware as the 5 percent; however, they use their "knowledge wisdom and understanding" to deceive the 85 percent mass and are thus designated "blood suckers of the poor."[28] Grounded in the most esoteric teachings of the Nation of Islam, a Muslim sect founded in the 1930s by W. D. Fard Muhammad in Detroit, Michigan, the Five Percenters are made up largely of alienated black youth who are apart of an ever-expanding lumpen-proletariat stratum in search of material and spiritual resources that will assist in combating and overcoming the death, disease, and destruction that is commonplace in inner cities across the United States. Through ciphers (or gathering circles in which members exchange knowledge and information pertaining to the teachings of Clarence 13X) and the informal acquisition of lessons, "a body of esoteric teachings" that are composed of a complex collage of scientific trivia, numerology, and a critical mix of Nation of Islam religious principles, Five Percenters actively pursue membership from the most aggrieved sections of the African American community, arming them with a corpus of teachings intended to lead to a more refined and "civilized" way of life. Five Percenter praxis is "relentlessly individualistic" and places a premium on the supremacy of Eastern philosophical teachings as offering keys to the liberation of Asiatic peoples (which include all people of African descent) from the tyranny of the streets.[29]

The Wu-Tang Clan's affinity for kung fu films grows out off their preoccupation with the East (both real and imagined) as holding the keys to freedom and self-determination for the Asiatic black man. Beyond the Wu-Tang Clan's own obsession in surreptitiously spreading the teachings of the Five Percent Nation of Islam through their music, kung fu films, generally, serve as a critical pop-cultural resource for poor black youth existentially dogged by the tyranny of the streets. In an essay exploring the etymological roots of the term *thug* and examining the core teachings of the Five Percent Nation of Islam, Melvin Gibbs discerned that the relentless individualism of the sect allowed for each man (referred to as a God or Allah) to control his own cipher or sphere of knowledge and information. Each God's interpretation of the world gained "validity through an assertion of self" and, much like Chan Buddhism, was different for each individual person.[30] What mattered was that the Supreme Mathematics (zero to nine) be foundational to each God and Earth's wisdom as they navigated the world around them. For instance, when the Wu-Tang Clan emerged as a group, they had nine members. Although there were other Clan members beyond the nine-member core, the nine held significance because it was the number for Born.[31] Within the Supreme Mathematics, Born represents rebirth or the time that one came to be conscious of their Godliness or Earthliness.[32] As a group that was partly formed in response to the exploitative qualities of the record industry, the Wu-Tang Clan set out to ensure that their artists obtained greater financial and artistic control over their product in an attempt to provide better economic opportunities for artists who, under normal circumstances, had very little say in the marketing and distribution of their own artistic creations. Thus the nine-member core of the Wu-Tang Clan was also symbolic of the rebirth of a new type of artist with greater awareness of the financial stakes of the music business.

For utilitarian purposes, Five Percent ideology remained remarkably open-ended in terms of the incorporation of new ideas that conformed to the individual's interest and curiosity. To complete their cipher, each person was encouraged to engage in his or her own research and absorb whatever new ideas they considered to be useful and in line with the Supreme Mathematics, the universal glue that bound the Five Percenters as a Nation of Gods and Earths. The RZA noted that after he mastered the 120 lessons—the rudimentary teachings of the Five Percent—he "became a seeker of knowledge in general" and "wanted to find the answer, the truth behind everything."[33] It is within this context that I want to suggest that the religious form of the Five Percenters, shot through with hip-hop sensibilities that effortlessly appropriated shared cultural memories, allows for the assimilation of new ideas (like Chan Buddhism) into a self-identified and self-defined body of knowledge.[34]

Interestingly, Chan Buddhism and Five Percenter ideology share nonsecular interest through their professed atheism and radical engagement with the realities of the material world and everyday life. Indeed, the RZA placed great emphasis on the Buddha's axiom: "Believe nothing, no matter where you read it, or who said it, no matter if I have said it, unless it agrees with your own reason and your own common sense."[35] Each person's spiritual practice placed the burden of obtaining enlightenment on the individual and asserted that self-realization was a prerequisite for higher spiritual consciousness. In this regard, I want to suggest that part of the Wu-Tang Clan's obsession with kung fu films, particularly their fetishizing *The 36th Chamber of Shaolin*, springs from deeper spiritual yearnings that serve as armor and psychic protection in the absurd world of the modern U.S. ghetto.

To illustrate this point further, let us turn to the music of Jeru the Damaja, the Brooklyn-based emcee who made his musical debut in 1993 with the underground classic *The Sun Rises in the East*, produced by the enigmatic and prolific beat alchemist popularly known as DJ Premier, one-half of the group Gangstarr. Although Jeru was not a self-described member of the Five Percent Nation of Islam, he did employ some of the teachings of the Five Percenters in his lyrics. It should be noted that the rudimentary teachings of the Five Percent Nation of Islam that regard all whites as devils and the black man and woman as God and Earth, respectively, form part of a generalized popular interpretation of Five Percent ideology that circulates among nonmembers of the Islamic sect.[36] For our purposes, Jeru's political and ideological insights into the problems that plague the African American community sit at the cross section of a hybridized Islam and a millenarian Afrocentrism, peppered with urbanized Rastafarian sensibilities that draw their sustenance from a long history of religious radicalism that crisscrossed the African diaspora. Throughout his debut album, *The Sun Rises in the East*, Jeru makes explicit reference to the films produced by Run Run Shaw and effortlessly melds kung fu motifs and metaphors into his artistic representation of the problems that plague black communities and the people who live in them.

In the lead single, "Come Clean," Jeru challenges all self-professed gangsta rappers to a battle that will showcase the superiority of one's skills (or lyrical flow/ability) on the microphone. He insists that his lyrical prowess is superior to the gun-toting emcees who make a habit of reminding audiences that their gangsterism can and, if necessary, extend beyond the performativity of the sound booth and into everyday life. Chastising hypermasculine emcees for their preoccupation with physical confrontation over verbal artistry, Jeru employs his own homophobic jibe that feminizes gangsta rappers and subverts them of their power to define the terms of hip-hop aesthetics and everyday life. Repeatedly, he asserts the importance of utilizing the mind as a liberatory agent free of the inherent self-destructive logic of gangsterism. Indeed, mental discipline is revered; however, Jeru reminds his foes that he is "a true master" and, if necessary, will "kick like kung fu flicks by Run Run Shaw." Although so-called gangsta rappers may assert themselves as the authentic voice of the ghetto, Jeru assures them that he, too, hails from the same socioeconomic status that they do yet prefers to employ more life-sustaining measures for resolving conflict.[37]

Throughout *The Sun Rises in the East*, Jeru continues to champion the mind. No cut embodies this theme more than the song "My Mind Spray." In the first verse, Jeru carefully asserts his desire to return hip-hop to its essence, in which lyrical skill and ability take precedence over predictable formulaic songs that became commonplace as hip-hop became an ultracommodity and gained a larger mainstream audience. Moreover, Jeru's boast that he has "more styles than a Shaolin Monastery" and can "drop rhyme science like he was Imhotep" returns us to the ingenious ways in which hip-hop artists effortlessly meld Afrocentric sensibilities with kung fu tropes in an attempt to construct an imagined world where the dispossessed are empowered through a relentless pursuit of ancient knowledge and wisdom.[38]

To conclude, I want to return to the Wu-Tang Clan, more specifically to the group's founder, the RZA. In the September 1999 issue of *Kungfu Magazine*, the RZA graced the cover with real-life Shaolin Temple Sifu Shi Yan Ming.[39] Ming and the RZA had known each other for four years and developed a mutual respect due to their common interest in Shaolin kung fu. Ming, who had trained in a Shaolin temple since he was five years old, defected to the United States in 1992 after he came as an emissary representing the Chinese government. "At the conclusion of that historic tour, Shi Yan Ming risked everything" and opened up a Shaolin temple in Manhattan.[40] The RZA became an avid student of Shi Yan Ming and assumed a student-teacher relationship that led him to training three days per week with the Shaolin master. The RZA admitted that before meeting Ming he had "no actual martial arts background besides a lot of reading of philosophies" and a steady diet of martial arts movies. Ming was impressed enough with the RZA's humility and vast knowledge of Shaolin kung fu that he took him on as a student.[41]

Yet "some in the martial arts world believed that it was inappropriate for a Shaolin temple monk to be associating with a rap star because the music is "drenched in violence, obscenity and drugs." In spite of the criticism, Shi Yan Ming relished his relationship with the Wu-Tang Clan mogul and gleefully declared that "Shaolin is everywhere!" and that no one country or person had a monopoly on its teachings. In concurrence with Ming, the RZA asserted:

> I think all barriers of discrimination of segregation are dissipated by Chan Buddhism. For anybody that truly understands what Chan is, they know that there are no separations. There is no good, there is no bad. A Shaolin Monk can associate with a rapper, singer, murderer, or thief. Even Jesus hung out with thieves and exiles. I think it's beautiful to see a Shaolin Monk in hip hop culture. There's always been a relationship between hip hop and martial arts: take some of the names of the MCs like Grandmaster Flash, or the breakdance moves like the windmill and one handed spin. It all comes from martial arts. Now we see it not only from movies, but we have a physical representative, that's Sifu Shi Yan Ming.[42]

As an avid practitioner of the art, the RZA noted that what he enjoyed most about Shaolin kung fu was "the harmony that it can bring to your mind and your body. As well as the gracefulness of the movements and the infinite applications once a full understanding is grasped." Moreover, in standard hip-hop fashion, shot through with Afrocentric sensibilities grounded in the idea that blacks are Asiatic, the RZA suggested that African American youths' affinity for kung fu grows out of the idea that Bodhidharma "was part of the Dravidian tribe of Africans who migrated to South India. And that martial art forms that he taught and learned were originally from the continent of Africa." For the RZA, traditional African culture "makes [black youth] predisposed to communicate with the martial arts."[43] Although the RZA does not delineate on how African-derived martial arts practices were carried over to the Americas, he does argue, however, that emceeing, like the martial arts, requires strenuous breath control. For the RZA, "music is harmonious with life," and "how chi flows, music flows." He credits his success in the music industry to his "martial application" that "can't be defined, but can definitely be heard."[44]

In 1999, the RZA accompanied Sifu Ming to the original Shaolin Temple in China. In addition to being "the first MC to perform there," he also had the opportunity to visit Wu-Tang Mountain in Hebei Province and meet "the Abbot of the *other* Wu-Tang" and exchange music.[45] The trip was so profound that the RZA could only describe it as "Enlightenment" and remind himself that the most important sutra (teaching) offered by the Buddha grew out of the question: "What do you have to teach, Buddha?" The Buddha replies: "I have nothing to teach. You have to learn it on your own."[46]

The RZA's experience at the original Shaolin Temple is symbolic of hip-hop's ability to engage and absorb all cultural phenomena that it deems useful and necessary for its growth and development. Both Shaw Brothers films and hip-hop music are intensely dynamic commodities that circulate and carry the cultural practices of diverse communities to all sides of the globe. This chapter, however, has sought to engage the cross-fertilization of these seemingly distinct, yet similar, forms of cultural production that share a profound interest in history, myth, memory, and spiritual enlightenment. Indeed, this mutual interest can be discerned when the gaze is beyond the fight.

Notes

1. Literary scholar Tzarina T. Prather echoes my experience with her own remembrance of the kung fu craze in Boston in the late 1960s and early 1970s. According to Prather, she and her contemporaries watched three full-length kung fu films for $5.00 on Sunday afternoon and would spill out of the theater mimicking their favorite characters from the film through their best rendition of their kicks, chops, and flips. Moreover, Prather also recalled "the posters of Bruce Lee that my brothers, uncles and male cousins had on their walls" and the emergence of "more than one martial arts dojo" in her neighborhood. See Tzarina T. Prather, "'Old Man Your Kung Fu

Is Useless': African American Spectatorship and Hong Kong Action Cinema," *Post Road Magazine*, no. 2 (Spring/Summer 2001), available at http://www.postroadmag .com/Issue_2/Criticism2/Criticism2.html.

2. To corroborate my personal narrative of the importance of Bruce Lee to the African American community in the 1970s, see James Spady, Stefan Dupres, and Charles Lee, *Twisted Tales: In the Hip Hop Streets of Philly* (Philadelphia: UMUM/ LOH, 1995), pp. 40–46.

3. David Desser, "The Kung Fu Craze: Hong Kong Cinema's First American Reception," in Poshek Fu and David Desser, eds., *The Cinema of Hong Kong: History, Arts, Identity* (New York: Cambridge University Press, 2000), pp. 24–27.

4. For a brief exploration into *Kung Fu Theatre* as a pop-cultural staple among African American audiences, see Amy Abugo Ongiri, "He Wanted to Be Just Like Bruce Lee: African Americans, Kung Fu Theatre and Cultural Exchange at the Margins," *Journal of Asian American Studies* 5, no. 1 (February 2002): pp. 31–40.

5. Some disc jockeys have argued that analog sound is superior to digital. Disc jockey/producer DJ Quick noted: "[T]here is no sound in a computer. It only records information and spits out what it thinks it recorded. It does that by converting signals to digital information and then reconverting it back to audible." Analog-produced material, however, "passes a signal through the tubes, preamps, and solid-state circuitry," thus producing a fuller sound. See Johnny Mann, "Main Ingredient: Interview with DJ Quick," *Scratch: The Science of Hip-Hop*, May/June 2005, p. 67.

6. As a graduate student in New York City and resident of Brooklyn in the mid-1990s, I frequently purchased my kung fu films from small, dingy bodegas run by Senegalese merchants with equal recall, sophistication, and cultlike interest in kung fu cinema, particularly Shaw Brothers–produced films. Film scholar Gina Marchetti noted similar forms of subterranean marketing and distribution strategies of kung films in African American communities in Washington, DC. See Gina Marchetti, "Jackie Chan and the Black Connection," in Matthew Tinkcom and Amy Villarejo, eds. *Keyframes: Popular Cinema and Cultural Studies* (New York: Routledge, 2001), p. 138.

7. Hip-hop icon KRS-ONE made his ode to vegetarianism on the lead song, "My Philosophy," from the critically acclaimed album *By All Means Necessary* (Jive Records, 1988). In explaining his philosophy and reintroducing himself as the self-professed "Teacha" in hip-hop, KRS declared: "[H]ear it first hand from an intelligent brown man, a vegetarian no goat or ham, or chicken, or turkey, or hamburger, cause to me that's suicide self-murder. Let us get back to what we call Hip-hop, and what it meant to DJ Scot La Rock." Moreover, as the center of the Native Tongues Crew that extolled the virtues of healthy living and urban bohemia, the Jungle Brothers used their classic album *Done by the Forces of Nature* (Warner Brothers, 1989) as a mouthpiece for an alternative lifestyle that included vegetarianism and spiritual refinement.

8. In terms of hip-hop and the postindustrial decline, see Tricia Rose, *Black Noise: Rap Music and Black Culture in Contemporary America* (Hanover, Conn.: Wesleyan

University Press, 1994); Tricia Rose, "A Style Nobody Can Deal With: Politics, Style, and the Postindustrial City in Hip Hop," in Andrew Ross and Tricia Rose, eds., *Microphone Fiends: Youth Music and Youth Culture* (New York: Routledge, 1994), pp. 71–88; Robin D. G. Kelley, "Kickin' Reality, Kickin' Ballistics: Gangsta Rap and Postindustrial Los Angeles," in *Race Rebels: Culture, Politics, and the Black Working Class* (New York: Free Press, 1994), pp. 183–227. On the city and the socioeconomic dimensions of hip-hop identity and the modern U.S. ghetto, see Murray Forman, *The 'Hood Comes First: Race, Space, and Place in Rap and Hip-Hop* (Hanover, Conn.: Wesleyan University Press, 2002).

9. In his seminal tome exploring the evolution and development of black radicalism globally, Cedric Robinson argued that one of the distinguishing characteristics of African responses to oppression on the continent and across the diaspora was the consistent "absence of mass violence" by Africans. For Robinson, "Blacks have seldom employed the level of violence which they (the Westerners) understood the situation required," although there was a long tradition of self-defense. See Cedric Robinson, *Black Marxism: The Making of the Black Radical Tradition* (London: Zed Press, 1983), pp. 242–47.

10. George Lipsitz, *Dangerous Crossroads: Popular Music, Postmodernism, and the Poetics of Place* (London: Verso, 1994), p. 37.

11. Greg Tate, "In Praise of Shadow Boxers: The Crises of Originality and Authority in African American Visual Art vs. the Wu-Tang Clan," *Souls* 5, no. 1 (2003): pp. 131–33.

12. Desser, "The Kung Fu Craze," p. 38.

13. Yvonne Tasker, "Fist of Fury: Discourses of Race and Masculinity in Martial Arts Cinema," in Harry Stecopoulos and Michael Uebel, eds., *Race and the Subject of Masculinities* (Durham, N.C.: Duke University Press, 1997), p. 315.

14. Desser, "The Kung Fu Craze," p. 38.

15. Kelley also noted that black people's fascination with antiquity reflected a genuine desire "to find a refuge where *black people* exercised power, possessed essential knowledge, educated the West, built monuments, slept under the stars on the banks of the Nile." See Robin D. G. Kelley, *Freedom Dreams: The Black Radical Imagination* (Boston: Beacon Press, 2002), p. 15.

16. Tate, "In Praise of Shadow Boxers," p. 132.

17. The RZA, *The Wu-Tang Clan Manual*, with Chris Norris (New York: Riverhead Freestyle, 2005), pp. 72–78.

18. For commentary on the Wu-Tang Clan's entrepreneurial interest, see the skit interview following "Can It All Be So Simple" on Wu-Tang Clan, *Enter Wu-Tang (36th Chamber)* (Loud Records, 1993).

19. "Wu-Tang: 7th Chamber" on *Enter Wu-Tang (36th Chamber)* (Loud Records, 1993).

20. "Liu Chia Liang (Lau Kar-leung) Interview with *Les Cahiers du Cinema*" (2000), available at http://www.shawstudios.com/liuchialianginfrenchtext.html.

21. Ibid. See also Stephen Teo, *Hong Kong Cinema: The Extra Dimensions* (London: British Film Institute, 1997), p. 108.

22. Teo, *Hong Kong Cinema*, p. 92.

23. "Philosophy of Shaolin," available at http://www.shaolin.com/shaolin _philosophy.aspx.

24. Ibid.

25. "History of the Shaolin Temples," available at http://www.shaolin.com/shaolin _history.aspx.

26. "Liu Chia Liang (Lau Kar-leung) Interview with *Les Cahiers du Cinema*," available at http://www.shawstudios.com/liuchialianginfrenchtext.html.

27. "The Development of Chan (Zen) in China," *Philosophy of Religion: Buddhism* (n.d.), available at http://www.hku.hk/philodep/courses/religion/Buddhism.htm.

28. Mimeographed copy of "The Lessons" and "The Father" in the possession of the author (n.d.). Five Percent materials are not available in book form but are generally passed along informally as photocopied lessons. I obtained these lessons in college through a roommate who was a member of the Five Percent Nation of Islam. For more detailed material regarding the Five Percent, see http://www.allahsnation.net.

29. Melvin Gibbs, "Thug Gods: Spiritual Darkness and Hip-Hop," in Greg Tate, ed., *Everything but the Burden: What White People Are Taking from Black Culture* (New York: Broadway Books, 2003), p. 91.

30. Ibid.

31. The Supreme Mathematics consist of: (1) Knowledge, (2) Wisdom, (3) Understanding, (4) Culture/Freedom, (5) Power/Refinement, (6) Equality, (7) God, (8) Build/Destroy, (9) Born, and (0) Cipher. Born also refers to completion. To move from (1) Knowledge to (9) Born is a marker of bringing closure to one's cipher that is represented by zero.

32. For details on the nine basic tenets of the Five Percent, the Supreme Numbers, the Supreme Alphabet, and the Supreme Science, see the RZA, *The Wu-Tang Clan Manual*, pp. 44–49.

33. Ibid., p. 50.

34. The RZA noted that in 1993 the film *Zen Master,* a movie that told the story of Bodhidharma, the founder of Chan Buddhism, profoundly moved him. He was particularly impressed with how Bodhidharma used martial arts to assist the Shaolin monks in attaining enlightenment. After the film, "I started reading the *Tao Te Ching* and the *I Ching* . . . because I was looking for the common thread of knowledge between what was going on then and now." See the RZA, *The Wu-Tang Clan Manual*, p. 50.

35. Ibid., p. 39.

36. The hip-hop artist Nas captured the ubiquity of Five Percenter ideology in the song "No Ideas Original": "Radios on card tables, Benetton, the Gods buildin', ask for today's Mathematics, we Allah's children, and this was going on in every New

York ghetto, kids listen, Five Percenters say its pork in Jell-O." See Nas, *The Lost Tapes* (Columbia Records, 2002).

37. Jeru the Damaja, *The Sun Rises in the East* (Payday Records, 1996).

38. Ibid.

39. Gene Ching, "Hip Hop Fist: Wu-Tang Clan's RZA and his Sifu, Shaolin Monk Shi Yan Ming?" *Kungfu Magazine*, September 1999, pp. 1–5. See the online version at http://ezine.kungfumagazine.com/magazine/article.php?article=100.

40. Ibid., p. 3.

41. Ibid. It should be noted that Sifu Shi Yan Ming is featured in an interview on the Shaw Brothers reissue of *The 36th Chamber of Shaolin* on DVD. Throughout the interview, Ming emphasizes the importance of understanding the spiritual aspects of kung fu and tells listeners that true kung fu is not about fighting but about spiritual enlightenment. See DVD reissue, *The 36th Chamber of Shaolin*, limited collector's edition (Shaw Scope, 1978).

42. Ching, "Hip Hop Fist," pp. 4–5.

43. Ibid., p. 2. For an introduction to Afro-Asian exchanges, see Robin D. G. Kelley and Betsy Esch, "Black Like Mao," *Souls*, Fall 1999, pp. 6–41; Bill V. Mullen, *Afro-Orientalism* (Minneapolis: University of Minnesota Press, 2004). In terms of kung fu, see Vijay Prashad's *Everybody Was Kung Fu Fighting: Afro-Asian Connections and the Myth of Cultural Purity* (Boston: Beacon Press, 2001). See also Ellie M. Hisama, "Afro-Asian Crosscurrents in Contemporary Hip Hop," *ISAM Newsletter* 32, no. 1 (Fall 2002): pp. 1–8.

44. Ching, "Hip Hop Fist," p. 4. The RZA noted that he and Clan member Old Dirty Bastard "started to get deep into what they were saying about chi energy. We got into the idea of channeling chi. It rejuvenates your body, but it's also philosophical. It's about finding balance," the RZA recalled. See the RZA, *The Wu-Tang Clan Manual*, p. 52.

45. Ibid., p. 55.

46. Ibid.

11

Reminiscences of the Life of an Actress in Shaw Brothers' Movietown

CHENG PEI-PEI

(*Translated by Jing Jing Chang and Jeff McClain*)

The martial arts film hero Ti Lung (Di Long)[1] in an interview once said: "The Shaw Brothers Movietown (Shaoshi yingcheng) was my paradise." In fact, the Shaw studio was not just Ti Lung's paradise but was the paradise of each and every young person who found themselves there in the 1960s. It was at that studio that each of us lived out our dreams.

In 1961, I immigrated to Hong Kong from Shanghai. In order to find a group of friends who shared my passion for performance, I enrolled, in 1962, in the Performing Arts Training classes at the Shaw Brothers South China Experimental Drama Center (Nanguo shiyan jutuan). At that time, the Center was still located on the fifth floor of the old Chi Lik Building, in Kowloon, on Nathan Road near Waterloo Road. The Chi Lik Building was exactly as actress and dancer Jiang Qing described it: desolate and shabby. When we entered the Center, our paradise still seemed a long way off. Little did we know that we were entering through its main gates.

Immediately after graduation from the Center in 1963, I signed the basic seven-year actor's contract with the Shaw Brothers. Shortly afterward, South China moved to the newly constructed Movietown at Clear Water Bay (Qingshui wan). It was then that I moved into the Shaw Brothers Studio dormitory. I am in full agreement with actress Ching Li's (Jing Li)[2] oft-stated claim that "It was there that I spent the most beautiful times of my youth."

Whenever there is discussion about how we all lived together in the Shaw Brothers dormitory, many people, especially Americans, look at me with a very awkward expression and ask, "Is it really true that Shaw Brothers actors were all locked up in the company's dormitory and completely cut off from the outside world?" Indeed, it is true that we were almost entirely ignorant of what went on outside of the Shaw studio. Unlike today's young stars, whose lives are constantly displayed in front of the cameras, without even a bit of privacy, however, we most definitely benefited from protection from this sort of harsh media frenzy.

The company often worried that what went on in our private lives might influence box office results. For instance, we were forbidden to date at too young of an age. When the story of the love between actor Kang Wei and Jenny Hu (Hu Yanni)[3] broke, it caused a tremendous commotion at the studio. Still, the experiences of today's generation of rising stars do not appear in any way better than ours. They, too, do not have true freedom, nor do they have the power to choose whom to love. Every one of their gestures is constantly under the surveillance of the paparazzi.

Compared with today's young actors, we were fortunate not only because of the cloistered protection provided by the Shaw Brothers, but also because of the studio's investment of resources toward our continued training. When the Center moved into Movietown at Clear Water Bay, it was like having a classroom in our own homes. Any one of us who wanted to continue learning in order to develop our acting potential was allowed to take courses. Where can we find a manager today that would possess the perseverance and audacity to groom a star in the face of endless challenges? Nowadays, as soon as a fledgling star shows his or her potential for market success, their manager quickly jumps at the chance to get a stranglehold on the young talent, working it until every living breath of the young star is squeezed out.

Back in those early years, we frequently spent all of the twenty-four-hour day in our paradise. We had no reason to step outside of the studio campus. When we had movies to make or notices of upcoming film projects, we would receive coupons for our meals. With these, our food-catering amah would prepare for us home-style meals. The amah's cooking was, in fact, often much more delicious than meals we had in our own homes. Even when we were not making films, if we did not feel like cooking for ourselves, we could eat our three meals at either one of the two restaurants located at the studio.

During the early 1960s, the Shaw Brothers Studio began construction on a residence complex. The first-generation residence hall (now long since demolished) was shabby, but quaint. In the beginning, only a very few Shaw Brothers employees moved into the residence building. I remember that Ivy Ling Po (Ling Bo)[4] was part of the first wave of employees to move in there.

Also among the first to move in were even some of the company's management and staff. Later on, director Ding Shanxi also came to live in the complex, followed by actress Li Ting. It was in that building that she committed suicide. It was, however, only when actor Yueh Hua[5] moved into the first residence hall that I began to pay casual visits there.

I still do not understand why Yueh Hua moved into the original residence building. At that time, most of those who were living in the first-generation residence hall were in the process of moving into the second residence hall. In the beginning, we did not care what the new residence building was called. The new residence complex was closer to the studio's front gates. From the old residence (also known as Number One Residence Hall), we had to pass by our South China classroom before we could get to the new residence building. As a result, the old residence hall always seemed to give us a sense of alienation and desolation. The new residence was much more spacious. It was a six-story structure, shaped as an *H*. For the convenience of all the actors, the Shaw Brothers built one of its first elevators in the middle section of the new residential complex.

One can still find this second residence hall, but, of course, it is no longer new. It has now been transformed into TVB's[6] martial arts direction department's storage area. After my daughter, Marsha Yuen (who returned to Hong Kong from the United States to pursue an acting career), became the first runner-up at the 1999 Miss Hong Kong Beauty Pageant, she took a few swordplay lessons in the building.

The original impetus for the building of a second residence hall was that Shaw Brothers was recruiting many film workers from Taiwan, and they all needed housing. Among the first émigrés from Taiwan were directors, actresses like Jenny Hu and Lily Ho (He Lili),[7] as well as all types of film crew personnel. Eventually, more and more people moved into the second building, including some native Hong Kong actors and directors. In the beginning, the tenants at the second residence hall were divided by gender, men on one floor, women on the other.

Little by little, the facilities at the residence hall improved without our being aware of it. When I first moved into the new residence hall, I had only one bedroom. I did have, however, my own private bathroom. Many rooms were not equipped with private bathrooms or cleaning facilities of any sort. Public bathrooms were located on the bottom floor of the building, directly facing the elevators. Those without private bathrooms had to take their showers, do their laundry, and wash their vegetables at these public facilities.

At that time, I had two directors as my next-door neighbors: Yan Jun lived on one side and Qin Jian on the other. Director Yan had family in Hong Kong, but the transportation system in Hong Kong was not as convenient as today, and transportation on the island side was even less convenient. If one wanted to cross the sea after midnight, he or she had to take a little motorboat. Therefore, in order to make things more convenient, Yan requested a room for sleeping in from time to time. Whenever Yan stayed over at the company residence, his wife, the famous actress Li Lihua,[8] would also move in with him to take care of his daily needs. Li Lihua was extremely capable both as a wife and as a professional woman.

In quite the opposite situation was director Qin Jian. When Qin first moved in next door to me, he had just recently separated from his wife, actress Jeanette Lin Cui,[9] and was already a very solitary and depressed man. Although his *Till the End of Time* (1966) was a smashing success (it was also the film that catapulted Jenny Hu into stardom), and Shaw Brothers continuously assigned him new film projects, very few people would ever hear him laugh or tell jokes. Therefore, even though we were neighbors for several months, we hardly exchanged any words. After I moved to the fifth floor, he hung himself by a rope tied to the pipe that ran between our bathrooms.

The Shaw Brothers renovated the fifth and sixth floors of the building into two-bedroom and three-bedroom luxury suites. This new development led to a division by class among the tenants. There were four units on both the fifth and the sixth floors. Due to the fact that the building was shaped as an *H*, two units of luxury suites would be facing each other. Aside from myself, only directors or company managers lived in those luxury suites. As a result, a certain distance developed between myself and the other actresses.

Due to the social unrest that took place in Hong Kong in 1967,[10] my mother, stepfather, younger brother, and sister all immigrated to Australia. Subsequently, my grandmother moved into my two-bedroom suite. Except for Jenny Hu, who was already married at the time, Li Qing, Qin Ping, and Lily Ho were each accompanied by their mothers. Later on, Lily's entire family from Taiwan moved in with her as well.

When I was young, I never enjoyed going out to have fun. Kang Wei later confessed to me that everyone thought I was a very strange person. How could there exist a young actress such as myself who would behave so seriously all day long? Even when I did not have movies to make, I would do voice dubbing or give dance lessons in order to make a little extra money. I also studied dressmaking and took English and ballet lessons. Today, my former dance teacher still uses me as an example of a studious dancer that all her students should follow as a role model. She tells her students how I would rush to ballet class immediately after work and how I worked hard enough to eventually receive the British Royal Ballet diploma. Somehow, I would always find ways to fill up my day.

Although I was making movies for a living, my favorite pastime remained going to the movies. I could easily watch four or five movies in a single day. On occasion, I would even write movie reviews. Perhaps because of the environment of the Shaw Brothers Studio, I felt that my entire life belonged to the world of movies.

In 1988, after having left behind the movie business for twenty years, I was

Cheng Pei-pei as Golden Swallow in *Come Drink with Me*. (Courtesy of Celestial Pictures Ltd.)

given a second chance to return to the cinematic paradise that was once mine and to once again search for dreams that were yet to be wholly fulfilled. At that time, the last remaining residence hall was the third one, which was built in the 1970s. After having already constructed two generations of residence halls, the new residence hall was even more improved. I think the company was by then fully convinced of the benefits of a residence complex in providing a stable environment for its staff members. This third residence hall was more like a vacation villa. When I returned to the former Movietown that year to make *Painted Faces*, I moved into one of the two-bedroom units. Although the unit was smaller than the luxury suite I used to have, it had more of a sense of home.

During the 1980s and 1990s, the Shaw Brothers were no longer making as many films as before. Yet there remained quite a number of old Shaw Brothers employees who were living out the remainder of their lives in the company's residence halls. For instance, famous martial arts film director Chang Cheh (Zhang Che)[11] lived there until he died. The year before he passed away, the Twenty-First Hong Kong Film Awards bestowed upon him the Lifetime Achievement Award. Because he was not able to walk far, we all went to his apartment at the studio in order to complete the award ceremony. That was the last time that I stepped into the building. Later on, whenever we shot films or other projects, we would only take shots from the exterior. Those who once lived there have now almost all moved away.

The husband-and-wife team of Alex Law (Luo Qirui) and Mabel Cheung (Zhang Wanting) are my very good friends, even though they joined Shaw Brothers much later than I did. When I asked them about their memories and feelings about Shaw Brothers, they told me, "When we first arrived at the Shaw Brothers Studio, we felt that it was overwhelmingly huge. It seemed that it would take half a day to cross the large campus and reach the harbor. Looking back today at Movietown, its grandeur and impressiveness are forever etched in our minds."

It is strange how things always seem larger in the memories of one's youth. In my memories, only one little tree, by the sidewalk near the studio, did not seem so large. When I returned to Shaw Brothers to make *Painted Faces*, I found myself once again walking from the company office building toward the studio. I discovered that the little tree had now grown to be a very tall tree. The feeling I had was akin to the one you would have were you to see your child all grown up after many years of absence. When I saw that tree again, I was suddenly hit by a pang of melancholy.

Truthfully, I do feel a sense of loss. The Shaw Brothers Movietown was constructed during the late 1950s, when I had not yet entered the movie business. Today, hardly anything remains from those bygone days. Now what we recognize as the Shaw Brothers Studio was actually built in the 1970s by Mona Fong (Fang Yihua).[12]

I remember that back in those early days of the Shaw studio, actors rarely had to shoot two films at a time, especially if they were lead actors. If we had to be in two films at the same time, it was a very big deal. When I made Xu Zhenghong's martial arts film *The Thundering Sword* (1967) and Xue Qun's musical *Blue Skies,* the production schedules of the two films would sometimes overlap. On occasion, I needed to work for both these films in a single day. At that time, I was still young and did not feel tired whatsoever. Indeed, sleeping a few hours less was really no big deal. Yet my mother would not stand for this. She would come to the studio office to complain that the company did not treat me like a human being, that they abused and exploited me. Because I was not yet twenty-one, not yet an adult, I could not sign my own contracts. Thus, the company finally had to give in to my mother's demands. They once even agreed with her demand that I be sent to Japan for further training. Without a doubt, the reason they willingly submitted to the whims of my mother was because they wanted to be able to keep me at their studio until I was able to make my own decisions.

When I interviewed martial arts actress Hui Ying-hung,[13] who joined the Shaw Brothers in the 1980s, after I returned to Movietown, I found that her acting experience at Shaw Brothers was completely different from mine. She told me how she sometimes had to shoot several films a day. Luckily, most of her films were martial arts films. Therefore, all she often needed to do was change her headpiece, and she would instantly become a different character from another martial arts film. Sometimes, she played the main character; other times, she had only cameo roles. There even were some films in which she appeared without ever knowing their titles. Of course, many of her films she never watched, and she confessed that at times she could not even remember which films she had made.

The actor Anthony Lau Wing (Liu Yong) was even more amazing. He told me that he would say to the company's chief executive officer, Wong Kar-hei (Huang Jiaxi), "I am made of steel anyway, you can assign me to whichever and however many films you please." As a result, he would work from morning to afternoon, afternoon to night, and night to morning. Oftentimes, it would be days before he could lie down on his own bed.

I feel very fortunate. When I was at Shaw Brothers, it was truly the best of times for the company. Although the period was not glamorous, each and every one of the films we made was truly a film of which we can be proud. Each one can be said to have reached a high standard of quality.

After the remarkable success of Ang Lee's *Crouching Tiger, Hidden Dragon*, I frequently gave interviews in different parts of the world. I was asked time and time again whether I felt any different while making *Crouching Tiger*. If I were to say that I felt exactly the same, that would be, of course, impossible. After almost forty years, since the time I played Golden Swallow in the Shaw Brothers martial arts classic *Golden Swallow* to the time I became Jade Fox, we have made many technological advances, which alter the experience for the actor. For instance, many of King Hu's (Hu Jinquan)[14] once carefully choreographed martial arts sequences are now done with computer programs. And yet, somehow, I still feel as if I have indeed returned to yesteryear. During the twenty years that I was away from the movies, I led a completely different life. That life had absolutely no relation to Cheng Pei-pei. Now that I have returned to film, it is as if Cheng Pei-pei has come back to life, returning once more to the world of martial arts.

Notes

1. Ti Lung was one of the principal martial arts actors at Shaw Brothers. He starred in many of director Chang Cheh's films, including *The Return of the One-Armed Swordsman* (1969), *Have Sword, Will Travel* (1969), and *The New One-Armed Swordsman* (1971). More recently, Ti has appeared alongside Chow Yun Fat in John Woo's *A Better Tomorrow* (1986), and *A Better Tomorrow 2* (1987), and with Jackie Chan in *Drunken Master II* (1994).

2. Ching Li began her acting career in Taiwan and joined Shaw Brothers in Hong Kong in 1967. Her films include *The Anonymous Heroes* (1971), *Duel of Fists* (1971), *The Boxer from Shantung* (1972), *Blood Brothers* (1973), and *The House of 72 Tenants* (1973).

3. Jenny Hu (born 1946) starred in many of the Shaw Brothers romantic dramas, including the film that made her a star, *Till the End of Time* (1966). She also stared in a number of melodramas, including *Madam Slender Plum* (1966) and *Four Sisters* (1967).

4. Ivy Ling Po (born 1940) appeared in many Huangmei opera genre films, often in male roles. One of her most famous roles was her portrayal of Brother Leung in Li Hanxiang's *Love Eterne* (1963).

5. Yueh Hua starred with Cheng Pei-pei in *Princess Iron Fan* (1966) and *Come Drink with Me* (1966). More recently, he appeared with Jackie Chan in *Rumble in the Bronx* (1995).

6. TVB is Hong Kong Television Broadcasting Ltd. Established in 1967, it was Hong Kong's largest and arguably most popular television station. Run Run Shaw is currently TVB's president.

7. Lily Ho (born 1952), originally from Taiwan, moved to Hong Kong and joined Shaw Brothers in 1967. She often played the role of the sexy femme fatale, her most memorable performance being her role as the lesbian love slave in Chor Yuen's *Intimate Confessions of a Chinese Courtesan* (1972). In 1974, at the peak of her career, she retired and married a business executive.

8. Li Lihua (born 1924) began her acting career at the age of eighteen, when she joined Shanghai's Yihua Film Studio. Li moved to Hong Kong in 1948 and in 1955 starred in the city's first color film, *Blood Will Tell*. She signed with Shaw Brothers in 1960 and appeared in films such as *The Magnificent Concubine* (1960), *Empress Wu* (1963), and *Vermillion Door* (1964).

9. Jeanette Lin Cui (1936–95) was born in Shanghai and moved with her family to Hong Kong in 1949, where she pursued an acting career. She married Qin Jian in 1959, and they divorced in 1967. Her Shaw Brothers films include *He Has Taken Him for Another* (1957).

10. Hong Kong in 1967 saw a series of demonstrations and riots by trade unionists and communist sympathizers against British colonial rule, sparked in part by the Cultural Revolution then taking place in the People's Republic of China.

11. Chang Cheh (1923–2002) was one of Hong Kong's most talented and prolific martial arts film directors, directing more than ninety films, including such kung fu classics as *The One-Armed Swordsman* (1967), *Golden Swallow* (1969), and *The Water Margin* (1972).

12. Mona Fong (born 1931 in Shanghai) met Run Run Shaw in 1952 while performing in a cabaret in Singapore. Fong gradually moved up in the Shaw Brothers organization, becoming head of the production department in 1973, joining the board of directors in 1981, and being appointed senior executive director in 1990. In 2000, Fong was listed as one of Hong Kong's richest women.

13. Hui Ying-hung starred in twenty-three Shaw Brothers films between 1978 and 1984. She earned the Best Actress Award at the Hong Kong Film Awards for *My Young Auntie* (1981).

14. King Hu (1931–97) is the legendary director of such films as *Come Drink with Me* (1966), *A Touch of Zen* (1970), and *Legend of the Mountain* (1979).

Select Filmography

LANE J. HARRIS

Included here are films that have been discussed in some detail in the book. For a more complete filmography of Shaw Brothers movies, see Yu Mo-wan, Angel Shing, and Lee Chun Wai, "The Shaw Filmography," in *The Shaw Screen: A Preliminary Study*, edited by Wong Ain-ling, 346–352 (Hong Kong: Hong Kong Film Archive, 2003).

Baijin long (*White Golden Dragon*). Tianyi, 1933. Dir. Sit Gok-sin.

Bi yun tian (*Blue Sky*). Shaw & Sons, 1952. Dir. Wang Yin.

Biancheng san xia (*The Magnificent Trio*). Shaw Brothers (HK) Ltd., 1966. Dir. Chang Cheh (Zhang Che).

Bu liao qing (*Love without End*). Shaw Brothers (HK) Ltd., 1961. Dir. Doe Ching (Tao Qin).

Busan (*Goodbye Dragon Inn*). Homegreen Films, 2003. Dir. Tsai Ming-liang (Cai Mingliang).

Chun guang wuxian hao (*A Mellow Spring*). Shaw & Sons Ltd., 1957. Dir. Li Han hsiang (Li Hanxiang).

Dongjing Xianggang miyue lüxing (*Hong Kong Tokyo Honeymoon*). Cathay/Shochiku, 1957. Dir. Nomura Yoshitaro.

Duliqiao zhi lian (*The Merdeka Bridge*). Malay Film Productions, 1959. Dir. Chow Sze-luk (Zhou Shilu).

Guobu xinniang (*Bride from Other Town*). Malay Film Productions, 1959. Dir. Chow Sze-luk (Zhou Shilu).

Hang Tuah (*The Story of Hang Tuah*). Malay Film Productions, 1956. Dir. Phani Majumdar.

Huimie (*Destroy!*). Shaw & Sons Ltd., 1952. Dir. Bu Wancang.

Jefri Zain dalam Gerak Kilat (*Jefri Zain in Operation Lightning*). Malay Film Productions, 1966. Dir. Jamil Sulong.

Jiangshan Meiren (*The Kingdom and the Beauty*). Shaw Brothers (HK) Ltd., 1959. Dir. Li Han-hsiang (Li Hanxiang).

Jin laba (*The Golden Trumpet*). Shaw Brothers (HK) Ltd., 1961. Dir. Doe Ching (Tao Qin).

Jing wu men (*Chinese Connection*). Golden Harvest/Pagoda Films, 1971. Dir. Lo Wei (Luo Wei).

Liang Shanbo yu Zhu Yingtai (*Love Eterne*). Shaw Brothers (HK) Ltd., 1963. Dir. Li Han-hsiang (Li Hanxiang).

Liulian piao xiang (*When Durians Bloom*). Malay Film Productions, 1959. Dir. Chow Sze-luk (Zhou Shilu), Ng Dan (Wu Dan).

Longmen kezhan (*Dragon Inn*). Union Film/Shaw Brothers (HK) Ltd., 1967. Dir. King Hu (Hu Jinquan).

Manbo nülang (*Mambo Girl*). Cathay (MP & GI), 1957. Dir. Yi Wen.

Mingri zhi ge (*Song of Tomorrow*). Shaw Brothers (HK) Ltd., 1967. Dir. Doe Ching (Tao Qin).

Ni nabian jidian (*What Time Is It There*). Arena Films/Homegreen Films, 2001. Dir. Tsai Ming-liang (Cai Mingliang).

Penarek Beca (*The Trishaw Puller*). Malay Film Productions, 1955. Dir. P. Ramlee.

Qingchun guwang (*King Drummer*). Shaw Brothers (HK) Ltd., 1967. Dir. Inoue Umetsugu.

Raja Bersiong (*The King with Fangs*). Malay Film Productions, 1968. Dir. Jamil Sulong.

Sambiki no samurai (*Three Outlaw Samurai*). Shochiku, 1964. Dir. Gosha Hideo.

Seruan Merdeka (*Cry of Freedom*). Malay Arts, 1946. Dir. K. R. S. Kristy.

Shaolin sanshiliu fang (*The 36th Chamber of Shaolin/Master Killer*). Shaw Brothers (HK) Ltd., 1978. Dir. Lau Kar-leung (Liu Jialiang).

Singapura di Waktu Malam (*The Song of Singapore*). Malay Film Productions, 1947. Dir. Wu Cun.

Taohua jiang (*Songs of the Peach Blossom River*). Hsin Hwa, 1956. Dir. Zhang Shankun, Wang Tianlin.

Tianxia diyi Quan (*Five Fingers of Death*). Shaw Brothers (HK) Ltd., 1972. Dir. Cheng Chang Ho.

Wu hu zang long (*Crouching Tiger, Hidden Dragon*). Asia/Columbia Pictures/Good Machine/Sony Pictures Classic/United China Vision, 2000. Dir. Ang Lee.

Xia nu (*A Touch of Zen*). Shaw Brothers (HK) Ltd., 1969. Dir. King Hu (Hu Jinquan).

Xiang jiang hua yue ye (*Hong Kong Nocturne*). Shaw Brothers (HK) Ltd., 1967. Dir. Inoue Umetsugu.

Xingdao hongchuan (*The Opera Boat in Singapore*). Malay Film Productions, 1955. Dir. Ku Wen-chung (Gu Wenzhong).

Yang Guifei (*Empress Yang Kwei Fei*). Shaw Brothers (HK) Ltd., 1962. Dir. Li Han-hsiang (Li Hanxiang).

Contributors

TIMOTHY P. BARNARD is associate professor of history at the National University of Singapore. He is the author of *Multiple Centers of Authority: Society and Environment in Siak and Eastern Sumatra* and editor of *Contesting Malayness: Malay Identity across Boundaries*.

SUNDIATA KEITA CHA-JUA is director of the African American Studies and Research Program and associate professor of history at the University of Illinois, Urbana-Champaign. He is the author of *America's First Black Town, Brooklyn, Illinois, 1830–1915*.

JING JING CHANG is a PhD student in Chinese history at the University of Illinois, Urbana-Champaign. Her research focuses on the history of Hong Kong cinema and immigration.

CHENG PEI-PEI is an actress, video producer, and television personality. She began her acting career in the Shaw Brothers Studio in the late 1960s. Cheng is most famous to fans around the world for her roles in musicals such as *Hong Kong Nocturne* and martial arts films such as *Come Drink with Me* and *Crouching Tiger, Hidden Dragon*.

RAMONA CURRY is associate professor of English at the University of Illinois, Urbana-Champaign with affiliations to programs on cinema and gender studies. She is author of *Too Much of a Good Thing: Mae West as Cultural Icon*.

POSHEK FU is professor of history and cinema studies at the University of Illinois, Urbana-Champaign. He is the author of *Passivity, Resistance, and Collaboration: Intellectual Choices in Occupied Shanghai, 1937–1945* and *Between Shanghai and Hong Kong: The Politics of Chinese Cinema* and co-editor of *Constructing Nationhood in Modern East Asia* and *The Cinema of Hong Kong: History, Arts, Identity.*

LANE J. HARRIS is a PhD student in the Department of History at the University of Illinois, Urbana-Champaign. His dissertation concerns the history of the modern Chinese postal services.

LILY KONG is professor of geography and vice-provost (education) at the National University of Singapore. Author and editor of numerous books, her most recent publications include *Globalisation and Territories in Asia Pacific Contexts, The Politics of Landscapes in Singapore: Constructions of "Nation," Landscapes: Ways of Imagining the World,* and *Singapore: A Developmental State.*

LAW KAR previously worked as a programmer for the Hong Kong Film Archive. A film critic, editor, and stage writer, his most recent book in English is *Hong Kong Cinema: A Cross Cultural View.*

SIU LEUNG LI is associate professor of cultural studies at Lingnan University, Hong Kong. He is the author of *Cross-Dressing in Chinese Opera* and coeditor of *Hong Kong Connections: Transnational Imagination in Action Cinema.*

JEFF MCCLAIN is a PhD student in Chinese history at the University of Illinois, Urbana-Champaign. His research focuses on missionary knowledge production and archeology in republican China.

PAUL G. PICKOWICZ is professor of history and Chinese studies at the University of California, San Diego. He is the author of *Marxist Literary Thoughts and China: The Influences of Ch'u Chiu-pai;* coauthor of *Chinese Village, Socialist State* and *Revolution, Resistance and Reform in Village China;* and coeditor of *Popular China, Unofficial China: Popular Culture and Thought in the People's Republic, New Chinese Cinemas: Forms, Identities, Politics,* and *China's Cultural Revolutions as History.*

FANON CHE WILKINS is associate professor of history in the Graduate School of American Studies at Doshisha University in Kyoto, Japan.

WONG AIN-LING is former programmer of the Hong Kong International Film Festival and now research officer at the Hong Kong Film Archive. Among her many publications are, most recently, *An Age of Idealism: Great Wall and Feng Huang Days* and *Shaw Screen: A Preliminary Study.*

SAI-SHING YUNG is associate professor of Chinese studies at the National University of Singapore. He is the author of two books on Chinese drama, Cantonese opera, and Cantonese gramophone culture in Chinese.

Index

The University of Illinois Press
is a founding member of the
Association of American University Presses.

University of Illinois Press
1325 South Oak Street
Champaign, IL 61820-6903
www.press.uillinois.edu